Edward Phelan and the ILO

The life and views
of an international social actor

INTERNATIONAL LABOUR OFFICE   GENEVA

Edward Phelan and the ILO: The life and views of an international social actor

International Labour Office – Geneva: ILO, 2009

ISBN 978-92-2-121983-5

biography / ILO Director General / role of ILO / history
01.03.7

ILO Cataloguing in Publication Data

Cover photo © World Trade Organization, reproduced by kind permission.
Inside photos © International Labour Organization.
Photocomposed in Switzerland   JMB
Printed in Switzerland   GEN

With my warmest wishes
of happiness and my
gratitude.

Antoinette Juvet-Miz.

Edward Phelan and the ILO

Preface

Centred on Edward J. Phelan's unfinished memoirs, this book is part of the International Labour Organization's Century Project, devoted to exploring and documenting the ILO's history. Edward Phelan was a key member of the small group of people who mapped out the design of the Organization during the Paris Peace Conference in 1919, a staff member of the ILO from 1919 to 1948, and its fourth Director (and first Director-General) from 1941 to 1948.

The first foreword, by former Irish Taoiseach Seán Lemass, and the introduction and postscript, by former ILO Director-General C. Wilfred Jenks, were written in the late 1960s. The second foreword was prepared especially for this volume by the present Taoiseach, Brian Cowen.

To set the scene for the memoirs of this unusual man, who played such an important role in the birth of the ILO, the well-known Irish labour historian Emmet O'Connor has contributed a biographical essay.

The volume continues with an extensive selection of passages from Phelan's memoirs. Explanatory editor's notes have been inserted in the text where necessary to maintain the thread of Phelan's story. Editorial footnotes, identified as such by the final element '(Ed.)', have also been added to explain historical events and names. Phelan's own notes are identified by the addition of his initials '(E.J.P.)'. The uncut and unedited memoirs can be found on the website of the ILO Century Project at: http://www.ilocentury.org

As the hitherto unpublished memoirs do not go beyond the early days of the ILO, the volume also includes three articles Phelan wrote for the Irish review *Studies* in the 1950s, providing his perspective on the Organization's later development.

The book concludes with a selected bibliography of Phelan's writings and a list of further reading on the history of the Organization.

Editorial work for this volume was undertaken by Julie Wolf. Project oversight was the responsibility of Jasmien Van Daele. A financial contribution from the Irish Government towards the cost of this publication is gratefully acknowledged. Thanks are also due to Patricia O'Donovan, ILO Executive Director, for her interest in and support for this work, and to Remo Becci and Fiona Rolian and the staff of the ILO's Historical Archives for providing some of the basic materials used in this project, including the memoirs themselves, and assisting in the preparation of the footnotes.

GERRY RODGERS
INTERNATIONAL LABOUR OFFICE

Table of contents

Foreword
Seán Lemass

Edward J. Phelan became one of the first of the international civil servants when he joined the International Labour Organization on its establishment in 1919. He was thus a pioneer in a profession which has since grown enormously in size and status as the world has found need for more and more international organizations to enable it to cope with its ever-increasing political, social and technical problems.

These memoirs give the background to Phelan's early life and include a graphic description of his childhood days in Ireland. They also outline his earlier career, mainly in the British public service, before he was called on to take part in what became his life's work in the ILO.

Edward Phelan took part in the drafting and editing of the text of the section of the Treaty of Versailles which created the International Labour Organization. He was one of the principal authors of the ILO Constitution. He organized the First Session of the International Labour Conference, which opened in Washington in October 1919, and became Head of the Diplomatic Division of the new Office in January 1920.

In this position, as subsequently in those of Assistant Director, Deputy Director and Director (which he became in 1941), Phelan saw his task as that of developing and consolidating the institution he had helped to create.

During the years from 1941 to 1948, he shouldered the entire responsibility of directing the International Labour Office, a task which demanded not only administrative experience but also great political acumen and diplomacy to ensure the survival of the ILO. Phelan was a man of vision, and all during the war years he worked and planned for the post-war reconstruction of the Organization.

In 1944, in Philadelphia, he convened a regular session of the International Labour Conference and presented his proposals for a wide range of future activities; they led to the adoption of the historic Declaration of Philadelphia. This Declaration not only guided all subsequent growth of the Organization but also inspired, to a large measure, the work of the United Nations in social and economic fields.

In 1946, the 99th Session of the Governing Body meeting at Montreal, wishing to honour the work that Edward Phelan had carried out during the Organization's most difficult period, conferred on him the title of Director-General of the ILO.

The longest period of contact I had with Edward Phelan was when, as Minister for Industry and Commerce in the Irish Government, I headed the Irish delegation to the 1937 International Labour Conference for that year and had the honour of being elected President of the Conference. I was tremendously impressed by his dedication and zeal and above all by his vision of the ILO as an enduring instrument in the cause of peace and social justice throughout the world.

One of Phelan's lesser-known contributions (but one which was to have a major influence on the working of the ILO) was that he was the innovator of the ILO "tripartite" formula which forms the basis of representations at International Labour Conferences. Each country's delegation includes, not only government delegates, but also representatives of workers' and employers' organizations, who have the same status in the Conference's deliberations as the government delegates. Phelan foresaw at an early stage that the work of the newly created Organization would be vastly more fruitful if representatives of workers and employers were personally involved in the formulation of international standards of social justice.

The memory of Edward Phelan will live on as long as the ILO, the instrument he did so much to create and fashion, continues to develop its now traditional role of setting ever higher standards to be applied to persons in employment in all countries, and as long as it shows its dynamism by taking on new tasks – as it has done in recent years in the field of technical assistance to developing countries – for which it is uniquely fitted in an era of unprecedented change and development.

SEÁN LEMASS TD
TAOISEACH OF IRELAND 1959–66

Foreword
Brian Cowen

When the former Taoiseach, Seán Lemass TD, penned his foreword to Edward Phelan's memoirs in 1968, his vision of economic transformation and change were already leading to a more prosperous and confident Ireland. His bold economic plan, crafted with the able assistance of Dr Ken Whittaker, had significantly shifted the economic trajectory of the country. Most importantly, in moving away from protectionism it had laid the foundation for Ireland's membership of the European Economic Community in 1973 and for the economic and social success story that Ireland became in the 1980s and 1990s.

The innovative and constructive role played in this transformation by the social partners in Ireland, particularly from 1987, when the first of a series of social partnership agreements was signed, is firmly rooted in the tripartism of the ILO. Edward Phelan is credited with developing the concept of tripartism, which is the cornerstone of the ILO and makes it unique in the United Nations system. He nurtured the development and evolution of tripartism from the time he joined the ILO as the "first international civil servant" in 1919 until his retirement in 1948, having served as its fourth Director and first Director-General.

Edward Phelan's life story is a fascinating one, and not only to his compatriots in Ireland. He was born in 1888 in Tramore, Co. Waterford, the son of a seafarer. His life story is that of a British civil servant: during the First World War he worked for the Board of Trade, gathering data on the cost of living in working-class areas throughout Britain, and subsequently was appointed secretary of the labour section of the British delegation to the peace conference in Versailles which, as part of the wider peace treaty, gave birth to the ILO in 1919. But it is also the story of a man of great personal courage, professionalism, dedication to public service, and diplomatic and political skill. Edward Phelan steered the ILO through its darkest moments during the Second World War and masterminded its relocation to Montreal in the summer of 1940. This not only ensured the survival of the ILO but enabled it to emerge stronger and reinvigorated with the adoption of the Philadelphia Declaration in 1944. As pointed out by Seán Lemass in his foreword, the Philadelphia Declaration "not only guided all subsequent growth of the Organization but also inspired, to a large measure, the work of the United Nations in social and economic fields".

Like all countries around the world, Ireland is now facing major economic, social and political challenges. However, unlike many other countries, Ireland continues to believe in the fundamental importance of its social partnership in solving problems and finding solutions that bring fairness and balance to economic and social decisions. In 2008, the social partners reviewed together the ten-year social partnership agreement Towards 2016 and concluded a Transitional Agreement for 2008–09 which adapts and adjusts the ten-year agreement to respond to the new challenges. Tripartism and social partnership have played a pivotal role in Ireland's economic and social development over 30 years of remarkable economic growth, improved living standards and better public services, and now form an indispensable framework to our decision-making during this difficult period.

As the ILO celebrates its 90th anniversary, it is very fitting that the life and work of Edward Phelan should be marked with this publication. The Irish Government is very pleased to have been associated with bringing this project to fruition. I am proud to join Seán Lemass in paying tribute to this remarkable Irishman, who combined his Irish and British identities with great ease and left an indelible mark on the wider international world.

BRIAN COWEN TD
TAOISEACH OF IRELAND
January 2009

Introduction

C. Wilfred Jenks

Edward Phelan had an impact on the social history of the twentieth century greatly exceeding that of many men who have left a far clearer image in the public eye. Among the creators of the International Labour Organization his was the most fertile mind and the most continuous and decisive role; he was for a generation the intellectual backbone of the ILO; he was the captain who piloted it safely, alone among the League of Nations organizations, through the storms of the Second World War and its immediate aftermath; he was the first in point of time, and had the longest record of uninterrupted service, of the first generation of the new breed of international public servants who began to play during the League of Nations period a distinctive part in world affairs. From the age of 30 onwards the ILO was his life, and its continued growth in authority and influence remained so throughout the 20 years of his retirement; but his vision was always broader and encompassed the wider tasks of the creation of an organized world community. With no taste for theoretical plans for world order which had no foreseeable practical application, he was always attracted by the vanguard of original thought expressed in practical terms.

Taking the world as a whole, the impact of the ILO on social policy in the twentieth century has been comparable to that of the most far-reaching social changes in individual countries: the social transformation of Britain, the European socialist movements, the Soviet Revolution, the American New Deal, the far-reaching changes in the Third World, the economic growth and cultural renewal of China. Without the dramatic quality of any of these, the impact of the ILO has been a continuing and worldwide stimulus to peaceful but positive and persistent social change, influenced by all of these major political trends and influencing all of them in greater or lesser degree at some stage of their development. This influence can be traced in varied fields of social policy: in the broad concept that economic policy is essentially a means of attaining social objectives; in the recognition that human resources are the most valuable of all resources; in the broadening scope of equality of opportunity; in an approach to earnings, work, rest and leisure designed to ensure that the fruits of progress are fairly shared; in measures to promote health, safety and welfare at work; in the provision of comprehensive social security and medical care; in the practice of government–labour–management cooperation as an essential element in a dynamic policy of economic growth and social progress; and in the acceptance of a whole series of economic and social rights, ranging from "freedom from forced labour", "freedom of association" and "freedom from discrimination" to "the right to work", "the right to just and favourable conditions of work" and "the right to social security", as important corollaries among human rights to the basic civil liberties.

The origins of these developments in social thought and practical action are of course much older than the ILO, but the extent of their present acceptance owes much to the ILO. International organizations, like governments, are rarely the first pioneers in any field; they can play constantly a major role in reducing the time lag before bold initiative becomes accepted policy, but their opportunities for wholly new initiatives, while not unknown, are rarer. They are nevertheless potentially one of the most powerful instruments of necessary social change by peaceful means in response to the thrust of dynamic growth. Through their action the controversially new, purged of the eccentricities and exaggerations of its birth, becomes the conventionally respectable. The distinctive character of the impact of the ILO has been the manner in which it has transcended ideological conflicts, differences of party and divergences of economic interest and has contributed to the broad consensus which has made the development of the welfare state in many varied forms the outstanding contribution of the twentieth century to social policy and one of the leading features of political evolution throughout the world.

There is, of course, no conceivable technique of precise measurement of this far-reaching impact on the varied fortunes of mankind as they work themselves out in the daily lives of ordinary folk. No figures of conventions ratified, laws passed, labour departments, inspectorates, employment services and social security funds created or developed, employers' and workers' organizations brought into a new relationship with each other and with the State, can give more than a fraction of the picture. The influence of the constant succession of reports, meetings, negotiations, standards, judicial and quasi-judicial enquiries, operational activities and educational programmes is so completely intermingled with,

2

as to be inseparable from, the general current of economic and social history. The fundamental nature of the changes which have occurred and their worldwide incidence are no longer a matter of controversy. "To most people," as Harold Macmillan has said, "because it affects their lives so closely, the coming of the welfare state is perhaps the most marked of all the changes that the last 50 years have brought." [1]

Edward Phelan masterminded for a generation the creation and development of the worldwide institutional framework through which many of these things have been and continue to be achieved; much of the policy pursued through the framework bore the impress of his resourcefulness. The young official of the early years had no prophetic vision of all this. His strength was that he was seeking solutions for immediate political and practical problems to which his political and official chiefs, burdened with other responsibilities and preoccupations, had to give an immediate answer. It was this pressure of the immediate which gave a practical turn to his naturally inventive imagination. It was the practicality of what he achieved that made it durable.

How did it come to pass that so considerable a figure has left so effaced an image? The explanation is fourfold.

Fundamentally, Edward Phelan was a solitary, who could enjoy but never surrendered himself to gregariousness. I did not know him in what Geneva legend described as his gay youth, but from the early 1930s onwards he led an increasingly retired life. It was a common saying in those days that the staff of the ILO fell into three groups: the small and privileged group of those who had spoken to Phelan; the larger group of those who knew what Phelan looked like; and the still larger group of those who had never seen Phelan, whose hours of arrival at and departure from the office were somewhat unusual by conventional standards. What was chiefly significant was that there was never a fourth group of those who had no clear picture of who Phelan was; the magnetism of his influence was known and felt throughout the Office and there were few important files in which the initials E.J.P. did not constantly recur. He sought and achieved detachment without distance. He had and kept throughout his career a full grasp of all but the most technical details of everything of significance which had happened in the ILO and everything significant which was happening in the world which could affect the ILO, of the political context of each problem, its significance for social policy and its administrative and financial aspects. The length and richness of his experience was compounded by a quick intelligence, a capacious and retentive

---

[1] Harold Macmillan: *Winds of change, 1914–39* (London, Macmillan, 1966), p. 2.

memory, fertility of resource, and a clarity of thought which found expression in a gift for lucidity of exposition. He had, at one time or another, dealt with everything, had for those days travelled widely, and in the latter part of his career invariably knew the full history and background of every question which arose for decision. It was, of course, a much simpler world than that of today, in which practical experience and the wisdom and intuitive judgements derived therefrom were a much surer guide to public policy, but his grasp of successive problems was nevertheless a remarkable achievement and his apparently effortless mastery of them never ceased to command admiration.

The effortlessness was never more than apparent; it was achieved through constant strain. Edward Phelan always had more intellectual than physical vitality. He was spare of physique, ate lightly, and for at least the last 40 years of his life was of delicate and at times precarious health. He had no resource of abundant energy on which to draw in emergencies. With great wisdom, he jealously guarded his strength for the task of his life. It was to prove providential that he had done so. The war years, when he bore the full weight of responsibility in exceptionally diffi-cult circumstances with the equivocal authority of one still serving in an acting capacity, scant and precarious resources, and no readily available Governing Body to share the burden, stretched his resistance to the uttermost. He barely survived what was throughout an ordeal. Yet at no point did he lose his grasp of everything essential. He was certainly entitled to say, as he did in 1948 on relinquishing office, that he was handing over after weathering the storms of war and the even graver perils of the immediate post-war period, with the Constitution of the Organiza-tion "revised and strengthened, its activities expanded, its membership increased, its staff and equipment reconstructed, its finances solid, its independence assured, its place in the general effort of the United Nations honourably recognized, and its faith in its mission more fervent than ever". [2] His task had been successfully completed against overwhelming odds, but it had taken an almost mortal toll of his vitality. It was several years before some resilience returned and by that time, although his task had been so triumphantly completed and he was free to enjoy life, the habit of jealously guarding his strength had become so settled that it had developed into an almost hypochondriac strain.

Temperament and health were, however, only part of the explanation for the impersonal nature of Phelan's legacy to the ILO and through the ILO to the world. Training and philosophy were at least as significant.

---

[2] ILO: Conference of the International Labour Organisation: 31st Session, San Francisco, Record of proceedings (Geneva, 1948), p. 241

Edward Phelan thought it more important to achieve things than to get the credit for them. He believed profoundly, and acted for many years on the belief, that the price of achieving something is often to allow the person who, by rank or influence, is in the position to act most effectively in the circumstances of the time to take the whole or most of the credit for it. He had no illusion that he had, or could have, any personal authority comparable to that of such major political figures as George Barnes or Albert Thomas, Frances Perkins or Ernest Bevin, and he was well content to have them take, and in certain cases to allow their spokesmen to take, credit for initiatives the seeds of which came from his own fertile mind. James T. Shotwell, who worked in intimate cooperation with Phelan in 1919 and remained in close touch with both Phelan personally and the ILO for 30 years thereafter, bore emphatic witness to his possession of this quality. "The International Labour Organisation", Shotwell wrote, "owes more to him [Phelan] than will probably ever be widely known, for both as planner and negotiator he worked impersonally in order to work effectively."[3] This was apparent to perceptive observers at a very early stage. Phelan himself took special pleasure in stumbling accidentally after the lapse of 30 years on a letter from Harold Laski to Justice Holmes of 22 August 1926 in which Laski said of the ILO, "the real genius of the place is an Irishman named Phelan who has a good deal of Felix [Frankfurter]'s quick nervous charm".[4]

Phelan's lifelong belief in the greater effectiveness of the impersonal approach was enhanced by the special circumstances of the years when he held the chief executive responsibility. They were years when personality counted for much less on the ILO scene than the fact that, as Phelan himself said, the ILO "embodies in its aims and in its actions some of the most profound aspirations of mankind".[5]

The personal memories of one who played such a part, and played it with such reserve, are a historical document of no little importance. These memories, as Edward Phelan has placed them on record, are not a history of the ILO so much as a sketch of the world in which it was created and an account of the intellectual development of himself as one of its creators. They range over his early life as a young Irishman in Liverpool, his administrative apprenticeship in the varied social experiments of the Lloyd George New Deal which laid the foundations of the British welfare state, his first venture into diplomacy as a member of Bruce

---

[3] James T. Shotwell: *The autobiography of James T. Shotwell* (Indianapolis, Bobbs-Merrill, 1961), p. 97.

[4] *Holmes–Laski letters: The correspondence of Mr. Justice Holmes and Harold J. Laski, 1916–1935*, ed. Mark de Wolfe Howe (London, Oxford University Press, 1953), p. 870–71.

[5] ILO: *Conference of the International Labour Organisation: 31st Session, San Francisco, Record of proceedings* (Geneva, 1948), p. 243.

Lockhart's mission to Russia in 1918 and his personal report to Balfour on his return, his part in the inception of the ILO, the negotiations for the establishment of the ILO at the peace conference in 1919, and the manner in which Albert Thomas, when appointed as the first Director of the ILO in 1920, took over the handiwork of the peace conference and developed it into something of altogether larger proportions and more far-reaching significance. The story, as Edward Phelan has recorded it, is reasonably complete for the vital formative period of his own life and the creation of the ILO.

To gauge its significance we must place Phelan's work in the context of his relationship to his predecessors as Director and his achievement as their successor.

There were four outstanding figures in the International Labour Office during its first 30 years, each of whom held in turn the highest executive office: Albert Thomas, Harold Butler, John Winant and Edward Phelan. It was my privilege to serve with and know all of them and to work intimately with the last three. They differed widely in personality and gifts; for much of the time, at successive periods, Thomas, Butler and Phelan, and then Butler, Phelan and Winant, and subsequently Winant and Phelan, complemented each other, not always in full agreement on policy or wholly congenial in personal outlook, but working together as colleagues for a common end in a manner which placed an indelible stamp on the whole Office and gave it a cohesion of purpose, team spirit and discipline which constituted its strength. Each, in his time, made a distinctive contribution to the development of the ILO which none of the others could have made so well.

Albert Thomas made the ILO "a far greater thing" than its creators had imagined. For the men of 1919 the ILO was the heir to the pre-war movement for international labour legislation and an answer to the claim of the labour movement for a voice in the peace settlement; beyond that they had no clear vision. For Albert Thomas, who did not come upon the scene until 1920, the ILO was the social conscience of mankind; it was the forum of the ordinary man in world affairs; it was a hope of achieving social revolution by peaceful means as an alternative to the violent disruption of society. The outcome, as Harold Butler was afterwards to say, was that in the course of 20 years the ILO became "a beacon to which millions looked in the hope that, if not for them, at least for their children the struggle for existence might be less harsh, the daily toil lighter and the reward in the shape of comfort and happiness less niggardly than providence had so far vouchsafed to the majority of mankind".[6] By the time Albert Thomas died, on

---

[6] Harold Beresford Butler: *The lost peace: A personal impression* (London, Faber & Faber, 1941), p. 13.

7 May 1932, he had created a tradition with a life of its own, the future of which no longer depended on the incomparable vitality of his own personality.

Albert Thomas loved crises; they showed to advantage his gifts of oratory and diplomacy and you could often achieve through a crisis something for which it would be tedious to await a long and uncertain process of slow growth. Harold Butler was an accomplished master of the pen with much less taste for the platform. He preferred avoiding incidents to resolving them and anticipated in some measure the cult of quiet diplomacy, but while he was not disposed to make heavy weather of unessentials he had a real tenacity of purpose combined with a broad and long view in which realism and shrewdness tempered each other. He made no attempt to emulate Albert Thomas' infectious enthusiasm, but he inspired the confidence of the wary, and by so doing greatly widened the effective geographical horizon of the ILO. Albert Thomas travelled throughout the world but European socialism had remained the core of his intellectual outlook and interest. Harold Butler, whose intellectual background was All Souls College Oxford and Whitehall, was already sensitive in the thirties to the new currents which were to shape the developing world in the forties and fifties. The great event of his Directorship, and the fulfilment of his fondest ambition, was the entry into the Organization in 1934 of the United States. Harold Butler had been an Eton classmate of John Maynard Keynes and it was primarily through his influence that the ILO became in the League of Nations world the acknowledged international platform of the Keynesian revolution.

John Winant's tenure of the highest office was much the briefest but forever memorable. Winant was no administrator. In normal times he would not have been a good Director. He knew at that time little of the world outside the United States and had no grasp of the procedures or technical work of the ILO. He read little except Sandburg's Lincoln and similar historical biographies, wrote nothing, and, while persuasive in conversation, was at times almost inarticulate in speech. His personal affairs and arrangements were intensely disorganized to an extent which was a perpetual embarrassment to himself, his friends and his staff. Outside the range of the morally challenging and the weighting of political trends he was apt to judge an issue by his estimate of the person who posted it; when he gave his confidence he gave it in full and not always wisely, and bothered little with the details of the advice on which he acted. It was therefore not surprising that the sophisticated were apt to underestimate the man. It was the great good fortune of the ILO that the man and the hour were providentially matched to each other.

Winant had in a supreme degree the two qualities which the situation which confronted him required – political intuition and personal magnetism. He was faith and warmth incarnate in a manner which inspired faith and warmth. He had the capacity of the great to inspire the confidence of the great and the ordinary, leaving the sophistication of the competent and well-informed unmoved or sceptical but incapable of inspiring any comparable response. It was Phelan who prepared the plans which enabled the ILO to survive the war, but it was Winant who shot the rapids with success. Two elements in his personal contribution were of decisive and permanent importance. No other man could, in reducing the staff of the International Labour Office from 400 to 40, have held the personal loyalty to the ILO of those not retained in so decisive a grip that the vast majority of those suspended from its service remained among its most steadfast champions throughout the war and, by becoming the core of the subsequent reconstruction of the Office, made possible the continuity of its tradition. No other man would have assumed personally the full responsibility for transferring the working centre of the ILO to belligerent Canada in the late summer of 1940; the move may have been almost the only one which remained possible at the time but was nevertheless a masterstroke of genius. These tasks completed, Winant had made his indispensable contribution, and as Phelan took over from him in February 1941 there was again a providential matching of the man to the hour.

When Phelan took over, the qualities of imagination and inventiveness which he had always shown in so exceptional a measure had been alloyed by experience with an equal measure of tact, patience and endurance. The dramatic decision which had saved the ILO by maintaining its freedom of action had been taken by Winant; it was Phelan's infinite resourcefulness which turned to good account the opportunity so created. That resourcefulness had matured during the intimacy of his cooperation with Albert Thomas, Harold Butler and John Winant.

C. Wilfred Jenks
ILO Director-General 1970–73

Part I
Phelan, the man

Edward Phelan:
A biographical essay

Emmet O'Connor[1]

Edward Joseph Phelan was born, officially, on Thursday, 26 July 1888, the eldest son of Thomas and Bridget Phelan, née Carroll, at Summer Hill, Tramore, County Waterford, in the south-east of Ireland.[2] In an irony that would have tickled his sense of humour, the life of this meticulous bureaucrat began with a clerical error. His true birthday was 25 July; at least his parents were of that opinion.[3] Phelan or Whelan, Anglicizations of Ó Faoláin, *faol* meaning wolf in Irish, were ancient and common names in Waterford, but not beyond. Tramore was then emerging as a popular seaside resort and largely middle-class dormitory of Waterford city, a major port, seven miles to the north on the River Suir. Bridget's father was "a prosperous businessman who had established the first mineral water factory in Waterford".[4] Her son was more impressed by the fact that his father, like his father before him, was a master mariner. Seafaring was his starting point. His memoirs, grounded on the conviction that his eventual career was the outcome of a mentality rather than a plan, and written to explore the patterns of that mentality, began with the sea and never got far beyond the

---

[1] Dr Emmet O'Connor is Senior Lecturer in History and International Affairs at the University of Ulster. He has published widely on Irish labour history, including *Reds and the Green: Ireland, Russia, and the Communist Internationals, 1919–43* (Dublin, University College Dublin Press, 2004).

For help with this article, the author is obliged to Jasmien Van Daele and Cyrena Beranek, ILO; Dr Attracta Halpin and Nóirín Moynihan, National University of Ireland (NUI); Professors John Horne and Eunan O'Halpin, Trinity College, Dublin; and Teena Casey and Dr J.M. Hearne, Waterford.

[2] Birth record, Registry of Births, Waterford.

[3] The entry on Phelan in *Who Was Who, 1961–1970*, Vol. 6 (London, A.&C. Black, 1972), p. 890, written by himself, gives his birthday as 25 July.

[4] Unless otherwise stated, the quotations are from Edward Phelan's memoirs.

establishment of the ILO. Psychologically, that made sense. His life to 1919 was a series of unlikely accidents, and yet, he believed, their very diversity prepared him to be "the first international civil servant", and the choices he made at each juncture reflected a pattern. By 1919 the mentality had matured, and his course was fixed for the ILO. It would see him appointed Chief of the Diplomatic Division in 1920, then Assistant Director in 1933 and Deputy Director in 1938, and finally Acting Director in 1941 and Director-General in 1946.

Man and boy

Edward's childhood in Waterford, though of short duration, had a formative effect, and his early memories were dominated by Cheekpoint, a fishing village on the Suir. As his father was usually at sea, Edward's mother allowed him to spend much of his time from the age of four at Fairymount, the home of his paternal grandfather at Cheekpoint. Fairymount also involved a measure of separation from Bridget. Tramore was connected to Waterford city by rail. Cheekpoint lay a further eight miles east over bumpy roads. Bridget in any case rarely visited because of "some estrangement between her and my father's sister". Edward's solitude was reinforced by the social gulf between himself and the children of the village, whose lives left little time for leisure. Deprived of a normal childhood, he grew fond of his own company and spent happy hours playing on the Minaun, a 400 foot volcanic rock above Cheekpoint, which offered a spectacular panorama of the estuary. Delighting in his imagination, he never tired of watching the traffic on the Suir, or the paintings of ships and faraway ports in Fairymount. From introversion, independence and the shipping, he acquired two lasting character traits: a self-contained persona and a desire to travel "to places that were distant rather than to places that were foreign". Coincidentally, a few miles south of Cheekpoint lay an army barracks built on land acquired in 1783 for an industrial colony of 1,000 Genevese watchmakers and jewellers. An advance party of 20 Swiss arrived in Waterford in 1784, but the project collapsed. Geneva barracks earned some notoriety as a prison for insurgents in the aftermath of the 1798 rising, and enduring infamy in the rebel ballad "The Croppy Boy".

In 1895, Thomas Phelan decided to shift from sail to steam and seek a job on a regular shipping line with a fixed home port at which he could settle his growing family. The decision took the Phelans to Liverpool, Britain's second busiest port, with a vast, casual dock labour force that made it a centre of substantial Irish immigration. It was a trying time for Edward's parents. Thomas was obliged to start again on the promotional ladder as an officer, and the Phelans had hardly adjusted to lodgings in Bootle, near the north-end docks, when his vessel was sunk in a collision. He spent "a long period ashore" during which the family – augmented with the arrival of twin baby boys – lived on his small savings. Forced into the "strictest economy", they rented a "tiny house" in Tuscan Street, Seaforth, a coastal resort and expanding suburb a mile or two north of Bootle. Much to the relief of Bridget's social sensibilities, they were able to move after a few months to the more salubrious Durham Road in the Waterloo district of Seaforth – not far away, but a road, not a common street – and bring her piano over from Waterford.

Unaware of his parents' financial trials, Edward found the changes stimulating. His sense of isolation persisted. His father kept his few volumes of literature and Irish history in his shipboard cabin. His mother, despite an education at "an expensive boarding school" in Dublin, had no leisure pursuits other than a woman's magazine and her beloved piano. Outside the classroom and the playground, Edward had little contact with the pupils at the nearest available Catholic elementary school, most of whom lived in poor or slum areas. He amused himself with reading, graduating from newspapers and comics to "penny-dreadfuls" and the fare in Waterloo library, where he devoured the adventure stories of Manville Fenn, Jules Verne, Captain Marryat and, especially, G.A. Henty. It says something for his independence of mind that, Henty's effusive imperialism notwithstanding, he backed the Boers against the Empire in what was the Vietnam War of its day. Ultimately, Edward progressed to knowledge per se. Indifferent as to subject, he purchased half the letter 'A' of the *Harmsworth Encyclopaedia*, intending to proceed to 'Z' until he discovered that an entry on chemistry had been overtaken by new discovery. Each summer he returned – alone – to Cheekpoint for the holidays. Secondary education, at St Francis Xavier's College, Everton, reinforced his voracious, catholic reading and his solipsism.

Promotion for Thomas allowed the Phelans to trade up to a larger house in Liverpool. A further change of circumstances ensued when Thomas Phelan's ship was bought by a German company which wanted to retain him in command. As the ship was to ply between Hamburg and Boston, Thomas decided to relocate the family to Hamburg. Much to Edward's disappointment, it was decided that the young teenager should remain in Liverpool with the Jesuits, dedicated men of formidable intellect in the eyes of Irish Catholics. He had the consolation of trips to Hamburg, which he prized for the opportunity they provided to travel independently and sample life abroad. From enquiries in Ireland, his mother found him an "Irish home" near St Francis Xavier's with Miss Ely, an old lady from New Ross, near Cheekpoint. Through Miss Ely, an agent who collected weekly subscriptions for a friendly society (one of the voluntary mutual companies which provided insurance for the poor against death or incapacity), Edward gained his first insight into the oppressive financial world of working-class people, an experience which would later prove "of value and ... not the least important part of my education".

Cocooned in his intellectual bubble, Edward had little idea of his abilities until brilliance in any subject he applied himself to brought him a string of exam successes and a city council scholarship to Liverpool University in 1906. He still had no understanding of the practical relevance of knowledge, and no preference for one field of study over another. Out of sheer curiosity as to what it might entail, he chose mathematics. Coasting through his first year, he took a "particular interest" in the debating society, surmounting shyness to develop as an effective public speaker. His confidence was boosted further by travel. He had spent the summer of 1905 in France, and for the long vacation of 1906 Thomas got him a berth on a merchant voyage to the Mediterranean and the Black Sea, which partly fulfilled a filial need to emulate his father. There followed the novel shock of failure in his mathematics exams in 1909, the result of poor tuition and misjudgement of the curriculum. With typical resourcefulness, he responded by diversifying, taking a diplôme supérieur in French at the University of Rennes, and returning to Liverpool to read French, economics and physics. He also found time to edit the students' magazine, *The Sphinx*; serve as treasurer of the Council of the Guild of Undergraduates; and enjoy "some forms of sport". Politics too – or political oratory, at least – formed part of his social life. His memoirs reflect the cultivated reticence of the British civil servant where political opinions are concerned, but he is less guarded on things Irish. He felt, as he later put it, "very Irish", supported Home Rule (the Irish demand for self-government within the United Kingdom) and was proud of Liverpool's own Irish Nationalist MP, T.P. O'Connor.[5] On social matters, he was a keen observer of the labour process, whenever he encountered it at close quarters. Yet he undertook lectures for the Workers' Educational Association only under pressure from his economics professor and to supplement his income when his scholarship ran out. Founded by university dons in 1903, the Association was "taking on a great extension", but Edward was not seduced by the romance of bringing education to the masses, or impressed by the upsurge of trade union militancy in England during these years. On the other hand his memoirs reveal a deep concern with the living conditions of working-class people which he later encountered in his work as a civil servant. Ideologically, he appears to have been a social liberal rather than a socialist.

---

[5] "Man of the week: Head of the ILO", *Standard* (Montreal), 1 Nov. 1941.

In 1910 Edward completed his Bachelor of Science degree in physics, and in 1911 he graduated with a Bachelor of Arts in mathematics and French, and a Master of Science degree. Before graduation he had set his sights on the civil service, his ambition being to enter the Indian civil service, purely because "successful candidates in the examination were given a year at Oxford to study oriental languages, and I saw no other way of getting there": a testimony to the mesmeric lure of Oxford and Cambridge, or "Oxbridge", in the English university system. He was "painfully" disappointed by his results, and the offer of a post in the Fiji Islands, where the prospects for promotion were slim. By chance, the Board of Trade, in effect an ancient department of government which was adding an expanding range of labour and social responsibilities to its traditional economic remit at this time, was looking for investigators for a cost of living enquiry. And so he went to London and Whitehall, the centre of the British civil service.

From statistics to statecraft

It was an exciting time to be in the Board of Trade, in so far as that adjective can be associated with the "antiquated air" of its headquarters at Gwydyr House. Britain was finally catching up with Germany in developing the rudiments of a welfare state. The Liberal Government elected in 1906 introduced old age pensions, trade boards to fix minimum rates of pay in "sweated" industries (where employees worked long hours at low pay and in poor conditions), labour exchanges, unemployment insurance and a national health insurance scheme. Phelan's job was to compile price indices for the cost of living in working-class areas. One half of his time took him to all parts of Britain; the other half was spent in London, where he entertained himself with the best of public speaking and debate on the topics of the day, notably the third Home Rule crisis of 1912–14, when Unionists threatened armed rebellion if Ulster were brought under a Dublin parliament. A casual encounter with D.L. Kelleher, a Cork man and prolific author of poems and travel books, whom he had first met in Liverpool, led him to lodgings in Hampden Residential Club, behind St Pancras railway station. Known as "The Toffs' Doss House", the club had an extraordinary clientele of down-on-their-luck peers, professionals, artists and the like. Phelan felt the seedy surroundings "helped to complete my education and to bridge the gap between my academic knowledge and the realities of adult life". While London offered "many opportunities to pursue my hobby of public speaking", he loved the weekly debate in the Hampden as, whatever the subject, "there was always someone who could argue from personal experience". His London life would earn him a legendary reputation in the ILO for being a youthful bohemian.

The Hampden Club also introduced Phelan to George and Edward Lunn, brothers of Henry, head of Lunn's Tours. The pair now operated a rival company, and offered the Irishman a position as a tour guide, escorting travellers from London to Switzerland and northern Italy. Bored with his job, disappointed with a failure to secure promotion and attracted, as ever, by travel, he accepted. It was as a guide that he first saw Switzerland, finding its scenery "unbelievably beautiful". As a guide, too, he wrote his first book, *Milan*. The holiday, as he called it, lasted 12 months, until the Board of Trade offered him a post as chief investigator. Feeling that the work was of greater importance, he reluctantly forsook the splendour of Venice for foggy Whitehall. Back in Gwydyr House, he was delighted to be given responsibility for a major enquiry into housing, as part of a wider government initiative to improve public health. The enquiry was suspended with the outbreak of world war in August 1914, but war service would see him rise from middle-ranking obscurity to proximity to the highest offices of state.

Phelan's disappointment in being denied permission to apply to join the colours – in a serious breach of regulations, he went so far as to appeal to John Redmond, MP for Waterford – was soon assuaged with "highly interesting work" arranging contracts for army supplies. Later he was assigned to what he regarded as "the most comic administration" of the Ministry of National Service under the "disastrous" future Prime Minister Neville Chamberlain. By 1916 he had come to the notice of Tom Jones, adviser to David Lloyd George, who had recently become Prime Minister. Following discussions with Jones he was appointed to organize the Intelligence Division of the Ministry of Labour, newly created by Lloyd George. Phelan remained unhappy about his absence from military service, the more so as his father had deferred retirement on the outbreak of the war and was a prisoner in Germany, his ship having been torpedoed in the Atlantic. Arrangements for induction into the naval reserve were afoot when Phelan was asked to join the secret British mission to Bolshevik Russia in 1918 as labour attaché, probably at the suggestion of Jones. This most unexpected adventure would be the final link in the chain of unplanned events that led a middle-class civil servant, with no provenance in the labour movement, to the concept of the ILO. It also gave a standing in foreign policy to one without a background in the diplomatic service, public school or "Oxbridge". On his return to London, Phelan found himself seconded to the Foreign Office as a consultant on Russia. For three weeks he held the Government to the line that Britain ought to collaborate with Russia against Germany. His belief that the Bolshevik regime would survive prompted him to think afresh on labour as a determinant of foreign policy, and draft memorandums on "Democracy and diplomacy", the appointment of labour attachés to embassies and the creation of some form of permanent international labour machinery. His status in the Foreign Office and the Ministry of Labour enabled him to make the connection between international and labour affairs with some authority, even if some elderly mandarins wondered whether he had not gone a trifle "Bolshie".

Building the ship

With Bulgaria's request for an armistice on 28 September 1918, it was clear that the world war was drawing rapidly to a close. It was equally obvious that trade unions would seek to have social principles included in the post-war treaty as a quid pro quo for workers' wartime sacrifices, and that belligerents would be anxious to accommodate them, if only to defuse social unrest and thwart the spread of communism. Anticipating a Cabinet request to the Ministry of Labour for counsel, Phelan had the Ministry's Intelligence Division discuss the options. His contribution to the birth and form of the ILO lay partly in his advocacy of a permanent international labour body, and in his conception of tripartism and of the formula by which governments, employers and labour would be represented, and partly in the fact that he was exceptionally well situated to give effect to these proposals.

Improving working conditions through international action – to forestall any one State undercutting others – was a dream as old as utopian socialism, and had acquired concrete expression in the establishment of the International Association for Labour Legislation (IALL) – a non-governmental agency – at Basle in 1900. In a tribute to the IALL, Phelan acknowledged that the ILO "may in one sense be traced to the Berne Convention of 1906 for the prohibition of the use of white phosphorus".[6] Initially he shared the general view in the Ministry of Labour's Intelligence Division that the peace treaty should consolidate the work of the IALL by incorporating protections for labour but, realizing the complexity and variety of the labour question in different countries, he came to favour a permanent international labour body instead. He was by no means alone in this conclusion. The idea had been suggested by Léon Jouhaux, Secretary-General of the French Confédération générale du travail from 1909 to 1947, in a report to an Allied trade union conference in Leeds in 1916, and attracted extensive support on the social democratic left – the Bolsheviks being opposed implacably to any

---

[6] E.J. Phelan: "The International Labour Organisation: Its ideals and results", *Studies: An Irish Quarterly*, Vol. 14, Dec. 1925, p. 614.

truck with capitalism. Phelan's proposals were set out in a memorandum on 9 October 1918. The IALL and Jouhaux notwithstanding, various British Ministry of Labour chiefs staked a claim to paternity of the seedling ILO. According to Phelan's senior colleague, Harold Butler, "I began to work out a programme for the peace conference with the able assistance of Edward Phelan, the youthful head of the Foreign Intelligence Section of the Ministry, which he had brought to a fine point of efficiency."[7] And according to George Barnes, Labour MP and Minister of Labour, "the germ" of the ILO resulted from "conversations between myself and Messrs. Butler and Phelan, and Sir David Shackleton [Permanent Secretary at the Ministry]".[8] To the roll of honour Phelan would have added C.K. MacMullan, Sir John Hope Simpson and Hector Hetherington, colleagues in the Intelligence Division, and Malcolm Delevingne, the Home Office's expert on occupational health.

The concept of tripartism was more original to Phelan. Bipartite employer–labour councils for the improvement of industrial relations were being introduced in Britain, following the report of J.H. Whitley in 1917, but tripartism was a step beyond Whitleyism, and Phelan's memoirs make it clear that his thinking was dictated by the dynamics of the proposed ILO. Tripartism was also controversial in its rejection of trade union demands for a body composed of delegates of governments and unions only, and in equal measure. Offending the unions, Phelan was told by his colleagues, would be self-defeating, the whole point of establishing the ILO being to appease the social democratic left and keep workers out of communism. Again, from Phelan's memoirs it is evident that he was prepared to dismiss political expediency, convinced that an organization without the backing of all interested parties could not deliver practical results.

> Having thus arrived at the conclusion that it would be impossible for the peace conference to take any effective action on the substance of the trade union proposals, I tried to imagine the kind of body which would be competent to do so. The principal features of such a body were evident. In the first place, it would have to bring together technically qualified representatives of the interests involved, namely workers, employers and government departments concerned with industrial matters. In the second place, it would have to have the power to frame its decisions in the form of international conventions which would give rise to binding international obligations. And in the third place, it would have to be a permanent institution

---

[7] Harold Butler: *Confident morning* (London, Faber & Faber, 1950), p. 157.
[8] George N. Barnes: *From workshop to War Cabinet* (London, Herbert Jenkins, 1924), pp. 247–48.

functioning continuously so that it could take account of changing conditions. Such a body could only be brought into existence and endowed with the necessary powers by an international treaty, and the meeting of the peace conference would provide a unique opportunity when this could be done.

When the Government agreed, Phelan assumed his work was done. Much to his surprise, he was appointed secretary of the labour section of the British delegation to Paris, which also included Barnes, Butler and Delevingne.

On 2 January 1919 Phelan arrived in Paris to establish contact with the other delegations and find some precious space in the Hotel Astoria, the working quarters of the entire British Empire contingent. Barnes followed in mid-January, having obtained the Cabinet's approval to secure three objectives in the peace treaty: an international organization on labour questions, of permanent character, and with representation from employers and workers as well as governments. He and Delevingne became the British members of the conference's 15-man Commission on International Labour Legislation, with Butler as a substitute member. Proposals for a permanent international labour organization were submitted also by the Belgian, French, United States and Italian delegations, but none were as detailed as those from the British. When the Commission set to work on 31 January, memoranda by Phelan and Butler formed the basis of its discussions. Phelan's memorandum, dated 15–20 January, suggested that the proposed International Labour Organization have two organs: a secretariat for collecting and disseminating information and a conference to adopt legislation. Pragmatically, he recognized that the desire for supranationalism would have to be moderated to obtain the compliance of governments. At the same time, he wanted employers and workers to have direct and equal representation alongside governments in the ILO. His solution – and his third big idea for the ILO – was the "2:1:1" formula. As Phelan conceived it, each government delegate would have two votes, and each workers' or employers' representative one each. Facing stiff opposition from the Americans, French and Italians, who favoured a "1:1:1" formula, Barnes assented to two modifications to Phelan's scheme. From the Belgian representative, Emile Vandervelde, he accepted a proposal that the government votes should be given to two delegates, not one; and he further agreed that "2:1:1" should apply in the International Labour Conference (ILC) and "1:1:1" in committees. To reconcile ILO authority with State sovereignty, Phelan proposed that the ILC could reach a decision by a two-thirds majority, but that such decisions would have to be referred by governments to their national parliaments. Butler later proposed the creation of an executive. Barnes was primarily responsible for steering the British proposals through the 36 sittings of the Commission and getting their substance accepted unanimously; he would treasure the Labour Chapter of the Versailles Treaty as his greatest achievement and devote much of his time on retirement to promoting the ILO, tripartism and harmony in industrial relations.

Phelan beavered away behind the scenes, the only one of the British team able to devote his full attention to the Commission. James T. Shotwell, librarian of the US delegation — though, as a member of the quasi-secret "Inquiry", President Woodrow Wilson's foreign policy advisory group, he was more influential than that designation implied — found him

> a loyal colleague, fertile and creative of suggestion, one who was never lacking in the understanding of the difficulties confronting the American delegation, perhaps aided by his Irish sense of humour. The [ILO] owes more to him than will probably ever be widely known, for both as planner and negotiator he worked impersonally in order to work effectively. [9]

Characteristically, Phelan developed a greater rapport with Barnes, a former official of the Amalgamated Society of Engineers, than with his fellow mandarins. He also felt a certain political sympathy for Barnes, who came to be vilified in British Labour circles for his anti-leftism and who projected the ILO as an alternative to doctrines of class conflict. But he shared nothing of Barnes' revanchist attitude towards Germany. At a personal level, the conference was enormously beneficial for Phelan. Initially intimidated in the company of world leaders, he soon grew in self-confidence and blossomed in the cosmopolitan milieu.

Phelan regarded the peace conference's adoption of the legal–institutional framework of the ILO on 11 April 1919 as the beginning of the ILO, and of his involvement with it. The peace treaty provided that the First Session of the International Labour Conference would meet in Washington, DC: the Conference was to appoint the Governing Body, which would elect a Director, who would then appoint his staff. The Conference's organizing committee in London was in practice the labour section of the British delegation to Paris, funded by a loan from the Treasury, and so the "peculiarly British" stamp on the ILO at this formative phase persisted. Phelan, as assistant secretary of the committee, requisitioned premises and assembled a secretariat. Starting from scratch was no mean task, as the legendary disorganization of the Washington Conference would demonstrate. The British influence was confirmed in Washington, though other delegations also came to the fore, and, to the annoyance of Lloyd George, English candidates

---

[9] James T. Shotwell: *The autobiography of James T. Shotwell* (Indianapolis, Bobbs-Merrill, 1961), p. 97.

Edward J. Phelan (1888–1967).

Albert Thomas, first Director of the ILO, and
British Prime Minister David Lloyd George.

The Commission on International Labour Legislation at the Paris Peace Conference,
February–March 1919.

First delegation of Ireland to the Sixth Session of the ILC, Geneva, June-July 1924.

From left to right:
Michael MacWhite (Permanent Irish representative to the League of Nations),
B. Stafford (Government adviser, Ministry of Industry and Commerce),
Ronald J.P. Mortished (Workers' adviser, Assistant to the Secretary of the Irish Labour Party
and Trade Union Congress), Alfred O'Rahilly (Government delegate, Professor,
University College, Cork), Thomas Foran (Workers' delegate, Member of the National
Executive of the Irish Labour Party and Trade Union Congress), R.C. Ferguson
(Government delegate, Director of Industries Department of the Ministry of Industry
and Commerce), Andrew O'Shaughnessy (Employers' delegate, Managing Director,
Dripsey Woollen Mills, Ltd.), Edward J. Phelan (Chief of the ILO Diplomatic Division).

Opposite page, bottom
The Organizing Committee of the First Session of the ILC (Washington, DC), London, 1919.

First row, from left to right:
William Rappard (Switzerland), Ernest Mahaim (Belgium),
Sir Malcolm Delevingne (United Kingdom), James T. Shotwell (United States),
Arthur Fontaine (France), Ethelbert Stewart (United States),
Minoru Oka (Japan), Guglielmo Emanuele di Palma Castiglione (Italy).

Second row:
Edward J. Phelan (United Kingdom), Harold B. Butler (United Kingdom),
John B. Andrews (United States), Shunzo Yoshisaka (Japan).

From left to right:
Albert Thomas, (Director),
Edward J. Phelan, (Chief of the
Diplomatic Division) and
Georges Fleury (Chief of the Office
of the Director), Geneva, 1922.

From left to right:
Edward J. Phelan (Deputy Director),
Harold B. Butler (Director)
and John G. Winant (Assistant
Director), Geneva, June 1938.

ILO's temporary premises at The Presbyterian College of Montreal (now Morrice Hall), McGill University, Montreal, August–November 1940.

US Secretary of Labor, Frances Perkins, presenting Edward J. Phelan with the original sketch by the cartoonist F.O. Alexander entitled "Above the Storm", published in the *Evening Bulletin* on 20 April 1944, Philadelphia, 12 May 1944.

President Franklin D. Roosevelt addressing the final sitting of the New York Conference at the White House, Washington, DC, 6 November 1941.

C. Wilfred Jenks (Legal Adviser) and Edward J. Phelan at the 26th Session of the ILC, Philadelphia, 20 April–12 May 1944.

Edward J. Phelan signing the Declaration of Philadelphia at the White House in the presence of (left to right) President Franklin D. Roosevelt, Cordell Hull (US Secretary of State), Walter Nash (President of the 26th Session of the ILC), Frances Perkins (US Secretary of Labor) and Lindsay Rogers (ILO Assistant Director), Washington, DC, 17 May 1944.

Edward J. Phelan and David A. Morse,
newly elected Director-General,
San Francisco, 12 June 1948.

Mrs. E.J. Phelan and Mrs. L. Rogers at the 28th Session of the ILC, Seattle, June 1946.

lost elections for the two most important posts in the ILO to the French: Arthur Fontaine defeated Delevingne for Chairman of the Governing Body, and Albert Thomas defeated Butler for Director of the International Labour Office, the civil service of the ILC. In Phelan's maritime metaphor, "Barnes, Butler and Delevingne built the ship … But Albert Thomas was the Captain chosen to take her on her voyage across uncharted seas." [10]

Phelan had served as principal secretary of the Conference, and devised rules of procedure which, with few amendments, became the standing orders of future sessions of the ILC. He was now respected as possessing an unrivalled grasp of the ILO's Constitution. In January 1920, Thomas took him aside after a meeting in London, where the ILO was in temporary quarters, and offered him a post in the Office. Subject to further discussion on terms, Phelan accepted without hesitation. His first task was to evict civil servants from the ILO's offices in Parliament Street, recruit clerks and messengers, and find typewriters, tables and stationery!

First officer

Phelan's appointment was confirmed formally at the next meeting of the Governing Body, which concluded in Paris on 28 January 1920. Shortly beforehand he helped defuse a potential crisis, arising from a British Government insistence that Butler be Deputy Director of the ILO and Thomas' refusal to have a deputy imposed on him. Phelan's suggestion that the British nominate Thomas for Director and that he be allowed to choose his own deputy – who turned out to be Butler – was accepted.

As the first appointee to the Office, Phelan's duties were "all-embracing". His immediate responsibilities were to deal with finance and engage a staff, but he also found himself handling the most minor of administrative problems, and each day brought a novel emergency. He would recall the period from February to May 1920 as the busiest of his life – a perception which may have been influenced by the death of his father, after a brief illness, on 10 March.

As he embarked on his ILO career, Phelan regarded himself as a functionary, and mentally was something of a Whitehall man on secondment. Strategically, he saw his job as the welding of the two main bureaucratic influences on the ILO

---

[10] E.J. Phelan: *Yes and Albert Thomas* (London, Cresset Press, 1936), p. x. The book is a valuable account of Phelan's time in the ILO under Thomas' directorship.

– the British and the French – and he was convinced of the superior efficiency of the former. Used to a system in which ultimate authority lay with a principal, and the duties of subalterns were defined exactly, the British were bewildered by the Rapport – the daily policy discussion of senior officials – and suspected the Cabinet – the Director's team of personal advisers – as a cabal. The continental members of the Office were no less confused by the British practice of dealing with issues through files rather than allocating them to individuals. At the same time, Phelan was enthusiastic for administrative innovation: in his Ministry of Labour days he had invited expertise from outside the civil service to collaborate on policy exploration and argued that the modern public servant should be proactive rather than regulative. Above all, he was excited by the ILO's tripartism and supranationalism, and hugely impressed by Thomas. Temperamentally and ideologically, the reserved Anglophone civil servant and the strident French socialist politician were an unlikely pair. But they recognized a complementarity in their strengths and weaknesses, and Phelan warmed to the energy and vision of Thomas. Slowly he developed a better appreciation of the French approach, even to the point of cultivating a more continental appearance and, perhaps in emulation of his hirsute boss, a moustache.

The British had envisaged the Office as no more than a secretariat. Thomas had a grander plan. Inspired by Jouhaux, he resolved that the ILO should concern itself not merely with securing an equilibrium in systems of labour legislation, but with social justice. To that end, the Office was to be organized in three divisions, diplomatic, research and political, and to have its own network of legations in member States, dealing directly with workers and employers. The Diplomatic Division was to be responsible for meetings of the Governing Body and the ILC, relations with governments, the League of Nations and other international bodies, and all matters pertaining to Conventions and the ILO Constitution. Delighted with Thomas' scheme, Phelan was at once flattered to be offered the position of Chief of the Diplomatic Division, and confident of his ability to do the job.

When the ILO settled in Geneva in July 1920, Thomas took more effective control, and Phelan became, de facto, the third official, running the Office in the absence of the Director and his deputy. As Thomas was usually abroad for 20 weeks of the year – liaising with governments, trade unions and employers in the member States – Phelan acquired considerable experience. He also accompanied his boss on trips to the United States, Canada, the Far East and various European countries, and Thomas' zest for direct engagement with politicians and the public ensured that he acquired first-hand knowledge of what government ministers, employers and workers thought of and wanted from the ILO. He was no longer just an official. Harold Laski, one of England's leading political theorists, observed, after a visit to Geneva in August 1926:

> The League [of Nations] itself was not especially impressive … On the other hand the International Labour Office does impress. One has the sense that fertile thinking is on foot and that really effective work is being done. The real genius of the place is an Irishman named Phelan who has a good deal of Felix [Frankfurter]'s quick nervous charm. He has a power of speculation that kept me up till four one morning. [11]

Phelan had no reputation as an early riser.

The evolution of Phelan's thinking is evident in his first four publications on the ILO. A talk to the League of Nations Union summer school at Geneva in August 1923, published by the Union as *The necessity for international labour organisation*, made a practical case for permanent machinery to deal with the negative consequences of industrialization for workers, and cited a moral imperative that governments repay their wartime debt to labour. By contrast, three articles in *Studies*, an Irish Catholic social review, in 1925–26 took these arguments for granted, and projected the real significance of the ILO as lying in its supranationalism and tripartism. The first article was republished by the League of Nations Non-Partisan Association in New York as *The International Labour Organisation: Its ideals and results*. Its primary thesis was that the traditional concept of state sovereignty was obsolete in the interdependent post-Versailles world: "the first effective condition of modern sovereignty is Membership [or the right to membership] of the League [of Nations], the possession by a State of what may be called international citizenship and the international franchise". The ILO went further in this respect, in departing from the old principle of unanimity in international decision-making and thereby opening up "possibilities of wider and more rapid international agreement", which might ultimately lead to "a measure of international democracy". Tripartism, Phelan felt, had had "a profound effect on the development of employers' and workers' organisations throughout the world", and been of particular benefit to trade unions seeking recognition and an acceptable programme in developing countries. [12] It also offered an alternative to

---

[11] *Holmes–Laski letters: The correspondence of Mr. Justice Holmes and Harold J. Laski, 1916–1935*, ed. Mark de Wolfe Howe (London, Oxford University Press, 1953), p. 870–71. Frankfurter was a colleague of United States Supreme Court judge Oliver Wendell Holmes (see Ch. 6, n. 38 below).

[12] Phelan: "The International Labour Organisation: Its ideals and results", p. 621; id., "Ireland and the International Labour Organisation", *Studies: An Irish Quarterly*, Vol. 15, Sept. 1926, p. 397.

23

communism and its trade union international, the Profintern, which was strongly opposed to the ILO. The optimism was moderated a little with acknowledgement that initial expectations of the ILO had not been realized, and that it faced an increasingly difficult economic environment, in Europe especially.

Expanding on the theme of sovereignty, Phelan published an article in *La Revue des nations* in 1927, defending the claim of the Irish Free State – which had been legally established on 6 December 1922 following the Anglo-Irish Treaty – to be a sovereign entity despite its status as a dominion of the British Empire. He rested his case on its membership of the League of Nations, its competence to make international treaties and its ratification of eight ILO Conventions. He had, moreover, been a covert agent in making these a reality. To the annoyance of the British, Phelan emerged as an ardent Irish Nationalist in Geneva, a brave decision which risked his prospects of advancement in the ILO and scuppered his chances of crowning his career with one of the orders of chivalry customarily conferred on distinguished Whitehall men. He enlisted Thomas in the cause. In February 1922, both attended the Irish Race Conference in Paris, one of a series of conventions which sought to rally the Irish diaspora. Phelan was a valued friend to all Irish visitors to Geneva, and his role was neither confined to the ILO nor passive. He corresponded with the Free State President, W.T. Cosgrave, and various Cabinet ministers, met them personally on visits to Dublin and tendered advice on tactics in the League, suggesting ways in which "we" could assert "our" independence at Geneva and loosen ties with Britain in the Imperial Conference. He was on intimate terms with Michael MacWhite, Irish representative to Switzerland from 1921 to 1923 and to the League from 1923 to 1928 and Vice-President of the ILC in 1928, and with Seán Lester, his replacement as representative to the League. Lester described Ned, as he called him, as "a man of influence with the Government ... I at regular intervals take Mr Phelan completely into my confidence regarding our League affairs. He of course reciprocates...".[13] Two other confederates were Alfred O'Rahilly, an Irish Government delegate to the ILCs in 1924–25 and 1932, and Ronald J.P. Mortished, Assistant Secretary of the Irish Labour Party and Trade Union Congress, who joined the ILO staff in 1930.

Phelan formed a lifelong friendship with the bumptious O'Rahilly, a professor of mathematics and physics at University College, Cork, polymath, politician and doughty Catholic apologist. Their minds met precisely on Ireland, the League of Nations and the ILO, and both regularly pressed their opinions on Irish officials.

---

[13] Lester to Walshe, 15 May 1930, in Ronan Fanning et al. (eds): *Documents on Irish foreign policy*, Vol. 3: 1926–1932 (Dublin, Royal Irish Academy, 2002), p. 539.

It was probably not coincidental that President Cosgrave took the ILO seriously, despite the conservatism of his Cumann na nGaedheal party, which had been formed from the right wing of Sinn Féin in 1922. Cosgrave provided what was virtually a state funeral for the Labour Party Senator Thomas MacPartlin, who died suddenly in Geneva while a member of the first Irish delegation to the ILO. And it was in the ILO rather than the League that Ireland first asserted its diplomatic independence of Britain. When the Free State joined the ILO in 1923, copies of all Conventions were sent to Dublin. Six Conventions adopted by Britain before the establishment of the Free State were ratified by the Irish Parliament, as were two not adopted, and all were registered with the League without referral to London. Phelan and O'Rahilly also pleaded with Dublin to register the Anglo-Irish Treaty with the League. Cosgrave agreed gingerly in July 1924, knowing His Majesty's Government would protest strongly that the Free State was an imperial dominion, not an independent country. Phelan remained concerned, gripped almost by a personal anxiety, that his wily old chums in Whitehall would whittle the Free State into a Home Rule province. A typical example of his jealous watch for Ireland followed a dinner with the Romanian minister in London.[14] Discovering, by chance, that the minister considered himself accredited "as much to Dublin and Belfast as to London", Phelan promptly notified Dublin that here was

> a dangerous ambiguity which damages our status, and which might perhaps figure among the points of status to be cleared up in London. If the Roumanian and other Governments consider that their Ministers in London are entitled to deal with their relations with Ireland it is not difficult to imagine that they can hardly regard us as independent at Geneva.[15]

It was as if, outside the protocols, he had difficulty in restraining his nervous energy. While the Cabinet and its tyros in Geneva were thrilled to have a friend at court, civil servants in Dublin took a more jaundiced view of his interventions, and the overly intense lobbying did not serve him well in the long run. He would make the same mistake with the US, Canadian and British Governments as Acting Director.

---

[14] In the diplomatic service, a minister was a grade below an ambassador. Small diplomatic missions were often headed by ministers from the 1920s to the 1940s. In the case of the Irish Free State, the appointment of ministers rather than ambassadors had the added advantage of minimizing difficulties with the British Government, which did not regard Ireland as a foreign country until it left the Commonwealth in 1949.

[15] Phelan to MacNeill, 16 Oct. 1926, in Fanning et al. (eds): *Documents on Irish foreign policy*, Vol. 3, p. 70. Phelan's letters to Irish Government officials are in the National Archives, Dublin, Department of the Taoiseach, S 5685, Correspondence with Mr E.J. Phelan, ILO.

With his ingrained detachment from the world of party politics, Phelan made a second error of judgement in getting too cosy with the Cumann na nGaedheal leaders. The general election of 1932 brought Éamon de Valera's Fianna Fáil party to power for the next 16 years. Socially radical and republican, Fianna Fáil would have been more robustly in tune with Phelan's prescriptions for Ireland and the ILO. "It is curious to note what a unique status Ireland could have in both the League of Nations and the International Labour Conferences," noted de Valera's paper, the *Irish Press*, in a front-page article after the new Government took office. "It is in Geneva that the freedom of Ireland can best be shown to be an international asset." [16] Seán Lemass, then Minister for Industry and Commerce, was elected President of the ILC in June 1937, and would write the foreword to Phelan's memoirs. Phelan continued to liaise with Irish diplomats in Geneva. He admired de Valera's speeches at the League and thought him "very pleasant and approachable". [17] But he was not as close to de Valera's people as he had been to Cosgrave's, and his hitherto frequent missives to Dublin ministers tapered off after 1932.

With the hectic period of the ILO's itinerant existence behind him, Phelan's duties became more manageable. He liked to work late, which allowed him to avoid disturbance and early morning starts, but never took papers home, preserving the evening and weekends for relaxation and socializing. Geneva was losing the cosmopolitan atmosphere it had acquired from its wartime refugees, and Phelan missed his raffish London pleasures. Talk was his "favourite amusement", and he had had few opportunities for banter, debate and witticism since the Hampden Club. With a few acquaintances he founded the International Club in 1922, which became instantly popular with associates of the League of Nations, the ILO and the diplomatic corps: 300 applied to join initially. Within this microcosm of global rivalries, protracted international wrangling ensued over the choice of a club president, culminating in unanimous backing for the Waterfordman. MacWhite was so impressed with the near-universal lack of animosity towards an Irish candidate – and its effect in silencing British objections to a "Sinn Féiner" – that he advised Dublin that here was a lesson for strategy in the League! The club moved into a former casino leased from the municipality, and offered a billiards room, a bar, a restaurant and a library, as well as introducing the American practice of lunches with guest speakers. The clientele gradually clustered in coteries, each devoted to food, drink, news or talk. Phelan ate sparingly

---

[16] *Irish Press*, 16 April 1932.
[17] Quoted in J. Anthony Gaughan: *Alfred O'Rahilly: Controversialist*, Part 1, *Social reformer* (Blackrock, Kingdom Books, 1992), p. 119.

and treasured the club for the conversationalists, ever alert for a good anecdote and never passing up the chance to assure incredulous journalists that the ILO was far more interesting than the League. He presided over the International Club for 12 years.

By the 1930s Phelan's health was beginning to fail, and he preferred to harbour the remaining energy in his thin frame. There remained a select social life with his partner Fernande Croutaz. Born in Nanterre, near Paris, in September 1899, to a Swiss mother and an "unknown" father, she had lived in Switzerland since the age of seven. It was a romantic union, Fernande's only assets being her beauty and personality. By all accounts, her "vivacity and sparkle balanced his more serious, reflective disposition".[18] They married in Genthod, a village just north of Geneva, on 10 June 1940, to enable her to accompany him in the ILO's wartime evacuation to Canada. The ceremony was a civil one: Fernande had been divorced in 1925, and Laski noted of her partner that he had "a hatred of organised religion that gave me immense pleasure".[19] The extent of the anti-clericalism is unclear: Phelan had bridled at criticism of Catholic devotion in his days as a tour guide in Milan and was buried according to Catholic rites; and it was not so pronounced as to affect his relations with O'Rahilly, who died a monsignor. The Phelans, as they were known in some circles even before their marriage, enjoyed a weekly bridge game with Seán and Elsie Lester, sampling a different wine each time. Other diversions included skiing, walking, trips to Ireland and, above all, yachting on Lake Geneva. The private side of Phelan's life became increasingly remote from his staff. Wilfred Jenks, who joined the ILO in 1931, remembered him as "a solitary, who could enjoy but never surrendered himself to gregariousness".

> It was a common saying in those days that the staff of the ILO fell into three groups: the small and privileged group of those who had spoken to Phelan; the larger group of those who knew what Phelan looked like; and the still larger group of those who had never seen Phelan, whose hours of arrival at and departure from the office were somewhat unusual by conventional standards.[20]

Nonetheless, there was no one in the ILO who was unaware of his influence, or of the ubiquitous 'EJP' annotated on ILO files.

---

[18] Documents re the Phelan estate (no call number), NUI, Dublin; Phelan Endowment draft, Pension Fund nominal file No. 708, ILO Historical Archives.

[19] *Holmes–Laski letters*, p. 871.

[20] See p. 3 above.

First mate

At 3.30 a.m. on 8 May 1932 Phelan was woken with the news that Thomas had collapsed in a café in Paris and been rushed to hospital, where he was pronounced dead. Phelan described the news as "shattering", and wrote an outstanding memoir of their years in harness: issued in 1936, in Paris as *Albert Thomas et la création du BIT* and in London as *Yes and Albert Thomas*, it was his most substantial publication and the one of which he was most proud. Butler took over as Director, and Phelan was appointed Assistant Director in 1933. It was the start of the second trimester of his ILO career, in which he would emerge as a personality in his own right. Hitherto, Thomas had been the public face of the ILO, and Phelan was seen as his private secretary. Butler was very different from Thomas, and Phelan's relations with the new Director were never as intimate as they had been with the old. They had Whitehall in common, but not much else: Butler was an Eton and Balliol man, married to the daughter of a former assistant inspector-general of the Royal Irish Constabulary, and a social Tory, nostalgic for the sweet serenity of Edwardian England. Nonetheless, himself shy and reserved, he allowed Phelan a greater role in acting, speaking and publishing for the ILO. He was also convinced that the ILO could best be strengthened by persuading the United States to become a member. In consequence, North America rather than Europe became Phelan's lodestar, and his sense of mission expanded commensurately with the challenge of the Great Depression. In collusion with Professor Shotwell of Columbia University and the Carnegie Endowment for International Peace – with whom he had collaborated intermittently since the Paris Peace Conference in 1919 – he worked to raise the profile of the ILO in the United States, and set out its role in the economic crisis and maintaining world peace.

Measured in style, Butler made no attempt to match Thomas' visionary drive. Phelan reckoned he did as well as could be expected – there was none to equal Thomas in his eyes – and praised Butler for his high intelligence and for sustaining Thomas' achievements in the worsening economic and political circumstances of "the devil's decade". With Franklin D. Roosevelt's election to the presidency towards the end of 1932, Butler saw an opportunity for bringing the United States into the fold. Not wishing to alarm US isolationists with a personal visit, he despatched Phelan, ostensibly on a mission to Canada and Mexico: New York and Washington, of course, lay in between. Phelan had some familiarity with the United States, having attended the Washington Conference in 1919 and toured North America with Thomas. In 1931 he had delivered the Harris Memorial Lectures at the University of Chicago, speaking on "unemployment as a world problem" with J.M. Keynes, the British economist who would exert a profound impact on post-war economic thinking in the Western world, and Karl Pribram, former chief statistician in the ILO's Research Division. He had had friends in New York since the Paris Peace Conference, notably Shotwell. In Washington he availed himself of MacWhite, now Irish minister to the United States, to make contacts in the diplomatic corps. An admirer of the American "can-do" attitude, he was astonished by the informality, energy and efficiency of the officials of Roosevelt's Administration, nonplussed by their frank aversion to the League of Nations and cautiously encouraged by their attitude to the ILO. On 20 August 1934, the United States became the 59th member of the ILO, Butler and the ILC having made it clear that accession would involve no obligations to the League. For Phelan it was a moment of wider significance. He and Shotwell hoped it would signal the re-emergence of the United States from isolationism. Both were then collaborating – along with Butler and Delevingne – on *The origins of the International Labor Organization*, sponsored by the Carnegie Endowment, and in 1935 the Endowment's monthly, *International Conciliation*, devoted an issue to papers by Phelan, Shotwell and the eminent law professor Manley O. Hudson on the possibilities opened up by US membership of the ILO. More specifically, Phelan welcomed the implicit affirmation of the ILO's independence from the League, believing it a prerequisite for the development of a broader role for the ILO. He had always supported the ILO view – contested by the League's Secretary-General – that while affiliation to the League ought to imply membership of the ILO, the ILO should be free to admit other States. He deemed the consequential deterioration in relations with the League – happily of brief duration – to be unfortunate but a price worth paying. He welcomed, too, the implication that in the long run the ILO would have to take responsibility for its own finances.

In 1938 Butler resigned, to avoid clashing with the French Government over an appointment to the ILO's Paris office. He suppressed the real reason for his departure, subsequently explaining that "In the critical position that then existed in Europe it was not even possible to thresh the matter out in public."[21] In this fraught context, Phelan put himself forward for Director. He reckoned he could count on 14 votes in the Governing Body, mainly from employers' and workers' representatives, but he knew that the other candidate, John Gilbert Winant, would probably win 16 votes, mainly from government representatives. Gil, as he was known, was a former Assistant Director of the Office and a senior official in the Roosevelt Administration, and ILO chiefs believed that a seasoned

---

[21] Harold Beresford Butler: *The lost peace: A personal impression* (London, Faber & Faber, 1941), cited in Antony Evelyn Alcock, *History of the International Labour Organisation* (London, Macmillan, 1971), p. 155.

American politician would be a major asset as Europe descended into crisis. As a narrow victory would be an inauspicious start for the new man, Phelan was persuaded to withdraw. He dismissed a deal which would have guaranteed him the job of Deputy Director with additional powers, but accepted the post from Winant after the election. Unlike his colleagues, Phelan had misgivings about what was, in effect, an external appointment. Winant spent much of his time in the United States, and was preoccupied with American politics, even in Geneva. At a personal level the two men got on well. Phelan appreciated Winant's abilities and "sympathy for all in distress", but deemed his methods "oblique ... and often baffling in the extreme". His recollections in *Studies*, which, unlike his memoirs, normally avoided criticism of his colleagues, included the subtle disparagement that there was "no opportunity to discover how [Winant's] unusual gifts and a background of experience so different from those of his predecessors would have influenced the ILO's development". [22]

Winant's "one great service", in Phelan's opinion, was arranging for the relocation of the ILO in the summer of 1940. It was a painful imposition on the staff, which left them divided and open to accusations of flight and betrayal. By contrast, the League of Nations secretariat resolved to "sit it out". But Phelan shared Winant's belief that the ILO must be free to pursue its social goals and maintain contact with affiliates if it was "to escape paralysis or possibly even extinction", and Winant saved the ILO from going the way of the League. [23] Phelan had pressed for evacuation plans as early as March 1939, and when the time came the ILO was better prepared for departure than the League. After a proposed move to Vichy was overtaken by the French collapse, Winant appealed, without success, to the State Department for an invitation to the United States. Given the ILO's need for good communications and up to date research facilities, the only realistic alternatives were London or Canada. Lisbon was ruled out for its regime, and Dublin received the damning judgement: "communications ... impossible". [24] Jenks suggested Canada: a belligerent, but less obviously so than front-line Britain. When Canada agreed on 26 July 1940, Phelan received a coded message from Winant to proceed immediately with 40 members of staff on the sole remaining escape route via Lisbon. The last group slipped out of Geneva on 7 August, without being told their ultimate destination. It was feared that once Germany got wind of the shift to enemy territory, it would compel Vichy France

---

[22] E.J. Phelan: "Some reminiscences of the International Labour Organization", *Studies: An Irish Quarterly*, Vol. 43, No. 171, Autumn 1954, pp. 241–70 (reprinted in this book), at p. 256.

[23] Ibid., p. 259.

[24] Memorandum, Documents re the Phelan estate, NUI, Dublin.

or Spain to close the borders. Phelan himself delayed for another week in a vain effort to get the League Supervisory Commission to approve the ILO's budget for 1941. He then set off with his compatriot Mortished and a few jerrycans of petrol. They reached the Spanish frontier on 15 August, unaware that General Franco had closed the border to League and ILO staff two days earlier. Anticipating trouble, Phelan motored along a secondary road to a minor customs post and pointed to "Diplomatic" on his unfamiliar Irish passport; the guards waved him through, thinking he was the Irish minister to Madrid. On 18 August, the ILO announced publicly that it was moving to Canada.

Portugal was pleasant after the gloom of defeated France and destitute Spain. Lisbon enchanted Fernande, which was fortunate as her husband tarried again until the Supervisory Commission managed to meet over three days in late September. The ILO's budget for 1941 was approved and, with hours to spare, Phelan embarked on the *Excambion* for New York and Montreal, where the ILO was to be accommodated in McGill University. Accustomed to palatial working quarters in Geneva, the cramped and spartan rooms in McGill came as a shock. Conditions gradually improved, and Phelan was very grateful for the hospitality of the Canadians, who were struggling to cope with the severe shortage of space in wartime Montreal.

Taking the helm

Winant's announcement of his impending resignation as Director in February 1941, to take up the post of US Ambassador in London, came as a bombshell. Phelan had no appetite for the top job in wartime. He was acutely aware that he lacked Winant's political clout, with the now crucially important US Government in particular, and feared that without it the ILO would not survive the war. Moreover, there was no possibility of the Governing Body meeting to appoint a successor in the foreseeable future, which would leave "a mere de facto Chargé d'Affaires", as he put it, trying to speak for the ILO without the required imprimatur. Repeated pleas to Winant to be invested with "the fullest authority" before his departure met with a procrastination that Phelan found as bewildering as it was dispiriting. Winant told his deputy, "I have never had such splendid loyalty and such valuable help," and yet declined to make any recommendations as to the succession. [25] To avoid the Directorship being replaced with a commission, which

---

[25] E.J. Phelan: "The ILO sets up its wartime centre in Canada", *Studies: An Irish Quarterly*, Vol. 44, No. 174, Summer 1955), pp. 152–70 (reprinted in this book) at pp. 158, 162–3.

he believed would cripple the ILO, Phelan resolved on unilateral action. Immediately on receipt of Winant's letter of resignation, he notified all members of the ILO that he was assuming command, pro tem. Four days later, Carter Goodrich, Chairman of the Governing Body, announced that Phelan was Acting Director as from 16 February.

Phelan considered his achievements as Acting Director to be the most important of his life. His entry in Who Was Who, which he wrote himself, is purely factual apart from the following: "kept ILO in active operation during War, 1941–44; secured adoption of Declaration of Philadelphia and its insertion in revised constitution of ILO and obtained recognition of ILO as a Specialised Agency of United Nations …".[26] Distracted by the circumstances of Winant's departure, he had given no consideration to how he would lead the ILO. On reflection, he concluded that the Office was doing as much as it could, but that its relations with governments needed to be revitalized, and that the "fundamental danger" lay in the "disintegration in the peripheral machinery", that is, the ILC and the Governing Body. His first major initiative was therefore to secure backing – from the United States, Britain, and the Governing Body especially – for a special session of the ILC, which assembled in New York in October 1941. He was particularly pleased that Roosevelt made a very public gesture of solidarity in inviting the closing meeting to convene in the White House. Phelan was satisfied that the ILO had "turned the corner".[27] The Conference had agreed to make the ILO "a clearing house" for measures of post-war reconstruction, and that agenda was soon invigorated by America's entry into the war. With an Allied victory assured, however long and arduous the journey, thoughts would turn increasingly to reconstruction, the United States would have a captain's part in the process, and as the only other international body was the League of Nations, Washington would inevitably make use of the ILO.

Marooned in Geneva – and partly in Vichy – the League of Nations secretariat could only look enviously at the success of "Ned's people", and swallow its frustration as Phelan undertook publicity initiatives to dissociate the ILO from the stricken League.[28] In April 1942 the League Treasurer, Seymour Jacklin, warned Lester, Acting Secretary-General of the League since September 1940, that any clash between the Supervisory Commission and the ILO would be resolved to

---

[26] *Who Was Who*, 1961–1970, p. 890.

[27] E.J. Phelan: "The ILO turns the corner", *Studies: An Irish Quarterly*, Vol. 45, No. 178, Summer, 1956, pp. 160–186 (reprinted in this book), at p. 163.

[28] Stephen Ashworth Barcroft: "The international civil servant: The League of Nations career of Seán Lester, 1929–1947" (PhD thesis, Trinity College, Dublin, 1973), p. 273.

the advantage of the latter.[29] There are odd coincidences in the circumstances of "Ned" and "Seán", which deepened their friendship without moderating the chronic friction between their respective organizations. Matters came to the boil at a meeting of the Supervisory Commission in Montreal in August 1942. Exploiting his mastery of procedure, and the ILO's better standing with member States, Phelan prevented the Commission from applying cuts in the League's budget to the ILO. At issue, he believed, was the principle of whether the ILO's finances should reflect the political fortunes of the League, or the services demanded of it. Between 1940 and 1945 the ILO's share of the League's budget rose from under 30 per cent to 50 per cent. Breaking the "financial nexus" in August 1942 marked the zenith of Phelan's standing. Tellingly, his recollections of the ILO in *Studies* did not venture beyond this point.

To the dismay of the Workers' Group especially, the ILO failed to exploit the opportunities created by the New York Conference, and was instead increasingly marginalized in the machinery of reconstruction. Phelan came under mounting criticism for his alleged lack of drive and ambition. He himself felt hobbled by two difficulties. First, there was the question of his appointment as Director. Given his 30 years as a bureaucrat, and scrupulous respect for regulations, it was natural that he would feel inhibited by his "Acting" designation, and once the Governing Body was able to meet, the failure to formalize his status could only be taken as indicative of a want of confidence in his abilities. Initially the Workers' Group favoured his appointment, while the British Government had the strongest reservations. It did not help that he had identified so stridently with Irish assertions of sovereignty in the 1920s, that Winston Churchill took Ireland's wartime neutrality as a personal affront and that another Irishman headed the other international body. In pressing his case, he merely alienated the United States and Canadian Governments, and made the issue something of an embarrassment. The second inhibiting factor was finance. Demands on the ILO were outstripping the capacity of its coffers. Ultimately, Phelan believed, the results would be disastrous, and he was not prepared to take on commitments and trust that the resources would follow. A third problem was that the ILO had its enemies. In the League of Nations, among employers and in governments, there were those who never liked the existence of this concession to labour. Most serious – and ironic in view of Phelan's long-standing advocacy of collaboration with Moscow – was the hostility of the emergent superpower, the Soviet Union: partly because of its

---

[29] Seymour Jacklin (1882–1971) was Secretary of the Public Service Commission in South Africa when he was appointed Treasurer of the League of Nations in 1926. He was promoted to Under Secretary-General of the League of Nations in 1944 and left in 1946.

connection with the League, and partly because communists equated tripartism with corporatism.

By 1943 Phelan was being criticized by the Governing Body for inactivity, and by workers' delegates for a lack of nerve. Work which might have gone to the ILO was routed instead to new United Nations (UN) agencies.[30] The establishment of the UN Relief and Rehabilitation Administration in 1943, to provide aid in territories liberated from the Axis, amounted to a direct challenge to the role envisaged for the ILO at the ILC in New York in October 1941. Phelan also misread a UN Conference on Food and Agriculture in 1943, assuming it would confine itself to technical aspects of food production and supply. He learned in the press that it dealt with a wider range of issues, including living standards and welfare. In 1945 it became the Food and Agriculture Organization of the UN.

As alternative agencies consolidated, Phelan feared that the ILO would be swept away with the League of Nations. It was essential to re-establish its mandate and secure credentials from the nascent UN. The first objective was achieved at the 26th Session of the ILC at Philadelphia in April and May 1944. The Declaration of Philadelphia extended the 1919 Labour Charter of the ILO by giving it a more comprehensive social remit. Realizing the second objective was more tortuous. The ILO was not discussed at the Dumbarton Oaks conference in August and September 1944, at which the UN Charter was drafted. It was another embarrassment for Phelan. John Hearne, Irish minister to Canada, spoke to him soon afterwards, and reported, with a knowing smile, "I avoided Dumbarton Oaks."[31] Whatever humiliation might await at the UN's inaugural conference in San Francisco in 1945, it was vital for the ILO to remain in the frame. Powerful support for its inclusion came from the British Trades Union Congress; and powerful opposition from the Soviet Union. Phelan lobbied the US State and Labor Departments, and got their approval for an unofficial presence. Unfortunately for the ILO and League delegates, the conference organizer was Alger Hiss, later uncovered as a Soviet agent, and every effort was made to belittle them. The Soviets refused to allow Phelan to speak, on the ground that he was a citizen of a neutral country. The fate of the ILO continued to hang in the balance until May 1946, when negotiations were concluded on its status as an agency of the UN.

The ILO resumed its legislative work in October 1945 at the 27th Session of the ILC in Paris. Forty-eight states were represented, two more than in 1939,

---

[30] Between 1942 and 1945, "United Nations" referred to the wartime allies.
[31] Quoted in Michael Kennedy: *Ireland and the League of Nations, 1919–1946: International relations, diplomacy, and politics* (Dublin, Irish Academic Press, 1996), p. 147.

and ten Conventions were adopted, the first since 1939 and the biggest annual tally to date. Its future was assured, but doubts remained as to its role and relation to the UN. To clarify these issues, Phelan's address was published in pamphlet form as *The ILO and the United Nations*. In February 1947 the Genevese press acclaimed the "triumphant" return of the "exiled" ILO staff, and Phelan's role in restoring a slice of the city's international stature would be remembered locally with gratitude. Later that year a proposed series of Asian conferences was inaugurated at New Delhi. Phelan's message to the Asian delegates implicitly hoped that the ILO would be an intrinsic part of the project of decolonization. His last significant achievement was Convention No. 87, which recognized freedom of association and the right to organize. Adopted in 1948, it is one of eight Conventions subsequently identified by the ILC as fundamental rights at work. The delicate matter of his status was finally settled in September 1946, when the Governing Body assented to Phelan's nomination as Director-General, with effect from 16 February 1941. In return, the Director-General yielded to the consensus that the ILO needed a leader with political clout to take it into a changed world: it was understood that he would retire on reaching 60. And so, with the kind of compromise for which he had earned his reputation for ingenuity, Mr Phelan ended a working life of public service.

Envoi

Ingenuity and continuity are usually cited as the key elements of Phelan's special contribution to the ILO. Continuity and tradition alone, he concluded, "can imbue newcomers to the staff with an effective sense of the nature of international service and thereby inspire and perpetuate that loyalty without which an international institution cannot hope to function successfully or in the long run even to survive". [32] As leader, his approach was empirical and consensual, believing that the success of the ILO was due to the fact that

> from the outset it has attempted to deal with concrete questions which have been carefully defined: this has facilitated the adoption of practical measures for the improvement of labour conditions, after a free exchange of views between representatives of Governments and organised employers and workers and by voluntary agreement between them. [33]

---

[32] Phelan: "Some reminiscences of the International Labour Organization", p. 256.
[33] *Preparatory Asiatic Regional Conference of the International Labour Organisation, New Delhi, 1947: Report of the Director-General* (New Delhi, International Labour Office, 1947), p. 1.

His gifts as a facilitator and administrator, juxtaposed with his difficulties as Acting Director, have led him to be pigeon-holed, unfairly, as a bureaucrat. If his mentality had matured by 1919, his professional intellectual development was at that point just beginning. Three photographs capture this evolution.[34] In the first, he stands slightly astern of the organizing committee of the Washington Conference in 1919, looking like a wide-eyed young clerk among his seniors. In the second, he sits with Thomas, cigarette in hand, affecting the pose of a sophisticated European in the Gothic style of a decade that taste forgot. In the third, as Director-General, he is alone, composed and thoughtful, dressed like an American college professor, complete with bow tie. He had come a long way since his Whitehall days, and his very attire and manner attest to his adaptability. He embraced Thomas' mission wholeheartedly, and was determined to carry the ideals as well as the structure of the ILO into the post-war era. It was politics, arguably his perennial blind spot, that caused him to falter in the final furlong.

After retirement, Phelan continued to live with Fernande in their lakeshore villa, La Pernette, Chemin Voile 9, Genthod, where he enjoyed reading, writing his memoirs and sailing his 30-square-metre skall. In 1955 he was recalled to active service by the President of the International Court of Justice in The Hague, to chair a special consultative committee, following allegations of irregularities in employment at UNESCO. Decorated by diverse governments and universities, he was particularly pleased to have been awarded a Doctorate of Laws (LL.D) by the National University of Ireland (NUI) in July 1944, O'Rahilly making the presentation to the Chancellor. It was a rare accolade from his native land, and Ireland's republican frugality in conferring honours ensured that his fame in the puissant echelons of academe, state and industrial relations did not percolate beyond that golden circle.

Phelan died on Friday, 15 September 1967. Of immediate family, he was survived by his sister Millicent and brother Harold, both of whom lived in England. At 10.30 a.m. on Monday, 18 September, the hearse entered the courtyard of the ILO, where the Director-General and members of the Governing Body and staff waited in the rain to pay their respects. Then, after a semi-cantata requiem mass in the church of St Rita in Bellevue at 11 a.m., Phelan was interred in the cemetery of Genthod. The funeral was attended by a wide range of representatives from the ILO, the UN, Switzerland and Ireland. Fernande died in Geneva in May 1996. She instructed that she be laid to rest beside her husband, after similar rites, in

---

[34] The photographs, reproduced here, accompany Brian Hillery and Patrick Lynch, *Ireland in the International Labour Organization* (Dublin, 1969; see pp. 14–15, 30), which was published by the Irish Department of Labour to mark the golden jubilee of the ILO.

a similar coffin. They had no children. In accordance with her husband's wishes, Fernande bequeathed a portion of her estate to the International Institute for Labour Studies of the ILO, to whom he had given the copyright of his memoirs, and a portion to the NUI "to promote the study of international law by appropriate means associated with the name of my husband in order to keep his name alive in his country".[35] The International Institute for Labour Studies has since established a Phelan Fellowship. The NUI Senate now meets in the Phelan Room, which is dedicated to the memory of both Mr and Mrs Phelan, and the university awards an E.J. Phelan fellowship in international law.

---

[35] Mrs Phelan's will, 1 July 1970, Documents re the Phelan estate, NUI, Dublin.

Part II
The memoirs of Edward Phelan:
The birth of the ILO

Young Irishman in Liverpool 1

The difference between an autobiography and a book of reminiscences is that, whereas the former may be expected to cover the whole of the author's life, the latter can be made up of a selection of such incidents in it as he may believe, rightly or wrongly, will be of interest to others than himself.

When I first began to think of recording some such incidents in my own career I thought that no account of my early years need be included, but as little by little my story took shape I became aware of a certain pattern that seemed to underlie many of its features and perhaps, in some measure, to have determined them. As I looked back, it seemed that certain elements in that pattern could be discerned among my first coherent memories and that to bring them into my story would make it more intelligible.

Even when I was well beyond the age at which most young men have a fairly definite idea of what they are destined to do or what they would wish to become I had no chosen objective and consequently no plan whereby I might advance towards its achievement. How I came to do what I did is a story of one thing following another. So, of course, is every story of a career; but the sequence is usually defined, or at all events readily understood, against a background of family environment or an ambition to enter some profession with a long history and recognizable traditions. I eventually found my career in the international civil service which I entered at its inception. I can in fact claim to have been the first international civil servant in the modern sense of the term and to have played some part in the setting of precedents and the laying down of rules that govern what is now an established profession. My initiatives and reactions were therefore essentially personal in their origin and, for that reason, some account of the kind of person I was, of the way I matured, and of the equipment I had derived from an unusually varied experience, has perhaps some interest. I propose to confine it to describing any special features which I now have reason to believe may have influenced my outlook or actions in later years.

Since I came from a seafaring family I began with an international background in the limited sense that even as a very young child I was always aware of the existence of a world beyond that which formed my immediate surroundings. When I was four or five years old much of my time was spent at the home of my grandfather in Ireland. He lived at Cheekpoint, a small village on the River Suir exactly opposite its junction with the river Barrow.[1] Cheekpoint was a very small village indeed, so small that it had no church, no post office, no school, nothing that could be called a shop and in fact nothing that resembled a street. It is difficult in these days of motorized transport to imagine its isolation. The church and the school were a couple of miles away at the entrance to the huge park that surrounded Faithlegg, the home of Mr Power, the owner of the whole countryside. The parish priest lived over eight miles away; the nearest available doctor was at Dunmore, more distant still; and neither could be summoned except by a messenger sent on foot. Seven miles of a hilly road connected the village with the city of Waterford which could also be reached by a small paddle steamer which maintained a daily service between Dunmore, at the mouth of Waterford Harbour, and the city, calling at Cheekpoint on its way.

My grandfather's house, standing high above the river in a charming garden, seemed to me a very grand place compared with the miserable cottages in which the villagers lived, and they shared my opinion of its importance. The great mansion of the Powers, with its conservatories and stables, its housekeeper and its cook, its butler and its coachman, its gardeners and gamekeepers, and the army of lesser beings who assisted these domestic aristocrats, belonged to another world, and was only to be compared with Curraghmore and Lismore Castle and other famous residences of a quasi-regal character.[2] To the villagers, Fairymount, as my grandfather's house was called, represented a standard of comfort, and indeed of luxury, far beyond anything to which they could ever aspire – a height as much above theirs as Faithlegg was above ours. In fact our house was modest enough, containing on the ground floor only a very large parlour and an equally large kitchen, the two being separated by a wide hall from which a staircase led to a corridor on the floor above giving access to four bedrooms. A small dairy

---

[1] Cheekpoint is in County Waterford, south-west of Dublin.
[2] These residences are all located in County Waterford.

and a stable with stalls for two cows completed the establishment. There was no running water and a supply had to be carried in pails from a well situated in one of the fields some 200 yards away.

Simple though the house was, it was well furnished; my grandfather had brought home from abroad furniture inlaid with rare woods, and oil paintings of the ships he had commanded and the foreign ports to which he had traded adorned the walls of the hall and the parlour. I never grew tired of looking at these pictures – they took the place of picture books and in a sense they were my companions. There were other boys in the village, but though I knew them by name I rarely saw them, and when I did our intercourse was limited to a friendly greeting. This was not because there was any class barrier; it was simply that these youngsters had no leisure. When they were not at school they were kept busy digging potatoes, mending nets, collecting dead wood for fuel, fetching water, or occupied by any of the innumerable odd jobs that have to be performed when life is poor and primitive. The result was that I had no boy friends and games had no place in my existence.

I was, however, quite unaware that I was alone because I never felt lonely. The river had for me all the attraction of a theatre and, although I knew that each performance would resemble the last, I waited each day with excited anticipation for the curtain to rise once more.

At about nine in the morning the little paddle steamer, the *Vandeleur*, would appear on her way up to Waterford. Shortly afterwards her sister ship, the *Ida*, would come down the Barrow from New Ross in County Wexford,[3] would round the wood point of Snow Hill and follow her predecessor upstream. Towards six in the evening I would be on the lookout to see them return. And a little later would come a far greater thrill. I would hear from far off the thudding of much more powerful paddles growing steadily louder until the Great Western Railway's Mail Boat with its bright red funnel would come into view heading down the harbour at what seemed a prodigious pace bound for the Irish Sea and Milford Haven. All through the week there would be other steamers to watch: the *Lara*, the *Comeragh* or the *Dunbrody* on their regular service to Liverpool; Clyde Shipping Company's steamers bound for Glasgow; and, once in a while, some strange tramp, rusty and ill-kempt, would appear, or a small schooner would make her way up the river under sail helped by the tide.

Like all small boys I found other amusements and distractions: I climbed trees; I scrambled over the Minaun, the rocky hill behind the house, where gorse

---

[3] New Ross is 15 km north of Cheekpoint.

and heather made a glorious combination of colour and where rabbits abounded; I helped, or was allowed the illusion of helping, to bring in the cows or make butter with a primitive churn by the process of pounding the cream with a wooden instrument like a pile-driver. But the river was never far out of sight and the coming and going of the ships on its waters had a predominant place in my day. Having no friends of my own age I played a perpetual game of imagination in which one or other of these ships carried me off to the strange places to which I ordered them to sail. Glasgow and Liverpool and Milford Haven were to me only names. But Naples with its volcano and Hong Kong with its mountain and its Chinese junks were real places with which I was familiar from my grandfather's pictures and it was to them that I directed my steamer to take me. In a sense they were more a part of my life than was the village, which inspired no such thrilling dreams.

Thus was born, perhaps, the germ of an ambition to travel, but in its earliest stage it took the form of a desire to go to places that were distant rather than to places that were foreign. To me one foreign place was no more interesting than another; my preference was for those which were furthest away. I had a very definite idea that sailors who made the longer journeys were somehow superior to those who ventured less far afield. The Captain of the Mail Boat was a person of great importance in my childish eyes, but he never went further than Milford Haven, and I would see him coming in again in a couple of days. Splendid and enviable though he might be, he was very low down in the scale compared with captains like my grandfather whose voyages had kept him away for years at a time.

So far I have made no mention of my father for the reason that he had no place in my life at this period. Ever since I remembered being aware that such a person existed, he had been off on long voyages. My mother I knew well but I saw little of her, for she rarely came to Fairymount because of some estrangement between her and my father's sister. She was glad, however, to let me stay there because she was very fond of my father's parents to whom my presence afforded immense pleasure, and because, since I had no other grandparents living, it was a convenient arrangement at a time when she was much occupied looking after my infant sister.

This explains how it was that in these early years, lacking the environment in which the majority of children develop, I was led to build up a world for myself. In one way or another, somewhat similar conditions continued to prevail during most of my formative years and no doubt produced a lasting effect.

The next phase of my existence began with what was for me a great event; with my mother and sister I boarded the SS *Lara* at the quay in Waterford in order to make the voyage to Liverpool where we were to live. My father had some time before come to the conclusion that the day of sail was over and that he would be wise to transfer into steam. It must have been a hard decision to make for he had been in command of full-rigged ships making ocean voyages ever since he was in his early twenties, and, on going into steam, he would have to step down the ladder and begin his career again. His progress, however, was rapid and he was able in due course to attain one of his ambitions, which was to get into a regular line with a fixed home port at which he could establish his family. Hardly had we settled into lodgings in Bootle than he encountered misfortune; [4] the ship in which he was first officer was sunk in a collision; times were bad and ships were being laid up; his service with the company had been brief; the first opportunities for re-employment would naturally go to officers with greater seniority and he therefore faced a long period ashore during which he must maintain himself and his family on such small savings as he had been able to accumulate.

The strictest economy was necessary as my mother had just presented him with twin sons. Most of this I only learned long afterwards. All I knew at the time was that we made a new and exciting change. We moved from our lodgings in Bootle out to Seaforth, [5] where our home was a tiny house, the rent of which was five shillings a week. Personally I thought it was a great improvement on the much larger house we had left. For one thing it was *our* house and we were no longer in what I considered the inferior position of lodgers; for another, the front room on the ground floor was completely empty and made a grand place to play in wet weather – I did not realize that this, to me, entirely desirable feature must have been a severe blow to my mother's pride. Her father had been a prosperous businessman who had established the first mineral water factory in Waterford, and she had been educated at an expensive boarding school in Dublin. To descend below the parlour level was to descend very far indeed in the social scale, and she must have felt this more than any other of the economies which had become necessary.

She must also have been rather appalled by our new surroundings which to my eyes were tremendously exciting and wholly delightful. Tuscan Street, for that was our new address, was in process of coming into existence and as yet only two houses in addition to our own had any tenants. When one stepped out of our front door, one stepped directly into a chaos of bricks and mortar, wheelbarrows, odd planks, lime pits, ladders, and all the other impedimenta that litter a building site. Everything seemed to have been thrown about in a haphazard fashion and, perhaps because children are natural rebels against order, this gargantuan

---

[4] Bootle is 6 km north of Liverpool.
[5] Seaforth is 2 km from Bootle.

untidiness filled me with joy. Moreover, when one explored it, cautiously at first and then with increasing daring, little islands of activity could be discovered where something interesting was going on – a bricklayer slapping down mortar from his trowel with a careless gesture and with his other hand deftly banging a brick into the bed he had prepared for it; his mate mounting a ladder with a hod of bricks on his shoulder and when he had reached the top giving a curious shrug which shot them into a heap within reach of his superior; navvies digging trenches; carpenters, plasterers, plumbers and slaters all displaying some fascinating skill which I was prepared to watch for hours. Groups of children from neighbouring streets who occasionally invaded the site were chased away without ceremony; but, no doubt because I lived in the street, my presence was tolerated and in time welcomed when it was found that I gave no trouble and was only too pleased at being asked to hand up a tool or run an errand. I got to know the workers by their Christian names and to regard them as friends, for they seemed always ready to answer my innumerable questions and to take pleasure in my company.

It was with great regret that, after a few months of this happy existence, I learned we were to move again, and I could not understand why the prospect gave my mother such evident pleasure. I was totally unconscious that we had been living in conditions approaching poverty; I had always had plenty to eat and I had had the run of the most magnificent playground any child could imagine. I did not realize that my close association with navvies and builders' labourers was not precisely the environment which my mother desired for her eldest son at his most impressionable age, and that the freedom with which I had been allowed to pursue it so completely had only been granted because it kept me away from the neighbouring streets which were slums with which it was desirable I should remain unacquainted.

We did not move very far. The slums were still only a stone's throw away, but Durham Road was a road and not a street – and in that area the distinction was important. The house, instead of rising flush from the pavement with a flat frontage, had a garden – no more than a couple of yards in depth but possessing a railing and a gate – and its front rooms on both floors had bow windows. It also had many more rooms and these my mother, no doubt with great satisfaction, was now able to furnish in adequate fashion, even to the extent of having her piano brought over from Ireland. There had been an unexpected turn in my father's fortunes and he was again at sea with prospects which he felt justified the setting up of the home which he and my mother had so long desired.

Here we remained for some years during which I attended the nearest Catholic school. It needs no special description for it resembled, I imagine, most of the other elementary schools in Liverpool in that period. There were, however, features about my schooldays there that combined to leave me once more isolated from any close companionship with boys of my own age. All but very few of the pupils came from poor and even slum areas. I met them of course during the brief recreations during the morning and afternoon when for ten or fifteen minutes we raced round the school yard or played some simple game; once school was over they departed to their homes and I saw no more of them until we met at school the following morning. It took me something over half an hour to make each of my four daily journeys to and from the school and so I never had time to make any close acquaintances in my own road.

I had pretty well exhausted the possibilities of the Waterloo Library when I reached the top standard at my school and it was decided that my education should be continued at St Francis Xavier's College in Liverpool. This meant an exciting change in my life in many respects. I became the proud possessor of a season ticket entitling me to travel back and forth between Seaforth and Liverpool by train; I acquired a satchel and books, and a blue serge cap with a shield worked in gold thread and the letters S.F.X. embroidered in its centre; and, even more important, as indicating that I could now take care of myself like a grown-up, I was given a daily allowance of six pence with which to purchase for my lunch whatever I might fancy.

All this novelty had hardly begun to fade when another change came. My father was promoted to the command of one of his company's larger ships engaged in the Atlantic trade and, as this brought him home more frequently, we moved to a larger and more conveniently situated house in Liverpool itself. I regretted losing my railway journeys and the freedom to choose my own menu for lunch; but I was the gainer by a diet more varied, and certainly more healthy, than the Eccles cakes to which I had become addicted for my midday meal, and the gift of a bicycle did much to compensate me for the loss of my season ticket.

Although I now lived much closer to the college, any real contact with my classmates remained restricted to our brief recreations during school hours. At the end of the day we scattered and, as none of them lived in my neighbourhood, I had to find my own amusements in the evenings and at weekends. Books were my main distraction but I now extended my reading to a newspaper. Earlier, along with other boys in Waterloo, I had taken a lively interest in the South African war and, although I was strongly pro-Boer, I had collected cigarette cards and buttons bearing the portraits of British army commanders. We followed their fortunes by hearsay or from the placards displaced outside newsagents' shops. It never occurred to us to seek further information in the newspaper itself; and, indeed, newspapers in those days were stodgy affairs which offered no attraction to youthful readers. A new era of journalism began with the *Daily Mail* and with its provincial edition which penetrated all over the country. A copy came by chance into my hands and I found its dramatic accounts of the Russo-Japanese war so absorbing that I insisted we take it regularly. The attention with which I perused its correspondents' stories, illustrated by maps and photographs, certainly added to my knowledge both of geography and of current events, but the paper has its place in these reminiscences for another reason.

A series of large and eloquent advertisements appeared in its pages announcing the forthcoming publication of the *Harmsworth Encyclopaedia* and I learned for the first time what an encyclopaedia was. The idea that there could be a book from which one could find out everything about anything left me spellbound; and when I discovered that it was a book which it would be within my means to acquire – it was to be published in fortnightly parts at a shilling each – I thought it was too good to be true.

I bought the first number which covered about half the letter "A" and, following my usual procedure, I proceeded to read it straight through. I found this a far more formidable task than I had expected but I struggled on day after day, appalled at the variety and difficulty of the subjects I encountered and humbled by the extent of my ignorance. Finally I came to "alkali", and then I got a shock. The advertisements had laid repeated stress on the fact that the new encyclopaedia would be up to date; many new discoveries had been made since other encyclopaedias had been published; the *Harmsworth Encyclopaedia*, with the aid of the world's greatest experts, would contain authoritative information on all these new developments. I had accepted the claim that all other encyclopaedias had accordingly been rendered obsolete and I was amazed at discovering that, so far as alkali was concerned, it was false. My knowledge of chemistry was limited to what one learns at school in a little over a year, but my chemistry master was a man who took a real interest in his subject and a week or so previously, after having described the processes employed in the manufacture of caustic soda, he had briefly outlined a new electrolytic process which was beginning to be used. The *Harmsworth Encyclopaedia* had somehow missed this important development. I was less perturbed at not receiving the promised value for my shilling than excited at having discovered an omission that had escaped the eye of the omniscient editor. Had my spare time been occupied with boy friends and the usual distractions of boys of my age I should, no doubt, have been little concerned by my discovery, if indeed I had made it at all. As things were, and as the *Daily Mail* advertisements continued to make their confident claim, I decided to write to the editor and draw his attention to the defect in the article.

I spent some hours in the Picton Public Library in order to make sure of my ground and, having found a full account of the new process in a chemical journal,

I set about writing my letter. Never having conducted any correspondence except with my parents, the composition of a letter to so important a person as the editor presented a serious problem. After many attempts I produced a draft which, as I now look back on it, was not without some diplomatic quality. I began with congratulations on the excellence of the first number and a reference to the great educational value of an encyclopaedia which could secure a wide distribution because of its moderate price – this was of course derived from the advertisements which I knew by heart – and then went on to say that I was afraid the reputation of the publication might be damaged by the omission from the Alkali article of any reference to a new manufacturing process of great importance. I ventured to enclose a short note on the essential features of this process which could be inserted in a later number in, for instance, the "E" pages under the heading of "Electrical processes".

When, after a fortnight, I had received no reply, I assumed that my letter, written on some pages torn out of an exercise book, had been consigned to the editor's wastepaper basket, and I put the matter out of my mind. Great was my surprise on receiving a typewritten letter on paper with an impressive heading conveying the editor's thanks for my communication and asking me if I would undertake to revise the whole article. This was more than I had bargained for; so I wrote back saying that the rest of the article seemed to me admirable and that all that was required was to make the addition I had suggested. A further letter from the editor expressed his satisfaction at learning that I had no criticism to make of the rest of the article and enclosing a cheque for two guineas for my manuscript which he assured me would be used in a later number.

I was delighted with the two guineas, which to me was an enormous sum, but I had common sense enough to realize that this was an exploit I could not hope to repeat, and my main feeling was one of relief at having emerged unscathed from a rather risky adventure. I was by no means sure that if the editor had discovered that he had been apologizing to a boy of 12, I might not have found myself in trouble.

Shortly after this incident there came another change in my mode of life. My father's ship was sold to a German company which wished to keep him in command and, as she was to ply between Boston and Hamburg, he decided to take his family to the latter port. I was disappointed beyond words on being told that, since my education must not be interrupted, I would have to remain in Liverpool. I protested strongly but I had to accept my father's decision. I gained, however, two important concessions, first that I should accompany the family on its journey to its new home, and secondly that I should join them for my Christmas, Easter and summer holidays.

My first independent journey to Hamburg was, of course, an exciting event. I felt that I had now become a real traveller and not just a package delivered on board at one end and lifted off at the other, as had been the case on my journeys to Ireland. I had to buy my own tickets, travel across England to Grimsby, find my way from the station to the dock and then set sail over the North Sea to a foreign port. On the first occasion when the ship docked at Hamburg there was no one to meet me. I was secretly delighted for, having already become a little familiar with the town when I had accompanied the family to their new home, I was confident that I could find my own way and was thrilled at the opportunity of doing so. I waited until the last passenger had disembarked, and then, having told the steward that if anyone enquired of me he was to tell them that I had gone home, I set out on my own. I found the nearest tram without difficulty, changed in the centre of town to a tram for Eimsbüttel, and reached the house to learn, as I expected, that my mother had gone to meet me. Half an hour later she arrived and her relief at finding me safe preserved me from the scolding my thoughtless conduct deserved. The evidence of this ability to take care of myself doubtless made her feel happier about the journeys I had now continually to undertake and which must have caused her no little anxiety. I have many pleasant memories of my holidays in Hamburg but, apart from the fact that they gave me some experience of life in a foreign country, I do not think that they had any particular effect on my subsequent development, certainly not as much as the conditions in which my education now continued.

I was still a day boy – St Francis Xavier's had no accommodation for boarders – but unlike my schoolfellows I did not live at home. I lodged with Miss Ely, an old lady who lived close to the college in one of a row of small houses typical of the surrounding streets. She had originally come from New Ross in County Wexford and my mother had discovered her through some chain of enquiry which she had made in Ireland with the object of finding some Irish home in which I could be safely left and be sure of being well fed. Miss Ely proved to be a small dignified lady, much looked up to in the neighbourhood as the owner of two BOOKS – the word was always pronounced with a respect that can only be indicated by capital letters. What these mysterious BOOKS might be greatly intrigued my curiosity until I discovered what they were. A BOOK, I found, was the foundation of the Friendly Society system, on which Lloyd George's scheme of health insurance was later to be built. The Friendly Societies were the insurance companies of the poor whom they insured against death, sickness and other eventualities when a lump sum would be a godsend to families whose incomes were so low and precarious that they could never accumulate savings on which they could draw in an emergency. Premiums for these benefits amounted to only a few pence a week. The owner of a BOOK was the agent who went from house to house collecting these precious pence, of which he retained 20 or 25 per cent, and paid the remainder to the Society; in the case of a new policy the collector was entitled to the whole of the premiums for the first six months. A BOOK was therefore a valuable property; not only did it produce a regular income, which could be increased if the collector was energetic, but it was the collector's property and could be sold to a person (approved by the Society) for a considerable sum.

Young as I was, I found the system shocking, and particularly the proportion of the premiums that remained with the collector. But, as I learned more about it, I realized that it met a real social need which, at that time, could have been met in no other way. These people would never have kept up their contributions without the collector's visits and, in the absence of this form of insurance, there would have been no way in which, for instance, funeral expenses could have been met and the pathetic fear of the terrible disgrace associated with a pauper's burial removed. Moreover, the collectors, far from being regarded with dislike, were generally looked on as friends of many years' standing who had been associated with the household since it was formed, who had watched the family grow up, who were the confidants of the wife or mother in her unending struggle, and whose weekly visits were looked forward to as a welcome break in the dreary round of a drab existence. My insatiable curiosity extracted from Miss Ely and her assistant (for Miss Ely's original BOOK had grown into two) many case histories, as they would now be called, of the families they visited; and without any deliberate purpose I acquired an amount of authentic information about how the poor lived in the slums of Liverpool. Years later this knowledge was to prove of value and it was, perhaps, not the least important part of my education.

Education, in fact, was a word which for me had no meaning at that time. It simply meant going to school and doing what one was told lest worse befall. I had no idea that education was a preparation for a career or that it involved any obligation to study, other than the performance of such tasks as might be set as homework. I neither liked nor disliked lessons; and it never occurred to me that I might be either more stupid or more intelligent than my classmates. At the end of the college year I sat, along with the rest of my class, for the Preliminary Oxford Local Examination. These examinations were held all over England, and those sitting for them were given the same papers to answer. There were three such examinations, Preliminary, Junior and Senior, corresponding to different grades of secondary education, and schools attached importance to the number of their pupils who passed them with success. Beyond having a vague feeling that this was rather a solemn affair because the questions were presented to me in print and I had to write my answers on unusual paper, I was not otherwise much concerned;

and, when the examination was over, my thoughts turned to the much more attractive subject of my departure for Hamburg where, I was told, the result would reach me in August.

I happened to be alone when the postman delivered to me a fairly thick book which, on being unwrapped, revealed itself as the list of successful candidates in the Oxford Preliminary. I thumbed the volume over, mildly excited at the prospect of seeing my name in print for the first time; it did not occur to me that it might not be there. The book consisted of something like 100 pages containing thousands of names in small print arranged in alphabetical order. I was disappointed when I could not find my name. I checked carefully all the names beginning with "P", only to be obliged to accept the fact that I had failed to pass. I looked for the names of some of my classmates and finding they had been successful, I became concerned about my mother's probable reaction. I did not dare destroy the book but I put it away out of sight where I hoped it would be overlooked, perhaps, if I was lucky, until after the end of my holiday, and then I went out for a walk. On my somewhat cautious return I was warmly embraced by my mother and was at a loss to understand what could be the reason until, puzzled by what she thought was my indifference, she said, "Why did you go out? Why didn't you wait until I came in to tell you the news? And why did you throw the book behind those newspapers? Don't you realize your father will be delighted?"

Apparently I had passed after all, and I felt very foolish. I muttered something about it not being all that important, and took up the book from the table to discover how I had made so stupid a mistake. "Not important!" cried my mother, "And there you are on the first page and all those thousands of boys behind you! You are a strange boy."

This gave me a clue and I opened the book at the first page. I at once noticed that here the names were not in alphabetical order but I could still not find my own. Wondering if all this was some queer kind of a dream I continued staring at the page until at last it dawned on me that I was looking at page 2, and that the list started on the inside of the cover where, under the heading "Passed with Honours", my name occupied the second place.

My pleasure at having scored so remarkable a success was tempered by the belief that I must have had some peculiarly lucky break and my fear that my performance on this occasion would lead to disillusion for my parents and embarrassment for myself later on. When I returned to school I was of course congratulated but otherwise no special interest seemed to be taken in my prowess and I was unaware that the college authorities, believing that they had a pupil of exceptional promise in their hands, were considering how best they could equip him for future successes.

In my last year at St Francis Xavier's I seemed to do little else than sit for exams. In addition to the Senior Oxford Local, there were a number of examinations conducted by the Royal College of Science for which I was entered – I gathered that the number of successes obtained in these examinations had some bearing on the grant which the college received to subsidize its teaching in science. But the most important examination so far as I was concerned personally was that for a City Council Scholarship at Liverpool University. With so many examinations to be faced I was not expecting to do anything extraordinary in the Senior Oxford Local; I came out seventh and, as I also won my scholarship, this was regarded as more than respectable.

Meanwhile my family had come back to Liverpool in circumstances that again illustrated the risks and uncertainties of a sailor's life. During the winter my father's ship on her way from the United States to Hamburg encountered gales of exceptional severity. Her whole cargo of pig iron broke through the between decks and crashed down into the lower hold. By some miracle it did not go right through the bottom of the ship but she was almost completely disabled, listing dangerously and leaking badly through her strained plates. My father succeeded in bringing her into the Mersey where she was dry-docked at Birkenhead. There was no wireless in those days and my first news of this accident was the arrival of my father at my bedside in the middle of the night anxious to assure me of his safety before I saw the news of the disaster in the morning papers. The next day I was able to see for myself the condition of the ship which was spectacular enough to attract wide attention. Photographs of the hold and its chaos appeared in the press and much publicity was given to the feat of seamanship which had saved the ship and her crew; and what was more important, Lloyd's surveyors were impressed by the achievement of the master who had prevented the ship and her cargo from becoming a total loss, for the opinion of Lloyd's is not without influence on the career of a master mariner. Instead of being out of employment for many months while the ship was being repaired, if repair should prove possible, my father was at once offered a command in his old company and Liverpool became again his home port.

One result of the change was to put an end to my trips to Hamburg, and a summer holiday in North Wales, where my mother had rented a cottage, seemed an unexciting substitute. To travel, however, appeared to be my destiny, for hardly were we installed in our cottage near Llangollen than I received a letter from my old French master asking me if I would like to spend my holidays with a family in France; my travelling expenses would be paid and my only obligation would be to give two boys of about my own age, who were to go to Beaumont College in the autumn, some practice in talking English. I jumped at the chance of visiting another foreign country and the additional attraction of undertaking alone a more complicated journey than I had yet had to face. Hitherto I had been able to rely on a boat to deposit me at my continental destination; a land journey across France to La Bourboule, a remote spot in the mountains of Auvergne, was a new and far more thrilling enterprise.

My hosts, Colonel Picard and his wife, were charming people; the boys and their two sisters were friendly and welcomed the arrival of a stranger. La Bourboule was a small place frequented by people who, like Madame Picard, were undergoing a cure; it offered no attractions save the medicinal waters, the pure mountain air, and the wild scenery. The young members of the family found it unbearably dull and my appearance was an event of major interest.

After a month or so at La Bourboule we proceeded to Paris, with which the colonel wished his sons to be better acquainted before leaving for England. His plan for acquainting them with Paris was drawn up with all the precision of orders for a military operation and exacted for its execution as much energy. The boys soon had more than enough of it and would much have preferred sitting outside cafés and watching the fascinating life of the boulevards. But the colonel thought that they had done quite enough lounging at La Bourboule, and since one was to enter the army and the other the navy after their time at Beaumont, he was inexorable. I had no inclination to protest, for he was a highly cultured man with a detailed knowledge of French history and consequently a most interesting guide to the historical monuments with which Paris abounds.

We moved on from Paris so that the boys might bid goodbye to some of their more important relatives, and I was given an even more fascinating glimpse of some of France's past glories, for we stayed for a week with Madame Picard's aunt who, I gathered, was the head of the aristocratic family from which she came. The old countess lived in a many-towered chateau which might have come straight out of a fairytale. Meals were ceremonious affairs served by liveried servants by whom I was at first rather daunted but whose presence did not interfere with my appreciation of the numerous dishes they placed before me nor with the series of wines by which they were accompanied. In the intervals between these repasts we boys roamed through the surrounding forest; and when on returning from these excursions I re-entered the chateau over the bridge that spanned the moat I found it difficult to believe that I was not dreaming.

A fortnight spent in the Vosges and a visit to Strasbourg brought the holiday to an end and I accompanied the colonel and his sons to London. There I had expected to take leave of them, but the colonel, who knew no English, asked me to remain for a week while he did some shopping and showed the boys some of the sights. These, he probably did not realize, were as new to me as to them.

When I finally said goodbye and headed back to Liverpool, I felt I had been away at least a year and that I had learned a lot. I had become acquainted with another country and I had had the experience of gracious living at a higher social level. It had all been extraordinarily pleasant but it was not a world to which I could expect to belong. The more modest world to which I was returning offered something more attractive, the thrill of starting on my university career and of discovering what paths would open before me and to what personal destiny they would eventually lead.

Student life

2

My scholarship at the University of Liverpool covered my lecture fees for any course of study I might choose to pursue during three years and gave me in addition an annual grant of £60. The normal holder of one of these scholarships had, I imagine, a fairly definite idea of what he wanted to do in later life and the studies he should undertake. I, however, had no ideas at all on the matter. The only career I knew anything about was the sea, but I had no desire to make it my profession. My father, I think, took it for granted that, since I lived onshore, I would get to know more about life on land than he did and would be better able to judge of the opportunities it offered. He did not realize, nor did I at the time, that the family in the various moves it had made had been cut off from friends and relations in Ireland, that I had never had any contact with people in other professions and that, consequently, I had had no chance of discovering whether I had any particular ambition. With no goal before me I had thus no idea that this was the moment when I should take my first steps along some chosen road.

On my return from France I studied the university calendar in the isolation of North Wales as if it was a sales catalogue out of which I could pick whatever took my fancy. All the subjects seemed attractive and it was difficult to make a choice. I could form a pretty clear idea about further study in one or other branch of the humanities – it would mean acquiring more and more of such knowledge as I already possessed, and that did not seem particularly exciting. Of what advanced mathematics might consist I had no notion; here was a mysterious realm which aroused my curiosity and which it would be fascinating to explore; and so I decided to read for an honours degree in that subject.

When I told my father what I proposed to do, he did not question my decision, but he asked rather diffidently whether I had considered taking political economy, adding that he thought the subject would become increasingly important. I wondered how he could have got hold of such a peculiar idea. In those days the term "political economy" conveyed little to the ordinary person; if he had heard of it at all, he associated it with a branch of philosophical speculation as remote from practical affairs as metaphysics. My idea of philosophers was drawn from Marryat's portrait of Midshipman Easy's eccentric parent;[1] and it did not lead me to suppose that philosophy was a career, or that the study of any of its branches could be of value. However, I bought a copy of Nicholson's *Textbook of Economics* in order to find out, if possible, what foundation my father might have for his opinion. My impressions were not favourable. The subject seemed incredibly dull – at one and the same time ridiculously easy and stupidly difficult. Nevertheless, since the lectures my own course of study required me to attend by no means filled my day, and as I could take any other lectures I pleased, I added economics to my list.

My first year at the university was extremely pleasant, for I found that I needed to do very little in the way of serious study. The standard I had reached for my scholarship and for other examinations in my last year at college was approximately that required for the intermediate examination at the end of my first year as an undergraduate. I had, therefore, plenty of leisure to explore student activities and I took a particular interest in the proceedings of the Debating Society. Lack of close companionship during my schooldays had intensified a natural shyness and, though I admired and envied the confidence with which others intervened, I was sadly convinced that I should never muster up enough courage to speak myself. I can never be sufficiently grateful to the energetic secretary of the society who finally overcame my hesitation and persuaded me to break the ice.

Although I could not know it at the time, this was really an important event in my career. Once I had got over my initial nervousness I found that I had a certain ability for public speaking and that it offered fascinating possibilities. Previously I had been told that I was good at this or that, but these judgements expressed by others never wholly convinced me; it was quite a different experience to discover in myself an unsuspected talent, and I sought to develop it, not only by constant exercise but also by going to hear, whenever possible, recognized masters of the art. The campaign preceding the General Election of 1906 gave me numerous opportunities to attend political meetings, and of these I took full

---

[1] Frederick Marryat (1792–1848) was an English novelist known for tales of sea adventure, including *Mr Midshipman Easy*. (Ed.)

advantage. I heard T.P. O'Connor,[2] the well-known Irish Nationalist, address his enthusiastic constituents in the paradoxically named Scotland Division of the city; and I went to conservative and liberal meetings in other constituencies to listen to other candidates. Most of them I thought were not particularly good. T.P. O'Connor and F.E. Smith, the young and then practically unknown lawyer who was later to become a famous political figure as Lord Birkenhead,[3] were the only two whom I considered first class; T.P. O'Connor I thought was the greater orator, and F.E. Smith the more effective debater.

Many other students took a keen interest in the electoral struggle. One of them, after hearing "F.E.", asked me if I did not agree that he was the best platform speaker in England. I suggested that, since he was a fervent conservative, his opinion was prejudiced, and that before being so dogmatic he should first go to hear T.P. O'Connor. Being an extremely fair-minded person he agreed to do so. When I met him the morning after T.P.'s meeting I was eager to learn his impression:

"Hello, Sammy," I said, "Did you go to hear T.P.?"

"Yes, I did."

"Well, what did you think of him?"

"Huh! Of course I didn't agree with a word he said. But … well … I was cheering."

This was, perhaps, the most extraordinary tribute ever paid to the spell that T.P. could cast over an audience, since Sammy was a tough young Yorkshireman not easily carried away. I sat beside him once in the gallery of the Arts Theatre while Sir Oliver Lodge delivered an address in celebration of Lord Kelvin's centenary.[4] Sir Oliver had a dominating presence; over six feet tall, with his high domed forehead and silver hair, he was an almost awesome figure. In a passage describing Kelvin's intellectual precocity he led dramatically up to the statement that the boy had matriculated at the University of Glasgow when he was only 12 years old. While he paused to emphasize this astonishing achievement, Sammy's voice shattered the silence with the derisive comment "What a rotten university!"

---

[2] Thomas Power O'Connor (1848–1929), an Irish journalist and politician, was President of the Irish National League of Great Britain (1883–1913). He was well known for his great wit and ability as a public speaker. (Ed.)

[3] Frederick Edwin Smith, Earl of Birkenhead (1872–1930), was a British lawyer and Conservative politician, serving as Lord Chancellor from 1919 to 1922. He was a very good friend of Winston Churchill and an excellent public speaker. (Ed.)

[4] Sir Oliver Joseph Lodge (1851–1940) was a physicist who worked on electromagnetic and radio waves and took part in the development of wireless telegraph. He was a renowned lecturer in his scientific field.

William Thomson, Baron Kelvin (1824–1907), was a physicist and engineer who gave his name to the kelvin temperature scale. The centenary took place in June 1924. (Ed.)

One other lecture that I attended during this period resulted in an acquaintance that was to grow into a lifelong friendship. By chance I happened to see a handwritten announcement on the notice board that a lecture would be delivered by a Mr D. Kelleher on "some modern Irish writers".[5] I had never heard of the lecturer; I knew nothing about literary movements in Ireland or anywhere else; and I went prepared to slip away if I found it boring. The attendance was depressingly small; it consisted of scarcely more than a dozen students, and I had the impression that their presence, like my own, was due to a vague sense of national solidarity.

The speaker, who was a small man rather shabbily dressed, seemed quite unconcerned by this meagre audience. Instead of the lecture I had anticipated he delivered an informal talk stringing together casual, effortless comments on a number of Irish authors in an attractive Cork accent. He expounded no thesis and made no attempt at oratory but, on me at all events, he produced an extraordinary effect. Simple words, with which I thought I was familiar, suddenly seemed to take on a new significance and to be far richer in meaning that I had hitherto perceived. In fact, although I would not have put it in that way at the time, I discovered that language had an unsuspected dimension which the poets could help one to explore.

After the meeting I got into conversation with him and found that his personality was as fascinating as his talk. We continued to meet from time to time and I was always amused, and sometimes startled, by a behaviour which set him apart from anybody I had yet encountered. The story of his first visit to Liverpool will serve to show how unlike his reactions were to those of other people. Convinced that literature was his destined vocation, he regarded earning a living as no more than a troublesome necessity. After being unemployed for some weeks in London he obtained a temporary post in Liverpool and walking out of Lime Street Station got his first view of the city. Most people are impressed, for St George's Hall is considered by architects one of the finest buildings in Europe, and it stands in a noble square. Kelleher apparently saw nothing but the grime which makes it as black as coal, and his impression was unfavourable. "But what did you think of the Mersey?" I asked as he told me the story. The river crowded with shipping is a spectacle which no other port in the world can surpass.

"I never saw it," he replied. "I walked a couple of hundred yards down Lime Street, and it got worse and worse. So I went back into the station, and waited for the next train back to London."

---

[5] Daniel Laurence Kelleher (1883–1958) was a playwright and poet who wrote travel sketches. In 1911 he published *Poems twelve a penny*. (Ed.)

[Editor's note: The complete text of the memoirs continues with accounts of Phelan's student holidays, during which he travelled extensively.]

My first years at the university presented no special feature; I matured a little, participated with more confidence in student activities, did a fair amount of work, and obtained my ordinary degree without difficulty. I was now qualified to enter on the studies leading to an honours degree and, though I was well aware that I must be prepared to work a great deal harder, the prospect of discovering some of the secrets of higher mathematics was attractive. I was soon disillusioned. Professor C inspired no enthusiasm. With his ragged gown half slipping off one shoulder, he would come hurrying across the quad in a queer jerky run, each rapid little step just enabling him to keep his balance without falling face downwards on the path. Arrived in the small room where we awaited him he would bustle up to the blackboard and cover its surface with algebraic formulae so rapidly that only with the greatest difficulty could we keep pace with him in our notebooks. The board was small; every few minutes he was obliged to clean it with a duster, an operation he performed with such energy that by the end of the hour he might have been mistaken for a baker. He never referred to doing a problem but to "doing it down"; sometimes it was not the problem which went down before his assault but he himself who was vanquished. This I found infinitely discouraging. If the professor was unable to extricate himself from the labyrinth in which he had lost his way, how could we unfortunates be expected to make our way out of some similar maze in an examination?

Things became brighter when the mathematical staff was strengthened by the addition of Professor W.H. Young, who was an authority on modern geometry.[6] In every respect he was a great contrast to Professor C. He was a tall, handsome man with a flaming red beard, always faultlessly attired, and I found his lectures fascinating. A small incident confirmed me in the belief that with Professor C I was wasting my time. At the end of two lectures Professor C had failed to solve one of his boring problems and had abandoned it saying, "You can see how to attack it. All you have to do is to carry on, and it will come out." Having spent some hours that evening working at the thing with no better result, I took the problem to Professor Young and asked him if he could give me a clue to the best way to set about it. "Can't you do that?" he asked, smiling. "It's quite easy. Look."

He wrote nothing down. He held a piece of chalk delicately between finger and thumb and used it only to gesture with. "You know so and so … " – he

---

[6] William Henry Young (1863–1942) was a mathematician who worked on measure theory and differential calculus. (Ed.)

stated a geometrical principle with which I was familiar from his lectures. I nodded. "Then it follows that ... " – I nodded again. He spoke three or four more sentences drawing deductions perfectly easy to follow; and there was the solution, logical and inescapable.

Immensely impressed by this demonstration I paid less and less attention to Professor C's lectures, and endeavoured to map out a course of studies of my own. I ought, I suppose, to have had more sense. I ought to have realized that mathematics was so vast a subject that the honours examination could deal with only one of its branches and that Professor C's pet subject would necessarily figure predominantly in the papers set. This was exactly what happened. Not a single question on modern geometry was included; my independent studies enabled me to deal with a few problems, but most of the questions required for their solution the manipulation of complicated algebraical apparatus. I understood well enough how to attack them but having neglected to acquire sufficient facility in its exercise I was hopelessly beaten by the element of time.

When the results were published I was not surprised to find that my name did not appear on the list. So far I had had an unbroken record of scholastic success, and failure was a new and unpleasantly humiliating experience. I tried to assess my responsibility as honestly as I could. Although I had devoted a good deal of time to a variety of occupations: to debating, to editing *The Sphinx* (the students' magazine), to membership of the Council of the Guild of Undergraduates, and to some forms of sport, I had nevertheless put in a lot of solid work. My failure was due not to idleness but to a lack of judgement for which I could blame no one but myself.

Under the rules I could not sit for the examination a second time. Something, however, could be salvaged from the wreck by taking the examination for the degree of Master of Science in a year's time and presenting mathematics as my subject; it would not carry the same distinction as an honours degree, but it would at least be evidence that I had pursued my mathematical studies far beyond the pass degree level. I rejected this idea for two reasons: I should be wasting a year going over a second time ground that I already knew, and I should have to work under Professor C, a prospect which I did not find attractive. The alternative was to try for an honours degree in another subject, and physics was the obvious choice, if Professor Wilberforce was willing to let me enter for the examination after a year's study.[7] He listened sympathetically to my proposal, and

---

[7] Lionel Robert Wilberforce (1861–1944) was Professor of Physics at University College, Liverpool from 1900 to 1935. He worked on the vibrations of loaded spiral springs and invented the mechanism known as the 'Wilberforce Pendulum'. (Ed.)

readily gave his consent. I had still to get my father's approval, and I awaited his return with some concern. My scholarship had come to an end, but I had been able to save enough to see me through the university for another year if I could continue to live at home. He might quite reasonably have taken the view that the time had now come when I ought to earn my own living; my relief was great when he raised no objection to the course I proposed to follow.

I thought this was very generous, and I hesitated to broach another idea which was that I might devote my summer vacation to perfecting my knowledge of French. I still had no notion of what I would do when my studies were over. The time, however, was clearly approaching when I should have to get a job of some kind, and a knowledge of a foreign language would presumably be an asset. After returning from my holiday in France three years earlier I had acquired a cheap edition of *The three musketeers* – it cost me two shillings, and I bought it more out of curiosity to see if I could read a French book, than for any other reason. At first I made slow progress looking up in the dictionary every word I did not know, but soon I became so enthralled in the story that I appealed to the dictionary only when I lost the thread of events. Having got through two volumes in this way I bought volume after volume, and in the course of some two years I read pretty well all of Dumas' novels. This method had the advantage that I learned French mainly by meeting words over and over again in contexts that revealed their meaning, and not through memorizing them after looking up their English equivalents. Although I thus came to read French with ease I had no practice in speaking it, but I thought I had a foundation on which I could build if I undertook some serious study.

After examining all the information I could collect I decided in favour of a summer course at the University of Rennes for two reasons: the programme suggested that the standard was high since at the end of two months a diploma could be obtained, holders of which were recognized as qualified to teach French abroad; and the courses were held at St Servan in Brittany where living would be cheap. My father not only approved the scheme, but gave me fifteen pounds towards its cost. My friend Hugo Rutherford decided to join me, as did also one of his cousins, and so we made a party of three.

[Editor's note: A full account of Phelan's time at the University of Rennes can be found in the complete text of the memoirs.]

The exam results exceeded my expectations. When we were called up one by one to receive our diplomas the presiding professor made a little speech complimenting me on my performance and announcing that the Board had unanimously decided to accord me the *Diplôme supérieur avec mention honorable.*

I was greatly pleased, not only at the success itself, but because I felt I had in some degree repaired my failure at Liverpool.

That failure I also retrieved by passing my honours examination in physics twelve months later. Once again I was faced by the problem of a future career, and once again I found that I had no ideas on the matter. I was offered a post as assistant lecturer in physics. This was flattering, but I could not feel that I was ready to commit myself. I had taken to physics only for the reason that it offered the way to an honours degree in the Faculty of Science, and not because the subject had for me any special attraction. I had a vague feeling that I had not yet got the material on which to make a decision and that I should not find the material in Liverpool. Why I should have thought that I should see things more clearly from Oxford I do not know, but that was the reason that led me to decide to have a shot at the Indian Civil Service, not because I had any desire to make my career in India, but because I had learned that successful candidates in the examination were given a year at Oxford to study oriental languages, and I saw no other way of getting there.

I was not given any encouragement. I was told that, with rare exceptions from Dublin, Glasgow and Edinburgh, all the successful candidates had come from Oxford and Cambridge, that no one had ever entered from Liverpool or any of the modern universities, and that my chances of success must be regarded as nil. Nevertheless, as I could think of no other objective, I decided I would take my chance.

The examination had some peculiar features: candidates made their own choice of the subjects in which they wished to be examined; the number of marks accorded for each subject was specified, and the only limitation was that the total obtainable on any combination chosen must not exceed 6,000; a candidate was given no credit for any subject in which he failed to secure more than a certain minimum of marks.

The subjects in which I might expect to make a reasonably good showing were mathematics and physics, and to these I added a selection of other subjects in order to bring the possible total of marks to 6,000 in the hope that in some of them I might score more than the minimum, and thus swell my total. Since the standard in all subjects was high, I realized that my chances of success were exceedingly small; if I was to spend another year at my studies, I wondered whether it would be possible for me to pick up another university degree so that in any event I should have something to show for my work.

I accordingly applied to the Dean of the Faculty of Arts for permission to read for the degree of Master of Arts in French language and literature. He replied that permission could be granted only to those who had obtained a Bachelor of Arts. I had expected that this would be his reply, and I called his attention to another rule which provided that a graduate of another university might be given the permission I sought, and I pointed out that the nature of the degree he must hold was not specified. I argued that I possessed two Liverpool degrees, that a Liverpool graduate ought to be entitled to the same privileges as a graduate of another university; the condition laid down in the rules was clearly intended to ensure that those to whom permission was given were qualified to enter on the studies in question, and my Rennes diploma was sufficient evidence in this connection.

The Dean happened to be the Professor of Philosophy, and perhaps for this reason he gave me a patient hearing.

"There is a good deal in what you say," he said, "but I very much doubt if the Faculty will agree. However, I am prepared to go this far. If the Professor of French is willing to take you, you can begin, but on the clear understanding that this unprecedented point will have to be decided by higher authority."

The Professor of French accepted me, and for some five months I worked under his direction. During this time I heard nothing more of the matter, and I assumed that all was well. Meanwhile, much had been going on behind the scenes, and the decision that was finally communicated to me seemed to me wholly illogical. I was told that my application was refused but that, in view of the fact that I had been acting on the Dean's provisional decision, the University had decided to let me sit, as a quite exceptional measure, for the Bachelor examination at the end of the year. I protested to the Dean that the decision could not be defended; the University, in order to refuse a request which the rules allowed it to grant, was giving me a permission which violated the rules.

"That is not the position," said the Dean. "The matter had to go from the Faculty right up to the Council of the University. The Council is the rule-making authority. The Council has made a special rule for you. That's a feather in your cap, for there is no precedent. You may as well take advantage of it."

There was, of course, nothing else I could do. Once more my propensity for getting off the beaten track had landed me in a mess. I had now only some four months in which to prepare for the Bachelor of Arts examination. My whole plan of work was disorganized since I must concentrate on getting the degree, and leave aside other subjects which I required for the Indian Civil Service examination. My problem was further complicated by other time-consuming activities. I had become the treasurer of the Guild of Undergraduates, a post which was no sinecure because the Guild was responsible for the upkeep of the sports grounds and for expenditure on a number of other student enterprises. Moreover, as my savings were insufficient to see me through this additional year at the university,

I had to eke them out by doing a certain amount of coaching. Neither of these occupations could be considered a waste of time; as treasurer I learned a good deal about business; and, when coaching, I had a slightly guilty feeling because I felt I learned more than my pupils – one never really understands a subject until one tries to teach it to someone else. A third affair that also made demands on my time was the Workers' Educational Association (WEA).

I had continued to attend lectures on economics during my scholarship years, and I had taken up the subject again as one in which I might pick up some marks in my Indian Civil Service examination. In spite of my having done little real work on the subject, Professor Gonner and his assistant, J.H. Jones, took an interest in my progress and, no doubt because of my reputation as a speaker, roped me in for WEA lectures. The movement, at that time, was taking on a great extension, the demand for lecturers in economics was difficult to satisfy, and I agreed to take a class one evening a week in Lancaster. This led to my spending a weekend in Oxford with a group of WEA lecturers, and it was thus that I made the acquaintance of Arthur Greenwood,[8] Alfred Zimmern,[9] Henry Clay and others,[10] all of whom were destined to attain celebrity in different fields, and who were my first links with a wider world.

In spite of these miscellaneous occupations I got through my Bachelor examination, not only without difficulty, but with distinction in three of my subjects, and then I set out for London to face the infinitely more difficult hurdle of the Indian Civil Service.

During the six weeks that remained before the examination was due to begin I proposed to put myself in the hands of Wren's, the famous coaching establishment to which, I understood, most candidates had recourse. Here also my reception was not encouraging.

"When do you intend to take the examination?" the Principal asked.

"Next month," I replied, surprised at his question.

"I meant whether you thought of taking it next year or the year after," he said dryly. "Most of our students come to us for two years."

"I have no choice," I said. "Next year I shall be over the age." I did not add that a year's fees at Wren's would have been beyond my means.

---

[8] Arthur Greenwood (1880–1954) was Labour Minister of Health from 1929 to 1931. (Ed.)

[9] Sir Alfred Eckhard Zimmern (1879–1957) was a British historian and political scientist specializing in international relations. He was known for his involvement in international relations summer schools, often referred to as "Zimmern schools". He contributed to the founding of the League of Nations Society and also of the United Nations Educational, Scientific and Cultural Organization (UNESCO) in 1945. (Ed.)

[10] Sir Henry Clay (1883–1954) was a British economist who later worked for the Ministry of Labour (with Harold Butler) on industrial relations (1917–19). (Ed.)

"In that case," he replied, "I am afraid we can't do anything for you. Of course, if you would like to come to us for a few weeks you can. But honestly I think you would be wasting your money."

Nevertheless I thought it worthwhile. I knew nobody with any experience of the examination, and I might pick up a few tips which would guide my own cramming in the most profitable directions. Even one or two extra marks in what I called my make-weight subjects might carry me over the minimum line, and mean a considerable gain. For instance, I had put down chemistry as one of my subjects, but I had little practical experience of inorganic analysis, and some work in a laboratory might make all the difference.

The examination was certainly an ordeal. That summer London sweltered in the hottest weather ever recorded. In a temperature well over 90° in the shade I went back and forth from my diggings in Bayswater to Burlington House wondering each time if I should find myself confronted by something completely beyond me. The examination went on throughout the whole of August, but there were often two or three days between one paper and the next – not that these afforded any great relief, for they had to be devoted to a last hasty cramming on the subject next to be faced. I was an experienced examinee, and I could judge pretty accurately the marks I would receive for each paper I handed in. In order to be on the safe side I was very conservative in the estimates I made, and at the end of the examination I was greatly encouraged to find that they gave me a total much higher than I had expected.

Success did not depend on reaching some fixed standard but on the number of vacancies to be filled; these vacancies included the higher posts in the Home, Indian, and Colonial services, and their number varied from year to year. The candidate emerging at the head of the list was given his choice; the next man took his pick of the posts remaining; and the process continued until no more posts were available. The number of Home posts was very small – usually not more than half a dozen – and these were taken, as a rule, by those at the top of the list. I had no hope of obtaining a Home post, and it was not my objective. I was, therefore, more than satisfied when my calculations indicated that I should find myself well up in the group to which the Indian posts would go.

The results reached me in the form of a printed document which first listed the candidates in the order of the total marks received and then gave similar lists for each subject. I was painfully disappointed to find that my estimate of my total had been wildly over-optimistic. Wondering how I could have miscalculated so badly I looked at the classification by subject to discover where I had overrated my performance. In mathematics my marks corresponded very closely with my guess. In all my make-weight subjects I had secured figures far superior to those which I had credited myself – my English essay had obtained only one mark less than the highest given to any candidate; in economics, economic history, English literature, French, and chemistry, I was among the first ten. In physics, however, I had obtained only a few marks above the minimum, and had barely escaped getting nothing at all. This was the figure that had thrown out all my calculations, and I had every reason to be convinced that it must be wrong.

In accordance with the usual practice the paper set in physics contained ten questions from which the candidate could choose the six he wished to answer; it was clearly stipulated that not more than six answers were to be submitted. To me the paper presented no difficulty; I could have answered all the questions if necessary, and my only problem was one of tactics. Answers to questions which were descriptive in character rarely, if ever, secured full marks – insufficient emphasis on some point, or the omission of some detail to which the examiner attached special importance, was likely to result in a score of 80 to 90 per cent. On the other hand, the answer to a question requiring the candidate to furnish a mathematical proof received either full marks or none. I had avoided one such question since it involved a long piece of mathematical analysis in which one might get stuck. After having answered the six questions I had chosen, and still having time, I tried my hand at the mathematical question, and worked it out successfully. I then crossed out one of my answers in which description was a prominent element, satisfied that by this substitution I had gained a few extra marks. I judged my paper to be worth at least 90 per cent, and it was inconceivable that, on the strictest possible marking, it could have been credited with only about a third of that figure. What made this result still more absurd was that my marks for chemistry, a subject of which my knowledge was superficial, were more than twice as high. The only possible explanation seemed to be that some of my answers (written in "books" marked only with a number and not with my name) must have been lost in the process of being transmitted to the examiner, and if this was the case there was no way of proving that they had ever existed.

The marks that I lost by this mischance, for mischance it must have been, would have put me somewhere near the top of the list, and the whole of my subsequent history would have been different. As it was, it was only when the Indian posts had been filled that I came into the picture. I was offered a post in the Fiji Islands but, after long consideration, I refused it, for Fiji was a small area all to itself, and the chances of promotion were small. Moreover, there was still a chance, though a very slight one, that I might yet get a post in India, since vacancies occurring up to within six months of the next examination were filled from those on the old list for whom a place had not been found. So I decided to wait, wondering if I should be left high and dry and be compelled to take up school-mastering, which seemed the only career likely to be open to me.

Within a few weeks two other openings unexpectedly appeared. Professor Gonner, under whom I had studied economics, had served on a number of official commissions, and was well known in governmental circles. When the Board of Trade was looking for investigators, [11] and when the National Health Insurance Commission wished to recruit lecturers to aid in bringing the Act into operation, [12] he was asked to nominate candidates, and he sent in my name. Summoned to be interviewed by these two departments, I set out for London with two, and possibly three, roads before me not knowing which I would be called on to follow nor to what it would lead.

My farewell to the University of Liverpool was as unorthodox as some parts of my career within its walls. I arrived from London for the degree ceremony at St George's Hall just as the Registrar and his aides were marshalling the procession. The organ was pealing, and the procession was about to start, when I got hold of the Registrar, and asked what place I was to take.

"You've got your list, and it shows your place," he said impatiently, "get into it at once."

"I've got the list," I replied, "but I'm in it twice. Which place do you want me to take?"

"Impossible," he cried angrily, thinking I had been celebrating the occasion, and looking keenly at me to see if I was sober. "Don't you realize that graduation is a most serious ceremony? Once the Chancellor utters the words 'I admit you to the degree of Doctor of Divinity', you are a Doctor of Divinity although you may have come up to be made a Doctor of Science, or Music, or whatever it may be. It is vitally important that people go up in the proper place. Find your place on the list, see who is in front of you and who follows you, and make certain you are between them. Hurry up. The procession must start."

"I'll do whatever you say," I replied, "but the point is that I am getting two degrees, and I can't, with the best will in the world, walk in your procession in two places at the same time."

The harassed Registrar almost tore his hair.

---

[11] The Board of Trade was a British government department, or ministry, which up until 1917 included responsibility for labour matters. It evolved into the Department of Trade and Industry in 1970. The latter was replaced in 2007 by the Department for Business, Enterprise and Regulatory Reform and the Department for Innovation, Universities and Skills. (Ed.)

[12] The National Health Insurance Act of 1911 introduced Britain's first limited scheme of national health insurance. The scheme was administered by four National Health Insurance Commissions for England, Scotland, Wales and Ireland. (Ed.)

This situation arose out of the special permission I had been accorded to take my Bachelor examination in the circumstances already recounted. I therefore figured among those to be admitted to the degree of Bachelor of Arts. But having obtained an honours degree in science a year previously, I also figured among those on whom the degree of Master of Science was to be conferred. It had never happened before that degrees in two different faculties fell to be conferred on the same person at a single graduation ceremony. The lists for each faculty had been carefully checked, but it had not occurred to anyone to check over the list as a whole, and it had not been noticed that my name appeared twice.

For a moment the Registrar was completely nonplussed. Then he grabbed an undergraduate and ordered him to walk in my place among the Bachelor graduates. I went up to be made a Master of Science, hurried down off the platform, dived underneath it, did a quick change into another gown and hood, relieved my much embarrassed proxy in the procession, and walked up again to the Chancellor to be admitted as a Bachelor of Arts. I imagine the nerve-racked Registrar was glad to see the last of me.

Apprenticeship with the Lloyd George New Deal[1]

3

Gwydyr House in Whitehall, where I reported to begin my work with the Board of Trade, had an antiquated air. The steps that led up to its shabby doors were worn and so was the flagged passage inside. The whole building had a depressed look about it and seemed badly in need of cleaning and painting. I was courteously received and given a huge volume containing the report of the Enquiry into the Cost of Living,[2] which had been made in 1906, and which was now to be brought up to date by the investigation in which I was to take part. Having presented me with this volume, the official who received me seemed exhausted by his effort and suggested that I should take it home and get fully acquainted with its contents. Though I had expected something different this seemed on the whole a sensible suggestion and, having been told at what hour I was to appear next morning, I went off.

I opened the volume with some curiosity. At first sight it seemed to contain nothing but hundreds of pages crammed with columns of figures giving the retail prices of pork chops, potatoes, cheese, tea, sugar and other items of a similar kind. I looked at these in some despair. I could not imagine how I was to carry out my instructions to "get acquainted with" such a mass of detailed material, nor what possible use it would be to me if I did.

---

[1] David Lloyd George's first ministerial position was as President of the Board of Trade, when he entered the new Liberal Cabinet of Sir Henry Campbell-Bannerman in 1906. He went on to become Chancellor of the Exchequer in 1908 and Prime Minister during the First World War. (Ed.)

[2] The full title of the publication was: *Cost of living of the working classes: Report of an enquiry by the Board of Trade into working class rents, housing and retail prices, together with the standard rates of wages prevailing in certain occupations in the principal industrial towns of the United Kingdom.* (Ed.)

I turned to the beginning of the volume and there I found some pages of ordinary print which I attacked more hopefully. The volume began with three letters: the first was from the Permanent Secretary of the Board of Trade to the President of the Board; the second, which was twice as long, was from the Director of the Labour Department to the Permanent Secretary;[3] the third, which was longer still, was from the Director of Labour Statistics to the Director of the Labour Department. But all three letters only said in substance: "Here is the report."

Apparently the Circumlocution Office had a real existence. Here were three very important officials occupying neighbouring rooms writing to tell one another what they all perfectly well knew, and then printing their letters in such a way that the story unfolded in reverse order and the reader found himself moving backwards in time like the man in H.G. Well's *Time machine*. Fortunately the letters were followed by an Introductory Memorandum from which I was able to gather some information about how the figures had been collected and how they had been combined to calculate the index numbers for the 100 towns which had been investigated. I noticed without any particular interest that Dundee figured at the head of the list.

When the actual work of investigation began I found it interesting enough. I was given a card bound in leather, rather like a small passport, which certified that I was an officer of the Board of Trade and requested all concerned to give me every possible assistance in my work. This was particularly useful in securing the help of local authorities for the purpose of inspecting working-class dwellings and measuring the rooms they contained so that the rents paid for similar accommodation could be compared. So far as prices were concerned I could get along on my own. I had with me the figures obtained for the previous enquiry, and I had only to visit the same shops and get them brought up to date; if the shop had ceased to exist I had to choose another shop doing a working-class trade in the same neighbourhood. Working-class districts were familiar to me and it was easy to get the information I wanted without giving offence or seeming unduly inquisitive. I learned to judge the moment when shopkeepers would be neither too busy nor too tired to give me their attention. What I wanted to know were the prices paid by their customers on a specified date some months before and, since most of these small tradesmen kept no detailed records, their replies were often vague or covered too wide a range to be of use for statistical purposes. With

---

[3] The Labour Department was part of the Board of Trade at that time. It became a separate ministry in 1917. (Ed.)

a little gentle persistence, however, something sufficiently definite could usually be obtained.

After I had finished my enquiries in a town I would bring my material back to London to assist in its examination and tabulation in case any points arose that needed to be cleared up. I was astonished by the care with which this examination was carried out. Lengthy discussions were often necessary before it could be decided whether a figure could be accepted or put aside as needing further investigation. It was a long time before I realized that, since the results of the enquiry would directly affect the pay of postal officials in the different towns and influence other wage rates, what seemed an exaggerated fuss over a farthing in the price of this or that item might really involve enormous sums.

When returns were in from practically all the towns, most of the investigation staff was dispensed with. Three only, of whom I was one, were retained in order to undertake any further supplementary enquiries that a still further check of the whole material might reveal to be desirable. This did not necessarily imply that I had made a better showing than those who were not kept on. Many of them were young economists who had only agreed to be available for a limited period and who had to return to their universities; one of these was Hugh Dalton, [4] then a lecturer at the London School of Economics, with whom I had become friendly, and whom many years later I was to meet again when, having reached almost the topmost rung of the political ladder, he was Chancellor of the Exchequer.

My earlier investigations had been confined to a single area but now, as one or other figure called for final confirmation, I travelled to all parts of the country and my knowledge of provincial England became extensive. One town had been left severely alone because it presented a special problem and that was Dundee. Dundee had been classed in the 1906 report as the town with the highest cost of living in Great Britain and its citizens had protested against a result which they refused to accept as correct and which they considered injurious to their interests. The Board of Trade had not been unduly perturbed, since some town or other was inevitably destined to occupy that unenviable position and whichever it proved to be could hardly be expected to be content. A new factor, however, entered into the situation in 1908 when Winston Churchill, [5] having been appointed President of the Board of Trade, had under the rules then operating to

---

[4] (Edward) Hugh John Dalton (1887–1962) was a Labour Party politician, serving as Chancellor of the Exchequer from 1945 to 1947. (Ed.)

[5] Sir Winston Leonard Spencer Churchill (1874–1965) was President of the Board of Trade (1908–10) before he became Home Secretary (1910–11) and Secretary of State for the Colonies (1921–22). He was later British Prime Minister from 1940 to 1945 and again from 1951 to 1955. (Ed.)

seek re-election to parliament; after a defeat in his old constituency he turned to Dundee where he was successful. During his election campaign he was made well aware of Dundee's grievance and, though he had moved from the Board of Trade to become Home Secretary, the officials of the Board were nervous lest the present enquiry should lead to further protests from his constituency. Moreover, the Dundee City Council, wishing to be well prepared to challenge the new figures if necessary, had expended several thousand pounds on an enquiry of its own. In these circumstances the investigation in Dundee had been left to the end, but the time had now come when it could no longer be postponed.

I was in Glasgow checking some figures when I received instructions to proceed to Dundee and carry out the enquiry. I was as surprised as I was pleased at being entrusted with this responsibility, but I realized that my task would not be easy and that obstacles of one kind or another might be put in my way.

It was, therefore, with a good deal of apprehension that I made my call on the Provost to inform him of my arrival and to make my usual request for assistance from the local authorities. To my immense relief I discovered that the Provost was as much afraid of me as I was of him; my position as the representative of the Board of Trade endowed me with enormous prestige in the eyes of the authorities of a city as remote from London as Dundee. It had produced no effect whatever on small shopkeepers in different parts of the country – I was asked on more than one occasion if it was a trade union – but on the Provost of Dundee it made a very great impression indeed; so much so that I imagine he did not notice my schoolboy appearance and saw only what he thought such an important person must necessarily look like.

When, after having introduced myself, I said I understood that Dundee had been carrying out a cost of living enquiry of its own, he looked alarmed. Perhaps he was afraid that the city had been flouting the prerogative of His Majesty's Government by conducting investigations far beyond its own boundaries and that a severe reprimand was imminent. Anyway, he hastily disclaimed any responsibility, saying that the matter had been decided at a meeting of the Council over which he had presided but that otherwise he had had nothing whatever to do with it and that the enquiry had been carried out by the town clerk. When I asked if I could see the latter I was told that he had been taken ill and would not be back in his office for a week. I suspected that this sudden indisposition was not unconnected with my arrival; and indeed the Provost's tone suggested that he shared my suspicion and that he felt he had been basely deserted when he should have had every support.

I was anxious to learn as much as possible about the town's investigation so that I might take all precautions on the items that they might be expected to challenge, and I therefore persisted, asking whether there was not an assistant town clerk whom I could see. The Provost greeted this suggestion with relief; there was such an official; he had acted as secretary to the committee of the Council which had dealt with the matter and could give me all the information. This proved to be over-optimistic. The assistant town clerk was even more flustered than the Provost and equally anxious to wash his hands of the whole affair; all the documents, he informed me, were in the hands of Bailie Stewart, the chairman of the committee, and it was to him that I must apply. The Bailie, I gathered, was, in private life, the head of a commercial college, and was regarded as an authority on statistics.

When I at last secured access to him I was sure that I had found the moving spirit behind the whole enterprise. He sat at his desk surrounded by stacks of neatly labelled files and a document, which was evidently his draft report, lay open in front of him. It all had the appearance of having been arranged to create an impression of efficient organization by a professional hand. He, at all events, showed no sign of being intimidated. On the contrary I sensed a self-confidence that was more than a little arrogant and a readiness to do battle if necessary. I therefore opened the conversation in the most conciliatory fashion. The Board of Trade, I told him, had no axe to grind; it was a matter of complete indifference to it which town might come out with the highest index. The Board had been interested to learn of the enquiry Dundee had conducted; any additional evidence that could be made available from any quarter could not be other than helpful. If any of his figures did not agree with ours we should only to be too glad to check over our results in the light of any evidence he could produce.

Flattered by this approach he proceeded to give me a description of what he had done. He had not, of course, attempted to investigate every town for which the Board of Trade had published figures – that would not have been financially possible and, in any case, it was not necessary for his purpose; it was sufficient to make a thorough enquiry in a number of sample towns situated in different parts of the country. He mentioned, no less than three times, that these enquiries had extended as far afield as Southampton, which the town clerk had visited personally. Southampton, I gathered, was to Dundee the other end of the world and convincing proof of how serious and comprehensive the investigation had been. The results of these enquiries, which had taken over twelve months, showed conclusively that a great injustice had been done to Dundee in 1906. He was now embodying them in his report which, after it had been printed and presented to the town council, would be made available to the Board of Trade.

While he had been giving me this exposition, which he delivered rather like a professor addressing his class, I had been looking at the mass of his files and asked if I might examine one or two of them to see the returns they contained.

"Certainly," he said. "You will see that we used the same forms as you used for your 1906 enquiry. Personally, I should have made a different selection of the items for food, but since our object was to test your results we were careful to secure prices for the same articles."

I took up another file hardly daring to hope that I should discover a repetition of the mistake I had noticed in the first.

"You read the 1906 report before you began?" I asked.

"Naturally," he replied impatiently. "I told you that we copied from it the forms we used."

"So you did," I said apologetically, "and then you worked out average prices for the different food items for each town?"

"Of course," he said, astonished at such an obvious question, and evidently wondering how the Board of Trade could have chosen to represent it anyone so stupid.

"I'm afraid", I said, thumbing through another file, "you didn't read our report with sufficient care, otherwise you would have noted that we don't average the figures we obtain for prices. What we extract from the returns for a town is the price most commonly paid for each article of food. The average price may be totally misleading. See what you have done about bread in Edinburgh." I handed him the open file. "Prices from nine shops have been averaged. Now look at the prices one after the other. They vary so much – one is twice that of some of the others – that they cannot refer to bread of the same character, and so an average price is meaningless. But apart from that, you can't determine which of these are typical working-class shops – some of them are clearly not – so you can't discover the price paid by working-class purchasers. What your investigators have obtained is the price at which bread was sold at certain shops, not the price paid by working-class purchasers. And even if you assume that the three lowest prices you have in this list are from typical working-class shops (and you can't of course build your figures on assumptions) you haven't enough material to enable you to fix the price most commonly paid."

He listened horror-struck while I took up file after file and gave further examples of how impossible it was to make any use of the figures they contained.

"But what am I to do?" he asked at last, completely overwhelmed.

"I don't know," I replied, and feeling rather sorry for him I added, "you've got a mass of miscellaneous information from which a trained economist might be able to extract something of interest. But you've got nothing which would enable him to arrive at comparisons of the cost of living. I can tell you, however, what you should not do; you should not publish the conclusions you have drawn from this material unless you want to make the town council and yourself a laughing stock."

Satisfied that the Dundee counter-enquiry had now been completely demolished, I went back to the Provost and informed him of the situation. He was greatly relieved and, I thought, by no means displeased at the disaster that had overtaken the Bailie. He agreed that no report should be published and offered me every assistance in the prosecution of my own enquiries.

On getting back to my hotel late in the afternoon I found a telegram which had arrived for me in the morning from the Board of Trade instructing me to take no steps in connection with the enquiry in Dundee pending the arrival of the Director of Statistics who was leaving London that night to take charge of the enquiry in person.

When I met him at the train the following day, a little concerned lest he should think I had assumed an undue measure of responsibility, I was surprised to find he was as relieved as the Provost to learn what had happened. He confined his activities to paying a formal call on the Provost and then returned to London, leaving me to pursue the enquiry alone.

Presumably as a result of my success in Dundee I was next entrusted with a special enquiry into Scottish rents. Working-class housing in Scotland had the peculiar feature that beds were most frequently located in recesses or alcoves in the kitchen or living room and that nothing that could properly be called a bedroom existed. For this reason no comparison between rents in England and in Scotland had been made in 1906, but this was an unsatisfactory situation and it was decided that an effort must be made to overcome the difficulty. Since London was the basic town with which all others were compared, a complete survey of working-class housing in the London area was necessary. I suppose I must be one of the few persons who have ever visited all the separate towns and urban districts of which the vast agglomeration called London is composed; for if I remember rightly they number something like 200.

I made one discovery that, to me at all events, was surprising. The worst slums and the most defective accommodation were not in the East End but in the West. In the East End the miles and miles of mean streets were infinitely depressing in their drab monotony; there was much poverty and overcrowding; but the houses were small. In the West End, tall basement houses with a flight of steps leading up to the door displayed an impressive exterior. They had been originally the expensive homes of rich families but, as other areas became fashionable, they had steadily descended in the scale until now they sheltered one or two families on each floor and, not infrequently, a family in each room. With the only water supply a tap in the basement, and with their successive flights of high and steep stairs, the carrying of even one pail of water to the upper rooms was a task demanding considerable physical effort. Any degree of cleanliness, material or personal, was virtually impossible, and their inhabitants could hardly be blamed if they lived in conditions of indescribable filth.

My survey finished, I was assigned the task of writing the section of the report explaining how the comparison of rents had been made. This was recognition, the importance of which I did not fully appreciate at the time, that I was deemed capable of work other than field investigation.

My activities in connection with the enquiry by no means comprised the whole of the experience which widened my outlook during this period. Although I did a lot of travelling, approximately half my time was spent in London, and London had much to offer in the way of instruction and amusement. I had begun by returning to the boarding house in Bayswater in which I had lived while making my attempt at the Indian Civil Service. It was Kelleher who, appearing suddenly out of nowhere, made me acquainted with the Hampden Residential Club to which I at once transferred. The Hampden deserves some description for it was a unique institution which in many ways helped to complete my education and to bridge the gap between my academic knowledge and the realities of adult life.

It had begun, I believe, as a kind of philanthropic institution but it was now a purely commercial enterprise. The premises occupied a whole block in an unsavoury area in Somers Town behind St Pancras Station. Three sides of the block consisted of the original houses which were identical with the other houses in the neighbourhood, but which now communicated with one another by a corridor which had been constructed at the back. The fourth side was a building originally intended for a gymnasium and still so called though it was empty. The space within the square formed by these buildings was partly occupied by a one-storey structure containing a large dining room and the kitchen; the remainder was covered with asphalt and had once been a tennis court but no net or markings survived. In spite of its unpromising exterior the club was comfortable enough inside. In winter a huge fire burned in the small carpeted entrance hall watched over by a uniformed porter; from the corridor beyond opened the reading room, the billiard room, and the dining room, all rather shabby but warm and comfortable.

The rest of the building with its stone corridors was chilly; but the bedrooms contained fireplaces and, as a large scuttle of coal could be obtained for a shilling, their occupants could keep themselves as warm as they pleased at small cost. A vast number of bathrooms had been installed in the basement and there was an unlimited supply of hot water. A bedroom could be obtained for nine shillings and six pence a week, this sum covering service and the use of all the club's facilities; a bed-sitting room could be had for slightly higher figures depending on its size – the largest, containing a sofa and a couple of armchairs, cost twelve shillings. The food in the restaurant was excellent and served by men waiters in evening dress. There was room for something like 200 residents; a large proportion were permanent, but there was a good deal of coming and going and there was never any difficulty in finding room.

The remarkable value the club provided more than compensated for its unattractive surroundings. The neighbourhood was sordid in the extreme. I was told by old members that no less than three murders had recently been committed in the street on which the window of my room looked out. I found no reason to disbelieve this story, for the spectacle presented by the street late on a Saturday night suggested that murder might be a common occurrence. Outside the half-dozen pubs men and women vomited in the gutter or relieved themselves of excess liquid in even less decorous fashion; viragos tore at one another's hair and, screaming obscenities, attempted to rip off one another's upper garments; men fought more silently but in bloodier fashion, while the onlookers cheered on the combatants with unholy delight at every brutal blow. What at first astonished me was to see members of the club, resplendent in evening dress and opera hats on their way home from the theatre, skirting round these rough crowds and exciting no hostile or jeering comment. The club, however, had long been accepted as a normal feature by the surrounding population who were accustomed to refer to it with a certain pride as "The Toffs' Doss House"; and perhaps the annual Christmas tree at which the club entertained the children of the neighbourhood helped to secure for club members an immunity which would not have been extended to strangers.

For me the great attraction of the club was the extraordinary variety of its membership. It included an ex-colonial governor, a dentist from New Zealand with pronounced revolutionary views, a man who had walked across mid-Africa armed only with a walking stick, a man who had attended the Tsar's coronation, a young violinist who was gaining a great reputation, a man who was reputed to be a cardsharper and to have served several jail sentences, an ex-Member of Parliament, a struggling dramatist, election agents, young barristers waiting for briefs, doctors looking for a practice, solicitors, commercial travellers, accountants, schoolmasters, and others whom I have forgotten.

The most remarkable feature of this mixed community was the liberty everyone enjoyed, a sort of ultimate tolerance in which not only one's acts, but one's humour, gay or morose, was equally accepted without question or criticism. It made no difference whether a man was shabby and down on his luck and obliged to confine his meal to the cheapest dish on the menu – I remember that a grilled herring with mustard sauce could be obtained for three halfpence. Ernest, the head waiter, would serve him with as much attention as the bookie sitting beside him who had had a good day and was doing himself well regardless of expense.

Meals could be obtained at all hours up to midnight but, as the evening wore on, tablecloths were removed and the dining room took on more and more the aspect of a café. Nobody cared whether you were drinking water or champagne, whether you were drunk or sober, talkative or silent. There was abundance of good talk; if you got bored with the subject at one table you moved to another, took your choice of music, art, horse-racing, philosophy, the latest stock exchange limericks, or you joined the journalists as they came in after having filed their stories and learned the news that would appear in the next morning's papers; and, if you enjoyed an argument, there was no need to break it off when the room closed at midnight – you adjourned to some hospitable bed-sitting room and carried on till dawn or later.

I saw much of Kelleher at this time. He liked the Hampden and its bohemian atmosphere suited him. He spent most of his time writing poetry and lived precariously from hand to mouth, doing odd teaching jobs and some freelance journalism. Finally he made a selection of short poems and got them printed free of charge by an acquaintance, an instructor in printing at a technical school somewhere in the Midlands. The first proofs were a hopeless mess in every respect, but after a number of efforts a correct text was achieved and he received a stock of slim volumes to which he had given the title *Poems, twelve a penny*. I do not know whether he ever succeeded in getting them put on sale – he had announced his intention of offering them to passers-by at the corner of the street – but he sent out copies for review. One or two reviews were faintly encouraging but one he used to quote with delight. It appeared in the Athenaeum, which prided itself on reviewing everything it received. The review contained only the following two sentences: "The poet assures us that these poems represent the fine fruit of his efforts. If so we can only dimly surmise the quality of the rejected verses."

I found many opportunities to pursue my hobby of public speaking in London. There was a weekly debate in the Hampden and, though the speaking was not noteworthy for its brilliance, the discussion was always interesting because, whatever the subject, there was always someone who could argue from personal experience. I also discovered the public gallery in the House of Commons; I thought it offered the opportunity to watch the most fascinating show in London; and it had the great advantage that admission was free.

Among my friends at the Hampden were a number of young lawyers and they invited me one evening to come and speak at a meeting of the Law Students Debating Society. They regarded practice in speaking as part of their professional training, and I was naturally glad to have an opportunity of measuring my ability against their sharp wits and legal minds. I had an immediate success, so much that I became a sort of honorary member of their society whose presence was welcome whenever I chose to attend.

Having dropped in casually on one occasion just as the proceedings were about to begin, I was asked if I would replace one of the openers who had telephoned that he was unable to come. Not in the least concerned at being totally unprepared to lead the opposition to a motion in favour of conscription I lightheartedly agreed. The proposer of the motion was a well-known solicitor, the mayor of one of London's most important boroughs who was something of a minor public figure and was credited with parliamentary ambitions. He was a stout, pompous man, overfull of his own importance and over-fashionably attired in a heavily braided morning coat and a white slip bordering the V of his waistcoat. He had his subject at his fingers' ends, but he spoke with a ponderous solemnity and made the mistake of talking down to his audience. In spite of the fact that he made out a strong case he alienated the sympathies of his listeners who, being mainly conservatives, would otherwise have been enthusiastically on his side. I realized that he had delivered himself into my hands. I made no real attempt to rebut his arguments; I merely restated them in a caricatured form which made him look ridiculous. This unexpected line of attack made him furious and stung him into imprudent interjections which only gave fresh material for my mockery. Finally, completely losing his temper and looking like an outraged turkey cock, he announced that he would take no further part in the discussion and stalked indignantly out of the room. I was afraid that I had overdone it, but the chairman's reaction reassured me. He said a few words condemning my opponent's conduct and ruled that the discussion should proceed. A few days later I received a letter expressing deep regret that I should have been exposed to such a display of unsporting ill manners at one of the society's meetings and the hope that I would not hold the society responsible.

In spite of this incident, therefore, I continued to be a welcome guest at the society's meetings and some months later I was invited to attend the society's annual meeting and reception. This was a very formal affair held in the great hall of the Law Society. It was attended by many of the heads of the legal profession and, since members were entitled to extend invitations to their families and friends, half the company was composed of ladies in evening dress whose presence made the occasion a brilliant social function. The main feature of the proceedings was a debate opened by some outstanding public figure.

When I arrived the hall was full and I slipped into an inconspicuous seat at the back to listen to G.K. Chesterton propose a motion arguing that parliaments are the greatest danger to democracy.[6] When he sat down members rose from all parts of the body of the hall eager to catch the chairman's eye and to display their talents before so distinguished an audience. The speeches were good; too good, for they had been carefully prepared and had little relevance to Chesterton's arguments which it would not have been easy to predict. They had high merit as pieces of polished prose but they were more like essays on a set theme than lively debating efforts and, as was inevitable, they tended to become monotonous and to echo one another.

After an interval of an hour for the reception, the debate was resumed. It had now become a rather dull affair except for those who were desperately anxious that it should not conclude before they had made their contribution. Suddenly I was tapped on the shoulder by the secretary who had come down from the platform with a message from the chairman asking me to speak.

"Tell him no," I said. "This is an important occasion for your members, and it would be rightly resented if I were to squeeze one of them out. Anyway, I didn't hear more than half of what Chesterton said."

He returned to the platform and I watched him whisper to the chairman who put the vice-chairman in his place and came down himself.

"Do me a favour and speak," he pleaded. "The thing is going dreadfully badly. Everybody is bored to death and Chesterton is falling asleep."

I understood his concern, and feeling that I owed him my help in return for the hospitality the society had so often extended to me, I agreed.

"Thanks," he said, "I'll call on you next," and he hurried back to the platform.

I had only a few minutes in which to decide what to say. One idea flashed into my mind and I grasped at it with a thrill. But it would clearly come best at the end and, after reviewing the few fragments of Chesterton's speech which I had been able to hear distinctly from my place at the back of the hall, I chose one with which I thought I could make some preliminary play. First of all, however, if I was to get my points over with effect, I would have to get and hold the audience's keen attention, and for this I was unfavourably placed since people would have to turn round to see me.

When I rose, the fact that I was wearing a dinner jacket while everyone else was wearing tails and a white tie aroused a faint curiosity. I deliberately assumed an Irish brogue which helped to stress the contrast with other speakers but which

---

[6] Gilbert Keith Chesterton (1874–1936), a prolific writer. His works included *The everlasting man* (1925), a reflection on the nature of Christ. He and his friend and literary ally Hilaire Belloc led strong attacks on both Liberal and Conservative Governments. (Ed.)

was also an essential part of my strategy. I have an accurate recollection of short speeches made after swift and intense concentration, and I remember this one in particular because I often thought it was the most successful I ever made. It ran as follows:

Mr Chairman,

I would not have intervened on this occasion were it not for one thing; there is one matter of great importance in connection with this motion to which no reference has yet been made.

I have the greatest admiration for the dialectical somersaults with which Mr Chesterton has entertained you this evening. But, surely, in discussing matters of gravity it is desirable that we should keep our feet on the ground. The danger in turning somersaults is not that the feet leave the ground. It is that they do not always return to it. From that danger, despite all his skill, our distinguished intellectual acrobat has not escaped. Up he went with amazing agility; and down he came, not on his feet but on his head – or rather he would have fallen on his head had he not landed himself in the soup. Into the soup he went – bang into the mulligatawny! [Heads turned to look again at the speaker and raised eyebrows manifested disapproval of this vulgar note.] Yes, bang into the mulligatawny so that the splash would hide from you his faulty footwork. And then, off he went, over the hills and far away, leaping like an overgrown chamois from one unstable foothold to another – marvellous to watch *and* impossible to follow. You, poor innocents, have been scrambling after him dizzy and dazzled; and now you don't know where you are, or how you got there. I suggest that you should not pronounce yourselves on this motion in that situation, standing precariously on a rainbow and clinging for support to Mr Chesterton masquerading as Peter Pan, the alpine guide.

I suggest that you get back to earth and see just where you were misled. Let us examine just where he slipped on his syllogism and sought salvation in the soup. We know where he began his argument; and we know the conclusion to which he asserts it leads. I will show you that there is no logical path that leads from the one to the other.

I had spoken slowly, the only way to make oneself clearly heard in a large hall in the days when there were no microphones. Everyone had turned round; Chesterton was fully awake and an occasional heave of his shoulders indicated an appreciative chuckle. I could now get to my argument, sure that it would be followed with attention. I went on, speaking now more slowly still.

But it is not only with a mistake in logic that I am concerned. I accuse Mr Chesterton of a deliberate attempt to deceive. I accuse him of having played fast and loose with the intelligence of this house. I accuse him of the callous betrayal of decent men for whom his long-professed sympathy is now revealed as disgusting hypocrisy.

These are grave charges and I should not put them forward unless I was satisfied that they could be substantiated to the full. I have one witness whose evidence cannot be challenged. That witness is Mr Chesterton himself.

What was his premise? He started by telling us that the literature of a country was characteristic of its people. He gave us examples and proof of this assertion of Chaucer and Dickens and other great names. But, if Chaucer and Dickens and the rest were no more than samples of their generations, how did they come to survive when millions of their fellows have been forgotten? They survived because they were exceptional and different.

But it is unnecessary to develop the argument. Mr Chesterton has, as you know, recently published a poem called *The White Horse*. It has been hailed by critics as one of the greatest poems of its kind in the English language. We may assume that Mr Chesterton was more serious when he wrote that poem than he was in the speech he delivered this evening. This is what he wrote on the point to which I have drawn your attention:

For these are the Gaels of Ireland
Whom the Lord God made mad,
For all their ways are merry
And all their songs are sad.

There you are. In Mr Chesterton's considered view the literature of a people does not reflect its ways.

There is no need to consider the rest of his case. He prides himself on his logic. A chain is no stronger than its weakest link. I have shown you that one link in the chain of his argument is missing. His whole demonstration falls to the ground. He has failed, and failed lamentably, to make out his case.

But I brought against him a graver charge. I accused him of hypocrisy. Let us leave aside all else. Let us forget that he has treated this honourable society with a levity more suited to the Holborn Empire than to this noble hall. Let us leave aside the fact that he has stumbled over his syllogisms and foundered in his fallacies. The most damning point against him is unaffected by the strength or the weakness of the arguments he has employed.

The fact remains that he has taken his stand squarely on the terms of his motion. He cannot deny that he has proclaimed his belief that parliaments are a danger to democracy.

I will ask him one question – one question which I defy him to answer to your satisfaction or to mine.

Why, if he believes that parliaments are a danger to democracy [I paused and, raising my voice, flung out an accusing arm], WHY has he been striving with might and main to thrust a parliament upon my unfortunate country?

The question was unexpected. There was silence for a second before the audience got the point; and then a storm of applause swept through the hall. Home Rule for Ireland was the burning political issue at that time. I had correctly guessed that the audience would be predominantly conservative, and that an attack on Chesterton's well-known support for Home Rule would rouse its enthusiasm.

The hour was late, and the chairman, judging that further speeches from the floor would not be welcome, called on the proposer to make his closing remarks. Chesterton could, no doubt, have torn me to pieces.[7] Instead he gave a delightfully humorous account of the enjoyment the discussion had afforded him, and with this the proceedings came to an end.

[Editor's note: The complete text of the memoirs continues with the author's account of the Bloomsbury Parliament, a mock government in which he took part.]

I was also glad to get free of my obligations in the Bloomsbury Parliament because the National Health Insurance Commission was making frequent demands for my services. On arrival in London, after being interviewed by the Commission, I had been subjected, along with some 30 or 40 other successful candidates, to a week's intensive cramming on the contents of the Act;[8] it contained, if I remember rightly, over 200 articles and was reputed to be the longest Act ever placed on the statute book. The ease with which the officials who had taken part in its drafting steered their way through its complexities excited my admiration. I was particularly impressed by Arthur Salter,[9] whose

---

[7] He must have recognized that I had misquoted the lines from his poem, the correct text of which would not have supported my argument. My misquotation was not deliberate. It was derived from my recollection of a review of his book in which some citations had been given. Whether there was a misprint in the review or whether my memory had played me a trick I do not know. What Chesterton had written was "For all their wars [not ways] are merry, And all their songs are sad". (E.J.P.)

[8] The National Insurance Act of 1911; see Ch. 2, n. 12 above.

[9] (James) Arthur Salter (1881–1975) was a civil servant and university professor specializing in insurance issues. From 1919 to 1920 he was head of the Economic and Financial Section of the League of Nations Secretariat. (Ed.)

mastery of his subject and whose power of lucid exposition were equally remarkable. We were encouraged to raise difficulties and I was one of his most persistent questioners, little thinking that our acquaintance would develop later in a sphere neither of us could then foresee.

I knew nobody among those attending the course. With six lectures a day we were kept far too busy to do more than nod to one another or exchange a few casual words. Many years after when I came to know a British Prime Minister I sometimes thought his face was familiar to me not only from press photographs but in some other association. It was only by chance that I discovered that Clement Attlee had been one of my companions at these lectures. [10]

At the end of the week we were put through a searching examination to test our knowledge of the Act. I had the satisfaction of being one of the few who acquitted themselves satisfactorily, the others being told that they must undergo a further period of instruction, and I was accordingly appointed by the Commission as an official lecturer on the Act. This meant that, subject to any absences from London, of which I must notify the Commission in advance, I might be called on at any time by telephone to deliver an evening lecture somewhere in the London area for which I would be paid travelling expenses and a fee of one guinea.

These lectures were interesting experiences, for the audiences varied from a meeting of all the workers employed by the Bovril Company to a meeting, which I addressed from the stage of His Majesty's Theatre, representing every occupation in the theatrical profession from scene-shifters to actor managers. After expounding the general provisions of the Act and their application to a particular group I had to reply to questions and, since the Act was extremely complicated, these often raised matters on which I had been given no guidance. It was impossible not to reply, and thus give the impression that the Government did not understand its own Act, and it was equally dangerous to give an interpretation which might be found to be mistaken. Exhausting intellectual concentration was always required when new and perplexing individual cases were put up, and I often thought that my guinea was a sweated wage. In fact I was being compensated by something far more valuable, experience in dealing with interpretations of an intricate legal text, which was to prove an important asset to me in my later career.

When the preparatory period was drawing to an end and the Act was about to be brought into application, lecturers were notified that a number of national

---

[10] Clement Richard Attlee (1883–1967) was leader of the Labour Party from 1935 to 1955 and British Prime Minister from 1945 to 1951. He promoted the welfare state and the new system of social security. In 1941 he attended the extraordinary ILO Conference in New York and Washington, DC as a British Government delegate. (Ed.)

health insurance inspectors would be appointed as part of the permanent organization. The salaries attached to these posts were twice as much as I was getting at the Board of Trade. Moreover I was attracted by the idea of joining a new department in which there would be prospects of promotion as it expanded. There was, however, one obstacle in my way and that was that I was below the minimum age specified for appointment. Apart from this, I had every reason to believe that I possessed all the necessary qualifications. My work for the Commission had been changing; instead of being deputed to deal with large audiences I was being sent more and more frequently to discuss with smaller bodies the conditions in which the institutions they represented could become "approved societies" under the Act and the amendments that would have to be incorporated in their rules to make this possible. Assignments of this kind indicated confidence in my ability and, hoping that an exception might be made in my favour, I went to see Arthur Salter.

"You can ask them to make an exception," he said, "and if I have any say in the matter I shall support you. I'm afraid, however, that it's a Treasury decision which the Commission cannot alter. But, if you are not accepted, don't be worried. Personally I think you would be wasted. You are young and something better will come your way in time."

I took this remark as a kindly effort to prepare me for a disappointment. Had I known Salter better I would have attached more importance to his words and been less discouraged when I was told that my candidature could not be taken into consideration.

Meanwhile, the work on the Cost of Living Enquiry had been completed; my draft of the section on Scottish rents had been approved and incorporated; proofs of the innumerable statistical tables were passed to me to see, but I had no means of checking them, nor did it seem to be expected that I should make any effort to do so. Since I had had no holiday for over a year, I put in an application for leave. I was told that the report was now with the Permanent Secretary who had to take the final responsibility for its contents, and that, until he had transmitted it with his approval to the president, I must remain available in case he should raise any question on the section I had contributed. In response to my enquiry how long I might expect to have to wait I was told that it was impossible to say; perhaps a couple of days, perhaps a month or more. I ought, no doubt, to have accepted the situation. As it was, I had nothing to do save reflect that statistics did not arouse my enthusiasm; that waiting on the convenience of a Permanent Secretary, whom I had never seen and who did not know I existed, was an utterly boring occupation; and that a career as a civil servant required qualities of patience which no ordinary human being could hope to develop. Moreover I was disappointed by my failure to get taken on by the Insurance Commission, disgruntled at being chained to my office while the weather was fine, and generally feeling irritated, frustrated and restless. All these factors combined to increase the temptation to throw prudence to the winds and to take advantage of an alluring offer of other employment which now presented itself.

[Editor's note: Phelan spent the next year as a travel guide for British visitors to continental Europe in the nascent business of group tourism, an account of which can be found in the full text of the memoirs. We rejoin the author on his return to the Board of Trade as Chief Investigator for an enquiry into housing.]

Wartime civil servant 4

The sentiment of satisfaction with which I resumed government service was increased when I learned the scope of the enquiry on which I was to engage. The initiative had come from Lloyd George, who had persuaded the Cabinet to envisage further social measures to improve living conditions. His Health Insurance Act provided a considerable measure of protection for the individual in case of sickness but other measures were required if the problem of public health was to be tackled in a really effective manner. The Factory Acts had done something to secure healthier conditions in industrial establishments; little, however, had been done about housing, which was generally regarded as a matter for private enterprise, and even the very limited powers given to local authorities were seldom used with any vigour.

As industry had expanded, housing conditions had grown steadily worse. Long hours of work, night shifts, the half-time system for children and the absence of transport facilities had led to the concentration of the working population in the closest possible proximity to the factory or the mine. Houses were mainly of the back-to-back type with no through ventilation and sanitary conditions were extremely bad. Housing of this type could be found even as late as 1912; but even where an improved type of house had been built with a small yard at the back, it had few amenities and fulfilled only the minimum sanitary requirements.

Lloyd George's approach to the problem was bold and imaginative. No doubt it was inspired by his knowledge of conditions in the Welsh mining valleys in which there was only room for the river, the road, the railway and one row of houses; with the result that the town, if town it could be called, consisted of one street which might be miles long.

Speaking in Glasgow in 1911 in the course of the "land" campaign after his famous budget of 1909, he evoked the problem in a characteristic peroration. He described how as a youth he had followed a funeral procession up a Welsh hillside and had watched the coffin being lowered with some difficulty into a grave that was not sufficiently wide because it was crowded by tombstones on either side. Then he told how the old Welsh minister with his white beard moving in the wind looked down into the grave and said, "Ah, Dafydd, my man, you have had a narrow lot in life, and you have a narrow grave in death. But one day, Dafydd, the Last Trump will sound, and you will rise up and you will cry 'Elbow room for the poor! Elbow room for the poor!'"

This was the central idea from which he later began to elaborate a housing policy; something which he saw must be of a more fundamental character than increased floor space and better sanitation for the individual house. With improved possibilities of transport it was no longer necessary for workers to live alongside their work; and he thought in terms of building whole new towns in pleasant surroundings from which the workers could travel to mine or factory and to which they would return at the end of their working day.

The preliminary enquiry in which I was engaged showed that conditions not unlike those prevailing in the Welsh valleys could be found in other parts of the country. In the Potteries, for example, "The Five Towns" were little more than a ribbon stretching for some 15 miles, a succession of mean houses and small factories which followed the line of the clay deposits from which the industry's raw material had been extracted. Although there was no physical obstacle, such as the steep sides of the Welsh valleys, to prevent lateral expansion, the general aspect of the "towns" was the same. But this was not the only feature which presented a problem. In the manufacture of pottery there is inevitably much breakage when the pots are fired; the fragments are known as schraf, and schraf is practically indestructible. The obvious way to get rid of it was to use it to fill the cavities from which the clay had been extracted and this is what was done. The consequence was that the houses built over these fillings stood on foundations honeycombed with crevices running down into the earth for perhaps hundreds of feet. No more perfect breeding ground for cockroaches could be imagined and they constituted a pest which it was impossible to eliminate.

When the war broke out in 1914, the enquiry was of course suspended. Along with my colleagues in the Department I received a notice stating that civil servants must not enlist without first obtaining permission; but, as my appointment was temporary, I assumed that, so far as I was concerned, permission would be a formality. I felt none of the enthusiasm which led so many young men to rush to the nearest recruiting sergeant, fearful lest the war would be over before they could participate in a great adventure; but, when Lord Kitchener predicted a three-years war and appealed for a million recruits,[1] I applied for permission to join up. My application was refused; and, believing that this must be a purely bureaucratic reflex, I wrote to John Redmond in the House of Commons asking him to intervene with the President of the Board of Trade.[2] The result was a severe reprimand for having contravened one of the strictest regulations of the Civil Service which forbids any attempt to invoke political influence. I was annoyed at what seemed a stupid and unreasonable attitude; I was of military age; I should have to go sooner or later; and I was irritated at not being allowed to carry out a decision at which it had not been easy to arrive. Before my discontent had time to become acute I discovered that the Department was far from being as unreasonable as I supposed and that my services were being retained because my special experience was rare and would soon be urgently needed.

To equip the Kitchener army the War Office had to acquire vast quantities of boots, belts, caps, buckles and every other article that a soldier might wear or use. The sources from which these items had previously been secured were incapable of providing the quantities now needed, and contracts had to be placed with other firms all over the country. All such contracts embodied the Fair Wages Clause whereby the wage rates paid were not to be less than those established by collective agreements or, if no such agreements existed, not less than those generally paid by good employers in the district for the same type of work. It lay with the Board of Trade to decide what these rates should be. In many cases the material in the possession of the Labour Department was sufficient for this purpose; but, when such material was not available, special enquiries had to be made.

In peace time enquiries of this character could be leisurely and exhaustive; with the advent of war not only was there a great increase in their number, but speed was of great importance. Moreover, the scope of the whole operation was immensely wider and the Board's responsibility correspondingly heavier. If the rates fixed were too high, vast sums of public money would be wasted and a chain reaction might increase expenditure in other directions; if the rates approved were too low, there might be strikes and the stoppage of production. Experienced investigators were, therefore, an imperative need; and it was this which explained why I was not given permission to enlist.

---

[1] Field Marshal Horatio Herbert Kitchener (1850–1916) was appointed Secretary of State for War by Prime Minister Herbert Asquith in 1914. Going against Cabinet opinion, he predicted a long war and began a massive recruitment campaign. He died in 1916, when his ship struck a German mine. (Ed.)

[2] John Edward Redmond (1856–1918) was an Irish nationalist politician who called for Irish involvement on the British side in the First World War. He had the third Home Rule Bill signed in 1914 but the advent of war prevented its entry into force. (Ed.)

It was highly interesting work demanding far more initiative and judgement than had been required for the Cost of Living Enquiry. Each case presented a new problem. I had to familiarize myself with different processes of manufacture and the skills they involved; I had to define the area within which a valid comparison could be made; if the precise article was not already being manufactured in the area, I had to discover if the same machines and similar skills were being used for the manufacture of other articles and decide whether they afforded a basis on which rates could be fixed. Much physical effort was also required. Rates had most frequently to be settled for small establishments making small articles with such equipment as they possessed, and these were often situated in remote parts of the country where no transport existed and where I might have to tramp from one little workshop to another, sometimes in mud and rain, only to find that I could get nothing of any use for my purpose. However, I learned much about small industry, small employers, the officials of tiny trade union branches and about life in communities much smaller than the towns in which my earlier enquiries had been conducted.

In time the number of these special investigations diminished. Other tasks were assigned to me and, as these involved no travelling, I could usually count on having free time in the evenings. I attended some lectures by Professor Bowley on statistical theory at the London School of Economics,[3] and I began to do some serious reading on monetary theory and on public finance. I also renewed my contacts with the Workers' Educational Association which called on me occasionally to address one of its meetings. One such invitation concerned a meeting at Nottingham where I was asked to replace a speaker who had been obliged to cancel his engagement; finding that it would be possible for me to leave London after I had finished my work at the office and get back to my desk the next morning at the normal hour, I accepted. The meeting proved a more important affair than I had anticipated. The Mayor of Nottingham presided in a large hall in which I could see no empty seats. My subject was "Some Aspects of War Finance" and I did my best to make it interesting for a popular audience.

Some days later I was told that Leach, the Assistant Director of the Department, wished to see me. It was the practice at the Board of Trade to collect and circulate for the information of its officials any articles appearing in the press of interest to the department. Leach handed me two of these cuttings and asked me if I had seen them. One was a lengthy article from the principal Nottingham

---

[3] Sir Arthur Lyon Bowley (1869–1957), a British statistician and economist, developed sampling techniques in the application of social studies. In 1919 he was appointed the first Professor of Statistics at the University of London. (Ed.)

newspaper giving extensive quotations from my address and the other was an editorial from the same paper drawing attention to the importance of some of the points I had made. This was more than a little startling. I knew that there was a strict rule forbidding a civil servant to write or speak in public on affairs connected with his department and, although a general exposition of the economic implications of war expenditure seemed harmless, the authorities might take the view that I had contravened the regulations. Inclined to be very cautious until I knew how the land lay, I limited my answer to the precise question put to me and replied that I had not seen the cuttings.

"Were you, by any chance, the lecturer?" Leach asked in a tone which I was relieved to find was quite friendly. I admitted that I was and explained that I had not anticipated that my remarks would be given publicity.

"We wondered if it could be you – yours is not a common name, you know – but we were puzzled because you had not been absent from the office."

I told him that I would not have taken on the lecture if it had interfered with my work, and he continued.

"The Department has no criticism to make of what you said. But if you should be asked to give any other lectures of this kind you might let us know in advance in case there should be any special points to which we might wish to draw your attention." Then, looking at me with a mixture of surprise and respect, he added: "I didn't know you were an economist."

Some months later I was greatly pleased at being given a permanent appointment to the post of Chief Inspector. Such permanent appointments were rare, as they required the special sanction of the Treasury, and a department had to be able to present a very strong case before the Treasury would consent to add to the number of its established posts. Whether the Nottingham incident played any part in this decision I do not know; many new tasks were being assigned to the Board of Trade, and my unusual and varied experience was, no doubt, my strongest recommendation. There was as yet no Ministry of Food, no Ministry of Munitions, and no Ministry of National Service; the matters which were later allocated to these and other new departments were, when they first arose, all dumped into the lap of the Board of Trade which seemed to be regarded as a kind of governmental maid of all work. So far as I was concerned, this process was all to the good, for it increased and widened my knowledge and gave me an acquaintance with other departments. The growing loss of ships from the submarine offensive made it urgent to obtain information on the stocks of certain essential imports, the rate at which they were being consumed, and the possibility of making economies or using substitutes. I was assigned to investigate the situation concerning the supply of pit props for the mines, and I was told that I could enlist the cooperation of the Home Office. After I had briefed myself with such scanty material as I could lay hands on, I called on the Chief Inspector of Mines and at the conclusion of our discussion I asked him to secure for me information on a number of points as soon as possible. Evidently, I impressed him with the importance of my mission, for a few days later a letter was delivered at Gwydyr House addressed to Edward Phelan, Esq., Timber Controller, Board of Trade. I was astonished that the Home Office, which prided itself on official exactitude, should have made such a mistake; and I was embarrassed lest my superiors should think that my assignment had gone to my head and that I had been giving myself airs. They drew no such erroneous conclusion and their only comment was a joking congratulation. The incident shows how great the pressure was and how on all sides red tape was being thrown aside.

While the inventory of stocks went on, the much more complicated problem of making an estimate of available manpower was also undertaken. The issue of conscription for military service dominated the political scene, but equally violent was the struggle that raged over the allocation of manpower between the fighting forces and industry, which had to provide the weapons and other supplies without which the fighting forces could not be equipped. When Lloyd George came into power he set up a Ministry of National Service to deal with the whole problem, and placed at its head Neville Chamberlain.[4] At that time little was known about him save that he was a member of a famous family, that he had been engaged in business in the West Indies and that, after his return to Birmingham, he had been active in municipal affairs. He seems to have held the curious, but by no means unusual, belief that experience in private business was the supreme qualification for the efficient conduct of public administration – 20 years later as Prime Minister, he applied this principle to the conduct of Foreign Affairs with disastrous results. His tenure as Minister of National Service was equally disastrous but, in the midst of all the war happenings which monopolized public attention, it attracted little notice.

St Ermin's Hotel, in which the Ministry was installed, sheltered the most comic administration which, I imagine, ever formed part of the governmental machine. It included no civil servants – they were naturally excluded as notoriously lacking the most elementary businesslike qualities. Different sub-departments were set up to deal with different groups of the population, and each of these was headed by someone drawn from the group concerned; Sir George Alexander, the

---

[4] (Arthur) Neville Chamberlain (1869–1940) was appointed Minister of National Service in 1916 to coordinate conscription and ensure the functioning of essential war industries with sufficient workforces; he resigned from this post in 1917. He was later British Prime Minister (1937–40). (Ed.)

well-known actor, for example, was to deal with theatrical employees and a musician was given the job of putting musicians to work on the land; a large body of untrained clerks was assembled to register the recruits for National Service who, it was assumed, would respond in great numbers to the Minister's appeal. The appeal brought little response for the reason that nobody knew what form National Service might take. Nevertheless, patriotic people did appear at St Ermin's anxious to render any service their country might demand of them. They filled up forms giving their names and addresses and indicating their occupation; in one case the man was subsequently allocated for work at the London docks – his occupation as "organizer" had been transcribed by an inexperienced clerk as "organ-grinder", and he had been sent to the docks on the ground that he was accustomed to an open-air occupation.

Few of these callers at St Ermin's were allowed to leave the building without being photographed by members of the Refugee Department, a proceeding which was all the more surprising as it was imposed on them almost by physical force by the members of that department who, in accordance with the principle on which the Ministry was organized, were typical refugees who spoke no English. The head of the department, himself a refugee, was subsequently found to have an espionage complex, and presumably believed that spies would make the secrets of the Ministry one of their main objectives.

Much of this deplorable and expensive nonsense went unperceived in the stress of the war, but there was a good deal of criticism when, after some weeks, the Ministry was unable to show that it had achieved any practical results. The Ministry thereupon rushed out a Restricted Occupations Order which made it an offence punishable by fine or imprisonment to engage any man under 60 years of age in certain occupations without the Ministry's permission. This was hailed by the press as vigorous and welcome action, and for 24 hours the Ministry basked happily in the sun of public approval. Then it had a rude awakening.

Van after van from the post office unloaded masses of letters asking for permits. No organization had been prepared to implement the Order and to deal with the individual cases which it ought to have been foreseen would arise. The businessmen were flurried; and, as the flood showed no signs of abating, and as angry telegrams began to arrive asking why no notice had been taken of earlier communications, they became panic-stricken. Finally, someone remembered that the list of occupations had originally been drawn up by the Board of Trade, and a despairing appeal was made to that Department for assistance. Late one afternoon I was sent to St Ermin's to clear up the mess.

Crabbed handwriting, eccentric spelling, and the inability of the writers to express themselves clearly made the examination of some scores of letters picked up at random from the mass that almost filled a room a longish job. What was evident was that the Order had created much hardship and distress. One man, for example, wrote that, after having been unemployed for some time and having now found a place, he had been told that his employer could not take him on without permission; he begged in simple but moving terms for this permission to be given at once since his wife was ill and his savings exhausted. Small employers were also in great difficulties; with the loss of employees to the army or to munitions factories they were finding it hard to keep going at all, and now they were forbidden to engage such men as might be available without becoming liable to fine or imprisonment.

How I and my colleague from the Board of Trade, C.K. MacMullan,[5] who joined me next day, got matters under control need not be told in detail. But as fast as letters went out, others came in and we got no real relief until the administration of the Order was placed in the hands of District Commissioners who were entitled to call for the help of the factory inspectors and the labour exchanges in the performance of their task. This arrangement was far from perfect since the factory inspectors and the labour exchanges remained under the orders of their respective ministries, but it was the best that could be devised in the circumstances.

The same arrangement applied in my own case; although I remained at St Ermin's, where I dealt with all matters concerning the Order referred to headquarters by the Commissioners, I was responsible to the Board of Trade and not to the Ministry of National Service. Many of these matters related to questions of interpretation, and here my experience with the National Health Insurance Act stood me in good stead; but I had also to exercise a general supervision over the operation of the Order and to attempt to eliminate, or at all events reduce, the friction which inevitably developed from time to time between the different parts of the improvised machinery.

The final comment on the farce of St Ermin's was enacted on its own doorstep. Auckland Geddes had made one condition on accepting his post,[6] and that was that the Ministry must be moved to another address; the name of St Ermin's was associated in the public mind with so much mess and muddle that he felt it placed him under an impossible handicap. Other premises were provided for him, and St Ermin's was taken over by the Tank Warfare Department of the War

---

[5] Charles Walden Kirkpatrick MacMullan (1889–1973) worked for many years at the British Ministry of Labour and was eventually appointed Principal Assistant Secretary. He had a successful career as a playwright under the pseudonym C.K. Munro. (Ed.)

[6] Auckland Campbell Geddes (1879–1954) became Minister of National Service after Neville Chamberlain's resignation in 1917. He subsequently served as Minister of Reconstruction and President of the Board of Trade from 1919 to 1920, and British Ambassador to the United States from 1920 to 1924. (Ed.)

Office. This was a hush-hush organization and after the process of moving out National Service and installing its own material had been completed, guards were placed at the doors and no one could enter without a special pass. As soon as these guards took up their duties they were assailed by a number of foreigners who protested that they had no need of passes as they were officials who worked in the building. Investigation revealed that they were the members of Neville Chamberlain's Refugee Section who had remained blissfully ignorant of the fact that the Ministry to which they belonged had moved elsewhere a fortnight ago.

The incidents recounted above give some indication of how varied, owing to war conditions, were the tasks and responsibilities that fell to my lot during the first years of the war, and how they gave me a far wider experience of governmental work than is usually accessible to a civil servant at the outset of his career. I was able to see the success with which professional civil servants tackled new responsibilities and the failure of the amateurs who arrogantly took it for granted that civil service methods and experience could be ignored. The whole problem of the structure and operation of the administrative machine appealed to me as a fascinating subject for study and analysis. This interest in public administration, although it arose in the beginning out of no more than my characteristic curiosity, was to lead to the next step in my career.

I must go back a little in my story so that the sequence of events may be clear. My admiration for the work of the Labour Department of the Board of Trade was not unqualified. An immense number of trade union publications, trade journals, collective agreements and other documents were examined; but after information on a limited number of specific items had been extracted, these documents were discarded and all the information they contained on other subjects was lost. The extension of the Department's activities during the war revealed that much of the information thus thrown aside would have been of great value, and much time and effort had to be devoted to retrieving it. It seemed to me that a fairly simple and inexpensive system could be devised whereby all this information could be stored and kept up-to-date. Even if such information might not be required for current purposes and might never be used in the preparation of published material, it would provide a basis on which questions of future policy could be reviewed. I put these ideas forward but, naturally enough, they received little welcome from officials overburdened with their day-to-day tasks.

I also became interested in the problem of administration at the other end of the scale, the problem of the distribution of functions between different ministries. With the creation of new ministries during the war, this had become a subject of discussion among economists and others interested in problems of government, and it naturally figured in the conversation of a small group of intellectuals who made a practice of lunching together once a week in Westminster. I do not remember how I first came to attend one of these lunches – presumably I was brought by Arthur Greenwood,[7] or by some other of my friends in the Workers' Educational Association – but afterwards I went to them pretty regularly. Among the new acquaintances I made at these meetings was Tom Jones,[8] at that time National Health Insurance Commissioner in Wales.

When Lloyd George replaced Asquith,[9] one of the first things he did was to summon Tom Jones to London where he was destined to remain as the trusted adviser of the new Prime Minister and of several of his successors. One morning I was a little surprised when Tom Jones, whom I knew only slightly, rang me up and invited me to lunch with him in a little restaurant in Soho; I was still more surprised when he asked me not to tell anyone of his invitation. The reason became apparent when during the meal he told me, under the seal of confidence, that the Prime Minister was preparing to set up a Ministry of Labour, and continued, "I understand you have been giving some thought to what such a ministry should do. I'd be glad if you would tell me your ideas because no one seems to have given the matter serious consideration."

On this I found plenty to say. The first step would obviously be to transfer to the new Ministry responsibility for labour exchanges, factory inspection, trade boards and labour statistics; but if nothing more than this was done, the change would amount merely to having another minister on the Treasury bench who would answer certain questions hitherto dealt with by the Home Secretary or the President of the Board of Trade. Labour questions, in my opinion, were going to take on vastly greater importance in the future. The new Ministry should be given the function of studying every aspect of them and watching developments both at home and abroad. It should, therefore, have, as an essential part of its equipment, a labour intelligence division which would keep under review the whole subject and be in a position to brief the Minister on matters on which the Cabinet would look to him for advice. There was a general case for providing all ministries with a division of this character because their officials were so overwhelmed by the urgency of their current tasks that they had no time to give adequate consideration to questions of long-term policy; but a division such as I had indicated was absolutely indispensable for a new Ministry called upon to

---

[7] See Ch. 2, n. 8 above.

[8] Thomas "Tom" Jones (1870–1955) was Deputy Secretary to the Cabinet under four prime ministers: David Lloyd George, Andrew Bonar Law, Stanley Baldwin and Ramsay MacDonald. (Ed.)

[9] Herbert Henry Asquith (1852–1928) was British Prime Minister from 1908 to 1916. He introduced government pensions and an extensive social welfare programme in 1908. In 1916 he resigned after a series of political and military disasters. (Ed.)

define its appropriate sphere of authority. Tom Jones listened to this exposition with attention and asked me if I would let him have a confidential memorandum for the Prime Minister; and this I naturally was only too eager to do.

What happened next was confusing and disconcerting. The task of defining the functions of the new Ministry was remitted to Arthur Henderson,[10] the Labour member of the War Cabinet; this was no doubt a political necessity but it had the disadvantage that Henderson had no ministerial experience and was consequently quite out of his depth. No one raised any objection to the inclusion of an intelligence division because it involved no sacrifice by any other ministry; as regards the other functions of the new Ministry there was a struggle. The Home Office succeeded in keeping factory inspection under its wing; the Board of Trade reluctantly surrendered labour exchanges and trade boards but only on condition that it be allowed to keep labour statistics.

This, as I pointed out to Tom Jones, made no sense. A division of labour intelligence divorced from labour statistics was a patent absurdity; since the new Ministry was now under the obligation to have an intelligence division, it would be compelled to duplicate at great expense work done by the Board of Trade. I explained in detail how a vast mass of material could be sifted for statistical and non-statistical information in a single operation and the economy which would result.

How Tom Jones set about getting the decision revised I do not know; the first thing that happened was that I personally was transferred to the Ministry of Labour where I joined MacMullan in getting the Intelligence Division organized; and shortly after, the Board of Trade surrendered the Department of Labour Statistics.

Montagu House, formerly the town residence of the Dukes of Buccleuch, which was assigned to the Ministry as its headquarters, was a palatial mansion in Whitehall almost directly opposite the entrance to Downing Street. At a time when accommodation for expanding government departments was extremely difficult to secure, this superb edifice so impressively situated in the heart of Whitehall was, no doubt, intended to demonstrate to Labour that the new Ministry was, so to speak, being given a seat in the front row.

Behind this imposing facade the Ministry, however, was less impressive. John Hodge,[11] the Minister, was an old style trade union leader from the steel industry

[10] Arthur Henderson (1863–1935) was leader of the Labour Party from 1914 to 1917. In 1916 he was appointed member of the "small war Cabinet" as Minister without Portfolio. He chaired the Geneva Disarmament Conference from 1932 to1934 and was awarded the Nobel Peace Prize in 1934. (Ed.)

[11] John Hodge (1855–1937) was a British trade unionist. In 1916 he was President of the British Workers' National League. In December 1916 he was appointed the first Minister of Labour, a post he held until August 1917. From 1917 to 1931 he was President of the Iron and Steel Trades Confederation. (Ed.)

with a forceful personality – amused civil servants recounted how, after he had asked to be left alone with the men's representatives in a wages dispute, his powerful voice, which penetrated to the corridor outside, was heard informing them that they were in the wrong and that they could take it from him that they would not "get a bloody farthing". Useful as such bluntness might be in handling an industrial dispute it was not in itself sufficient to equip him for the other duties of his post. Sir David Shackleton, [12] who was appointed as Permanent Secretary, was a man of much higher intellectual capacity and more varied experience. He had been one of the first Labour members of Parliament, had acted as Labour Adviser to the Home Office and had been chairman of the National Health Insurance Commission; but he was not a professional civil servant and nothing in his career had fitted him for the responsibilities a Permanent Secretary is required to assume. Both Hodge and Shackleton would undoubtedly have their hands full, for labour unrest was spreading and certain features of the shop steward movement were causing anxiety to both the government and the trade unions.

This was, though in a more marked form, the kind of situation I had envisaged when I had urged on Tom Jones the necessity for an intelligence division which could devote its whole attention to "thinking about" matters of general policy. The Division as actually constituted was small and its structure was simple. At its head was Sir John Hope Simpson, [13] a retired Indian civil servant; below him it was composed of two sections, one headed by MacMullan which dealt with home intelligence, and the other, dealing with foreign material, headed by myself. The system which I had suggested earlier in the Board of Trade, whereby information on all labour matters could be collected and kept constantly available, was worked out in detail and put into effect – its operation was so simple that it could be entrusted to a staff of temporary girl clerks with a minimum supervision.

In the light of the flow of information thus at our disposal, a weekly report was prepared jointly by MacMullan and myself and sent forward through Hope Simpson to the Minister, who circulated it to the Cabinet. The Division might also be called upon by other parts of the Ministry for information on some particular point arising in the course of their normal work; but the preparation of the weekly report for the Minister was the only specific task assigned to it. It was thus

---

[12] Sir David James Shackleton (1863–1938) was President of the Council of the Trades Union Congress from 1908 to 1909. He entered the civil service in 1910, and worked for the Minister of Labour from 1916 to 1925, first as Permanent Secretary and after 1920 as Chief Labour Adviser. He was a British Government delegate to the Fourth Session of the ILC in 1922. (Ed.)

[13] Sir John Hope Simpson (1868–1961) was a British Liberal politician and colonial administrator. He served in the Indian Civil Service from 1889 to 1916 and was Private Secretary to the Parliamentary Secretary of the new Ministry of Labour between 1917 and 1918. (Ed.)

left free to assume on its own initiative the more general function for which I had urged its creation. How it set about this more ambitious task can most easily be explained by an example.

In 1917, there were rumours that the idea of instituting a federal system of government for the British Isles had appealed to the imagination of Lloyd George as affording the possibility of a new approach to the question of Irish Home Rule; a general federal solution would attract support from nationalistic opinion in Wales and Scotland and thus cut across party lines. If the matter reached the stage of a Cabinet discussion, as it seemed that it might well do, and Ministers were asked for their opinion, what, for instance, should the Minister of Labour say about labour exchanges, trade boards, labour statistics and the other matters for which he was responsible – which of them should be decentralized to provincial authorities and which should remain under federal control?

Questions of so fundamental a character could not be adequately examined by the Cabinet on the basis of observations supplied by the officials administering these services under the existing system. The advantages or disadvantages of one or other solution could be weighed only in the light of a review which would include, in addition to the opinions of these officials, a study of the experience of federal States and of the success or friction with which the solutions they had adopted had in fact worked.

Because of our other occupations neither MacMullan nor I could undertake personally a job of this kind, but we could call in a member of what we called the "production staff", university professors and lecturers with whom the Division was in touch and who were always ready to render any service they could to a government department in war time. When one of these volunteers undertook a particular study, he participated along with Hope Simpson, MacMullan and myself in a discussion of the general lines it should follow; then all the information the Division possessed was placed at his disposal, and he was left free to conduct whatever other research might be necessary and to write the document without interference; when he had finished he would participate in another discussion in which his conclusions would be subjected to searching criticism. Thus some fifteen years before the Brains Trust of President Franklin Roosevelt attracted public attention, the Intelligence Division of the Ministry of Labour had initiated a system of bringing academic scholarship and administrative experience into collaboration to explore problems of social policy.

Once this machinery had been created and was working satisfactorily, I again became worried about my personal situation in regard to the war. The drastic measures that had to be taken to make good the appalling losses in France, such as sending back into the fighting line men who had been severely wounded several times, made me unhappy about my sheltered position. After my first abortive efforts to get into the army at the beginning of the war, I had accepted the principle that it was for the government to decide in what capacity each individual could render the most useful service. Its decision in my case had seemed to me reasonable, but, although my present activity was of long-term importance, it was far more remote from immediate war necessities than my earlier work had been, and I looked for some way of getting myself transferred into one of the fighting services in spite of the Ministry's power to hold me back. It was beginning to look as though the increasing success of the German submarine offensive might prove the decisive factor in the war, and I learned that the navy, in its endeavour to deal more effectively with this menace, was in urgent need of electrical engineers and physicists. Since I had an honours degree in physics, the Government might be forced to decide whether I could be more useful in the navy than in the Ministry of Labour, and I managed to secure an interview with the commander of HMS Vernon, the headquarters of the anti-submarine organization in Portsmouth. My qualifications were considered as more than sufficient and, after a medical examination which gave satisfactory results, I was told I would be given a commission as second lieutenant in the Royal Naval Volunteer Reserve.

"That's quite agreeable to me," I said, "but there is a difficulty since I am a civil servant. If you really think I can be of use, you will have to get the Admiralty to apply for my release from the Ministry of Labour."

"That can be arranged," was the reply. "I'll write to the Admiralty tonight and they will do what is necessary. It may take a little time but you ought to hear something in about a week or ten days."

On my return to London I told Harold Butler what I had done.[14] He was by no means pleased. I did not expect any more favourable reaction, for I knew that, as the senior professional civil servant at the Ministry's headquarters, he was heavily burdened. Although he ranked only as Assistant Secretary, because of Shackleton's lack of experience he was in reality the Second Secretary of the Ministry, and he viewed with dismay the weakening of the Intelligence Division which would result from my departure. In spite of his displeasure and his statement that there was no likelihood that the Ministry would consent to release

---

[14] Sir Harold Beresford Butler (1883–1951) started work in the Home Office in 1908 and was transferred in 1917 from the Foreign Trade Department to the Ministry of Labour to fill the post of Assistant Secretary to the Minister. In 1918 he, Phelan and Malcolm Delevingne drafted a programme for the Labour Section of the Paris Peace Conference. In 1919 he was appointed Secretary to the Organizing Committee and Secretary-General of the First Session of the ILC in Washington, DC. In the early years of the ILO he served as Deputy Director of the Office, with responsibility for administration and finance. In 1932 he succeeded Albert Thomas as Director of the ILO, resigning in 1938 to take up the post of Warden at Nuffield College, Oxford. (Ed.)

me, I was confident that a request from the Admiralty could not be refused, and I looked forward to the prospect of having some part in the anti-submarine warfare. In view of the fact that my father's ship had been torpedoed in mid-Atlantic and he himself carried off as a prisoner of war to Germany, no other form of active service could have seemed more appropriate.

I was working late one evening in Montagu House when my door opened and two figures came in. The room was completely dark because of the black-out, the only illumination being the small pool of light thrown on my desk by a shaded lamp. Peering into the gloom, I recognized Butler; his companion was unknown to me but his overcoat suggested he was someone from outside. Butler was about to speak but the stranger restrained him and they advanced to my desk in silence. The authority of the stranger's gesture, Butler's worried acquiescence, and this silent approach combined to create an atmosphere of mystery more suited to the stage than to a room in Montagu House. The impression was intensified when the stranger enquired in a curiously throaty whisper whether we could be overheard in the adjoining rooms. The question made sense, for my room was one of a temporary series constructed of lath and plaster, but I was at a loss to imagine what could be the nature of a communication that must not be overheard by my neighbours through whose hands passed all sorts of confidential papers. I was able to give the assurance that the rooms on either side were empty since my neighbours had gone home; and Butler then introduced my visitor as Bruce Lockhart from the Foreign Office,[15] who wished to speak to me on a highly confidential matter.

Lockhart, whose name conveyed nothing to me, went straight to the point. The War Cabinet, he said, had appointed him to head a secret mission to Bolshevik Russia. It had also decided that the mission should include someone well acquainted with the labour situation in Great Britain. He had been assured that I possessed this qualification but, before I gave him a reply, he felt bound to warn me that members of the mission might be exposed to some personal risk. The mission was urgent; it would leave within 48 hours. The Admiralty would provide a cruiser to convey it across the North Sea; but after that it would have to fend for itself. It might not get into Russia at all; if it did, it was impossible to predict what kind of reception it would encounter, and equally impossible to say

---

[15] Sir Robert Hamilton Bruce Lockhart (1887–1970) joined the British Foreign Service in 1911 and was posted to Moscow. He was acting British Consul General in Moscow when the Russian Revolution broke out in February 1917. In 1918 he was accused of plotting against the Bolshevik regime and was condemned to death. His life was spared in exchange for the return of the Russian diplomat Maxim Litvinov (see Ch. 5, n. 4 below). (Ed.)

how long it would be able – or be forced – to remain. It was essential that the affair be kept absolutely secret. Was I married? I shook my head. Who was my nearest relative? I replied that my father was a prisoner in Germany and that my mother lived near Liverpool. If I accepted, he continued, not even my mother might be told; I must just disappear. When I arrived in St Petersburg I would be able to send a letter home by bag, but until then nobody must learn what I was doing. Was I prepared to go?

At this point Butler, who had been looking increasingly troubled, intervened to say that he could not take the responsibility of letting an important member of the Ministry's staff go off for an indefinite period without the Minister's permission. Lockhart replied that Butler had been told of the matter on the clear understanding that the most complete secrecy was imperative. That was a War Cabinet decision, and it was deliberately intended to exclude any communication to Ministers. On no account was the Minister to be told; a leakage would be inevitable and the consequences would be disastrous. The Prime Minister had laid the greatest stress on this point.

This interchange gave me a few minutes in which to consider what I should reply. I had heard nothing more about my appointment to the navy; it might yet come through, but perhaps the Admiralty had decided not to pursue the question and if it did, the Ministry might refuse the request for my release. The present offer had an authority behind it which left the Ministry no say in the matter, and to accept it would put an end to these uncertainties. When Lockhart turned to me for my answer I accepted his proposal.

"Good," he said. "Here is a hundred pounds. Buy a revolver and a fur coat. It will be very cold, so make sure you get a good one; get a fur cap and snow boots as well. Have you a passport?" I nodded. "Apply tomorrow afternoon at the Home Office for an exit visa and get Norwegian and Swedish visas from the consular offices. Ask for the permit and the visas as a private individual stating you want to go to Norway and Sweden on commercial business; it will be arranged that you will get them without difficulty. Meet me at my flat at 6 p.m. and I will introduce you to the other members of the mission."

He shook me by the hand and disappeared with Butler into the shadows, leaving me dazed by these rapid instructions and by this sudden plunge into what seemed like a Phillips Oppenheim novel. Indeed, in the silence that followed their departure, I found it difficult to be sure that I had not been dreaming. Might I not have dozed for a few moments in my darkened room? And was not this fantasy of Russia and a cruiser the crazy pattern which my subconscious mind had constructed out of the news about Russia in the press and my hopes of joining the navy? What possible service could I render in Russia? I knew nothing of the country and not a word of the language. I felt in my pocket. There was nothing dream-like about the wad of crisp Bank of England notes that my fingers encountered. Tomorrow I would have to get my exit permit and my visas; I would have to acquire the articles Lockhart had specified, and presumably there were others I ought to think of for myself. I had never before purchased either a fur coat or a revolver, and I was not sure how best to set about doing so. As I walked home I tried to concentrate my mind on these practical problems but with no great success. They were small and unimportant beside the incredible, and yet undeniable, fact that I was going to Russia, the menacing and mysterious country where revolution was producing increasing chaos; and my imagination ranged wildly over all the probable and improbable things I might or might not encounter in that strange land.

Russia during the Revolution **5**

It is no part of my purpose to retell the story of Bruce Lockhart's mission to Russia in 1918. His book *Memoirs of a British agent*, published in 1932, gave an extraordinarily vivid account of his personal adventures; it secured a deservedly wide circulation and provided the title, though little more, for a successful film. All I propose to do is to recount my experience during the early part of his mission and, incidentally, to complete his narrative on some points that he omitted from his story, partly because his mind was concentrated on the political problems which he had to confront, and partly because they made little or no impression on one who was familiar with the Russian scene. I, on the contrary, was visiting Russia for the first time and my reactions were therefore more intense. What these reactions were will appear from the following pages, but before I recount them it will be well to recall what was the position in Russia which led to Bruce Lockhart's mission and how he came to be chosen to undertake it.

When, in October 1917, Alexander Kerensky was overthrown by the Bolshevik revolution,[1] and the new Government declared its intention of making peace with Germany, in defiance of the agreement between the Allies not to enter into separate peace negotiations, public opinion in England reacted violently. It was widely believed that Lenin and Trotsky were German agents; the Russian action, which would allow the Germans to transfer huge armies from the east and fling them against the hard-pressed line in France, was denounced as the vilest treachery; in the

---

[1] Alexander Fyodorovich Kerensky (1881–1970) was the leader of the Russian revolution of February 1917. He was appointed Prime Minister in July 1917, but in October of the same year his government was overthrown by the Bolsheviks and he subsequently fled to the United States. (Ed.)

face of this wave of indignation Lloyd George had announced that diplomatic relations with Russia had been broken off and that the ambassador had been recalled. Nothing less would have satisfied public opinion; but the consequence was that the British Government found itself with no direct channel through which it could receive information about developments in Russia and without any possibility of exerting any influence, however small, on the course of events.

Neither France nor the United States had taken similar action and Lloyd George was irked by a situation in which he was dependent on reports from Paris and Washington. His colleagues in the War Cabinet, and in particular, Lord Milner,[2] shared his view that some form of contact should be established with the Bolshevik Government provided the right person could be found to whom such a difficult task could be entrusted.

Lockhart had left Russia only a few weeks before the Bolshevik revolution and was home on sick leave after a brilliant record of service as Consul General in Moscow. He was known to Lord Milner who believed that he had all the necessary qualifications – a knowledge of Russia and the ability to speak Russian fluently, a wide acquaintance among the leading personalities in Russia up to the fall of Kerensky and, in addition, youth and energy and an acute political sense. At Lloyd George's request Milner brought Lockhart to a meeting of the War Cabinet where he made an excellent impression. The upshot was the decision to send him to St Petersburg in the guise of the head of a commercial mission but in reality as an unofficial ambassador to get into touch with the Bolshevik Government.

It was Lord Milner who suggested that the mission should include someone with knowledge of labour questions in Great Britain. It was known that there were many Russian revolutionaries in the country and that they were in touch with elements in the trade union movement. Milner's argument was that the Bolshevik Government would be receiving information from them about opinion in Britain, the accuracy of which Lockhart would be unable to judge. I do not remember ever asking Lockhart how he was led to seek me out in the Ministry of Labour. Day-to-day events crowded on one another too fast to leave room for curiosity about the past. But I have no doubt that the suggestion must have come from Tom Jones.

The other two members of the mission whom I met at Lockhart's flat the evening following my meeting with him at the Ministry of Labour were Captain

---

[2] Alfred Milner, Lord Milner (1854–1925), served during the First World War as a member of the War Cabinet. Chairman of the Russian Information Committee, he agreed to allow intervention in the Russian internal conflict and was in contact with Bruce Lockhart on the latter's mission to Moscow. In 1918 Winston Churchill replaced him as Secretary of State for War and Milner became Head of the Colonial Office. (Ed.)

Hicks and Edward Birse.[3] The former was an army officer who had spent most of the war period in Russia; the latter an Englishman who had been in business in Moscow all his life and who, as Lockhart put it, had spoken Russian from his cradle. The mission was remarkable for its youth. Lockhart's age was not easy to guess; not because he really looked older than his years but because his poise and personality suggested mature experience and judgement. In fact he was only a few months over 30; I was 29; Hicks in his early thirties and Birse, I should judge, a few years older.

Having made certain that all our personal preparations had been completed, Lockhart informed us that we were to leave London by the mail train to Edinburgh the next evening; our sleeping berths had been reserved for us but we were to board the train as individual passengers to all appearances unknown to one another.

Most of the next day I spent at the Foreign Office where certain formalities concerning my temporary transfer to that Department were completed and where I was given my official appointment as a member of the mission together with the unexpected and gratifying news that my salary would be a thousand a year. I also learned that in view of the disturbed conditions in Russia, no figure could be fixed for a subsistence allowance and all proper expenses incurred on this head would be reimbursed. Lockhart had insisted on this highly exceptional measure and events were to show how wise he had been.

At the end of the morning he took me off to lunch to meet Maxim Litvinov.[4] Years after, I was to know Litvinov well when he was the Foreign Minister of Russia; at that time most people in England thought of him as a rather comic figure who had emerged from obscurity in the East End to put forward a ridiculous claim to possession of the Russian Embassy. Nevertheless, Lockhart had rightly judged that to gain Litvinov's goodwill would be a first important step towards the accomplishment of his mission. He accordingly obtained an introduction to him and was so successful in winning his confidence that Litvinov gave him a letter addressed to Trotsky. This letter was an interesting document which gave evidence of much diplomatic skill on both sides. Litvinov's position was one of great difficulty. He was an isolated outpost of the revolution, cut off from its leaders and without any instructions on the policy they wished him to pursue. His letter was carefully worded. He disclaimed any knowledge of the

---

[3] Edward Birse was the commercial expert on Lockhart's mission to Moscow in 1918. (Ed.)

[4] Maxim Maximovitch Litvinov (1876–1951) was a Russian revolutionary and Soviet diplomat. He was living in London when the Russian Revolution broke out and was appointed Soviet Government Representative in Britain. In 1918 he was arrested by the British Government, but soon exchanged for Bruce Lockhart. Soviet Minister of Foreign Affairs from 1930 to 1939, he attended the Assembly of the League of Nations from 1936 to 1938 and again in 1946. (Ed.)

exact purposes of Lockhart's mission but expressed the opinion that it might be useful to both countries; skilfully and indirectly it conveyed a practical suggestion that if Lockhart could be granted permission to send messages in code, he, Litvinov, would be able to claim the same facilities in London.

I must have had some preconceived idea of what I expected Litvinov to look like for my first impression was one of disappointment. He seemed not only ordinary but utterly uninteresting. His clothes were ill-fitting and even grimy; of medium height, his figure was thickset and his movements almost clumsy; he spoke with a strong guttural accent which made his English at first difficult to follow; everything about him seemed shabby and sluggish and undistinguished. But as the conversation between him and Lockhart progressed, my opinion of him changed. Although he spoke slowly it was not from any hesitation or doubt about what he wanted to say; and if he used no emphasis the very ease and lack of any animation in his manner somehow suggested that none was needed. Only an occasional slyly humorous remark and the gleam in the eyes behind his thick glasses revealed that a lively intelligence was hidden underneath his unimpressive exterior.

On arriving back at the Foreign Office, I found myself in the middle of a scene of great activity. Birse had been included in the party so that his business experience might enable us to put up a convincing show as a commercial mission, and he was engaged in verifying a number of large wooden cases which contained stationery, typewriters, a roneo (printing machine) and all the other paraphernalia needed to give a substantial camouflage to our supposed activities. In another room on the ground floor, a couple of carpenters were hammering together some more cases to take our emergency rations. By all accounts, famine conditions prevailed in St Petersburg and Hicks had been deputed to secure a stock of tinned goods which we could fall back on in case of necessity. He had spent a couple of hours making an extensive choice from the shelves of Fortnum and Mason and had ordered his purchases to be delivered to the Foreign Office without specifying how they should be packed. The result was that they had arrived at the Foreign Office in the form of innumerable brown paper parcels each neatly tied with string and provided with the little wooden handle which makes them convenient to carry. Excellent though this contrivance might be for transport to the suburbs it was hardly appropriate for a journey to Russia, and additional cases had to be constructed in great haste. This incident, which at the time gave us considerable amusement, was later to cause us anxiety and even some danger.

Another packing process was also going on which I watched with great interest. Since we were to travel through Norway and Sweden as private individuals, we would have to undergo customs examination and we could not therefore take with us personally our revolvers, our secret code or any confidential papers.

These therefore had to be confided to a King's Messenger to be transported in a sealed diplomatic bag. This added the final touch of romance to the preparations for our journey, but my sense of economy and my curiosity led me to ask why a member of the mission could not act as a temporary King's Messenger and be given the necessary laissez passer. The Foreign Office official to whom I addressed my question seemed astonished at my ignorance and explained that, as the privileges extended to a King's Messenger were conditional on his not remaining for more than a limited number of days at his destination, they could not be enjoyed by a member of the mission.

On the assumption that railway porters would not be a prominent feature of railway travel in Russia I had limited my personal luggage to two small suitcases which I could easily carry. Consequently, when I arrived at King's Cross station I was wearing my fur coat, a garment so voluminous that it would have required a large suitcase all to itself. Remembering Lockhart's advice to get one which would really keep me warm, I had acquired, second hand, a genuine Russian article. I felt self-conscious as I entered the station, for I was sure that my appearance was peculiar. The coat's superb astrakhan collar conveyed an air of opulence which was not in itself especially disturbing; the trouble was that, being cut in Russian fashion, the coat extended down almost to my ankles and must, I thought, give the impression that it belonged to a much taller man. I drew a breath of relief when a policeman passed me with no more than a glance and made no move to arrest me on suspicion of being in possession of stolen property. The sight of another policeman, however, threw me into a panic for it dawned on me that if I were asked to account for my possession of the coat I should be in a hopeless position since I could not tell the only story that was at once true and convincing. Unable to make any reference to the mission, I would be bound to give some other explanation which would not stand up under questioning; I would be detained and the mission would go off without me. It was a dreadful thought. Blessing the fact that the wartime lighting in the station was dim, I sought the deepest shadows and made my way to the train as speedily as I could without showing undue haste.

On arrival at Edinburgh, we went to the North British Hotel to await instructions from the navy. We had nothing to do save go out for a few minutes from time to time to stretch our legs or sit in the lounge reading all the newspapers we could get hold of for news of events in Russia. It was by no means reassuring. Newspapers were just beginning to adopt the system of splashing their most dramatic items across the top of a page in heavy type and, during the two days we spent in Edinburgh, Russia monopolized the headlines. I remember one which read "Famine in St Petersburg. City has Food for only Five Days", and others told of increasing anarchy in the army and navy and the massacre of officers.

Lockhart and Hicks grimaced a little but did not seem greatly disturbed; no doubt having seen disorder in Russia before, they discounted in some measure these lurid reports. I, lacking their experience, and having a lively imagination otherwise unoccupied, gloomily pictured in detail the dangers and horrors we must expect to encounter.

[Editor's note: The author continues with a description of the Lockhart mission's trip to Stockholm, and then through civil-war-torn Finland, which can be found in the full text of the memoirs. We rejoin the narrative at the mission's arrival in St Petersburg.]

Lockhart had telegraphed during the day in order to secure if possible that we should find somewhere to sleep for the night. We were met by a servant from the Embassy who told us what arrangements had been made. Lockhart went off to stay with Rex Hoare, the second secretary; Hicks was also taken in by a personal friend; Birse and I had rooms reserved for us at the Hotel de France, and there we were joined by Waterworth and his orderly after they had deposited the bags at the Embassy. [5]

I could see little of St Petersburg on the drive from the station to the hotel; there were only a few dim lights in the streets and none showed in the houses. The roads seemed to be in an appalling condition. My sleigh went forward over a series of bumps and hollows and at times skidded sideways so that I was in perpetual danger of being thrown out. The Hotel de France had a dilapidated air though it stood on the Fontanka almost next door to the Ministry of Foreign Affairs and had once been a place of some renown. Dinner consisted of borscht, the famous Russian soup of which I had often read, and black bread. The soup was hot and palatable enough but it must have been the poor relation of the soup really entitled to that name for I could not believe that it was very nourishing. The bread on the contrary really lived up to its name; it was as black as coal and resembled treacle which had been mixed with chopped straw. It was strictly rationed and I was supplied with two pieces not much larger than a couple of postage stamps. The waiter served us in silence and almost as if he was walking in his sleep – the menu was open to no discussion and there were no orders to be taken; the other diners were equally silent; the electric lights gave no more than a faint red glow and seemed on the point of dying out altogether; the whole atmosphere was one of intense depression and hopeless apathy.

Next day, I accompanied Hicks who had been deputed by Lockhart to search for permanent quarters in which the mission might be installed. He was

---

[5] A member of the Lockhart mission to Russia, Waterworth was part of the Corps of King's Messengers, who hand carry confidential and important documents to British embassies. (Ed.)

characteristically gay and cheerful and did much to raise my spirits. Nevertheless, even in his company, the city seemed as gloomy in the daylight as the dining room in the Hotel de France the night before. No attempt had been made to clear the snow from the streets. The houses rose out of it like the palaces out of the waters of the Grand Canal in Venice but the effect was very different. Venice had all the attraction of fairyland; St Petersburg looked like an abandoned city into which sand had been steadily drifting from the desert beneath which it must eventually disappear. The curious wave-like formations which the snow had assumed strengthened this impression. There were few people in the streets and they seemed to avoid one another, each going his own way oblivious of his surroundings, apparently plunged in melancholy reflection.

It is impossible to give a description of St Petersburg as it was at that time which will not appear incoherent and contradictory; the word "incoherent" perhaps sums up the picture better than any other and explains why the contradictions could arise.

The Bolsheviks had taken over the Government but what they took over was already little more than a name. They were powerful only because groups far more numerous could find neither will nor unity to oppose them. They could exercise hardly any of the powers that a normal government, even though weak, has at its command; and they were wise enough not to try. Their real strength was that they understood the weakness of their position and had the will to consolidate it by the ruthless use of such powers as they possessed. Their plans, worked out long beforehand by Trotsky and Lenin, men of real political genius, were to cut away the foundations on which life in Russia reposed. Even in St Petersburg, where their authority was strongest, that was a formidable and lengthy task. They had first to destroy before they could build. For a period there was a void; and it is this which explains why life in St Petersburg in the spring of 1918 displayed on the surface so many contradictions.

Two houses which Hicks and I visited that morning in our search for premises showed how startling these contradictions could be. The first looked as if it might be suitable for our purpose. But behind its imposing facade it was a ruin; all the panelling had been wrenched from the wall and the stairs were filthy; families from the slums had invaded it and reduced it to conditions as bad as, and perhaps worse than, those they had left. Less than a hundred yards away we tried another house; externally it looked much the same but inside it retained all its ancient splendour.

Since it was here that the mission was eventually lodged, I came to know it well and I can still call to mind all its main features. Although it was referred to as a flat, and the term was perhaps technically correct, I doubt if flats on such a scale have ever been constructed outside of St Petersburg. The number and the size of the rooms it contained gave some idea of the lavish style in which the aristocracy had lived under the Tsarist regime.

Birse and I shared as an office the owner's study; a desk, several tables and no less than nineteen huge leather-covered armchairs failed to give the impression that it was overcrowded. Lockhart, as became his status as head of the mission, was installed in the "small" drawing room in surroundings of Louis XV gilt furniture which might well have adorned the Quai d'Orsay. The arrangement of the main drawing room was no doubt intended to allow guests to seat themselves in groups for it contained six sets of drawing room furniture each complete in every particular; the room always amused me because it resembled a showroom in a furniture store rather than a private salon. Beyond it lay the ballroom, a beautifully proportioned hall with a series of tall windows rising from its polished floor to its painted ceiling from which hung three enormous chandeliers of glittering cut glass. After all this splendour, the dining room seemed almost commonplace and left one unprepared for the disclosure that the flat also possessed a private chapel of impressive dimensions.

The sleeping quarters were curiously different from the rest. The bedrooms, situated at the back of the building over the kitchen and the other domestic offices, were only half the height of the other rooms and so small that they resembled cabins on a ship.

This palatial residence, complete with housekeeper, cook and some minor domestic staff, we rented for a ridiculously small sum – we could in fact have got it, or something even more splendid, for nothing. The presence of a diplomatic mission was a guarantee to its owner that his home would not suffer the fate of the house that Hicks and I had earlier visited. He was so satisfied with his bargain that he threw in the keys of his cellar which proved to be exceedingly well stocked. It should be added that in addition to all these advantages our front windows looked out straight across the Neva at the Peter and Paul Fortress, which with the slim golden spire of its cathedral makes one of the finest views in the city.

With a roof over our head and excellent vintages at our disposal, our only remaining material problems were food and fuel. Food was by far the more serious, for the reports of famine conditions had not been exaggerated. It was asserted that deaths from starvation and hunger typhus ran into thousands per day. There was no means of checking the accuracy of such estimates but, whatever the real figure may have been, signs far more striking than the miserable food in the Hotel de France were not lacking to show that the food conditions were desperate. Sleighs were difficult to find for few horses survived. Walking home one night from the Embassy I saw one emaciated beast lying dead in the snow where he had fallen.

When I passed the spot the next morning all the flesh had been hacked from the carcass and only the bones remained; the next day they too had disappeared.

All stocks of food had long since been consumed. Railway transport was hopelessly disorganized and the supplies that irregularly reached the city were insignificant in proportion to its needs. Moreover, a great part of these supplies were distributed to the soldiers, whom the Bolsheviks had to keep in good humour for they numbered something like 200,000 and were armed. The soldiers in fact were enjoying life as they had never enjoyed it before. They were well clothed and, in comparison with the privations they had endured at the front, well fed; they had no officers, were subject to no discipline and had no duties to perform. So far as they were concerned, the revolution was over and they would have resisted violently any attempt to deprive them of its fruits.

Peasants from the neighbouring countryside brought small quantities of food into the city but, in the absence of any police protection, they were often robbed of their produce and supplies from this source were no more than a trickle.

In these conditions our own food problem, much to our astonishment, solved itself without any effort on our part. On the first night that we spent in our new quarters we were awakened by the housekeeper at about 2 a.m.; loud and persistent knocking at the door of the flat had roused her and she was terror-stricken. We huddled into our fur coats and seized our revolvers; a demand for entry at such an hour seemed to bode no good. Lockhart opened the judas (with which the door was fortunately provided) and after the exchange of a few sentences in Russian drew back the bolts. On the landing outside stood a smiling soldier who offered to sell us a small sack of white flour. The revolution had abolished the whole statute book, but the law under which goods tended to flow to the most advantageous market still continued to operate. Supplies of other foodstuffs continued to reach us in the same way during the rest of our stay. The vendors were always soldiers and they always came at night; whether because there would have been some risk involved in carrying rare articles of food through the streets in daylight, or whether the address of clients such as ourselves, who were always ready to purchase, was a trade secret which some small group wished to keep to itself, we never knew.

Lockhart's mission was to explore the possibility of securing some form of Anglo-Russian collaboration against the Germans. A little more than 20 years later, in the middle of another world war, what was fundamentally the same question was swiftly and successfully resolved in a few hours. In 1918 Lloyd George's position was very different from that of Winston Churchill. Churchill came into power accepted on all sides as the obvious national leader at a moment of grave crisis; he had behind him at all times the full support of a united House of

Commons; and in military matters, despite a certain amount of grumbling at his impatience and his insatiable desire for action, his relations with the professional heads of the fighting forces were marked by mutual confidence and respect.

Lloyd George, on the other hand, stood on a political quicksand; he was distrusted by most of his own party, and Conservative and Labour support came to him only indirectly through his personal influence on individual leaders and not directly from the rank and file; his relations with the great majority of the army leaders were strained almost to breaking point; and he was thus far less able than Churchill to follow up in detail the carrying out of policies which he initiated. Having set on foot the Lockhart mission he left it to do the best it could; which meant that he left its future in the hands of the Foreign Office, which could not be expected to regard without some professional jealousy the sudden promotion by the Prime Minister of a junior consular official to a post of high diplomatic responsibility. This element would not in itself have been of great importance were it not that there existed a divergence of opinion between the Foreign Office and the Prime Minister on a point of fundamental importance. The Foreign Office was in agreement with the Prime Minister that Anglo-Russian collaboration against the Germans was desirable and should be sought by all practicable means. But the most influential personalities in the Foreign Office, remaining convinced that Lenin and Trotsky were German agents, believed that to negotiate with them was merely to walk into a trap; collaboration, they thought, could only be safely and usefully established when Lenin and Trotsky had disappeared from the scene. This was the reason why Lockhart's telegrams to the Foreign Office remained for the most part unanswered.

Things were equally confused on the Russian side. Events developed with disconcerting rapidity and violent differences of opinion arose among the Bolshevik leaders over the policy to be pursued in their relations with the Germans. When we arrived in St Petersburg a delegation was negotiating with the Germans at Brest-Litovsk. At the end of a lengthy discussion the Germans made no concessions and the terms on which they insisted were so severe that Trotsky refused to authorize their acceptance. A majority of the Central Executive of the Soviets supported his view in spite of Lenin's advice to the contrary. Trotsky set about raising a Red Army in the hope that the threat of a resumption of the war would lead the Germans to modify their terms. The Germans paid no attention, but the reaction of Russian opinion proved the accuracy of Lenin's judgement. For every ten workers that Trotsky succeeded in enrolling in his new army, hundreds deserted from the old. Any suggestion that the war might be renewed aroused the violent hostility of both soldiers and peasants. The futility of Trotsky's policy became apparent; Lenin's view prevailed; and it was decided to send plenipotentiaries to sign the German terms. The fact that Lenin appeared to be willing to hand over immense areas of Russian territory to the Germans confirmed the Foreign Office view that he was their confederate and that it would be madness to enter into any agreement with him. While the Bolsheviks had been vacillating the German armies had continued their advance and their troops entered Pskov,[6] not much more than a hundred miles from St Petersburg. There they halted; probably they had no desire to saddle themselves with the responsibility for a city in which well over a million inhabitants were starving and in which it would have been a huge task to restore any semblance of order. But no one had any illusion that the treaty, which had now been signed, would prevent them from occupying St Petersburg if at any time it might suit them to do so.

While these events were taking place, Lockhart's position became increasingly difficult. Although he remained on friendly terms with Trotsky, who did not doubt his personal sincerity, the Soviet leaders were by no means convinced that his mission might not have been designed to throw dust in their eyes while the British Government pursued in reality a counter-revolutionary policy. They were shrewd enough to realize that Lockhart's inability to tell them of any answer to his telegrams was an indication that he was not receiving the backing in London that he had confidently expected.

Although Lockhart's negotiations were thus brought almost to a standstill, he was nevertheless fully occupied in trying to keep himself as fully informed as possible of a situation which was altering almost from hour to hour.

The news of the crisis with the Germans gave something like an electric shock to the city. No doubt it only affected a small proportion of the population but the change was noticeable in many different ways. We began to receive streams of visitors all eager to learn if we had any news and bringing in exchange their own contribution to the innumerable rumours that were flying about. I do not know whether rumours are a special feature of Russian life or whether an appetite for them grows in a revolutionary period. Most of them seemed to be utterly improbable but they were recounted seriously and, since anything might happen, they could not be dismissed out of hand. In attempting to check them we of course helped to speed them on their way but we had no alternative. One had so curious a sequel that it deserves to be recounted. One morning two different visitors brought us the exciting news that serious fighting had broken out at the St Paul station between the new Red Guards and the soldiers, and that it

---

[6] Pskov is located about 20 km east of the Estonian border. German troops occupied the region from February to November 1918. (Ed.)

was developing into a regular battle with heavy casualties on both sides. Half an hour later a third visitor arrived – incidentally, when he divested himself of his overcoat I was surprised to see that he was wearing the uniform of a commander in the Imperial navy, and I wondered at his recklessness when groups of the sailors who had massacred their officers at Kronstadt were frequently to be met in the streets. We asked him if he had heard anything about the fighting at the St Paul station. "The St Paul station?" he asked incredulously. "That's utter nonsense. I've just come from there and everything is perfectly normal." He was well known to Lockhart and his statement could be accepted without question.

A couple of nights later some soldiers discovered the existence of a hidden store of liquor in some cellars in a street off the Nevsky Prospect which they proceeded to loot. The news spread and a considerable crowd of other soldiers and civilians arrived to seek their share of the treasure. Hitherto the authorities had made no attempt to interfere with any looting by the soldiers, but on this occasion the Red Guards appeared and ordered the mob to disperse. The soldiers resisted, and a regular battle ensued in which the Red Guards got the upper hand with the aid of armoured cars which mercilessly mowed down their opponents. The casualties, which were reported to have exceeded a hundred killed, may have been exaggerated but there was no doubt whatever that an encounter of a serious character involving many casualties did in fact take place.

No doubt it was a coincidence but I found it extraordinarily curious that a rumour so closely resembling what actually happened should have preceded an unpredictable event.

The most frequent, and by far the most interesting of our visitors, was Raymond Robins.[7] Officially he was the head of the American Red Cross in Russia, but in fact he was the American counterpart of Lockhart and it was he, and not the American Ambassador, who was in effective contact with the Soviet Government. He was a well-known public figure in the United States, having been the candidate for the Vice-Presidency as running mate to Theodore Roosevelt in the "Bull Moose" campaign of 1912, and his reports therefore received particular attention in Washington and were probably responsible for the benevolent attitude which President Woodrow Wilson adopted towards the Soviet system.

Robins' conviction, which Lockhart shared, that for the Allies to take an unfriendly attitude towards the Soviets was "to play the German game in Russia", was not the only reason that made his visits welcome. He produced always the

---

[7] Colonel Raymond Robins (1873–1954) arrived in Russia in 1917 as Deputy Chief of the American Red Cross. In 1918 he became Head of the American Red Cross but was also the unofficial representative of the American Ambassador to Russia. (Ed.)

stimulating effect of an unusually vivid personality. Even Lenin, who was cold and almost inhuman in his relations even with the closest of his Bolshevik colleagues, fell under Robins' spell and was readily accessible to him at all times. In those critical days Robins' information was always accurate and our contacts with him were invaluable. Whether it was information or opinion to which he gave expression he had a gift of pungent phrase which was always a delight. I remember his once being asked how he could be so sure that the Soviets represented the Russia of the future when anti-Soviet armies had been mobilized in the south.

"I've been down there," was his reply. "I've had a look at those armies. I've talked with Alexeiev,[8] and I guess I know a corpse when I see one."

The presence of the German army at Pskov across the main railway running straight to St Petersburg created an impossible situation both for the Soviet Government and for the Allied embassies. The city was now undefended and there was nothing to prevent the Germans taking possession of it whenever they pleased.

In these circumstances the Soviet Government decided to move to Moscow. The Allied embassies, which had no desire to fall into German hands, preferred to go to Vologda so that, if they were endangered by a further German advance, they could get out of Russia via Siberia and Japan. The British Government, however, ordered what remained of the Embassy staff and the British military missions to return to England. Lockhart was not included in these instructions, presumably because the Foreign Office felt it was for the War Cabinet to decide whether or not he should remain in Russia.

Lord Milner's supposition that Lockhart would need a labour adviser had proved unfounded and my inclusion in the mission had turned out to be unnecessary. As I could neither speak nor read Russian I could give Lockhart little assistance and he suggested that I should return to London with the staff of the Embassy, where he thought, since I was fully acquainted with his reasons for urging Anglo-Soviet collaboration, I might perhaps be able to do something to secure that his arguments were better understood.

It was one thing for the Foreign Office to order the British representatives home; it was quite a different thing for them to find ways of obeying. And it was an ironical comment on the Foreign Office's attitude to Lockhart that had it not been for the relations he had established with the Soviet authorities the British representatives would never have been able to get away. Tension had become acute and the Russian Foreign Office was determined not to let any persons

---

[8] General Mikhail Vasiliyevich Alexeiev (1857–1918) was a Russian general and a leader of anti-Bolshevik forces (1917–18). In 1917 he was Chief of Staff of the anti-Bolshevik forces under Alexander Kerensky. (Ed.)

whom they suspected of counter-revolutionary activities to leave the country. It was only Lockhart's personal intervention, in which he had to exercise all his gifts of persuasion with Petrov,[9] the Acting Minister for Foreign Affairs (Chicherin having gone off to sign the treaty with the Germans),[10] which secured the necessary visas for the British party. Even then it was not certain that these visas would be honoured, for, when the special train, which Lockhart had also managed to extract from the Soviets, reached Beleostrov on the Finnish frontier, the frontier officials declared they had no instructions and refused to allow anyone to go on. Lindley, the British chargé d'affaires,[11] managed to telephone Lockhart, who got in touch with Petrov. The trouble it seemed was that a certain number of visas had been forged. Once again Lockhart's persuasive powers were successful and Petrov came out to the frontier on a special train to clear the matter up. Finally, all the British party was let through; but a group of other passengers whose papers were suspect had to return to St Petersburg.

The Soviets were still afraid that some of their enemies had slipped through the net. The next evening, when we were dining in the grill room of the principal hotel in Helsingfors, the hotel was surrounded by Red Guards and we were all lined up in the hall for a further examination. It was an unpleasant experience. The fugitives were evidently people to whom the Soviets attached great importance and the Finns had clearly been asked to take extraordinary precautions. We stood for half an hour in a long line, each of us covered by a Red Guard with his rifle while our papers were being examined and while other guards searched the hotel from the cellars to the roof. The guards seemed keyed up to a high state of tension; the one opposite me was a youth of 17 or so who trembled with excitement – it was perhaps the first important operation on which he had been engaged and I was in a state of panic lest his trembling should extend to his finger hooked round the trigger of his rifle. Finally, after what seemed an eternity, the search proved a failure and we were allowed to resume our meal. I remembered afterwards having seen two of the diners leave the grill room a minute or two before the Red Guards made their appearance. Somehow they must have received a warning

---

[9] Peter Petrov was a Russian revolutionary who sought asylum in Britain after the 1905 revolution. He was interned by the United Kingdom in 1916 for supporting the enemy cause. His release was personally secured by Trotsky. He was Soviet Acting Under-Secretary for Foreign Affairs at the time of the Brest-Litovsk Peace Treaty (early spring 1918). (Ed.)

[10] Georgy Vasiliyevich Chicherin (1872–1936) was People's Commissar of Foreign Affairs in the Soviet Government from 1918 to 1930. He was replaced by Litvinov in 1930. (Ed.)

[11] Sir Francis Oswald Lindley (1872–1950) served as Embassy Counsellor in Petrograd (St Petersburg) from 1915 to 1918 when, on the withdrawal of the Ambassador, he was then given charge of the Embassy until 1919, at which point he was transferred to Vienna. (Ed.)

that they were being sought. Next day, I found them on the train totally unconcerned at their narrow escape; they were members of the secret service who were in the possession of documents which the Soviets were anxious to secure.

The next incident in our journey was an unusual and, I imagine, a rare experience. The struggle between the Whites and the Reds in Finland had now developed into military operations on a grand scale; the Whites held the northern half of the country and the Reds the south; the main Red and White armies faced one another ready for a major battle and their lines ran at right angles straight across the railway over which we had to travel. When we reached the little town in which the Commander-in-Chief of the Red Army had his headquarters our train was run into a siding, and we were told that it could proceed no further. Rolling stock and engines were of immense importance to both sides, and the Reds, though willing to give us every possible assistance, were not prepared to let our train fall into the hands of the Whites. Three of our party volunteered to reach the White Army in order to negotiate conditions for our passage, including a promise that the sleighs, which the Reds were willing to place at our disposal, would be allowed to return. Colonel Thornhill, the Military Attaché, accompanied by Professor Potter who spoke Finnish, and by Lieutenant Gerhardie, [12] set out on horseback on this rather risky mission. They carried a large white flag to announce their peaceful intentions and an equally large Union Jack; the latter had to be hurriedly manufactured with the expenditure of much labour and ingenuity from such scraps of coloured material as it was possible to find, but it was indispensable not only to indicate their nationality but also as an additional measure of protection since the white flag was practically invisible against the snow-covered landscape.

It was 36 hours before they reappeared and relieved an anxiety about their fate which had begun to become acute. They had been delayed by the reluctance of the officer commanding the front-line troops of the White Army to let them proceed to General Mannerheim's headquarters, [13] situated some distance to the rear, until he had sent a messenger to the General and received his orders. The result of their mission was, however, in every way satisfactory and fixed a timetable for our arrival at the White lines the next day.

---

[12] William Alexander Gerhardie (1895–1977) was a British writer. He joined the Royal Scots Greys in 1914 and was posted to the staff of the British Embassy in Petrograd from 1916 to 1918. From 1918 to 1920 he was a member of the British Military Mission to Siberia. (Ed.)

[13] Baron and Count Carl Gustaf Emil Mannerheim (1867–1951) was Commander-in-Chief of Finland's defence forces (White Guards) in 1918, fighting the Red Guards during the civil war. He was elected Regent of Finland in 1918, but after the defeat of Germany Finland became a republic and he was replaced by the first President of Finland. He served as President of Finland in his own right from 1944 to 1946. (Ed.)

That evening the Red Commander-in-Chief, whose name was Wesley,[14] gave a small farewell dinner to Lindley, the chargé d'affaires of the Embassy, and half a dozen of our party of which I was one. Wesley, a tall handsome Finn, wore the usual strip of red ribbon round his arm but no insignia marked his rank as Commander-in-Chief. The meal was a simple one served in a small room in the modest town hall by a couple of women. Wesley played his part as host with an unassuming cordiality which made the meal very pleasant. He spoke English quite well and without making any attempt to dominate the conversation lost no opportunity of putting the case for the Reds, asserting that it was the Whites who had begun the civil war and expressing the hope that the British Government would not lend any support to the Whites who were actively assisted by the Germans.

Next morning our train moved cautiously up to the Red front and there in a deep trench cut in the snow we took our places in sleighs, each driven by an armed Red Guard. When all was ready the signal was given and in single file the sleighs moved out of this shelter and headed for the White lines.

The White lines were only a short distance away and we were into them before we realized that we had crossed no-man's land. There our sleighs turned into a trench between two lines of White Guards who covered our drivers with their rifles. The latter scowled at their enemies and muttered what I took to be hearty curses and jeering taunts in Finnish – perhaps they felt that our presence allowed them to do so with impunity, or perhaps they were just keeping up their courage in a situation which was certainly unpleasant. The Whites scowled back but remained silent; I imagine they were itching to teach those impudent Reds a lesson but fortunately for us discipline held them in check. The White officers were evidently worried; they distrusted the Reds and seemed to fear that they might take advantage of the distraction caused by our arrival to launch an attack and were anxious to hurry us off from the front line as soon as possible. The atmosphere was tense and I think everyone was relieved when the Red sleighs turned round and headed back towards their own lines without incident.

That night a small group of us dined with General Mannerheim at his head-quarters. It was a much more formal affair than the simple meal with his opponent the evening before. An orderly stood rigidly behind the chair of each guest and a strict etiquette prevailed. Perhaps the General was following the traditions of the Imperial Russian Army or perhaps he merely wished to impress us with the contrast in military bearing and discipline between his troops and those of the Red Army.

---

[14] August Wesslin Wesley (1887–1942?) was Commander-in-Chief of the Red Guards in Finland in 1918. After the Finnish civil war, he fled to Estonia and served in the Estonian armed forces. In the description that follows, Phelan wrongly assumes that Wesley was among the traitors executed after the fall of Helsingfors. (Ed.)

In any case the ceremonial seemed excessive in the circumstances and detracted from, rather than enhanced, the strong personality he undoubtedly possessed. Nevertheless, it was an interesting, and I imagine a rare, experience to dine on successive evenings with Commanders-in-Chief of two hostile armies which were about to do battle. Both were impressive in very different ways. Whether Mannerheim's professional training and the discipline of his troops would have given him the victory, it is impossible to say. The Reds proved tough opponents and might well have got the upper hand had not a German army under General Goltz landed in their rear some weeks later and thus allowed Mannerheim to win the decisive battle of Tammerfors. He was then able to take Helsingfors, but his victory was tarnished by the revenge which the Whites took on their prisoners. Some hundreds were shot after a perfunctory trial as traitors and among them was Wesley, the Red Commander-in-Chief, who had been our host.

The remainder of our journey was uneventful. It was a thrill to be back in Sweden and to find a world untouched by anarchy.

We had to wait four days in Stockholm and while strolling through the town to get some exercise I thought I might as well discover whether I could get something for my rouble notes. I tried the first bank I came across only to learn that, as I expected, rouble notes did not interest them in the least. Merely in order to have an objective in my aimless strolling, I went into each bank I saw. From four of them, I received the same reply. At the fifth bank, however, the cashier displayed some interest. "Are they Kerensky notes or Tsarist notes?" he asked. "Tsarist notes," I replied; Kerensky notes I knew had no value in St Petersburg, where they were contemptuously referred to as "Whisky labels". "Are they in good condition?" he enquired, and on inspecting them added, "I think I can make you a quotation." He disappeared and when he came back he quoted a rate which seemed so incredible that I had to ask him to repeat it. The sum was so considerable that I felt it would be foolish to carry it with me on the trip across the North Sea where we should have to run the risk of being torpedoed; I asked him if he could transfer it to my account in London in pounds and this he said would present no difficulty. I walked out of the bank richer by £247. The explanation was that Stockholm was full of refugees from Russia who were anxious to get out relations; presumably this meant extensive bribery and for this purpose they had need of Russian currency. There was therefore a market for Tsarist notes, the only notes to which the Russians attached any value, and my aimless persistence had by chance led me to the bank which was dealing in them.

My reception at the Foreign Office, to which I at once reported on my return, was disconcertingly casual. On reflection, I realized that officials could hardly be expected to have any very definite recollection of someone they had met for no more than a few minutes three months before; and, since Lindley and the staff of the Embassy had also arrived and were available to give an account of conditions in Russia, they had no reason to suppose that a Labour Adviser could add anything of value to their reports. It was clear that I could consider my connection with the Foreign Office at an end and that after a few administrative formalities I would resume my duties at the Ministry of Labour. Lockhart's hope that I might be able to secure for his dispatches a greater measure of attention had obviously no chance of being fulfilled.

I walked across to Montagu House feeling somewhat damped by this very dull ending to an exciting episode. But if the Foreign Office was indifferent to my return the Ministry was not, and my reappearance aroused both interest and curiosity. Harold Butler carried me off to lunch, and Hope Simpson invited me to spend the night at his home so that he might devote a whole evening to hearing the story of my adventures.

He lived out in the country some 40 miles from London and he insisted that all talk about Russia should be postponed until we had dined. After our meal, we adjourned to the lounge and drew up our chairs before the fire. The house stood in an isolated spot some distance from the railway; the night was calm and not even a whisper from the trees outside penetrated into the room. It was a silence with a delightful quality of security and repose, very different from the silence of those nights in Finland and in Russia that had always seemed heavy with menace. I was conscious of the contrast as I embarked on my story; and perhaps it made my memory sharper and my narrative more vivid. In any case, Hope Simpson became wholly absorbed in my tale and we were both startled when the quiet of the room was abruptly shattered by the telephone. The clock on the mantelpiece showed that it wanted but a few minutes to midnight and, exclaiming impatiently that the local exchange must have put the caller on to the wrong number, Hope Simpson went into the hall to reply. I could hear his side of the conversation: "Yes … Yes, he's here with me now … Yes, I'll give him the message … No, that won't be necessary, I'll see that he gets there in time."

I listened, at first idly and then with growing bewilderment. As far as I was aware, nobody knew that I was at Hope Simpson's home. He might, perhaps, have told someone in the Ministry; but, if so, what possible reason could there be for telephoning, since we would both be coming in to Montagu House in the morning? And, stranger still, why on earth telephone at midnight when Hope Simpson might well be in bed and asleep?

I found it impossible to imagine what the explanation could be, and I waited with acute curiosity for Hope Simpson's return. His answer to my mute enquiry was as astonishing as it was unexpected: "The Prime Minister wants you at the

War Cabinet tomorrow morning. You are to be at Hankey's office at 11 sharp. [15] They've been telephoning for hours all over London trying to find you. Pretty good work to have tracked you down here," he commented, and this tribute to the efficiency and persistence of Hankey's staff, I thought, was well deserved.

Next morning, after I had waited for nearly an hour, Hankey appeared and told me that the War Cabinet would be unable to see me; grave news of the success of the great German offensive had been received from France and all other business had to be put aside. The Prime Minister had, however, asked Mr Balfour to see me, [16] and I was to go over to the Foreign Office at once. It was characteristic of Lloyd George that this information was conveyed as a personal message and accompanied by expressions of regret and of his hope of being able to have a talk with me at some future time.

When I was shown into the historic room of the Secretary of State for Foreign Affairs, Balfour got up from his desk and invited me to sit opposite him in front of the fire. There were two armchairs and, between them, a small chair with a straight back. I offered to take this modest and uncomfortable seat but Sir Louis Mallet, [17] who was evidently to assist at the conversation, firmly refused to allow me to do so and took it himself.

Balfour slid down in his chair with his legs stretched out in front of him in the attitude I had often seen him assume in the House of Commons – he looked exactly like Spy's famous cartoon. All morning I had been trying to guess what questions might be put to me and wondering how I could convey any coherent and convincing view of the situation in Russia in a series of answers that would have to be brief and that would probably have to deal with unrelated subjects. Much to my relief, Balfour opened the conversation by saying: "I want you to give me your impressions of Russia and the conclusions you draw from them. Don't feel that you have to hurry. Take as much time as you need and give me all the details you think significant."

I could not believe that this invitation was to be taken literally. Ambassadors, I remembered once having been told, were expected not to exceed 20 minutes, and I assumed that the most I could count on would be a quarter of an

---

[15] Maurice Pascal Alers Hankey (1877–1963) was a British civil servant. He served on the Committee of Imperial Defence (1908–1912) and created the Cabinet Secretariat, of which he was the first Secretary. (Ed.)

[16] Arthur James Balfour, later Lord Balfour (1848–1930), was British Prime Minister from 1902 to 1905. In 1916 he was appointed Foreign Secretary in Lloyd George's new administration, and in 1917 he penned the Balfour Declaration, promising the Jews a "National Home" in Palestine. He resigned from his post as Foreign Secretary after the Paris Peace Conference. (Ed.)

[17] Sir Louis du Pan Mallet (1864–1936) was a British diplomat and from 1907 to 1913 Assistant Under-Secretary of State for Foreign Affairs. (Ed.)

hour. I decided, therefore, to get in my main points in simple form and to turn back and elaborate them if time permitted. The result of these tactics was that my argument became something like a spiral and, at times, dangerously like a circle.

I began by saying that differences of opinion about the policy to be followed towards Russia derived fundamentally from the different views taken of the probable duration of the Bolshevik Government. Most people gave it only a few weeks, or at most a few months. My own opinion was that it would last for at least three years and, possibly, for much longer. This emphatic declaration seemed to take Balfour by surprise – at least he looked less languid, and it had the effect of securing his attention.

The trouble with Russia, I continued, is not that there is dispute about the facts but that, starting from the same facts, people reach exactly opposite conclusions. No one denies that the great factories along the banks of the Neva are at a standstill, that no smoke rises from their chimneys, and that scores of thousands of workers are without employment and that they and their families are starving to death. The conclusion drawn is that such a catastrophic situation cannot possibly continue; that it must inevitably and rapidly provoke an uprising that will drive the Bolsheviks from power. No doubt that conclusion would be justified for other countries if similar conditions arose. But the argument ignores what impressed me as being the fundamental fact in the Russian situation. In Russia there is an apathy such that normal reactions cannot be counted on; there is a spiritual paralysis far more significant than the economic paralysis on which these forecasts are founded. Eyewitnesses described to me the Bolshevik attack on the Winter Palace; how small, badly armed and incompetent were the Bolshevik forces; how they had only one piece of light artillery which they fired at the Palace across the square without ever once scoring a hit; how there were thousands of army officers on leave in St Petersburg at the time, and how not one lifted a finger; how Kerensky's only defenders were some members of a women's regiment and some boy cadets who, nevertheless, succeeded in holding off the attackers for the greater part of the day.

Possibly, these stories contained an element of exaggeration but the still more astonishing incident at Pskov, for which I had incontrovertible evidence, and my own experience of the attitude of the Russian soldiers at Helsingfors suggested that they were substantially true. All this was evidence of a spiritual bankruptcy in the mass of the Russian people for which it would be difficult to find a parallel.

It was a fact that there were areas in which there were efforts to organize active resistance to the Bolshevik Government; but these efforts lacked unity and were bedevilled by inefficiency and personal jealousy. All the advantages lay with the Bolsheviks not only because they controlled the central machinery of government, but because they alone knew what they wanted and possessed determined leaders. In the conditions prevailing in Russia, where all else presented a spectacle of decay and disunity, it was not surprising that the one group that had a definite purpose and resolute leadership should exercise an attraction. The extreme character of their programme, and the ruthlessness with which they pursued it, was a source of strength rather than of weakness. It was a mistake to argue about their chances of survival in terms of popularity or unpopularity as if they were a political party operating in a traditional political framework. No such framework had ever existed in Russia; its history was a history of despotism. It was said that when the priests had told their peasant congregations of the advent of the People's Republic, they had been asked: "What is the name of the new Tsar?" Bolshevism made a mystical appeal; it was more like a religious than a political phenomenon; its prospects of survival and success could not be measured in terms of normal political experience.

It was asserted that Lenin and Trotsky were German agents. Those who made this assertion pointed to the economic and military collapse of Russia and to the surrender of one-third of Russia's territory into German hands. But both these events were the inevitable consequence of the incapacity and corruption of the old regime. The Bolsheviks did not precipitate the collapse; they had been able to seize power only because the other groups were incapable of putting up any real opposition. As for surrendering vast areas to Germany, the Bolsheviks had no choice. This charge against them assumes that the other groups, if the Bolsheviks had not prevented them, would have kept Russia intact. Even if one supposes that they could have composed their differences and formed a common front against the Germans, they could not have overcome the fanatical pacifism of the army or the war-weariness of the mass of the people, and if they had made a military effort against the Germans the only possible result would have been that the latter would have become the masters of the whole of Russia. Lenin had realized this danger and he had wisely preferred to surrender territory which he could not hold and which was of no importance in comparison with what he had succeeded in retaining.

It was true that the Germans had facilitated the return of Lenin and Trotsky to Russia, and they had done so because they believed it would be to their advantage. They feared that Kerensky under Allied pressure would succeed in restoring Russia's will to fight. It was clear now, in the light of subsequent events, that the efforts of Kerensky and the Allies had had no chance of succeeding and that Russia, as a military power, was doomed before Lenin and Trotsky came on the scene. The Germans had miscalculated; all they had succeeded in doing was to put into power in Russia the only group in that demoralized country that had a strong will and a definite purpose.

It was argued that, whether Lenin and Trotsky were German agents or not, they were playing the German game by destroying the whole framework of Russia at the cost of immeasurable human suffering. But this argument was based on the assumption that if the Bolsheviks did not behave like a national political party they must necessarily be betraying Russia in some foreign interest. If, however, one assumed that their object was world revolution, and there was plenty of evidence to support this assumption, it was not difficult to understand their behaviour. Lenin was reported to have said: "We do not care if every man, woman and child in Russia perishes if the world revolution succeeds." Their doctrine was that destruction must come first, that only when capitalism had been extirpated could a communist regime be effectively created. Capitalism was the arch-enemy and they would shrink from no measures, however appalling, to destroy it. Here one encountered the mystical element to which I had previously referred.

No one could predict the future with certainty. One could only say that, if one looked at the whole picture coldly, one was driven to the conclusion that the Bolshevik Government was firmly established in Russia, and that there appeared to be no serious threat that any effective challenge to its existence would develop in the near future.

If that conclusion was correct, it followed that for the Allies to take a hostile attitude to the Bolshevik Government would be to play into the hands of the Germans. The Bolsheviks represented the only obstacle to the complete domination of all Russia and its resources by the Germans. As a war-time policy, it was the interest of the Allies to encourage the Bolsheviks to be anti-German. It would be foolish to suppose that any help given to the Bolsheviks would alter their fundamental objective; they would still consider revolution in the Allied countries as part of their programme. But Germany figured in that programme also, and Germany was a more immediate menace to them than England or France. The fact that they had destroyed capitalism in Russia did not mean that they wanted a weak Russia. They wanted a strong Russia in which they could build up their communist State and they had urgent need of agricultural machinery and foodstuffs. These the Allies could furnish. If the forecast that the Bolsheviks would remain in power proved to be false, a gift of this nature would help to alleviate the sufferings of the Russian people and would be remembered with gratitude. The alternative was to leave the field open to the Germans to whom Russia, Bolshevik or non-Bolshevik, would sooner or later be forced to turn.

I had been watching Balfour all the time, ready to break off as soon as I detected any sign of impatience. He had given no such sign and I had, therefore, gone on until I felt that I had given him a fairly complete picture. I now looked at the clock and, discovering that I had been talking for nearly an hour, I brought my remarks to a close with a few hasty words of apology.

"You don't need to apologize," he said. "Your account has been most interesting. Is there anything you would like to add?"

"I don't think so," I replied after a moment's hesitation. No doubt I might have presented my argument in a more balanced and effective fashion if I had known in advance that I was to be accorded so much time, but I had covered most of the ground, and I thought it better to leave things as they were. I assumed that the interview was over, but Balfour settled himself deeper into his chair and continued, "Well, if there is nothing you wish to add, would you mind if I asked you a few questions?"

His questions, which showed that, for all his languid air, he had followed closely everything I had said, asked me to develop more fully several points. Encouraged by his readiness to pursue the matter further, I replied at some length. After I had answered his last question, he remained silent. I looked at the clock; it showed half past one.

Balfour made no move to get up. "I have one further question," he said slowly. "Is there any question I have not asked that you would wish me to put?"

I was startled. There was one matter to which I had hesitated to make any reference. It was uncanny that he should seem to sense that I had left something out.

In spite of the opening he had given me, I still felt considerable hesitation. The subject was delicate, and by bringing it up I might well destroy the favourable impression I thought I had made. On the other hand, it was of real importance, and so I decided to put it frankly.

"As a matter of fact there is," I replied. "I don't know how to frame the question, but the answer to it is that the Bolsheviks believe that the British Government is playing a double game and that Lockhart's mission is merely a blind."

His reaction was immediate. He almost leapt out of his chair and, standing with his back to the mantelpiece, said angrily, "Do you realize that that is an accusation against my personal good faith?"

I rose to my feet and, appalled at the intensity of the feeling I had aroused, I tried to mollify him: "No," I said. "It is nothing of the kind. All I have said is that the Bolsheviks express that belief and assert they have reasons for holding it."

"I can assure you", he replied more calmly, "that there is no truth in such an accusation. On what grounds do the Bolsheviks pretend to hold that view?"

"They assert that the British Government is lending active support to counter-revolutionary movements in Russia, and they find it difficult to reconcile that with Lockhart's mission."

"But that comes to the same thing," he said, flushing. "They are accusing me of dishonourable conduct."

"No," I replied. "Not you or the Foreign Office, but the British Government."

"It's the same thing," he repeated, unmollified. "I am responsible for the conduct of the foreign policy of the British Government, and I assure you I would never countenance anything of the sort."

"I don't doubt that for a moment," I replied. "But may I say something else?"

"Certainly," he said.

"Nobody, I think, not even the Bolsheviks, would doubt your personal good faith. But other departments have agents in Russia. Is it not possible that some of them may have been engaged in activities that give the Bolsheviks ground for their belief? The Bolsheviks would have no hesitation in making a false statement if it would serve their ends. But it is difficult to imagine what they could gain by making a false statement on this point. If, as I believe to be the case, they would be willing to accept British help against the Germans, the last thing they would want to do would be to make accusations of this kind unless they believed them to be founded. Whatever else they may be, they are not stupid. They are intelligent and efficient, and they must have a good deal of information on what is going on in the counter-revolutionary areas."

I did not expect Balfour to reply, since he could hardly discuss with me matters in which other departments might be involved. I made an effort to get back to the earlier atmosphere of our conversation.

"The only reason I brought up this disagreeable matter is that it is an element in the situation, and you should have all the elements before you. If there is any real foundation for this Bolshevik belief, and if the British Government is in fact pursuing two policies in Russia, it must make its choice and pursue one or the other. If, on the other hand, the Bolshevik belief is a mistake or its suspicions unfounded, then the matter ought to be cleared up. That is the point I really wanted to make because, if it were decided to adopt anything in the nature of the humanitarian policy I have suggested, it would be difficult to pursue it successfully in an atmosphere of suspicion."

"I appreciate that," said Balfour in his old pleasant manner, from which all trace of irritation had disappeared. "I think you were right to bring it up. Now you will want to get some lunch. Lord Robert Cecil will see you this afternoon at half past three. [18] Tell him everything you have told me. I want to thank you

---

[18] (Edgar Algernon) Robert Gascoyne-Cecil, first Viscount Cecil of Chelwood (1864–1958), best known as Lord Robert Cecil, was a British politician and peace campaigner. He entered the Government in May 1915 and was appointed Parliamentary Under-Secretary of State for Foreign Affairs. From 1916 to 1918

once more for your exposition and for your full and most informative answers to my questions. I shall be grateful if you will talk to some of the other people here and give them your views; my secretary will make appointments for you and let you know."

And then came the most astonishing remark of all: "I have one more request to make to you before you go. Will you think over all you have told me and, if anything occurs to you that you feel you should have included, will you come back and see me again?"

As I hurried off to lunch – it was a few minutes after two – my mind was more occupied with Balfour than with Russia. His thoroughness in obtaining from me all the information I could give made a profound impression. I was to work with many other ministers in the years to come but I never met any who combined so extraordinary a degree of intelligence, patience, courtesy and the determination to master completely every aspect of the question he had to consider.

My interview with Lord Robert Cecil that afternoon lasted over an hour, but the atmosphere was quite different. Balfour's attitude had been detached and impartial; Cecil's approach was that of a barrister cross-examining a witness from whom he was bent on extracting some damaging admission. He was courteous but it was a formal courtesy that was rather intimidating. His hunched shoulders, his cold watchful air, and something vaguely ecclesiastical in his appearance suggested a Spanish inquisitor. I knew he was strongly opposed to the idea that any form of collaboration with the Bolshevik Government was either possible or desirable, and I felt I would need to keep all my wits about me in a contest with a formidable opponent.

He had, I imagine, expected me to be some kind of left-wing socialist sympathetic to the Bolshevik system, and he seemed rather taken aback when I took the line I had taken with Balfour, and said that I did not contest the description given by others of conditions in Russia but only the conclusions drawn from them. Nevertheless, all the advantages were on his side and he made full use of them. He attacked at the first opportunity, breaking in with questions and making it impossible for me to maintain any continuous thread in my argument. I soon came to the conclusion that this was of no importance; that his mind was closed; and that, no matter how clearly and convincingly my case might be presented, it would not modify his views. His questions showed that he was in search not of information but of ammunition, and I deduced that the policy

---

he held the post of Minister of Blockade. In June 1918 he became Assistant Secretary of State for Foreign Affairs and was therefore deputy to his cousin Arthur Balfour. From 1920 to 1946 he devoted his efforts to the League of Nations, and in 1937 received the Nobel Peace Prize. (Ed.)

towards Russia was being re-examined. He presumably feared that undue weight might be attached to my testimony, on the ground that I had actual experience of conditions in Russia, and he wanted to be able to urge that, on my own admission, my information was incomplete and my conclusions open to question. I, therefore, abandoned any attempt to present my argument in full, and concentrated on resisting his efforts to undermine it.

It was a long battle. Towards the end, having failed to make any breach in my position by a frontal attack, he endeavoured to outflank me by moving to wider ground.

"Do you know that the Bolsheviks are exporting food from Odessa?" he asked.

"No," I replied.

"Well, it is a fact. How then is it possible to believe that their statement that they are in need of food is honest?"

"I have no knowledge of what is happening in the south of Russia," I replied. "I do know that thousands of people are dying of hunger in St Petersburg."

"Yes," he said, pressing his point, "but how do you reconcile the actions of a government which is exporting food and at the same time allowing thousands of its people to die of hunger?"

"I don't reconcile them," I said. "I can't argue about facts that are unknown to me. I can only say that, if one had all the facts, it is possible that the conclusion you draw would not be sustained."

"What facts?" he enquired sharply. "I can assure you that the information about Odessa has been verified beyond question."

"I'm not referring to that," I answered. "I mean all the facts of the situation as a whole. The railway system is utterly disorganized and transport is almost impossible. Moreover, trains carrying food from the south would have to pass through areas where there are considerable White forces. These forces are reported to be short of supplies. Even if that is not the case, they certainly believe that famine in St Petersburg will bring the Bolsheviks down. I just don't know what the possibilities of the situation are. But the existence of famine in the north and an abundance of food in the south does not necessarily prove that the Bolshevik attitude is dishonest."

This ended the interview. I had gained nothing, but I had given nothing away. Against so formidable an opponent as Cecil, a draw was the best I could hope to secure.

During the following days I spent most of my time talking with one or other of the principal Foreign Office officials. The interest shown in these talks naturally varied, but it became more and more evident that a general examination of the Russian problem was being undertaken. Sir William Tyrrell not only saw me several times but invited me to assist at a number of conversations with people who had been associated with earlier missions to Russia, particularly during the Kerensky regime.[19] None of these, I thought, threw any great light on the actual situation, save in so far as they served to confirm how complete had been the Russian collapse before the advent of the Bolsheviks to power, nor did any of those who described this earlier phase of the Revolution seem to realize that the establishment of the Bolshevik regime raised wholly new problems.

After my talks with Balfour and Cecil, I took the first opportunity of having a chat with Tom Jones. He knew, of course, of what had been going on, and he told me that Balfour had made a very full report of his conversation with me to the Prime Minister, and that the latter had been keenly interested. "You seem to have made a great impression on Balfour," he added. Although I knew that Tom Jones was a model of circumspection and that his utterances were carefully guarded, I attached no special significance to this remark, which I took to be no more than a friendly compliment. I was, therefore, totally unprepared for what happened some few days later. At a banquet given by the Lord Mayor of London, in the course of a survey of foreign affairs, Balfour dealt at considerable length with Russia and concluded with a statement that preparations were being made to send several cargoes of food and agricultural machinery to St Petersburg in a humanitarian effort to alleviate the appalling conditions of famine that prevailed in that city.

This announcement created a sensation. The newspapers made it a major item; editorial comment was extensive, and, though often qualified by a note of caution, was on the whole by no means unfavourable. I was elated, but my elation was mixed with awe. All I had set out to do was to persuade the Foreign Office that the idea merited serious consideration. I knew I had aroused quite a measure of interest, but I was far from anticipating that interest might so rapidly develop into acceptance, and still less prepared to hear that immediate action was contemplated. But, startled as I was at the result, I was not so dazed as not to realize that I had been only one link in a long chain. To Milner and Lockhart belonged the credit of suggesting that this line of policy should be explored, and it was Lloyd George who, by a bold decision, had made its exploration possible. By chance I had become its successful advocate, the more effective, perhaps, because my personal acquaintance with Russia was limited to the period in which new issues

---

[19] Sir William George Tyrrell (1866–1947) served in the Foreign Office from 1889 to 1928. Between 1916 and 1919 he was Head of the Political Intelligence Department. (Ed.)

became more sharply defined and because my view of the new Russia that was emerging was not blurred by memories of the old.

My satisfaction, however, proved to be premature. It was reasonable to suppose that a policy backed by the Prime Minister and by a Foreign Secretary who was an ex-Prime Minister belonging to the other great political party represented a firm decision. This supposition had, however, no solid basis. Lloyd George was the leader of a coalition and controlled no majority of his own; Balfour, eminent though he was, was no longer the leader of the Tory Party. Lloyd George was in no position to make his will prevail. Although he appeared to dominate the scene, he was wholly dependent on the support of Bonar Law; [20] he knew that he could count on that support on all measures directed to the energetic prosecution of the war but that he must proceed with caution on any matter which would create a division in the Tory Party, the unity of which Bonar Law was determined to maintain. In these circumstances he felt compelled to play for time. Further consultations were undertaken by the Foreign Office with a number of outside experts on Russian affairs. The majority of those consulted had welcomed with enthusiasm the advent of a democratic system of government and it was hoped that their support for a new policy towards Russia would help to swing opinion in its favour. The fact that they had known personally and, in some cases, had been close friends of earlier leaders of the Revolution who had since been imprisoned or assassinated, made it emotionally impossible for them to believe that these crimes could go unpunished and that the Russian people would not rise against the Bolsheviks who were responsible for these atrocities.

Thus, the theory that moral indignation and economic catastrophe must inevitably unite "all the stable forces in Russia" in a victorious combination against the Bolsheviks received unexpected support, and nothing more was heard of the preparations to implement the Balfour policy.

It is, of course, idle to speculate what might have happened if the Balfour policy had been put into effect at the time it was announced. All that can be said is that the two main predictions on which it was founded proved to be correct. The Bolshevik Government proved not to be an ephemeral phase; it, and not its opponents, survived. The prediction that, if the Bolsheviks were antagonized by the Allies, they would turn to the Germans was fulfilled at the Genoa Conference in 1922. Lloyd George's plan for that Conference was, in fact, an attempt to return to the Balfour policy. It was then too late. The Treaty of Rapallo between

---

[20] Andrew Bonar Law (1858–1923) served in Lloyd George's War Cabinet as Chancellor of the Exchequer from 1916 to 1919. From 1922 to 1923 he was Prime Minister and Leader of the House of Commons. (Ed.)

Russia and Germany wrecked the Conference and dealt a moral blow to Lloyd George's prestige both at home and abroad.

Although the Balfour policy was never implemented, it was never formally decided that it had been abandoned. Even after British troops arrived in Murmansk and Archangel, the die was not finally cast in favour of outright military intervention. The belief that the presence of this symbolic force would precipitate union among and vigorous action by the counter-revolutionary armies proved an illusion; and, as relations between the Bolsheviks and the Germans became more and more strained, there was much to be said for reviving the Balfour policy.

The birth of the International Labour Organization   **6**

Icontinued for a time to occupy a room in the Foreign Office and to be consulted on various questions relating to Russia. Since I had a good deal of idle time, I devoted it to writing a memorandum on "Democracy and diplomacy" in which I summarized some general conclusions suggested by my limited but rather special experience in the Ministry of Labour and the Foreign Office. I drew attention to the increasing influence of two new factors on the determination of foreign policy: the growth of the trade union movement and the change in the functions of the press. I cited Lloyd George's lengthy discussion with the trade union leaders when he became Prime Minister as an example of the importance which now had to be attached to the opinion of organized labour; and I suggested that, although it had become evident that the press had largely ceased to be the obedient exponent of the views of one or other political party, the independent influence it could exercise had not been fully appreciated. I argued that it was no longer possible to follow intelligently, and still less to interpret with any degree of assurance, the foreign policy of countries in which these new factors were assuming increasing importance. The Revolution in Russia was only an extreme example of the political and social ferment produced by the war; in one form or another widespread social and political changes must be expected in the post-war period and new personalities would emerge from this background to dominate the political scene. The existing diplomatic machinery, evolved in very different conditions, would be ill-equipped for its task in a world so radically changed. I concluded by saying that, if these general considerations should prove to be of any interest, I was prepared to develop them in greater detail and to suggest ways of meeting the situation that might be considered. I had this memorandum registered and sent it to Sir William Tyrrell. I was beginning to think that I had seen the last of it when the file was returned. Tyrrell had sent it on to Balfour who had written a minute with his own hand saying that he had found the document very interesting and that I should be asked to put forward my suggestions. I accordingly wrote a second memorandum proposing that, in suitable cases, labour attachés should be appointed to embassies and legations, indicating the work they should perform, and suggesting that their activities should be coordinated with those of the Intelligence Department of the Ministry of Labour. Many years were to pass before such attachés came into being, and I imagine that at that time this memorandum of mine had been entirely forgotten.[1] I mention it here because it was the first time that I put forward officially a suggestion for governmental activity in the foreign field in relation to labour problems, though only for the purpose of gathering information. Such information would be of value to the Foreign Office, but only as one item among all the factors that department had to consider; but if it was made available to the Ministry of Labour, in the same way as the reports of commercial attachés were made available to the Board of Trade, it would create a link between the Foreign Office and the Ministry and help to secure for the latter a place of greater importance in the ministerial hierarchy.

I knew, of course, the history of the pre-war attempts at international labour legislation, but it did not figure in my preoccupations about the Ministry of Labour because it lay in the competence of the Home Office under which remained the responsibility for factory inspection, and it was not a matter in which the Foreign Office could be expected to take any interest. I was convinced that it ought to be developed on a more extensive scale after the war; I drew the attention of Alfred Zimmern, Arthur Greenwood and others to its importance in private discussions about post-war measures;[2] and I urged that the effort should in future be pursued continuously through some kind of permanent international machinery and not intermittently as in the past. Knowing that any idea they sponsored was likely to get a hearing in influential quarters, I hoped that in this roundabout way action by the Home Office might be stimulated and something useful accomplished.

The news of the Bulgarian request for an armistice, announced in the press on 28 September 1918, was responsible for setting in train a reconsideration of these ideas from an entirely new standpoint. The implications of this event

---

[1] In the course of a search in the archives of the Foreign Office in connection with the Shotwell volumes I was astonished to discover that the file containing my memorandum and Balfour's minute had been preserved. (E.J.P.)

[2] On Zimmern and Greenwood, see Ch. 2 above, nn. 9 and 8 respectively.

took shape in my mind during my journey from Hampton Court, where I was temporarily staying, to the Ministry of Labour to which I had reverted a few weeks before. At the meeting with Hope Simpson and MacMullan at which we reviewed each morning the news of the day to see if there was any item to which the Intelligence Division should devote particular attention, either for inclusion in the weekly report to the Minister or for other action, I set out the sequence of events which might now be expected: after the Bulgarian surrender the Germans would, sooner or later, be compelled to ask for an armistice; this would be followed by a peace conference; the Cabinet would soon begin to define its peace proposals; and at some stage the Minister of Labour would be asked if he had anything to say. My conclusion was that the Division should at once consider what advice it should give to the Minister.

We were familiar with the resolutions dealing with war aims adopted by the numerous labour and socialist conferences that had met during the war, since all their proposals had been examined in the ordinary course of the Division's work. For our present purpose we could leave aside those dealing with territorial and other questions of a political character, on which the Minister would have no claim to speak with a special authority, and concentrate on those which referred to conditions of work. Here, there was unanimity in demanding that the peace treaty should provide guarantees or lay down standards, applicable to the workers of all countries, as regards the right of association, the limitation of hours of labour, the protection of immigrant workers, industrial hygiene, safety, etc. and in some instances the measures desired were indicated in considerable detail.[3] It was realized that, if these standards were incorporated in the treaty, some form of supervision or control would be required to ensure that they were effectively observed, but in this connection the resolutions were vague and the solution put forward was that the International Association for Labour Legislation should be entrusted with this task.[4] This association was an unofficial body described by Ernest Mahaim,[5] one of its most active members, as "consisting of middle-class reformers sympathetic to the working classes". The trade union organizations

---

[3] See C. Riegelman, "The war-time trade-union and socialist proposals", in J.T. Shotwell (ed.): *The origins of the International Labor Organization* (New York, Columbia University Press, 1934), Vol. 1, pp. 55–79, and Vol. 2, pp. 3–96. (Ed.)

[4] The IALL was founded by an International Congress of Civil Social Reformers held in Paris in 1900. In 1901 its Central Office was opened in Basle. Its purpose was to research working conditions and to propose labour legislation. The Association is formally considered as the predecessor of the ILO. (Ed.)

[5] Ernest Mahaim (1865–1938), Professor of Law at the University of Liège, was instrumental in founding the IALL in 1900. He was Belgian Government delegate at the First Session of the ILC in Washington DC (1919), and subsequently was Belgian Government representative to the ILO Governing Body and delegate to the ILC until 1938. In 1930 he served as President of the 14th Session of the ILC. (Ed.)

had held aloof from it, with the exception of the British movement which had occasionally sent a delegate. It seemed unrealistic that the trade unions should now regard it as capable of performing with any real authority the functions of supervising the actions of governments, and there were other features in their proposals that gave them something of the character of political manifestos. Nowhere was there any suggestion that employers should, at any stage, be consulted, and the obvious necessity for some form of negotiation with governments, who after all would have to assume responsibility for the obligations created by the treaty, was only indirectly provided for by two suggestions, namely that all the governments should include a representative of labour among their plenipotentiaries, and that an international trade union conference should be held at the same time and place as the peace conference.

Thus, while, on the one hand, the trade union proposals included an admirable programme of desirable measures for the improvement of labour conditions, on the other hand, they provided no constructive suggestions as to how their programme could be implemented through the action of the peace conference.

This was how I viewed the problem as our discussion began. As explained earlier, it was our practice to include in discussions of this kind a member of our "production staff", which consisted of university professors and lecturers who had volunteered for service in the Ministry during the war, and our little committee accordingly included, in addition to Hope Simpson, MacMullan and myself, Hector Hetherington, at that time a lecturer in philosophy at Glasgow University. [6]

The general view, which I at first shared, was that the peace treaty should incorporate a series of labour guarantees and standards based on the proposals put forward by the trade unions, but as I tried to picture how this could be accomplished in practice, I became more and more conscious of the many difficulties that would be encountered. I knew from my experience of collective agreements that, even when only one industry was concerned and the points in dispute settled, long discussion was required before appropriate words could be found to define the exact obligations involved. The process would be infinitely more complicated when the scope of the obligations extended to all industries and all countries. Innumerable technical questions would arise, and it was certain that the peace conference delegations would not include members qualified to deal with them. The most that the peace conference could be expected to do would be to give its blessing to some kind of general declaration which, realizing that

---

[6] Sir Hector James Wright Hetherington (1888–1965) was a lecturer in philosophy at Glasgow University between 1910 and 1914 and Professor of Logic and Philosophy at University College Cardiff from 1915 to 1920. At the end of his career he became Principal of Glasgow University (1936–61). (Ed.)

it was treading on unfamiliar and dangerous ground, it would frame in cautious terms creating no real obligations. Moreover, and this seemed to me to clinch the argument, labour standards were not things that could be definitely fixed at any particular time; technical progress and social concepts were in constant development; for example, in 1917 the Berne labour conference demanded a ten-hour day and now, only twelve months later, there was growing pressure in several countries for legislation limiting the daily working hours to eight.[7]

Having thus arrived at the conclusion that it would be impossible for the peace conference to take any effective action on the substance of the trade union proposals, I tried to imagine the kind of body which would be competent to do so. The principal features of such a body were evident. In the first place, it would have to bring together technically qualified representatives of the interests involved, namely workers, employers and government departments concerned with industrial matters. In the second place, it would have to have the power to frame its decisions in the form of international conventions which would give rise to binding international obligations. And in the third place, it would have to be a permanent institution functioning continuously so that it could take account of changing conditions. Such a body could only be brought into existence and endowed with the necessary powers by an international treaty, and the meeting of the peace conference would provide a unique opportunity when this could be done.

The objection to this idea, strongly urged by Hope Simpson, was that, interesting as it might be, it would not be regarded by labour as meeting in any way the unanimous demand for immediate action by the peace conference. I argued, in reply, that this objection dealt with political tactics, a matter which the Minister should decide for himself. Before doing so, he should, however, be warned that to press for action by the peace conference on specific improvements on labour conditions, popular as such a course would be at the moment, involved the danger of subsequent disillusion and discontent, and that it was the function of the Intelligence Division to draw his attention to this risk and to suggest, if it could, some alternative line.

After a long discussion this view prevailed and it was left to Hetherington to embody our conclusions in the form of a draft memorandum. He produced in due course an admirably lucid document which, having been approved by all concerned, was sent forward by Hope Simpson to Butler with the suggestion that it should be submitted to the Minister.

---

[7] See Resolution IV of the International Conference of Trade Unions, Berne, 4 October 1917, in Shotwell (ed.): *The origins of the International Labor Organization*, Vol. 2, Document 7, pp. 45–46. (Ed.)

The policy of releasing key men first (who were precisely those who had been called up last) provoked grave resentment with riots in Glasgow and Belfast. Churchill insisted on a system based on length of service and number of wounds.

Other causes of discontent were the shortage of housing, rise in the cost of living, increase in unemployment, the dissatisfaction of munitions workers who had earned large wages finding themselves dependent on the dole, the resentment of ex-soldiers against those who had remained at home and earned good money, and the revolutionary ferment encouraged by events in Russia and in Hungary.

Once a brief memorandum had been prepared for the Minister in view of some contingency which might be expected to arise, the job of the Division was regarded as finished unless it should happen that it was asked to furnish supplementary material. On this occasion, however, I could not feel that such a detached attitude was appropriate. The proposal, I was convinced, had a long-term importance, and the unique opportunity that the peace conference would provide for its realization would not recur.

At the moment, it was unlikely to receive immediate consideration for the Ministry was preoccupied with the wave of unrest, sometimes violent in character, that swept over the country when the end of the war seemed in prospect. Some of its manifestations were due to real grievances; others were symptoms of tensions that had become unbearable during 18 months of unprecedented slaughter and strain; others were undoubtedly provoked by a small extremist minority. This confused situation, the gravity of which it was impossible to assess with any certainty, naturally monopolized the Ministry's attention. In great measure it proved to have been a kind of nerve storm resulting from overstrain, and it found another outlet in unrestrained rejoicing when the guns in Hyde Park carried to London the tidings that the long agony of the war was really at an end.

The Government's decisions on the points which it would raise at the peace conference now became a matter of urgency, and I was much concerned lest the Ministry should lose its chance of making its contribution. There was reason to fear that it might, for the vast and complicated problem of arranging the demobilization of the army so that it would key in with the changeover in industry from war to peace production was thrown on its shoulders and absorbed all its energies. I would have accepted a negative decision without question, but the idea that possibly the matter was being overlooked or forgotten in the pressure under which the Ministry was working was one that I could not passively entertain. I felt I must find out what the situation was, and since Hope Simpson was as much in the dark as I was myself, I went to see Arthur Greenwood, who had been appointed Deputy Permanent Secretary of the Ministry of Reconstruction and who, since the function of that department was to coordinate all aspects of post-war planning, was in a position to know whether the matter was receiving consideration. He, also, was unable to give me any information but he at once displayed the most lively interest. He remembered my earlier conversation with him on the subject; he declared that this was precisely the kind of thing the Ministry of Reconstruction wanted to see put forward; and he asked me to let him have a copy of the Ministry of Labour's proposals, to the existence of which I had referred only in general terms. This was further than I was prepared to go, and I suggested that, since the matter was now in the hands of my superiors, he should address an official request to the Ministry. A couple of days later he telephoned to say that he had the document and that he would like to discuss it with me.

The presence of Nash,[8] the Permanent Secretary of the Ministry of Reconstruction, at this meeting indicated that the matter was regarded as important, and at its conclusion it was evident that a serious consideration of the Division's proposals by the two ministries was certain to be undertaken. If the result should be favourable and the Government should decide to pursue the matter further, subsequent action would take the form of diplomatic negotiations at the peace conference. In these the Ministry of Labour would have no part, but it would have gained in prestige and, incidentally, the Intelligence Division would have given a striking demonstration of its utility. In any case, from now on the affair would be dealt with on another plane and could no longer be my active concern.

Whether Arthur Greenwood's intervention would have been decisive in itself it is impossible to say, for certain other happenings during the next few weeks, of which I only learned at a much later date, undoubtedly influenced the final result. Economic questions were certain to figure importantly in the discussions in Paris and the Board of Trade had therefore to be strongly represented in the peace delegation. Sir Hubert Llewellyn Smith,[9] the Permanent Secretary of that department, when he came to draw up the list of experts who would assist him, thought it wise to be prepared for all eventualities. Labour questions had been under his wing before the creation of the Ministry of Labour, and he was aware that the labour movement had made various declarations concerning peace policy. He therefore wrote to his opposite number in the Ministry of Labour,[10]

---

[8] Vaughan Robinson Nash (1861–1932) was a British economist. In 1916 he was appointed to the secretariat of the Reconstruction Committee in Asquith's coalition government and continued in this function under Lloyd George until 1919. (Ed.)

[9] Sir Hubert Llewellyn Smith (1864–1945) was the first Labour Commissioner for the Board of Trade (1893) and served as Permanent Secretary of the Board of Trade from 1907 to 1919. After the First World War he played a leading part in the reorganization of the Board. (Ed.)

[10] Sir David Shackleton: see Ch. 4, n. 12 above.

offering to include Butler in his list. Butler, to whom the letter was referred for observations, much as he was tempted by the idea of attending the peace conference, felt that the Ministry's prestige was involved. If the Ministry was to be represented at Paris, it was desirable that it should be on a basis of equality with other departments and not as a subsidiary of the Board of Trade. It was not important enough to claim separate representation but he remembered the memorandum of the Intelligence Division and he saw that if the Home Office and the Ministry of Labour combined they could put up a strong case for joint representation. He at once sent a copy of the memorandum to Sir Malcolm Delevingne,[11] his old chief at the Home Office, and suggested that the two departments should join forces and endeavour to obtain approval for the proposal it contained. Delevingne's response was favourable.

At about the same time, presumably on Greenwood's initiative, he, Butler and Delevingne, using the original memorandum as a basis, drew up a shorter document which, after signature by the Home Secretary and the Minister of Labour, was circulated to the Cabinet. Here again, chance intervened to favour, perhaps decisively, its reception, for it provided the Prime Minister with a political argument of no little value. When Lloyd George had sought Labour's support on forming his government he had agreed to the demand that Labour should be represented at the peace conference. He had no hesitation in giving this undertaking. He had already agreed to appoint to ministerial posts a number of members of the parliamentary Labour Party, and, when the time came, the peace conference delegation would necessarily include ministers from the different parties forming the coalition. Towards the end of 1918 it became evident that this solution would not be applicable. A general election was overdue and Lloyd George had decided to seek a mandate from the country before engaging in peace negotiations; Labour ministers had come under criticism and attack from their own movement, and a party conference adopted a resolution that they should withdraw from the Government when the session of parliament came to an end.[12] The Labour movement maintained that Lloyd George was, neverthe-

---

[11] Sir Malcolm Delevingne (1868–1950) acted as government delegate to international conferences on labour regulations in Berne in 1905, 1906 and 1913. In 1919 he was the British representative to the Commission on International Labour Legislation at the Paris Peace Conference and subsequently to the Organizing Committee of the First Session of the ILC. He represented the British Government in the ILO Governing Body between 1919 and 1920 and took part in the First, Fifth, 11th and 12th Sessions of the ILC. (Ed.)

[12] There was considerable dissension in the Labour Party at this time. Three of the Labour ministers, of whom George Barnes (see n. 13 below) was one, refused to obey this resolution and decided to remain as members of the Government until peace was signed. Barnes, although an official Labour Party candidate was nominated to oppose Lloyd George, easily held his seat in his Glasgow constituency and continued as member of the War Cabinet after the election. (E.J.P.)

less, bound by his pledge and that, whatever might be the composition of the new Government, he was under an obligation to include among the peace plenipotentiaries a representative chosen by Labour. Since only the Government would have constitutional power to enter into peace negotiations, this demand was unacceptable, but Lloyd George was concerned at the prospect that during the election campaign a charge of bad faith would be levelled against him and that it would be asserted that he had all along intended to renege on his promise by invoking the constitutional argument. The suggestion that the Government should urge the peace conference to depute the responsibility for dealing with labour matters to a separate international body in which the workers would be represented consequently appealed to his political sense as affording an argument with which he could make great play if the charge of bad faith became a dangerous issue. He gave the proposal from the Home Office and the Ministry of Labour his warm support and the Cabinet's approval followed.

I knew nothing of all this until Butler sent for me to tell me of the Cabinet's decision and of the creation of a special section of the peace delegation which, under the direction of Mr George Barnes, [13] the Labour member of the War Cabinet, was to deal with the matter in Paris. Sir David Shackleton and himself, from the Ministry, and Sir Malcolm Delevingne and the Chief Inspector of Factories, from the Home Office, he continued, would be the members of the section. [14] I was about to congratulate him on his personal good fortune when he took my breath away by adding that I had been appointed as the section's secretary and that, after making contact with Mr Barnes and the Foreign Office, I was to proceed at once to Paris to make all the necessary arrangements for the section's work.

I was rather intimidated by the Hotel Majestic. Both its external appearance and its internal appointments suggested that it was appropriately named and well fitted to house visitors of royal blood or others whose eminence set them in a class apart. The members of the British Empire delegation who were now its exclusive occupants were fully as distinguished as those for whose reception it had been designed. I had the list in my pocket; incredibly my own name figured in a document which included prime ministers, reigning princes from India, members of the British and dominion cabinets, ambassadors, generals and

---

[13] George Nicoll Barnes (1859–1940) was a British trade unionist and politician. In 1919 he was Vice-President of the Commission on International Labour Legislation and a contributor to the draft proposal for Part XIII of the Treaty of Versailles. He was a government delegate to the First Session of the ILC. Following his retirement in 1920 he continued to support the ILO, notably by writing *A history of the International Labour Office*, published in 1926. (Ed.)

[14] Only Delevingne and Butler actually went to Paris. Both the Home Office and the Ministry of Labour were overburdened at the time and could ill spare their higher officials. (E.J.P.)

all the most important officials in the civil service. I no longer looked on such personalities with excessive awe; I would have felt no diffidence in approaching any one of them on official business. But to find myself one of their company in the crowded lounge was altogether different. Everyone seemed to be on intimate terms with everyone else; I could see nobody that I knew; and I felt very much as though I had strayed into some old boys' meeting where my right to be present might be challenged. I was on the point of making off to my room to settle down with a book when Botha and Smuts entered. [15] To me, with memories of schoolboy's hero worship, they were legendary figures and I was staring at them so intently that my first thought on being tapped on the shoulder was that I was about to be reproved for breach of good manners. Looking round, I was greeted by Eustace Percy, [16] who told me he wanted to put me in touch with some members of the American delegation who were interested in labour questions. Next day, I accompanied him to the Hotel Crillon where he introduced me to Professor Shotwell and David Hunter Miller. [17]

After some discussion of the general labour situation in Europe, the conversation turned to labour and the peace, and Shotwell outlined a memorandum he had written proposing that a provision should be inserted in the peace treaty prohibiting child labour. This, he argued, was the one question of social reform which had no connection with class warfare, and one that made a universal appeal to humanitarian sentiment. "The Congress of Vienna banned the slave trade; the Congress of Paris must save the children," was his eloquent conclusion. Impressive though this was, his approach seemed to me to be curiously remote from the realities of the situation. To exclude from consideration all other questions of social reform on the ground that they were controversial was to make no

---

[15] Louis Botha (1862–1919) was the first Prime Minister of the Union of South Africa from 1910 to 1919. He played a moderating role at the peace conference.

Field Marshal Jan Christiaan Smuts (1870–1950) was a South African statesman. A member of the British War Cabinet from 1917 to 1919, he served as Prime Minister of South Africa from 1919 to 1924 and from 1939 to 1948. (Ed.)

[16] Eustace Sutherland Campbell Percy (1887–1958), a British politician, was assistant to Lord Robert Cecil from January to March 1919. He helped draft the League of Nations Covenant, after which he became Joint Secretary of the Inter-Allied Commission on the League. (Ed.)

[17] Professor James Thomson Shotwell (1874–1965), an American historian, was part of the "Inquiry", a study group set up by President Wilson to prepare peace negotiations. At the Paris Peace Conference he was a member of the Commission on International Labour Legislation. He wrote a history of the ILO's early years, published as *The origins of the International Labor Organization* (New York, Columbia University Press, 1934), 2 vols.

David Hunter Miller (1875–1961) was an American lawyer, member of the "Inquiry" and legal adviser to the American Commission to Negotiate Peace at the Paris Peace Conference. He participated in the drafting of the League of Nations Covenant. (Ed.)

effort whatever to meet the demands of organized labour. Moreover, the Supreme Court of the United States had declared federal legislation on child labour unconstitutional, and it hardly seemed likely that the Government of the United States would take the initiative in proposing international action on the subject.

The most interesting point about his exposé, however, was the indication it gave that the United States delegation had no wider proposals in mind, and I accordingly suggested that consideration should be given to the question whether the peace conference was a suitable body to deal with labour matters at all and whether it would not be better for it to set up a permanent organization which would be technically competent to do so. This approach to the problem aroused considerable interest, so much so that further meetings were arranged in which other members of the American delegation, including Professor Haskins, Mr Beer, Dr Bowman and Professor Young participated. [18] I felt that these were useful and that American opinion was steadily becoming favourable to the main principle underlying the British plan.

Meanwhile, I had not neglected my essential responsibilities as secretary of the labour section. The Hotel Astoria had been secured as office quarters for the British delegation and there I secured, after something of a struggle, three rooms in which the section could work and the services of a secretary–typist. One other question led to a dispute. The head of the Delegation Registry insisted that the files of the labour section must be dealt with as part of the papers concerning the League of Nations; I insisted equally strongly that the labour section was an independent entity and that its papers must be dealt with separately. The matter had therefore to be settled by higher authority and was eventually referred to Lord Robert Cecil. I had not seen him since my tussle with him some months before and I thought the chances were that he would incline to the Foreign Office view. However, after listening to my case he gave his decision in my favour. Although all that was decided was a minor matter of internal administration, it was the first occasion on which the question of the ILO's independence vis-à-vis the League arose; no one realized at the time how important the issue was to become during the peace conference nor that it would continue to give rise to dispute for many

---

[18] Professor Charles Homer Haskins (1870–1937) was an American historian and President Wilson's adviser on Western Europe. He was a member of the "Inquiry".

George Louis Beer (1872–1920) was an American historian, specializing in the history of British colonial policy. He was one of the American experts at the Paris Peace Conference and subsequently a member of the League of Nations Mandate Commission.

Dr Isaiah Bowman (1878–1950) was Director of the American Geographical Society (1915–35) and Chief Directorial Adviser to President Wilson at the peace conference.

Professor Allyn Abbott Young (1876–1929) was the economic adviser on the "Inquiry". (Ed.)

years after.

Butler arrived in Paris on 11 January 1919 and was followed a few days later by Barnes, who had remained in London until he could get the Cabinet's approval of the joint memorandum from the Home Secretary and the Minister of Labour. This approval covered three principles: (i) an international organization to deal with labour questions should be established; (ii) it should be of a permanent character; and (iii) it should admit representation from employers and workers as well as from governments. It was left to Barnes in consultation with the labour section to decide the form in which these principles should be submitted to the Commission which the British delegation would propose the peace conference should set up. Since the ultimate objective was to have the organization created by treaty, the task of the Commission would be to agree on provisions for incorporation in an international convention to be adopted by the peace conference. At this time, it was assumed that this procedure would be followed in the case of the League. When, later, it was decided that the Covenant of the League should form part of the peace treaty, the Constitution of the ILO came to be dealt with in the same way; until then the proposals for an ILO were referred to as the Labour Convention. It was, therefore, desirable that the British plan should be submitted in the form of a series of articles suitable for a Convention; but before this could be done the three principles had first to be expanded into a complete scheme defining the machinery to be set up and the rules under which it would work.

As soon as Barnes arrived, he called Butler and myself into consultation to settle the detailed outlines of a coherent plan of this kind. In our discussions that went on for three days and that continued during meals and far into the night, I was allowed to play a full part. I had already thought out the scheme in detail; I had considered variants of its possible features; and I was ready with all the arguments – pro and con – on any question that might be raised. This, of course, much simplified our task. Barnes and Butler had the more important role which was to probe and weigh the arguments I put forward and to decide on those they thought should be retained. When the process was complete I embodied in a memorandum the results arrived at.[19] The points covered were far too numerous to be listed here. It is, however, of interest to note that, with one exception, all the major features of the ILO's Constitution as eventually adopted were included at this stage, and in particular three points that marked a break with all previous

---

[19] See "Memorandum on the machinery and procedure required for the international regulation of industrial conditions, prepared in the British Delegation, January 15–20, 1919", in Shotwell (ed.): *The origins of the International Labor Organization*, Vol. 2, Document 25, pp. 117–25. (Ed.)

diplomatic tradition and practice, namely that the Conference could adopt international Conventions by a majority, that employers' and workers' delegates should be entitled to vote, and that the Conventions adopted should be laid before national parliaments and ratified if they approved.

Now that a complete and detailed plan was on paper, I felt we had made a decisive step forward. Delevingne had not participated in our discussions, but as we had arrived at unanimous conclusions, I assumed that he would give his approval. I said as much to Butler, but his reply banished my optimism.

"You don't know Delevingne," he replied with a grimace. "He won't accept anything he hasn't had a hand in himself. I'm afraid he's going to be difficult."

My acquaintance with Delevingne was limited to a telephone conversation just before my departure for Paris. Since Butler had a habit of understatement, the apprehension he had expressed led me to picture a formidable person who would imperiously brush aside all we had done and who would probably not be prepared to listen to anyone as unimportant as myself. I could scarcely believe my eyes when the next evening Butler introduced me to a frail-looking little man who entered the Majestic carrying an umbrella. I remember wondering whether it was the man who was abnormally small or the umbrella which was unusually long. At all events, there was something comic in the disproportion, and this comic effect was increased by a pince-nez, a squeaky voice, and an air of self-conscious import-ance that I found pathetic rather than intimidating. I imagine that the reputation that I later learned he enjoyed in Whitehall as a tyrannical and disagreeable chief derived from manifestations of an inferiority complex. My own experience of him was totally different. He was sometimes a little huffy and pretentious in a way that I found amusing but he was always courteous and considerate. He was pernick-ety about details and a stickler for exactitude; in this respect the standards I had learned to respect in the Board of Trade no doubt got me good marks. His personal association with the Berne Conferences of 1906 and 1913 had made him a fervent advocate of international labour regulation, [20] and my wholehearted enthusiasm for the same cause probably created a bond between us. In any case, nothing resembling the difficulties that Butler had led me to expect ever arose. Delevingne quite properly subjected all our conclusions to a careful and critical scrutiny. In general, he was well satisfied but he was shocked by the idea that workers and

---

[20] The IALL Technical Conference held in 1905 limited the night work of women in order to afford them a minimum of 11 hours' rest, and made the sale, importation and manufacture of white phosphorus illegal. The IALL Diplomatic Conference held in 1906 drafted and adopted the Conventions agreed upon at the 1905 Technical Conference. The IALL Technical Conference held in 1913 prohibited the employment of women and children in industry for more than ten hours per day. (Ed.)

employers should be delegates and proposed that they should be given the status of advisers, only government representatives being entitled to vote.

This was a difficult point which had been discussed at considerable length before his arrival. After much reflection, Barnes had decided that workers and employers must be full delegates and that the governments' position was sufficiently safeguarded by the fact that the final decision on whether a decision of the Conference should be applied or not in any country lay with the constitutional authorities in that country. Delevingne admitted that this gave the governments the last word, but he pointed out that with the scheme as it stood this last word would tend to be negative; governments would not feel that they had any real responsibility for decisions adopted by a body in which their representatives were in a minority; the national action which the organization was intended to secure would not follow, and no practical results would be achieved.

This argument, based on how the machinery would work in actual practice, was new and it made the problem seem insoluble. On the one hand, if the workers were made full delegates, the governments would not take the decisions of the Conference seriously; on the other hand, if the workers were not offered full delegate status they would not participate and the scheme, serving no political purpose, would fall on the ground.

Barnes pondered gloomily while we waited for him to make his choice. I had no great interest in his decision for each horn of the dilemma was equally deadly. Delevingne might hope that a purely governmental organization would carry on the work of the Berne Conferences in a more regular fashion but I felt he did not realize how much the world had changed during the war and how impossible it would now be to secure international labour legislation without labour's participation. Surely, there must be some way of getting round the difficulty. Suddenly, I threw out a suggestion, more with the idea of keeping the discussion alive than in the belief that I had a solution. "Why not give each government delegate two votes, and the employers and workers one each?"

I was a little nettled when Delevingne dismissed this with a shrug and a superior smile as no more than an amusing interjection; it might be too unorthodox to be acceptable but it was at least a theoretical solution which I thought deserved less summary treatment. His attitude roused my debating instincts and I embarked on an impromptu defence of the idea. As I proceeded, hurriedly marshalling such arguments as occurred to me on the spur of the moment, I began to see that there was perhaps more in my proposal than I had imagined. With the votes distributed in the way I had suggested, the composition of the Conference would reflect equally the economic elements of production and consumption; the employers and workers, representing the producers, would have 50 per cent of the votes, and the governments, representing the interests of consumers, would have the other 50 per cent. Moreover, since a two-thirds majority was required for the adoption of a Convention, no Convention could pass without substantial government support.

Delevingne, to whom Barnes turned for his opinion, would not go further than to say that the idea was ingenious. In reality his view, never explicitly expressed, was that only government representatives could adopt international Conventions; and consequently, he was not prepared to give his personal approval to any system under which non-governmental delegates would be entitled to participate in the voting.

Butler was equally non-committal, not because he shared the view that a fundamental principle was involved but because he was reluctant to oppose openly his senior colleague and redoubtable ex-chief.

Barnes, nevertheless, gave his decision in favour of including in the plan the new system of voting.

I was surprised by the quiet firmness with which he did so. I had found him a very likeable person. He had many characteristics that made it a pleasure to work with him; he was wholly unassuming, patently sincere, and painstaking to a degree. But I had wondered more than once whether he had the energy, political ability and intelligence to drive our scheme successfully through the peace confer- ence. Until now he had made no positive contribution to its elaboration; he had listened patiently until he had fully understood what was proposed and then he had given his agreement in the fewest possible words. Now that he had, for the first time, taken an important decision without the concurrence of his official advisers, I saw that I had underestimated his quality. This view was confirmed by the steps which he now took on his own initiative to obtain the support of the British workers and employers, and of the Dominions, for the plan. At his invita- tion, delegates of the Trades Union Congress (TUC) came to Paris and the main features of the scheme were laid before them. One important suggestion emerged from the meeting and that was that provision should be made for a council that would meet periodically during the intervals between conferences. This was the origin of the Governing Body, which was to prove such a valuable part of the ILO's machinery. The employers were unable to arrange for a delegation to come to Paris at such short notice but they sent certain observations in writing of which the most interesting was that they thought the organization would be of little use unless it was given mandatory powers.

While the TUC delegates were examining the plan, Barnes started his consultation with the heads of the Dominion delegations and, since Delevingne and Butler had returned to London, he asked me to be present. I knew that there was disagreement on many issues between the British and the Dominion delegates, and, at a moment when discussions were going on concerning fundamental questions of status and policy, it seemed likely that the Dominions would regard a scheme for international labour legislation with impatience and would give it scant consideration. I wondered what impression Barnes with his quiet gentle manner could make on strong personalities such as Sir Robert Borden, Prime Minister of Canada, and "Billy" Hughes, Prime Minister of Australia;[21] much was at stake, for unless he could get their support, everything would again be in jeopardy.

I have a vivid recollection of my anxiety when the first of these consultations took place with General Smuts. For some reason, the two ministers remained standing the whole time. Smuts, in his smart uniform with its red tabs and the gold insignia of his rank, was an impressive figure. Barnes was by no means a small man but in his ill-cut black suit he looked insignificant. Moreover, he had a curious habit of standing with crossed feet, an attitude which gave him an awkward appearance and which on the present occasion struck me as most undignified. My anxiety that we should put up a good performance made his opening sentences seem as clumsy as his posture and I thought that Smuts was frowning with displeasure. Then I realized that in simple unemphatic phrases Barnes was covering all the essential points in a way that rendered them readily intelligible to anyone to whom the scheme was being communicated for the first time, and that Smuts' frown denoted attention and not impatience. When Barnes had finished he asked a number of questions which I would have found difficult to answer without lengthy explanations. Barnes' replies were brief but they evidently gave satisfaction, for Smuts gave his unqualified approval to the plan and expressed his fervent hope that the peace conference would accept it. After this experience I never doubted Barnes' ability to justify our proposals to any audience, and I no longer cared whether he crossed his feet or stood on his head while doing so.

It proved impossible to arrange individual consultations with all the Dominions in the time available but Barnes found a substitute procedure which was both ingenious and politically highly astute. He invited the Dominion Prime Ministers to a joint meeting with the British trade union representatives, over which he presided. They not only came, but a long discussion ensued in which the Prime Ministers of Canada, Australia and New Zealand took an active part at

---

[21] Sir Robert Laird Borden (1854–1937) was Prime Minister of Canada from 1911 to 1920. He had insisted Canada be accorded its own seat at the Paris Peace Conference, thus ensuring that each of the Dominions would sign the Treaty.

William Morris Hughes (1862–1952) was Prime Minister of Australia from 1915 to 1923. (Ed.)

the conclusion of which they wished the scheme every success.

The next step was to cast the plan into treaty form. I made a tentative draft which was then worked over by a small committee composed of Butler and myself; Sir Robert Garran, the Solicitor-General of Australia; Sir Cecil Hurst; and Philip Noel-Baker. [22] No changes were made in the general structure but some modifications were introduced to take into account proposed provisions of the peace treaty concerning mandates, the establishment of an international court and so on. On 31 January 1919 this text was submitted to a full meeting of the British Empire delegation and received unanimous approval.

Meanwhile, the press in all countries had become increasingly critical of what was happening, or rather of what was not happening, in Paris; the delegations had been in Paris for weeks: no meeting had been held; and the newspapers had nothing to report other than that the whole operation of making the peace was paralysed by quarrels between the chief delegates of the great powers. This was true, and they had been reluctant to assemble the conference until they had composed their differences. The pressure of public opinion, however, made some action imperative and the first meeting of the conference was convened for 18 January. Its agenda comprised only three items, carefully chosen so as to precipitate no controversial issue: (i) the responsibility for the war; (ii) penalties for war crimes; and (iii) international labour legislation. [23]

The sitting amounted to little more than the formal bringing of the conference into being. After a speech of welcome from the President of the French Republic Raymond Poincaré, Georges Clemenceau, the French Prime Minister, was elected to preside. As soon as he could stem the attempts of the delegates to embark on long general speeches, he abruptly announced that they should communicate their observations on the questions on the agenda to the secretariat and declared the meeting adjourned. The only result achieved seemed to be the scene of wild confusion among the journalists who mobbed the departing

---

[22] Sir Robert Randolph Garran (1867–1957), first Solicitor-General of Australia (1916–32), served as part of the British Empire delegation at the Paris Peace Conference and contributed to the League of Nations Covenant.

Sir Cecil James Barrington Hurst (1870–1963) was a British lawyer. He served on the Philimore Committee, which prepared a draft for the Covenant of the League of Nations. He attended the Assembly of the League of Nations as a substitute delegate in 1922, 1924 and 1925.

Philip John Noel-Baker (1889–1982) served as assistant to Lord Robert Cecil and subsequently worked for Sir Eric Drummond, the first Secretary-General of the League of Nations. He was also Professor of International Law at the University of London (1924–29) and a lecturer at Yale University (1933–34). He was awarded the Nobel Peace Prize in 1959 for his campaign for disarmament. (Ed.)

[23] See the extract from the Preliminary Peace Conference, Protocol No. I, Session of 18 January 1919, in Shotwell (ed.): *The origins of the International Labor Organization*, Vol. 2, Document 26, p. 126. (Ed.)

delegates in a frantic, and generally unsuccessful, effort to discover what on earth international labour legislation might be.

The second meeting of the conference, held a week later, had a more realistic character. The question of the League of Nations figured on its agenda. The atmosphere was perceptibly different; one could feel that, the formalities now being over, there was real life in the assembly as it approached one of its major tasks. Clemenceau, who presided, had President Wilson on his right hand and Lloyd George on his left. The four seats next to Lloyd George were occupied by the other British plenipotentiaries, Bonar Law, Milner, Balfour and Barnes. From my seat immediately behind Barnes I had a clear view of all the eminent personalities who were ranged along the wings of the U-shaped table. The speeches of President Wilson, Lloyd George, Orlando and Léon Bourgeois were eloquent and moving appeals to the conference to fulfil the aspirations of mankind by establishing an institution to ensure permanent peace. [24]

After this first phase of the proceedings, there was a brief adjournment. I found myself caught up in the crowd of celebrities that surged out of the Salle de l'Horloge into an equally splendid apartment to partake of the French Government's hospitality. As a mere spectator, I doubted whether I was included in this invitation and I was idly watching the scene when Barnes asked me if I did not want a drink. We moved up towards the buffet, making for a place where the crowd seemed slightly less dense than elsewhere. I was inclined to draw back when it became apparent that we were heading straight for the spot where President Wilson, Clemenceau and Lloyd George had been respectfully allowed a modicum of elbow room, but Barnes went steadily on quite unperturbed. Wilson, who was biting into a sandwich, gave him a friendly nod and the greeting of his companions indicated that he would be welcome to join the group. Barnes replied with a gesture towards the buffet and moving in behind Lloyd George devoted his whole attention to securing for me a glass of champagne and one for himself. The incident illustrates features in his character which I found especially attractive: his complete unselfconsciousness, his indifference to any flattering mark of attention, and a singleness of purpose in small things as in great which was proof against all distraction.

The second half of the sitting revealed some of the strains and stresses

---

[24] Vittorio Emanuele Orlando (1860–1952) was the Prime Minister of the Kingdom of Italy (1917–19). Head of the Italian delegation at the Paris Peace Conference, he was forced to resign before the Treaty was signed. (Ed.)

Léon Victor Auguste Bourgeois (1851–1925) was French Minister of State and a member of the War Committee (1917–19). His diplomatic skills paved the way for the creation of the League of Nations and he became the first President of the League Council. He was awarded the Nobel Peace Prize in 1920. (Ed.)

existing beneath the surface of the superficial unanimity that had prevailed during the first. One after another, the representatives of the smaller nations rose to protest against the hegemony of the great powers and to demand a larger measure of representation on the commissions of the conference. Clemenceau made a scathing reply pointing out that it was his duty to keep the meeting strictly to its agenda and that he intended to do so. He then put to the conference the proposals for the appointment of the various commissions. As soon as the text of a resolution had been read, he rapped out in staccato fashion like a sergeant major hustling recruits through their drill, "You have heard the proposal – No objection – Adopted." On one occasion his own foreign minister rose in his place and waved his agenda paper to indicate that he wished to make an observation. Clemenceau's eyes glittered angrily and the sergeant major was transformed into the tiger. With a savage gesture he waved the unfortunate M. Pichon down and snapped "No one asks to speak – Adopted." [25] The last resolution subjected to this expeditious procedure provided that a Commission, composed of two members from each of the five great powers and five members to be elected by the other powers, should be appointed to consider the international adjustment of conditions of employment and the form of the international machinery to be set up to achieve this purpose.

Barnes and Delevingne were at once designated as the two British members. Other governments followed this example and appointed important members of their delegations. As the names came in we noted with satisfaction that the composition of the Commission would endow its recommendations with considerable authority; for instance, France appointed Colliard (Minister of Labour) and Loucheur (Minister of Industrial Reconstruction); [26] Belgium, Vandervelde (Minister of Justice); [27] Italy, Mayor des Planches (Commissioner General of Emigration); [28]

---

[25] Stéphen Pichon (1857–1933) served as French Minister of Foreign Affairs in 1906–11, 1913 and 1917–20. (Ed.)

[26] Pierre Colliard (1852–1925) was Georges Clemenceau's Minister of Labour from 1917 to 1920 and served as Vice-President of the Commission on International Labour Legislation.

Louis Loucheur (1872–1931) replaced Albert Thomas as French Minister of Munitions in 1917 and became Minister of Industrial Reconstruction in 1918. He was Georges Clemenceau's principal economic adviser at the Paris Peace Conference. (Ed.)

[27] Emile Vandervelde (1866–1938) was Belgian Justice Minister from 1918 to 1921. (Ed.)

[28] Baron Edmondo Mayor des Planches (1851–1920) was Italian Commissioner General of Immigration in 1919. He attended the First Session of the International Labour Conference in Washington, DC and was the Italian Government representative to the Governing Body in 1919 and 1920. In 1920 he was President of the Second Session of the ILC (Maritime). (Ed.)

Cuba, Bustamante (a noted international lawyer);[29] and Czechoslovakia, Edvard Beneš (Minister of Foreign Affairs).[30] President Wilson's action in nominating Samuel Gompers, the President of the American Federation of Labor (AFL), and Mr A.N. Hurley, an American employer,[31] came as a surprise and suggested that there must be some confusion in the American delegation concerning the task which the Commission was expected to perform.[32]

Since Barnes was the only plenipotentiary of one of the great powers appointed to the Commission, the British delegation took it for granted that he would be called on to preside. They were disconcerted when, without any previous consultation, Colliard proposed that Gompers be elected chairman.

It was clear that our efforts at liaison with the American and French delegations had been less effective than we had imagined. As regards the Americans, we were unaware that Shotwell and his colleagues, with whom we had been in such close touch, were members of a body known as "the Inquiry" set up by Colonel House to prepare studies on questions likely to come before the conference,[33] that its status in the delegation was ill-defined, and that it was regarded with little favour by the State Department, of whose actions it was not always informed. As regards the French, although Delevingne had kept in constant touch with his friend Arthur Fontaine,[34] he had not realized that the latter was not the equivalent of the permanent secretary in a British ministry and that there might be

---

[29] Antonio Sánchez de Bustamante y Sirven (1865–1951) was Cuban delegate to the Paris Peace Conference in 1919 and became Justice of The Hague Tribunal in 1921. (Ed.)

[30] Edvard Beneš (1884–1948) was Secretary of the Czechoslovak National Council in Paris from 1916 to 1918 and Minister of the Interior and of Foreign Affairs in the Czechoslovak Government from 1918 to 1935. He represented Czechoslovakia at the Paris Peace Conference. A member of the League of Nations Council from 1923 to 1927, and President of the Seventh Session of the ILC in 1925, he later became President of Czechoslovakia (1937–38; 1940–45; 1945–48). (Ed.)

[31] Samuel Gompers (1850–1924) was founder and President of the American Federation of Labor. During the First World War he was appointed by President Wilson to the Council of National Defense, where he chaired the Labor Advisory Board. He attended the Paris Peace Conference as an official adviser on labour issues and was appointed President of the Commission on International Labour Legislation.
A.N. Hurley was President of the American Shipping Board. (Ed.)

[32] Phelan does not mention the Japanese delegation (Otchiai and Oka) or the Polish delegation (Zoltowski and Patek). For a complete list of participants, see E.J. Phelan, "The Commission on International Labor Legislation", in Shotwell (ed.): *The origins of the International Labor Organization*, Vol. 1, pp. 128–30. (Ed.)

[33] Colonel Edward Mandell House (1858–1938) was President Wilson's foreign policy adviser until 1919 and his chief negotiator in Europe from 1917 to 1919. Along with Wilson he established the "Inquiry". He strongly supported American membership of the League of Nations. (Ed.)

[34] Arthur Fontaine (1860–1931) had been the first Director of the French Labour Office (1899–1920). In 1900 he took part in the creation of the International Association for Labour Legislation and represented France in several of its conferences. In addition to helping to draft the treaty creating the ILO, he was the first Chairman of the ILO Governing Body (1919–31) and French Government delegate to the ILC from 1919 to 1921 and again in 1931. (Ed.)

decisions by his minister of which he had no knowledge. The lack of coordination between the French members of the Commission was a permanent and disconcerting feature. Colliard and Loucheur never attended together, and it was not uncommon for one of them to strongly oppose the thesis that his colleague had defended vigorously the day before.

The decision to put Gompers in the chair proved to be fortunate. Only a chairman of exceptional ability and long experience could have presided with success over a meeting in which so many complicated issues had to be discussed. Moreover, Barnes was left free to devote his whole attention to steering the British proposals through the Commission, and this by no means easy task he performed with admirable parliamentary skill. The very fact that the scheme was a closely knit logical whole meant that a decision on one point often was linked to the decision that might be taken on some related point in another article and that amendments could not be considered intelligently without regard for the consequential amendments that might be required elsewhere. Barnes was never at a loss and members of the Commission were constantly amazed at the way in which he could sum up a discussion which had roved back and forth in the most confusing fashion, and lucidly set out the essential points at issue.

Every evening we reviewed in the Majestic the progress made and discussed the tactics to be employed the next morning. Departmental duties required Delevingne and Butler to return to London whenever possible. They were never away together but neither could keep in continuous personal touch with every phase of the discussions. Barnes attended all the meetings of the Commission but he had to keep himself informed of what was happening on other issues and take part in the regular meetings of the heads of the British Empire delegation. I was the only one of our little group who could devote his whole time to the affairs of the Labour Commission and I had two special tasks which obliged me to follow its proceedings with concentrated attention.

The peace conference had no comprehensive secretarial machinery such as is now a regular feature of all international gatherings. Each commission had to extemporize a secretariat as best it could with the help of such staff as one or other delegation might be able to lend for the purpose. On paper the secretariat of the Labour Commission looked impressive. Fontaine and Butler figured respectively as Secretary-General and Deputy Secretary-General; and the title of "secretary" was accorded to an American, a Belgian, an Italian and a Japanese; but in fact none of these ever undertook any secretarial duties. Fontaine and Butler were substitute members, and the others no doubt rendered services to their respective delegations the nature of which was not revealed. The Commission had, however, to have a minimum of practical assistance, and this was provided by myself and Camille Pône,[35] a young member of Fontaine's staff. To us fell the task of compiling minutes of the proceedings from such notes as we were able to take – no stenographic record was available.[36] This in itself would have fixed things in my memory, but I had also to dictate each evening a short report of the progress made for the information of the Dominion delegations. I had, therefore, a detailed grasp of how things stood at any time, and any views or suggestions I put forward in our discussions in Barnes' room at the Majestic consequently received serious attention.

On 28 February the Commission ended its detailed examination of the Convention and it then adjourned for ten days. This adjournment had a specific purpose. Matters on which there had been disagreement had been disposed of, for the time being, by taking a vote. Since it was desirable that the Commission should, if at all possible, arrive finally at a unanimous report, it was understood that its members would, during the interval, endeavour to secure from their governments instructions that would facilitate this outcome of their deliberations.

On most of the points on which differences prevailed, it could be reasonably expected that governments would be willing to bow to the view of the majority. But there were two points of importance on which opinions were strongly divided and to these it was essential that governments should give serious consideration.

The first related to the distribution of votes in the annual Conference.

The British proposal, as already recounted, had provided that of the three delegates from each country the government delegate should have two votes and the employers' and workers' delegates one each. A counter-proposal had been put forward providing that the three delegates should have one vote each. Yet a third proposal was advanced providing that each country should have four delegates, two for the government, one for the workers and one for the employers, and that each should be entitled to a vote. Since this gave effect to the principle of the British proposal, Barnes declared his willingness to accept it and it secured the support of the majority. The two systems were known as the 2:1:1 and the 1:1:1. The former had been carried but only by a narrow margin and the 1:1:1 system had been vigorously pressed by the Americans and the French.

---

[35] Camille Pône joined the Organizing Committee after completion of the work of the Commission and served in the Secretariat of the First Session of the ILC. In January 1920 he was appointed Section Chief of the Diplomatic Division of the ILO (under Phelan). In 1932 he became Butler's Chief of Cabinet. (Ed.)

[36] Stenographic records of the sessions were in fact kept by both English and French stenographers, as well as summaries of the meetings which were circulated following each session. The French stenographic record has been printed by de Lapradelle, in *La Paix de Versailles: La Documentation internationale*. For the minutes, see Shotwell (ed.): *The origins of the International Labor Organization*, Vol. 2, Document 34, pp. 149–322. (Ed.)

The second point was connected with the first but it was much more complicated. It related to the obligation of each country to apply a Convention adopted by the Conference unless its legislature expressed its disapproval. This provision was first attacked on the ground that it did not go far enough, and a counter-proposal was made to give the Conference mandatory powers. When this was defeated, objections were raised to the original proposal from the opposite angle. The Americans declared that it went too far and that the United States could not accept it for constitutional reasons. Neither Gompers nor Robinson succeeded in convincing the Commission that a constitutional obstacle really existed,[37] since the text left with the legislature of each country the final decision whether a Convention should be applied or not. After various efforts had been made to find a form of words that the Americans could accept, they put forward a text of their own the effect of which was to exempt federal States from the obligations by which all other States would be bound. On a vote the British text was adopted by 8 votes to 2, the two votes against being those of the Americans. This disposed of the matter for the moment. The importance of the American opposition was recognized but it was difficult to believe that it could remain so intransigent and it was hoped that full consideration of the matter by the American delegation during the adjournment would enable a satisfactory solution to be found.

When the Commission suspended its sittings our little group at the Majestic disintegrated. Butler returned to England; Barnes, after consultation with Lloyd George, also went to London to lay before the Cabinet the results achieved; and Delevingne fell victim to the virulent type of influenza which was then sweeping across Europe and had to take to his bed. As soon as I had completed the minutes of the last two sittings, I went to see Shotwell to learn what was happening in the American delegation. I discovered with consternation that Gompers had gone off to Italy for an extensive tour and that Robinson had also left Paris. I urged Shotwell to get the matter of the pretended constitutional difficulty brought to the President's attention since, unless some action was taken before the Commission reassembled there would be little prospect that the deadlock could be broken. Shotwell shared my concern but declared that it was impossible for him to intervene. "Since the appointment of the Commission," he commented rather bitterly, "we of the Inquiry have been given no information, and all we know of what has been going on is what we have learned through occasional contacts with the British delegation."

---

[37] Henry Mauris Robinson (1868–1937) was a member of the staff of the Council of National Defense (1917–18). In 1919 he was an American member of the Supreme Economic Council. (Ed.)

Much depressed, I returned to the Majestic and there I ran into Loring Christie of the Canadian delegation.[38] In the course of a casual conversation, he mentioned that Felix Frankfurter had just arrived in Paris.[39] I had never met Frankfurter but I had corresponded with him and I was aware of the great reputation he enjoyed. I knew that he was the President's trusted adviser on labour questions and that he was an authority on constitutional law. He was thus the ideal person to approach President Wilson; and having discovered his address and made an appointment by telephone, I went to see him at the Hotel Meurice. I found him in bed with the flu but this in no way seemed to affect the cordiality of his welcome or his lively interest in my story. When I had finished, he at once said that the constitutional argument which had been urged against the British proposal was unsound. This was encouraging but I told him that Gompers and Robinson claimed to have consulted the jurists in the American delegation and asked him if he would read the minutes of the discussions and give a considered opinion the next day. This he readily agreed to do and I left with him the necessary documents.

On returning to the Meurice the following afternoon, Frankfurter introduced me to two other American lawyers whom he had called into consultation. "On many constitutional points these gentlemen would disagree with the views I hold," he said, "but they will tell you that they entirely agree with the opinion I gave you yesterday." As soon as they had left I broached the question of his taking the matter up with President Wilson, stressing what a tragedy it would be if the project of establishing an international organization that could be of inestimable benefit to mankind were to come to naught owing to a misunderstanding on the part of the American delegation. Greatly to my disappointment, he said that personally he could take no action on the matter since he was in Paris to plead the Zionist cause; he would be seeing the President but it would be as a member of a Zionist deputation and it would be impossible for him to introduce any other subject. He was disinclined, however, to let the conversation end on this negative note and he cast about to find some alternative solution. Could I not get Lloyd George or Barnes to go to the President? I explained that Barnes was in London and that for many reasons I thought any intervention ought to be made by an

[38] Loring Cheney Christie (1885–1941) worked in the Canadian Ministry of Foreign Affairs as a legal adviser and helped Robert Borden (see Ch. 6, n. 21 above) to gain independent membership for Canada in the League of Nations. (Ed.)

[39] Felix Frankfurter (1882–1965) was Professor of Law at Harvard Law School when the United States entered the war in 1917. He chose then to serve as Special Assistant to the Secretary of War, Newton D. Baker. He was appointed to a commission to resolve major strikes threatening war production. (Ed.)

American. He agreed with this view and suggested that I should tell Shotwell and Hunter Miller about our conversation and convey to them his strong opinion that one or the other should insist on seeing President Wilson.

My talk with Shotwell and Miller seemed to take things no further. Although Miller joined with me in urging Shotwell to get the matter to the President, the latter still felt that he would be in a false position if he took such an initiative on a subject the responsibility for which had been taken away from him and placed in other hands.

However, some days later Shotwell called me up to say that he had an appointment to see Colonel House and asking me to come down to the Crillon to have a talk before the interview took place. I found him surrounded by the documents of the Commission and he told me the line he proposed to take. I doubted whether the kind of historical survey he had in mind would be appropriate and when he asked me for my opinion I suggested it would be wiser to begin at the end. "How do you mean?" he asked. "Colonel House", I replied, "is probably the most hard-pressed man in Paris at this moment. My suggestion is that you go straight to the point by showing him the paragraph in question and asking him whether there is a fundamental constitutional objection to it. My own belief is that he has never seen the text. If you can get him to read it you will save time and it will be easier to make your comments."

Shotwell thought this a good idea and he underscored the half-dozen lines of the paragraph with a blue pencil. He invited me to wait in his room till he came back and when he returned he gave me an account of what had happened.

His reception had been the reverse of cordial. Without a word of greeting, House had curtly expressed his annoyance at being bothered about the Labour Commission's affairs; Gompers, he said, had given him a full account of the situation; the proposal that an international body should be entitled to impose labour legislation on the United States was utterly preposterous; it could not be entertained for a moment and it was wasting his time to ask him to discuss it. Despite this brusque intimation that the interview could be considered at an end Shotwell put the text before him and asked him to read it. House accepted it with ill-concealed impatience and ran his eye over the marked passage. Having read it again more carefully he looked up and said in a very different tone: "This is not at all what I understood from Gompers. I don't say we could necessarily accept it as it stands, but it is something we would not be justified in refusing to discuss." He then instructed Shotwell to take the matter in hand and endeavour to work out an agreement. Shotwell was thus brought back into the picture with results which will be indicated later.

Barnes arrived from London the evening before the Commission was due to resume its meetings. [40] He, Delevingne and I dined together in the Majestic and he told us that the text in the form in which it had emerged from the Commission had received the approval both of the Cabinet and the Trades Union Congress. The Cabinet left him free to use his judgement as regards any amendments that might be put forward during the forthcoming meeting save on one point. In no circumstances would the British agree that the government delegates in the Conference should have less than 50 per cent of the votes. Barnes had drawn the special attention of the Trades Union Congress to this point and they had authorized him to state that they supported the maintenance of the 2:1:1 system.

I was alarmed to find that neither Barnes nor Delevingne seemed to anticipate any difficulty in making this view prevail. I reminded them that the 2:1:1 system had been carried by the narrowest possible margin and that the counter-proposal to give equal votes to the three categories of delegates had received important support. I added that the 1:1:1 system made a strong appeal to the workers whom the governments would have consulted and that it was by no means certain that, when the discussion was reopened, the decision would not go the other way.

"Nonsense!" said Delevingne, bristling. "The whole thing is a British proposal. When the other governments realize that the British Government has definitely decided that it cannot accept any scheme except on this condition they will give way."

"I don't think it's nonsense," I replied with some warmth. "Listen." I enumerated the countries on the Commission and gave my forecast of how they would vote. "In my opinion the 1:1:1 system will be adopted by a majority of one or two votes."

"You may be right," said Delevingne, in a tone that implied that he disagreed but was disinclined to continue the discussion, "but there is nothing we can do about it."

"You certainly can't just be sitting here and being foolishly optimistic," I countered. "You ought to go round and try to get the Polish and Czech votes. Everything will turn on the way they go."

Delevingne looked startled. "That would not be dignified," he protested.

"Dignity be damned," I burst out, and Delevingne winced at my language. "You will be a lot less dignified if Great Britain is defeated on a matter on which she has decided to risk her prestige."

---

[40] The next meeting of the Commission was fixed for 11 March 1919. The dates indicated in this and n. 43 are in line with the minutes of the Commission. Phelan appears to have condensed the period between the meetings of 11 and 19 March 1919. (Ed.)

"There is something in what Phelan says," said Barnes, who as usual was letting us fight out the argument before he made up his mind. "What do you think, Sir Malcolm?"

This was Barnes' gentle way of intimating that he had come down on my side. Delevingne, as a good civil servant, felt he must accept the Minister's view but that he was still entitled to draw attention to the practical difficulties involved.

"I'm afraid there is not much chance of doing anything at this hour, it is now half past ten," he said, and then, turning to me, continued: "Mr Barnes might lend you his car and you could try."

Delevingne, I was sure, was still unconvinced and had no desire to go driving round Paris so late at night on what he considered to be a fool's errand. His invitation to me was slightly malicious but I gladly accepted his challenge and set out alone.

It took me some time to locate Count Zoltowski, the Polish member of the Commission,[41] but I finally ran him to earth in a small and very modest hotel near the Arc de Triomphe. He had already retired for the night and he received me in pyjamas and a dressing gown. After I had apologized for disturbing him and explained the reason he promptly gave an assurance that he would vote for the British text. I had a feeling that he was taking the matter rather too lightly and I wondered what reliance I could place on a promise obtained so easily and so quickly. It was true that the night was bitterly cold and he had every reason for wishing to get back to bed in his unheated room with all possible speed. Nevertheless, I was not prepared to go without attempting to make certain that he would be as good as his word. I reminded him that he had not attended the last two sittings of the Commission but had been replaced by a substitute, Patek.[42] He replied that he would make a point of being present next morning and that if by any chance he was unable to do so, he would telephone to Patek. I was still not wholly satisfied. Telephoning in Paris was sometimes a troublesome business and Patek would have to be summoned out of the meeting to take the call. I suggested that it would be much better if Zoltowski would give me a letter which I could hand to Patek at the critical moment if that course should prove necessary. After a slight hesitation, he agreed, and, now confident that I had the Polish vote in my pocket, I set out for the Czech delegation.

---

[41] Count Jan Zoltowski was a member of the Commission on International Labour Legislation and a member of the Polish National Committee at the Paris Peace Conference in 1919. (Ed.)

[42] Stanislaw Patek (1866–1944) was the Counsellor of the Polish Court of Cassation in 1918. He was a member of the Polish National Committee at the Paris Peace Conference and of the Commission on International Labour Legislation after the departure of Count Zoltowski. He later served as Polish Minister of Foreign Affairs from 1919 to 1920. (Ed.)

I found Beneš still hard at work although it was well past midnight. He listened attentively while I explained my mission but his reply was discouraging. The conclusions arrived at by the Labour Commission had been subject to a serious examination by all the interests concerned; the workers had insisted that the 1:1:1 system be adopted, and the Ministry of Labour and the employers had concurred. In the presence of this unanimous attitude Beneš felt that it was impossible for him to take any other line. I pointed out that however much the Czech workers might be in favour of the 1:1:1 system, it could not be supposed that they would wish to maintain their view at the cost of destroying all prospect of the creation of the organization in which they desired to see it applied. It was understandable that the Czech Government should have accepted the result of the consultation which it had undertaken; but there was now an entirely new element in the situation and it would be justified in reconsidering its attitude in the light of the consequences to which it might lead. There were two possibilities: (i) the British proposal would be defeated; there would be no ILO; and the British Government would hardly feel cordial to the smaller powers who had contributed to a result which it would regard as a humiliation; (ii) the British proposal would be carried; the ILO would be saved; and the British Government would undoubtedly not be unmindful of the support it had received at a critical moment. Which of these two things would happen might well depend on the Czech vote. Rightly or wrongly, the British Government attached a fundamental importance to the matter. This had created a situation in which questions of general policy had to be given weight as well as the narrower considerations which previously might have been thought decisive.

Beneš walked up and down in silence for some moments. At last he said that he could not give me an answer without further thought. He promised, however, that he would personally attend the Commission in the morning.

When the Commission opened its sitting, Patek occupied the Polish seat and the Czech seat was empty. This was still the position when the discussion of the voting powers of the Conference delegates began. [43] Barnes made an excellent speech setting out with great force the arguments in favour of the 2:1:1 system. While this was being interpreted, I moved unobtrusively up behind Patek and placed Zoltowski's letter on the table in front of him. He opened it and, having glanced at its contents, turned round with an angry flush on his face to see who had delivered it. I hastily whispered that Zoltowski had asked me to give it to him if he found it impossible to be present.

---

[43] The meeting took place on 19 March 1919. See Shotwell (ed.): *The origins of the International Labor Organization*, Vol. 2, Document 7, pp. 291–93. (Ed.)

"Zoltowski!" he spluttered. "Who is Zoltowski?"

"I understood he was the Polish member of the Commission," I replied, very much taken aback.

"Nothing of the kind," he said indignantly. "I am the representative of Poland. Zoltowski is nobody, a mere junior official who sat here to keep my place until I could arrive."

I made a profuse apology for the mistake and expressed the hope that he would vote for the British text.

"Certainly not," he replied fuming. "Zoltowski is an idiot to think I could possibly accept it."

I looked round the room. Beneš had not put in an appearance; the vote might come at any moment; everything might depend on the Polish vote. It was a time for desperate measures and I saw one slim chance. As I moved back towards my place I stopped and whispered to Barnes, "Would you invite Patek to dine with you privately tonight? Beneš hasn't turned up and I think it's the only chance of saving the vote."

Barnes looked at me with a twinkle in his eye. "Sir Malcolm wouldn't think it very dignified," he replied, "but go ahead."

While whispering to Barnes, I had glanced at the list of speakers on Gompers' pad. Several names had been added and I could afford to wait a little before again approaching Patek and asking him to step outside for a moment as I had a personal communication for him from Mr Barnes. He had now cooled down somewhat and he agreed, though not very cordially. When I joined him in the hall I told him that Barnes was particularly interested in the Polish question (which was perfectly true) and that he had been anxious to find an opportunity for an informal discussion with a member of the Polish delegation. He hoped Patek would understand the pressure under which the British plenipotentiaries were working and would excuse an invitation at such short notice. He had been thinking of inviting Zoltowski as soon as the prospect of a free evening appeared, but he would naturally much prefer to talk with Patek, now that he realized that he had been misled about Zoltowski's position. Patek was obviously pleased and at once said he would accept. I made no mention of the vote but merely under-took to convey his reply to Mr Barnes.

About an hour later, while the discussion was still proceeding, Patek made a sign towards the door indicating that he wished to speak to me again. I followed him out and he told me that he had spoken over-hastily in announcing his opposition to the British text and that his statement had merely reflected his annoyance at Zoltowski's intervention. The discussion to which he had been listening had shown that the question was far less simple than he had supposed.

Could I repeat to him Mr Barnes' arguments which he was not sure had been adequately reproduced by the interpreter? "I think Mr. Barnes is right," he said when I had concluded my exposition. "Will you tell him privately that he can count on my support?"

Shortly after my return to the room, Beneš appeared just in time to participate in the vote which, as I had anticipated, proved to be a near thing. The 2:1:1 system was carried by 8 votes to 7. Had either the Poles or the Czechs voted the other way the British text would have been defeated. Each of the countries was often to claim in the future that without its vote there would never have been an ILO.

The equally important but more complicated issue of the American constitutional problem still remained to be dealt with. Consideration of it was postponed several times in the hope that with Shotwell's help some basis of agreement might be found. His efforts were hampered by the fact that, although he had been given a mandate to work for a solution, he had not been made a member of the Commission. In appointing Gompers and Robinson, the United States had adopted a system of representation which it was unable to alter. It could not replace either by someone competent to deal with the constitutional questions that had arisen, nor could it give them instructions on the line they were to take. Gompers had frankly stated to the Commission that, although he represented the American Government, he also represented American labour, and that if the interests of the two should conflict, he would be guided by those of the latter.

When at last the constitutional problem came up for discussion, Gompers put forward as obstinately as ever his thesis that the text proposed was in fundamental opposition with the American Constitution. The prospect of any compromise seemed as far away as ever, but Shotwell refused to give up hope and succeeded in persuading Robinson to ask that the question should be once more adjourned.

Eventually, owing to Shotwell's persistence, ingenuity and patience, the basis of a possible agreement seemed to emerge. It remained to be seen whether the principle involved could be translated into a text acceptable to the two sides and to the Commission as a whole, and this task was remitted to a committee composed of Mahaim, Delevingne and Shotwell. Delevingne was appointed reporter of the committee and his remarkable skill as a draftsman enabled it to lay before the Commission a brief report setting out with admirable clarity the modifications in the original text which would be required. These may be shortly indicated as follows. The obligation on governments to submit Conventions to their legislative authorities, and to ratify them if approved, was retained. The Conference was empowered to adopt decisions in a new form called a Recommendation which, like a Convention, had to be submitted to the national legislative authorities but, if their approval was given, the only obligation was to report the measures taken to carry it out and no question of ratification arose. This was no more than a useful addition to the powers of the Conference since there might be subjects for which a Recommendation would be more appropriate than a Convention. Lastly came a provision to meet the case of the United States and any other State in the same position. A federal State which was subject to limitations in its treaty-making power might elect to treat a Convention as a Recommendation if, and only if, the limitations applied in that particular case.

After presenting his report, Delevingne stated that the British delegation, having given the matter full consideration, had come to the conclusion that it could accept this new proposal and it therefore recommended it to the Commission for adoption. Gompers announced that the American delegation was also willing to accept it, and it was then adopted by the Commission, 10 votes being cast in favour and four delegates abstaining. The four abstaining delegates explained that their attitude was intended to mark their regret that the change had weakened the original text but that their abstention referred only to this point and not to the scheme as a whole. These declarations indicated the general desire of the governments to arrive at a unanimous conclusion and a willingness on all sides to accept with good grace the decisions taken on other points by a majority vote. There was, it seemed, good reason to suppose that, having now got over the most dangerous obstacle in its path, the Commission would be able to present a unanimous report to the peace conference.

This view proved to be overoptimistic. It left out of account Gompers' peculiar conception of his role. His declaration that he would be guided by the views of the American labour movement if they should conflict with those of his Government had not been taken seriously. It had been presumed that what he meant was that he would press his view energetically in the confident hope that his Government would follow him; but that he might go to the extreme of voting against the final report of the Commission, which all its members and his own Government were prepared to accept, seemed inconceivable.

Barnes was the first to realize that Gompers might in fact take this course. He knew a good deal about the history of the American labour movement and that Gompers had always been opposed to the idea of labour legislation. He believed that when Gompers had accepted his appointment to the Labour Commission it had been his assumption that the Commission's task was to draw up a "labour charter" to which the peace conference would give its blessing and that he had not anticipated that the Commission would put forward a scheme to secure the improvement of labour by stimulating the enactment of labour legislation.

The evening before the Commission was due to take the final vote on its report Barnes told me that it was quite possible that Gompers would vote against it. "I have done all I could to persuade him not to do so," concluded Barnes, "and I think he is hesitating and has not yet finally made up his mind. Do you think you could do anything by talking to some of his advisers?"

Gompers always arrived at the Commission escorted by half a dozen officers of the American Federation of Labor. He was punctual to the minute and I often chatted with him and his entourage while he was waiting for the Commission to assemble. I was, therefore, on friendly terms with all of the group and when I found them in the lounge of the Grand Hotel I told them frankly the object of my visit and of Barnes' concern about Gompers' attitude. We talked till well after midnight and they listened with interest to my argument that Gompers should take into account the situation in the whole trade union movement in Europe and that by throwing his weight behind the Commission's proposals he would immensely strengthen its moderate elements. When I asked them, however, if they would urge Gompers to take this line they replied that, while they would tell Gompers of the points I had made, "the Chief" would make his own decision and nothing they might say would have any influence.

I have no reason to believe that my visit in any way affected Gompers' decision but it had an importance at a much later date. It brought me into intimate contact with William Green, who was eventually to succeed Gompers as President of the American Federation of Labor, [44] and with others who were to become dominant figures in the movement, and at a critical period in the ILO's history they were to give it invaluable support.

The next morning the report of the Commission was adopted unanimously. [45] Gompers, in a moving speech, told how it was only after long hesitation that he had come to the conclusion that the scheme, if properly worked, would further the highest human interests and that, therefore, he had decided to use all his efforts to gain for it support. It was a decision requiring far greater courage than the members of the Commission could realize. Gompers was an old man who could well afford to rest on great achievements that had gained for him a respect amounting to reverence from American labour. He could foresee that he would encounter opposition and that he would be bitterly attacked for advocating principles which he had previously denounced. Such indeed proved to be the

---

[44] William Green (1870–1952) was the Secretary and Treasurer of the American Federation of Labor from 1916 to 1924 before becoming its President from 1924 to 1952. He was the Workers' Member of the Governing Body at its 51st Session in 1935. (Ed.)

[45] 24 March 1919. (Ed.)

case and it was only after a severe struggle that he was able to win a majority in favour of his policy at the next annual convention of the American Federation of Labor.

An essential element in the proposals adopted by the Commission was that the new machinery should be brought into immediate operation; the scheme therefore included the measures to be taken to enable the first International Labour Conference to meet in six months' time and fixed its agenda. In order that this programme might be carried out, it was necessary that the peace conference should give consideration to the Commission's report at the earliest possible moment.

Since Gompers had to leave for the United States, the task of securing the peace conference's approval devolved on Barnes as the Commission's Vice-President. A new crop of difficulties immediately confronted him. At the opening sitting of the peace conference, the delegations had been asked to send to the secretariat their proposals concerning labour legislation, and the documentation transmitted to the Labour Commission thus included in addition to the British proposal a number of others. These other proposals had one common feature; they all advocated the inclusion in the peace treaty of a "labour charter" proclaiming certain principles. In contrast with the British proposal, which had been carefully worked out, these other suggestions bore the marks of hasty improvisation and offered little more than a list of subjects on which some general pronouncement might be made. The decision of the Commission to take the British proposal as a basis for discussion was agreed to on the understanding that when it had been disposed of these other proposals would be considered.

Once the British scheme had been approved, no further action was logically necessary since the permanent organization for which it provided was the obvious body to deal with specific issues. It was natural, however, for the other countries to desire that, in one form or another, their proposals should find a place in the Commission's recommendations, and it was decided that an article should be included in the ILO's Constitution proclaiming that the consideration of certain principles was of special and urgent importance.

All the arguments I had originally put forward that the peace conference should not itself attempt to take decisions on labour questions now proved to be justified, for this article precipitated a crisis that threatened to wreck the whole scheme. Barnes, with his usual caution, sought the approval of the British Empire delegation before taking any further step. He assumed that this entailed little more than a formality; the scheme had been approved in its original form; the Dominions had been kept informed by my daily reports of all developments and they had formulated no observations and had raised no objections. To Barnes' dismay he now found an attitude that was frankly hostile. The Dominion delegations, led by Sir Robert Borden, expressed the most violent opposition to the principle in the Labour Charter dealing with equality of status for immigrant workers, and declared that unless this paragraph was eliminated they would refuse to approve the Commission's report.

In the angry atmosphere thus generated, other criticisms were raised which led to acrimonious disputes. Only one need be mentioned here because of its subsequent importance in the history of the ILO. Sir Robert Borden, like Barnes, was strongly in favour of the Labour Organization being an integral part of the League of Nations. The point had not been dealt with in the Labour Commission since it was assumed that it was a matter for the central drafting committee of the peace conference when it came to incorporate the Labour Convention in the peace treaty. This explanation satisfied Borden but it provoked a vigorous protest from the formidable "Billy" Hughes, who announced that Australia would have nothing to do with the ILO unless it was kept separate from the League. The reason for his attitude was that Japan was insisting on the inclusion in the Covenant of a statement about racial equality; if no such declaration was included it was probable that Japan would refuse to become a member of the League and in that case, if membership of the League and the ILO was to be identical, Japan would not be a member of the ILO. Australia attached importance to Japan's membership of the latter as affording some protection to Australian industry against the competition of low-paid Japanese labour, and New Zealand and South Africa shared this view.

Several meetings of the British Empire delegation were required before these and other difficulties could be got over – in particular it was agreed that the identity of membership in the League and the ILO should not be specified, and that Barnes might ask for approval of the organizational part of the Commission's scheme by the peace conference, the Labour Charter article being held over until a satisfactory wording could be found.

The road, however, was yet far from clear. The peace conference had been ready enough to set up the Labour Commission in January when it was anxious to give public evidence that it was at last getting down to its task. In April, labour questions were the last thing with which it wished to be bothered. The Council of Foreign Ministers, which acted as the steering committee, was unmoved by Barnes' argument that, if the first Labour Conference was to meet in October, an immediate decision of the peace conference was indispensable, and refused his request for a plenary session. Balfour, however, succeeded in securing that this decision should be reported to the Supreme Council on the ground that a question of policy was involved which only the heads of the delegations of the Great Powers could decide. It was by no means certain that President Wilson and his colleagues, harassed as they were at that time by acute disputes on most of the great political issues of the peace, would turn aside to consider a question of procedure or would be willing to overrule their foreign ministers. Barnes addressed a strong letter to Lloyd George pointing out how dangerous it would be if the impression was given that the plenipotentiaries were devoting all their attention to territorial questions and were taking no interest in matters which labour regarded as of fundamental importance. No doubt these considerations carried weight with President Wilson and the Prime Minister, and they may also have influenced Clemenceau and Orlando, who were becoming seriously concerned at the increasingly revolutionary temper of labour in their respective countries. In any case the Supreme Council decided in Barnes' favour and a plenary session was called for 11 April to receive the report of the Labour Commission.

In attempting to persuade the Foreign Ministers to agree to a plenary session, Barnes had argued that this procedure would secure for the ILO valuable publicity. Mr Lansing had sarcastically replied that he could not see what further publicity Mr Barnes was seeking to obtain,[46] seeing that the London *Times* had published the full text of the scheme the previous morning. "The workers", said Barnes dryly, "do not read *The Times*."

Now that it was certain that the approval of the peace conference would be forthcoming, Barnes wanted to be sure that the decision would be more than a formality and that its full significance would be made widely known. As the reporter of the Labour Commission, he would have the principal role at the plenary session and he could develop at such length as he pleased the argument that the ILO afforded the workers the practical machinery through which their demand for a Labour Charter could be effectively satisfied. But he knew that his was not the voice to which the left wing of the labour movement would be prepared to listen. During the war extremist elements in Great Britain had seized every opportunity to sow confusion and dissension in the ranks of labour and had sought in particular to discredit the more responsible and moderate leaders. Barnes had been one of their victims, not because they had any special animus against him but because the fact that he had taken Arthur Henderson's place in the War Cabinet lent itself to dramatic misrepresentation. On one occasion, Henderson had been kept waiting while Barnes had succeeded in dissipating a misunderstanding between him and other members of the Cabinet. Henderson had been slightly annoyed at the moment but this minor incident had no

---

[46] Robert Lansing (1864–1928) was American Secretary of State (1915–20) and headed the American Commission to Negotiate Peace in Paris in 1919. (Ed.)

connection with his resignation, which took place a fortnight later on a totally different issue. These two events were unscrupulously combined into the story that Henderson had resigned as a protest against the grossly humiliating treatment to which Labour had been subjected, and that Barnes, in agreeing to take Henderson's place in the War Cabinet, had acted as a "political blackleg". To anyone who knew Barnes the accusation that he had been guilty of dishonourable conduct was ridiculous, and in his Glasgow constituency, although the Clyde area was one of the principal centres of labour unrest, he continued to enjoy the confidence of his electors. Nevertheless, the story of "Labour on the door mat" and of Barnes' disloyal and despicable behaviour was successfully exploited up and down the country and gained so wide a credence that it possibly still survives. Those who swallowed it seem never to have asked how it was that the other half dozen Labour ministers, who were in a position to know the true facts, remained as members of the government with no sign that they had any sense of having been humiliated.

It must have been painful for Barnes to find himself, after a lifetime devoted to the trade union cause, the object of so wounding an accusation, but he was far too conscientious a man to allow himself to be distracted from his work as a minister, even in order to defend his personal reputation. The same singleness of purpose now led him to ask Emile Vandervelde to take the major role at the plenary session.

When, on the eve of the meeting, there was no news of Vandervelde's arrival from Belgium, Barnes was greatly concerned and at his request I went down to the Belgian delegation to seek information. After much telephoning to Brussels, it was discovered that he had started out by car – there was of course no railway communication: his car had broken down in the battle area where the roads were mere tracks over ruts and rubble; he was on his way back to Brussels and it would be useless for him to resume his journey in the morning since it would be impossible for him to arrive in time. I suggested that an aeroplane was the solution, but more telephoning revealed that the Belgians had no machine available and they asked whether the British could provide one. Barnes arranged that this should be done and a plane set out in the morning although the weather forecast was unfavourable. When the plenary session began there was no news of the plane's return, and it was only as Barnes was drawing to the end of his speech that a somewhat dishevelled Vandervelde took his seat at the peace conference table.

Barnes devoted his speech entirely to a matter-of-fact account of the Commission's work and to a summary of the proposals now submitted for the Conference's approval. Only in a brief introductory passage did he make any allusion to the fundamental issue before it. He had no prepared text and his phrases lacked polish; but they were not without a quality of natural eloquence and they may be quoted as a characteristic expression of the philosophy that had guided him throughout his public career:

> Some of us knew our labour at first hand, and we knew that there were many in it condemned to lives of penurious toil, relieved only by spells of compulsory idleness ... Age and want, that ill-matched pair, too often haunted the mind of the worker during his working life, and we must remember that the worker today still lives very largely in pre-war memories; he dreads return and is determined not to return to those pre-war conditions. Those pre-war experiences of labour have laid upon the world a heavy burden and a great danger. They have produced a worker who is class-centred, who ... has been deluded into the belief that the less work he does the more is left for his workmates. That feeling, and the practice based upon it, is demoralizing to the individual and harmful to the community. But it can only be eradicated by security against unemployment and improved conditions of employment. In saying that, I am not casting any stones at any class in regard to existing conditions. It has not been conscious cruelty, but rather the long arm of circumstances that has cast the devil's chain around the workmen of some countries. ... Nevertheless, it is true to say that the mass remains a misfit in their present conditions, a source of concern to all lovers of their kind and a menace to the peace of the world. It is that latter aspect of it that makes labour regulation, and I should say labour improvement, an integral and an urgent part in the work of a peace conference. [47]

After a short speech from Colliard, Vandervelde rose. There was a perceptible stir of interest round the table, for as one of the outstanding leaders of the socialist movement in Europe he was an international personality whose words would carry weight in many countries besides his own. A tall man with a somewhat stern and forbidding countenance, he had a commanding presence which was reinforced by the sharp and nasal tone of his voice and a grit of lucid expression that lent to his arguments a compelling power. The line he took was admirably calculated to secure Barnes' objective. One by one he took up the objections which had been made to the British scheme, objections which he stated he had shared, and then he gave the reasons that had led him to change his views and decide to defend energetically the Commission's conclusions. It was a masterly exposition and a brilliant achievement for a man who could have had little sleep

---

[47] Phelan quotes the beginning of G.N. Barnes' speech. For the complete address, see "Proceedings of the Preliminary Peace Conference", in Shotwell (ed.): *The origins of the International Labor Organization*, Vol. 2, Document 50, pp. 390–96. (Ed.)

during the last 36 hours, most of which had been spent in conditions of fatigue and discomfort. His closing words made a profound impression even in their translation by Paul Mantoux, [48] who could not reproduce the tone of authority which so greatly added to their force:

To sum up, I consider that the work of the Labour Commission has been one of fairness and moderation, of "give and take" and, if I may say so, one of transition between the absolutism of the employers, which was the rule of yesterday, and the sovereignty of labour, which I am ardently convinced will be the rule of tomorrow. For passing from the one to the other there are many roads: some are beset with violence and insurrection; others, on the contrary, give just as quick a journey, but without clashes and shocks. If I dared express my thoughts in a tangible way, I should say there are two methods of making the revolution which we feel is happening throughout the world, the Russian and the British method. It is the British method which has triumphed in the Labour Commission; it is one which I greatly prefer, and it is for that reason that with all my heart I support the conclusions of my friend, Mr Barnes, in expressing the hope that they may be accepted by the Conference, and that the events of today will show that the working classes, having been one of the decisive factors in winning the war, shall receive their due recompense at the moment in which we are about to make peace. [49]

There were a number of other speeches and then Barnes moved a resolution approving the Constitution of the ILO, requesting the governments to nominate their representatives on the Organizing Committee, [50] and authorizing that committee to proceed at once with its work. This resolution was adopted unanimously and by that act the peace conference brought the ILO into being.

The decision of the peace conference on 11 April 1919 marked the beginning of a completely new phase in the history of the ILO and, incidentally, resulted in a change of my functions that subsequently entitled me to claim that I was the first appointee to the international civil service.

---

[48] Paul Mantoux (1877–1956) was a French historian. He acted as an interpreter for Georges Clemenceau at the Paris Peace Conference and was co-founder with William Rappard (see n. 54 below) of the Graduate Institute of International Studies in Geneva. (Ed.)

[49] Phelan quotes the end of Vandervelde's address. For the complete address, see "Proceedings of the Preliminary Peace Conference", in Shotwell (ed.): *The origins of the International Labor Organization*, Vol. 2, Document 50, pp. 398–402. (Ed.)

[50] The Organizing Committee was created to help the US Government prepare the documents to be submitted to the First Session of the ILC, scheduled to take place in Washington, DC in October 1919. The Committee, composed of seven members, met for the first time on 14 April 1919. Its tasks were to collect and synthesize information about labour issues and to deal with the Conference's logistical questions such as the setting up of the procedures, the organization of the staff and preparations for the election of the Governing Body. The Committee was disbanded in October 1919 when the Conference began. (Ed.)

Years later, when a pension scheme was set up for the officials of the League, the ILO and the International Court of Justice, the date from which service should be counted as pensionable had to be determined in each case. It was taken for granted by the pensions administration that the earliest date applicable was that on which the Secretary-General of the League had assumed his functions but, on examination, the claim that my service was antecedent to that of Sir Eric Drummond had to be admitted.[51] I doubt, however, whether the transition from national to international service made any impression on me at the time, for it was accompanied by no formalities of any kind.

Since there was all too little time to prepare the ILO's first conference, it was imperative that the Organizing Committee should be set up at once. Butler was so busily engaged at the Ministry in London that he had been unable to come to Paris even for the plenary session of the peace conference, and it was to me that Delevingne turned to arrange for the Organizing Committee's first meeting. This was easy to secure as the governments concerned chose as their representative members of their delegations in Paris, namely Delevingne (Great Britain), Shotwell (United States), Fontaine (France), di Palma Castiglione (Italy),[52] Oka (Japan),[53] Mahaim (Belgium) and Rappard (Switzerland).[54] All, save the last named, had been associated with the Labour Commission and I knew them quite well; Rappard I also knew, for, because of Switzerland's historic part in the earlier efforts at international labour legislation, he had followed the proceedings at Paris on behalf of his Government and had been in frequent contact with our group at the Majestic. Fontaine was chosen as Chairman, Butler was appointed Secretary and I Assistant Secretary. It was decided that the Committee's headquarters

[51] Sir (James) Eric Drummond (1876–1951) was a British diplomat attached to the British delegation to the Paris Peace Conference. He was the first Secretary-General of the League of Nations (1919–33). (Ed.)

In July 1932, after several months of deliberations, Phelan was informed that, for pension purposes, his services should be counted as having begun on 14 April 1919 – the date of the first Meeting of the Organizing Committee. For further information, see League of Nations Pension Fund, Personal File of Member: Edward Joseph Phelan, No. 708, ILO Historical Archives. (Ed.)

[52] Guglielmo Emanuele di Palma Castiglione (1879–1947) was technical adviser on questions of labour and emigration to the Italian delegation at the Peace Conference in Paris. After serving as delegate of the Italian Government for the First Session of the ILC in Washington, DC, he went on to work at the ILO from 1920 as Chief of the Intelligence and Liaison Division and from 1933 as Assistant Director until his retirement in 1937. (Ed.)

[53] Minoru Oka (1873–1939) was Japanese delegate to the Paris Peace Conference and the First Session of the ILC in Washington, DC in 1919. He was Director of Commerce and Industrial Affairs in the Ministry of Agriculture and Commerce and later the Director of the Bureau of Commerce in Tokyo. (Ed.)

[54] William Emmanuel Rappard (1883–1958) was Professor of Economic History at the University of Geneva and co-founder of the Graduate Institute of International Studies in Geneva. He attended the First Session of the ILC in Washington, DC, was Swiss Government delegate to the ILC from 1947 to 1956, and served as President of the 34th Session of the ILC in 1951. (Ed.)

should be established in London and that it would reassemble in that city a couple of weeks later when the secretariat would have been able to lay before it detailed plans for its work.

On arrival in London I went to see Butler. The original demobilization scheme had given rise to such widespread protest that political pressure for its revision could not be resisted, and his whole attention had to be devoted to the complicated problems thus precipitated. On the other hand, Delevingne had written to him stressing the urgency of preparing the work of the Organizing Committee. Delevingne's wishes could not be lightly disregarded but they, too, raised problems of no little complexity. Not only had the precise task of the Committee to be defined, but no international funds existed from which expenditure for its operations could be met. Butler, therefore, applied to the Treasury, which placed £1,000 at his disposal as a loan to be eventually repaid, and from the Office of Works he obtained office accommodation in 53 Parliament Street, almost next door to Montagu House. Having informed me of these preliminary arrangements and added that I could use the services of the Ministry for such administrative purposes as the engagement of staff, he left me to my own devices, saying that if I met with any difficulty I could apply to him but obviously hoping that I would not disturb him unless there was real necessity. Much pleased at his confidence in giving me such a free hand and more than a little impressed by the responsibilities involved, I walked down Whitehall to install myself in my new quarters. Here, I immediately met my first problem. I had assumed that all I needed to do was to survey the different rooms, make my choice of the one I would occupy myself, and settle down to plan the staff I should require. This happy vision was dispelled when, on entering my new domain, I found it was fully occupied and humming with activity. The senior official readily admitted that he had been given notice to vacate the premises, but there were a great many matters to be cleared up, and it would be about a fortnight before he could actually move out. I knew by now how this kind of obstacle could be dealt with. I telephoned to the private secretary of the Minister of Works and explained that any delay in making the premises available would prevent the execution of a decision of the peace conference to which the Prime Minister attached the greatest importance. This produced the desired result with even greater rapidity than I had expected. The next morning the rather dazed occupants were hustled out along with their files and papers and I was able to take possession at the beginning of the afternoon.

It was less easy to decide what precisely the Committee should set out to do. The rules under which the ILO would work were clearly laid down in its Constitution, but the provisions for bringing it into operation had been added at the last minute and they were by no means free from ambiguity. The United States was "to make arrangements for the convening and the organization" of the first Conference, to be held in Washington in October, and it was "to be assisted in the preparation of documents for submission to the Conference" by the Organizing Committee. On the face of it, this wording entrusted all the responsibility to the United States and gave the Committee only a subsidiary role. On the other hand, the peace conference had instructed the Committee "to proceed with its work at once" and this decision seemed to entitle the Committee to act independently, at all events until the United States should actually convene the Conference. The first thing to be done, therefore, was to inform the governments officially of the Committee's existence and ask for their collaboration and assistance.

As I set to work to draft an appropriate letter, I realized that its contents required very careful consideration. It would put into operation for the first time some parts of a new piece of international machinery. The action governments might take would be important from the point of view of the Committee's immediate task, but it might well have a far greater importance in creating precedents which would profoundly influence the ILO's future methods. The letter would have to be addressed to the ministers of foreign affairs of the different countries. It could not be taken for granted that they would know much about the ILO and the departments called on to provide the information the Committee required might know nothing at all. In order that proper consideration might be given to the Committee's communication, it was essential that governments should realize that supplying technical information to the Committee was only the first step in a series of operations in which they would be concerned and in which their interests would be involved. In order that they might have the full picture before them, it would be necessary to enclose with the letter the complete text of the ILO's Constitution, and copies, in French and English, must at once be printed for the purpose.

Against this background it might be hoped that governments would reply promptly and with a due sense of responsibility to the questionnaire dealing with the different points on the agenda of the Conference. These asked for all available information on existing legislation and practice concerning hours of labour, measures for preventing or providing against unemployment, the employment of women, the employment of children and the generalization of the Berne Conventions of 1906.

The drafting of these questionnaires was undertaken by the appropriate technical sections of the Home Office and the Ministry of Labour. Fontaine and Delevingne could be counted on to submit them to a competent scrutiny and my only concern was to make certain that they would be ready in time. I attached, however, the greatest importance to the paragraph in the letter referring to them. Experience in Paris afforded a convincing demonstration of the advantages of furnishing to a committee or conference a carefully prepared text as a basis for its discussion and, if this procedure could be accepted for the Washington Conference, the likelihood of securing positive and practical decisions would be greatly enhanced. I, therefore, inserted a passage in my draft saying that the Organizing Committee would draw up suggestions for Conventions or Recommendations, based on the information received, for submission to the Conference as a basis for discussion. I hoped I could persuade Delevingne and Fontaine that the Committee ought to accept this responsibility and, if they agreed, I was pretty sure that their colleagues would also approve. When, in due course, the draft letter was submitted to the Committee the suggestion encountered no objections, and thus was initiated a procedure which became a regular feature of all subsequent meetings of the International Labour Conference and which undoubtedly contributed to their remarkable success.

I, of course, kept Butler informed of all that was going on. A messenger went back and forth between my office and his several times a day. Every proposed action of any importance was submitted to him in a file and all he had to do was to add his initials, if he approved, or indicate in a short minute what other course should be followed. The fact that he invariably gave his approval by no means signified that he did not take his responsibilities seriously, but only that he saw no occasion to intervene so long as he was satisfied that things were going all right.

After the Committee had approved the letter and the questionnaires, the subsequent steps to be taken were clear. The replies would have to be analysed and compared and, in the light of the information they furnished, a number of texts for submission to the Conference would have to be drawn up. This work would throw a heavy burden both on such technical and translating staff as it might be possible to extemporize and on the Committee itself, but all their efforts would be wasted unless governments could be afforded sufficient time to consider seriously the proposals made and frame instructions to their delegates. No air service for the carriage of either mails or passengers, of course, existed; it would take several weeks for the Committee's documents to reach the more distant overseas countries and an equally lengthy period must be allowed for their delegates' journey to Washington. The only possible way of planning a satisfactory timetable was to decide that the Committee's questionnaires and the text to be discussed by the Conference should be communicated to these countries by cable. This solution, however, presented Butler with an awkward financial problem. He was reluctant to appeal to the Treasury, which had a traditional dislike for expensive means of communication, and to which he must soon apply for a substantial loan with which to finance the expenditure on the Washington Conference. I suggested that the Foreign Office might help and he authorized me to approach that department and also the Colonial Office which might be prepared to send similar cables to the Dominions.

At the Foreign Office, I encountered no difficulty. Cabling was a commonplace procedure, and the magic words "peace conference" were a sufficient explanation of my request. The Colonial Office, however, was less receptive, and the Permanent Secretary to whom the question had to be referred was both annoyed and embarrassed. How, he asked, could he possibly authorize the sending of cables running to thousands of pounds when he had just been appointed to an interdepartmental committee to enforce a drastic reduction in official cabling, which was choking the wires and delaying commercial cables to an extent that had given rise to violent protests? The peace conference argument produced no effect, and it was only when I pointed out that Australia and New Zealand, whose prime ministers were keenly interested in the ILO, would resent being less favourably treated than other countries, that he at last grudgingly consented.

The governments, on the whole, replied with extraordinary promptitude to the questionnaires – no doubt the magic of the peace conference was still potent.

About this time the whole success of the Conference seemed gravely menaced by the action of the International Federation of Trade Unions (IFTU), the Executive Committee of which adopted a resolution demanding that Germany and Austria be entitled to membership in the ILO and that the workers' delegates to the Conference be nominated in agreement with the trade union movements in each country affiliated to the IFTU, and stating that, unless these demands were complied with, none of their affiliated unions would send representatives to the meeting in Washington. A deputation from the Executive Committee of the IFTU came to London to lay these demands before Barnes; in addition to the Frenchman Léon Jouhaux it included the Belgian trade unionist Corneille Mertens,[55] and the Dutch Jan Oudegeest and Edo Fimmen,[56] whose names were

---

[55] Léon Jouhaux (1879–1954) was an influential French trade unionist and Secretary-General of the Confédération générale du travail. He was a member of the Commission on International Labour Legislation in 1919 and subsequently the French workers' delegate to the First Session of the ILC. Elected workers' member of the ILO Governing Body in 1919, he remained on the Governing Body and served as French workers' delegate to the ILC until 1953. In 1951 he was awarded the Nobel Peace Prize.

Corneille Mertens (1879–1951), Vice-President of the International Federation of Trade Unions in 1919, was workers' delegate for Belgium at the ILC from 1919 to 1937 and Workers' Vice-President of the ILC in 1924 and 1936. He was also a workers' member of the Governing Body from 1928 to 1940. (Ed.)

[56] Jan Oudegeest (1870–1950), a Dutch trade unionist, was workers' delegate for the Netherlands to the First Session of the ILC in Washington, DC in 1919 and a member of the ILO Governing Body from 1919 to 1928. He was also Secretary of the International Federation of Trade Unions.

Eduard Carl "Edo" Fimmen (1881–1942) was Secretary of the Netherlands Federation of Trade Unions from 1916 to 1919. In July 1919 he served alongside Oudegeest as Secretary of the International Federation of Trade Unions. (Ed.)

familiar to me but whom I had not yet met. They were much taken aback when Barnes explained that there was nothing he could do to give them satisfaction since the Constitution of the ILO had fixed the membership of the Organization and the procedure by which the workers' delegates to the Conference were to be chosen, and, since the Constitution was part of the peace treaty, it was impossible for him or for anybody else to alter its provisions. Nevertheless, they persisted in their demands and in the threat that, unless some way of meeting them was found, their affiliated organizations would boycott the Conference.

Delevingne was greatly concerned and inclined to favour a proposal then being mooted that, for other reasons, the Conference should be postponed. Barnes, however, was determined to go ahead. He believed that it would be better to get the ILO started even if the IFTU carried out its threat, and he was convinced that once it was certain that the Conference would be held, the workers would realize that it was not in their interests to abstain from participation. He counted on the British trade union movement to give a lead in this direction and his judgement proved to be correct. He had throughout consulted the British Trades Union Congress and, as already recounted, they had approved all the steps he had taken in Paris. The Trades Union Congress in those days was a loose consultative body which was far from possessing the authority it has today. In the IFTU, the British unions were represented not by the Congress but by the British Trades Union Federation, a body that comprised only three or four unions, though they were important, and which was possessed of considerable funds and therefore capable of strike action if necessary. Barnes had rightly seen that the TUC was in reality the more representative body and his foresight in consulting it was now fully justified. It was not in any way bound by the decisions of the IFTU and it readily accepted the Government's invitation to nominate a delegate and advisers to the Washington Conference. This broke the line and the trade union movement in other countries followed suit. The IFTU did, however, obtain an important measure of satisfaction on its second demand. Jouhaux took the question of the admission of Germany and Austria to Clemenceau and the latter got the Supreme Council to declare that the decision should be left to the Washington Conference. That Conference did admit Germany and Austria to membership of the ILO but the decision it took had a far wider importance for it created a precedent which, although disputed, allowed the ILO to exert independence in admitting other States not members of the League of Nations.

During the earlier stages of the Organizing Committee's work, the fact that the United States took no action, save for the appointment of Shotwell as one of the Committee's members, caused no concern. The Committee was able to proceed with its task unhampered by any discussion of its precise mandate, and the confusion that might have arisen, had the governments received conflicting communications from two different sources, was avoided. As time went on, however, the complete absence of any sign of activity in Washington, and the news of the growing opposition in the United States to President Wilson and to the peace treaty, became disquieting. At last on 11 August the State Department made a communication to governments stating that "the President of the United States hereby convenes the first meeting of the annual Labour Conference to assemble in Washington at noon on 20 October 1919".

The Conference having thus been officially convened, I assumed that all cause for any major anxiety had been removed. I had yet to realize that no international agency, however limited and technical its activities, could hope to remain unaffected by the strains and stresses in the world around it. Nobody, save the little group with which I was working, worried about the effect which the political storm in the United States might have on the ILO as such. But there was widespread concern in influential quarters over the disastrous results which the failure of the ILO Conference might have on the fortunes of the League of Nations. The ILO was an autonomous body but it was nonetheless "part of the machinery of the League". The Washington Conference would be the first attempt to apply the League principles in one particular sphere. The prospect that these principles should be put to the proof in an atmosphere of violent political controversy of which the League was the centre aroused grave apprehension. The success of the Conference would be hopelessly compromised from the start, its purposes would be misrepresented, its mistakes exploited and its failure held up as conclusive evidence that the whole League idea was a dangerous dream.

These apprehensions led to the conclusion that the meeting of the ILO Conference ought to be postponed, and a suggestion to this effect was conveyed to President Wilson through an American channel. The Organizing Committee was again plunged into uncertainty until the President's reply was made known. It was categorical; authority to fix the date of the Conference had been entrusted to the United States which alone had the power to postpone it; in the exercise of that authority it had convened the Conference for 20 October and that decision stood; the Government of the United States would cooperate in every way possible to make the Conference a success whether it actually participated or not.

Meanwhile, the drafts to be discussed by the Conference had been dispatched to the governments, the main part of the Committee's documentary task had thus been completed, and it turned its attention to other questions which were, perhaps, not strictly within its terms of reference but which now had assumed an urgent character. The composition of the Conference was unprecedented, its agenda was heavy, the questions to be discussed were complicated and agreement might not be easy to secure. It was, therefore, important to provide that the machinery of the Conference should work smoothly and that, so far as possible, the task of the delegates should be facilitated by adequate secretarial arrangements, in particular for translation and interpretation. The experience of the peace conference had shown that effective arrangements of this kind could not be extemporized by drawing on such help as the delegations themselves could provide, and it was essential that staff with the necessary linguistic qualifications should be recruited without delay. These considerations raised the question of the appointment of the Secretary-General of the Conference, an appointment which the United States, as responsible for the organization of the Conference, might well have claimed should go to an American. The political circumstances, however, were such that Washington was by no means anxious to advance its claim and the Committee's suggestion that Butler should be considered for the post was readily approved.

To Butler, therefore, fell the responsibility of planning the Conference secretariat. Its actual recruitment, however, could not be centralized; stenographic and typing staff to work in English would be obtainable in Washington; the corresponding staff for work in French could only be secured in France, and Fontaine undertook to engage them; bilingual staff such as interpreters, translators and people capable of acting as secretaries of committees could best be sought in London, either directly or by borrowing from the League secretariat which was in process of formation. Little time was available for this last type of recruitment, but this did not greatly matter since experienced staff did not exist and the number of people who could be found possessing the necessary linguistic qualifications and appearing capable of adapting themselves to the work they would be required to undertake was so limited as to leave little choice. More difficult were the purely practical problems of fixing rates of salary, subsistence allowances in the United States and arranging for transatlantic passages; but finally these matters were disposed of and the next phase of our operations began.

With the convocation of the Conference, Washington had become the obvious centre at which all the final preparations for the meeting should be concentrated, and it was accordingly decided that the headquarters of the Organizing Committee should be transferred to that city, and that Butler and I should proceed to the United States as soon as possible.

[Editor's note: There is a break here in the author's manuscript, probably reflecting his intention to devote a chapter to the First Session of the International Labour Conference held in Washington, DC in 1919. This chapter, however, was never written. There are two accounts of the Conference by participants which remain of interest. Harold Butler, who was Secretary-General of the Conference, wrote about

the Conference's significance for the development of the ILO.[57] *Hector Hetherington wrote in 1920 at Harold Butler's request a more detailed and factual contemporary account.*[58] *Phelan's story resumes immediately after the Washington Conference.]*

---

[57] Shotwell (ed.): *The origins of the International Labor Organization*, Vol. 1, pp. 305–30.
[58] H.J.W. Hetherington: *International labour legislation* (London, Methuen and Co., 1920).

Albert Thomas takes over 7

The Treaty of Versailles came into force on 10 January 1920. This event, in the opinion of legal authorities, *ipso facto*, validated the decisions of the Washington Conference; and the Governing Body, in virtue of the powers delegated to it, declared the Conference closed. Thus, when Albert Thomas took office as Director on 27 January 1920,[1] not only was the structure of the ILO complete, but the Organization had acquired its full legal character.

This development had more than a merely technical significance. The Organizing Committee had, it is true, received from the peace conference an international mandate; and, in a sense, from the moment the Committee began its work the ILO came into existence. In fact, the Committee was little more than an international label attached to the continuance of the activities of the labour section of the British delegation at the peace conference; Barnes, Delevingne and Butler shaped and controlled all its decisions – premises, secretarial and expert staff were provided from British resources. In Washington, the predominant role of the British was less in evidence; other delegations took an active part in the proceedings and had their share in formulating the decisions arrived at; but, here again, British leadership, organizing ability and financial assistance provided the essential basis on which all else was built. The period during which the infant ILO had taken its first steps with this parental support was now over. With the

---

[1] Albert Thomas (1878–1932), a French socialist politician, was appointed Under-Secretary of State for Artillery and Munitions in May 1915, becoming Minister of Munitions the following year. At its First Session in 1919, the ILO Governing Body elected Thomas over Butler as first Director of the ILO. He remained Director until his death in 1932. (Ed.)

ratification of the Treaty it had come of age and, henceforth, it must stand on its own feet and fend for itself.

For this reason January 1920 is a decisive date in the ILO's history. But it is also important as marking the emergence of a new conception of the ILO's mission and of the methods by which it should pursue its aims.

Albert Thomas had taken no part in the ILO's creation, no part in the work of the Organizing Committee, no part in the Washington Conference. When he was approached by the workers to allow his name to be put forward for the directorship his knowledge of the Organization was almost nil. I once asked him if he had followed the various stages of its development. "No," he replied. "Each of the leaders of the socialist party in the Chamber of Deputies was responsible for studying one particular aspect of the peace negotiations; my assignment concerned the application of the principle of self-determination, and the ILO was the affair of one of my colleagues." When he came to look at the ILO, he had therefore no preconceived ideas; he saw it, so to speak, from without and not from within; and in this different perspective he saw it as something much bigger than its authors had ever imagined.

The story of how he led others to share this larger vision and how he transformed it into a reality is a story which I have told in *Yes and Albert Thomas*.[2] It is not a story that can be summarized; Albert Thomas' many extraordinary qualities and the power and charm of his personality cannot be conveyed in a few short paragraphs; no real picture either of the man himself or of his immense achievement can be given without recounting in circumstantial detail incidents that throw into relief the problems that faced him and the courage and resource he displayed in their solution. Here, I can only give a brief indication of the difference between his view of the ILO and that which prevailed before he came on the scene.

The authors of the Constitution started from the principle that "the failure of any nation to adopt humane conditions of labour is an obstacle in the way of other nations who desire to improve conditions in their own countries".[3] This approach had the advantage of being directed to a specific problem and of leading logically to the proposal that measures should be taken to secure that unfair economic competition, based on inferior conditions of labour, should not interfere with the adoption of some desired reform. The ILO, novel though some of its features might be, seemed to involve no revolutionary departure; it was regarded as a practical method

---

[2] E.J. Phelan: *Yes and Albert Thomas* (London, Cresset Press, 1936). (Ed.)

[3] See the Preamble of the ILO Constitution. This paragraph of the Preamble was not amended in 1946. (Ed.)

whereby the process of international labour legislation, hitherto intermittent and dependent on the chance initiative of some individual government, should henceforth become a regular and continuous international activity.

This limited conception of the ILO in no way diminishes the importance of what its authors accomplished. Had Albert Thomas never come into the picture, the ILO would, nonetheless, have constituted an immense advance in international organization. Moreover, had it not existed, there would have been nothing to set alight the flame of Albert Thomas' imagination, and no solid foundation from which he could have started to create an institution with more comprehensive aims.

For Albert Thomas international labour legislation was only one element in a problem that required international consideration. He was keenly aware that social forces were stirring in Europe with a new intensity. He was aware, too, that most of their energy was being dissipated in confusion and conflict with results that might well prove disastrous. If, however, that energy could be channelled into the ILO and there be concentrated on concrete objectives, doctrinaire differences would tend to become of secondary importance and real social progress could be achieved. For this to happen, the trade unions – for it was to the trade unions more than to the political movements that he attached importance – must be led to share his belief.

In the existing revolutionary temper of labour, *International Labour Legislation* was hardly the battle cry to which the workers could be expected to respond with passionate enthusiasm. They were by no means satisfied that the ILO had made, or could make, any substantial contribution to their aims; at best it was no more than a sideshow and, as Léon Jouhaux had thundered in Washington, it fell far short of what they demanded. In the desire to show that the activities of the ILO were complementary to those of the League of Nations and, therefore, deserving of the popular support which the League idea had called forth, there had been inserted in the Preamble to the ILO's Constitution a rhetorical phrase which asserted that universal peace could be established only if it was based on social justice.

Albert Thomas seized on these words; here was the battle cry which he needed; here was a principle that transcended doctrinaire differences; here was the appeal to which rival movements could rally while still maintaining their particular views of the objective to be ultimately attained. Straightaway he raised over the ILO a new banner on which was boldly inscribed *Social Justice*.

The most striking evidence of the novelty of this view of the ILO's mission at that time is furnished by the fact that his action attracted no attention. Although, in addressing the Governing Body after his election, and in the first documents he laid before it as Director, he emphasized that this was the principle by which the ILO should be inspired, his statements excited no remark. No doubt members of the Governing Body rated them as a piece of empty political eloquence devoid of any practical implications. The workers were not to be moved from their luke-warm, suspicious attitude by a mere declaration; the employers' and the government representatives, satisfied that they understood the Constitution of the Organization better than this newcomer, took it for granted that, when he knew more about it, he would realize that decisions on policy lay with the Conference and the Governing Body and that the function of the Office was limited to providing the administrative and technical assistance those authorities might require.

In arriving at this comforting conclusion, members of the Governing Body made the mistake of thinking that Albert Thomas' knowledge of the Constitution was defective. In fact, he was fully cognizant of the constitutional position; he was satisfied that the Constitution as it stood would serve his purpose; he had no desire to amend or evade its allocation of responsibilities; and, far from wanting to challenge the powers of the Conference and the Governing Body, he wanted to enlarge them. No objection could be taken to his assertion that the ILO was important; but what startled the members of the Governing Body was that he made the assertion to the Supreme Council in a letter addressed to Lloyd George in which he vigorously protested that the Council had no right to occupy itself with a matter the ILO had already taken in hand. The issue later ceased to have any practical significance but that did not alter the fact that the ILO had dared to call the Supreme Council to account, and that the Prime Ministers of Great Britain, France and Italy had been obliged to spend a whole afternoon discussing the ILO's intervention. This was the first of a number of interventions that served to demonstrate to governments the existence of a new international organization whose rights could not be bypassed or ignored; and which served also to make the ILO itself conscious of responsibilities that it must not evade or allow to go by default.

Many who watched these bold initiatives were inclined to discount their undeniable success. They admitted that Albert Thomas was "putting the ILO on the map" and securing for it a measure of public attention such as it had not hitherto received. But in their view, the claims he advanced were ridiculously exaggerated; the ILO could never hope to occupy effectively territory so extensive; and when this became apparent he would be compelled to abandon his overweening ambitions and restrict his efforts to the more modest task for which the Organization had been created.

They were wrong in supposing that he underestimated the importance of the ILO's work in the field of international labour legislation. On the contrary, he attached to it a special value because it provided a concrete example of what could be achieved by organized international effort. Where he differed from his critics was in his belief that international labour legislation was not an end in itself but only a step towards a greater achievement which the ILO's Constitution in nowise forbade and which it was urgently necessary to pursue. He knew full well that his initiatives would not bear fruit unless the Organization could be brought to understand his aim and furnish the support which alone could make its achievement possible. He set out to enlist that support where its real source was to be found, namely in the member States.

Nowadays, when regular air communications link all parts of the globe, it is difficult to realize the difficulties which this plan presented. In the 1920s they might well have been deemed insuperable; journeys that can now be accomplished in a matter of hours had then to be counted in terms of weeks or even months; there were areas where railroad communications were subject to interruption, sea routes over which steamer services were slow and irregular. Faced with these obstacles, it might have been supposed that he would have limited his programme to countries that were actually members of the Organization but he did not hesitate to expand it to countries that were outside the ILO. Visits to Russia, the United States, and to as many colonial territories as possible were included in a plan that he had almost completely fulfilled when he died in 1932.[4]

This vast programme of personal visits to every country on the globe illustrates how far his imagination ranged and the constructive spirit by which it was dominated. But before he could begin to seek support for the ILO in the member States he had first of all to tackle the problems that faced him at the centre of the Organization. With his appointment as Director, the constitutional structure of the ILO had been completed but, though the structure was complete, it was empty. There was a Director but there was no office for him to direct. All the provisional arrangements for staff, premises and finance which had been brought into being for the Washington Conference had now lapsed and a permanent machine had to be built to replace them.

Albert Thomas had prepared his plan. After providing for a central secretariat to deal with finance, personnel, translation and interpreting, typing and a registry, it proposed that the Office should be organized in three divisions, namely the Diplomatic Division, the Political Division and the Scientific Division. These titles sounded somewhat pretentious in English but in French they

---

[4] Albert Thomas' missions outside Europe took him to Canada and the United States (1922–23); Brazil, Argentina and Chile (1925); and the Soviet Union, Manchuria, China, Japan, Dutch East Indies, Indochina and Egypt (1928–29). (Ed.)

aptly described their respective functions; the Diplomatic Division was to deal with governments, the Political Division with workers' and employers' organizations, and the Scientific Division with publications, statistics and information; in addition there were to be a number of technical sections to deal with specific technical questions such as safety, industrial hygiene, etc.

The Organizing Committee had drawn up a more modest scheme, but this Albert Thomas had quietly shelved and no more was heard of it; the Governing Body very wisely took the line that, subject to its financial control, the Director was entitled to organize his staff in the way he thought best.

Once the Governing Body had given its approval to his proposals, Albert Thomas appointed me as Chief of the Diplomatic Division. I was naturally greatly pleased since he might well have hesitated to confer such wide responsibilities on a young man only 31 years of age. Those responsibilities were wide indeed: they covered the organization of all meetings of the Governing Body and of the Conference, all relations with governments, the League of Nations and other international bodies, all questions concerning the ratification and application of Conventions and, in general, all questions arising out of the ILO's Constitution. Although I was surprised, as indeed I had a reason to be, at the scope of such an assignment, I was not dismayed. I felt that I knew how these matters should be dealt with and I had no doubt of my ability to handle them to my own satisfaction.

This self-confidence was fortunate, for Albert Thomas unexpectedly asked me to continue in charge of the ILO's finances and I had immediately to set to work to translate his scheme of organization into terms of a budget that the Governing Body could approve for transmission to the League of Nations, from which the ILO must now draw its funds. I had no claim to financial knowledge but my experience at the Washington Conference gave me a basis on which to construct estimates for other conferences and for the work entailed in their preparation.

The Governing Body ended its meeting on 28 January 1920 and Butler and I at once returned to London where Albert Thomas had decided to establish the ILO's temporary headquarters. This decision, based on his desire to protect himself in some degree from the pressure to which he knew he would be subjected about French appointments to the staff, was to me particularly welcome. I had a formidable task in front of me which it would be easier to tackle in London than in Paris. The agenda of the second meeting of the Conference which was to open in Genoa on 15 June comprised four items relating to seamen.[5] On each of these

---

[5] Second Session of the ILC, Genoa, 15 June–10 July 1920. (Ed.)

items, questionnaires had to be addressed to the governments; reports, based on their replies, had to be compiled and texts prepared which the Conference could take as the basis of its discussions; these documents had to be produced in both French and English. This task was similar to that which I had previously performed for the Organizing Committee, but there was an important difference in that I could not now call on British Government departments for the assistance they had then provided, the full value of which I now appreciated. I had now to negotiate printing contracts, obtain supplies of paper and make my own arrangements for the distribution of the volumes as they issued from the press.

Two meetings of the Governing Body, to be held on 22 March and 8 June, required the production of still other reports and concurrently with all this, the official correspondence of the Office had to be dealt with, the secretariat of the Conference had to be organized, and Governing Body decisions carried out. This list, which could be extended, will give some idea of the burden thrown on the Diplomatic Division for which, apart from myself and Camille Pône, a staff had yet to be recruited. Certainly, the period February–May 1920 was the busiest I ever experienced. In the circumstances nothing could go forward smoothly, any breakdown in one operation – and breakdowns were inevitable – threatened to disorganize all the others, and hardly a day passed without the necessity for some emergency adjustment. If finally everything was accomplished within the time limits that had to be respected, it was owing to the fact that I knew exactly what required to be done, that Albert Thomas (whose final approval was necessary for every document) never held anything up, and that, partly by good luck and perhaps partly by good judgement, I managed to collect as the first members of the Diplomatic Division a small staff of remarkably high quality which responded with enthusiasm to the calls made upon it.

Other activities were, of course, being undertaken at this time; other parts of the Office were beginning to take shape; and other sections of the staff were being recruited. These operations were not my direct concern but I was able to follow their development as a member of Albert Thomas' Rapport, a meeting held every day when he was in London, attended by Butler, myself, Thomas' Chef de Cabinet (principal private secretary), and such other officials as might be called in for the discussion of any particular question. It was at these meetings that Albert Thomas expounded his lines of policy and told us of one or other initiative of his own such as his protest to the Supreme Council to which I have already referred. To me this was a novel procedure but I soon realized its practical advantages. I was fully informed of all that was going on and, in consequence, it was often unnecessary to ask for instructions which, had they been given by a written minute on a specific point, would have been far less illuminating; the knowledge I acquired at these meetings was of particular value in the preparation of papers for the Governing Body, and the time saved was of importance.

Time, indeed, was my essential problem and the difficulties to which it gave rise could, as a rule, be overcome by some exceptional personal effort which, with a youthful enjoyment in my responsibility, I was always ready to furnish. There was one matter, however, where this solution was of no avail and where my patience was sorely tried. So far as the control of expenditure was concerned, my Washington experience once again stood me in good stead, and I had the assistance of an able accountant in the person of F.M. Collins,[6] to whom I could safely leave the work of paying salaries, making other payments, and the book-keeping operations involved.

As regards income I had assumed that no particular difficulty need now be anticipated; the Treaty of Versailles had come into force and the League was under the obligation to pay the expenses of the ILO. This view proved somewhat over-optimistic. The League Treasurer, Sir Herbert Ames,[7] was well aware of the legal position, but he drew my attention to the wording of the Treaty which provided that the ILO's expenses were to be paid "out of the general funds of the League". No such funds, he added, yet existed since the Assembly had not yet met and no budget had been voted.

This unpromising opening to our first conversation came to me rather as a shock.

"But you must have funds," I protested. "The Secretary-General has engaged staff, and presumably that staff is being paid."

"No," he replied sadly. "I have no funds. I have only debts and overdrafts."

"Well," I said, "I've got to pay my salaries. Another little overdraft won't do you any harm."

This time it was Sir Herbert who was shocked. "You don't seem to under-stand," he said in a tone of reproof, "that an overdraft is a serious matter – a very serious matter indeed."

I realized I had made a bad mistake. No one speaking to a banker should ever refer with anything approaching flippancy to an overdraft, especially if it happens to be the banker's own. My unfortunate remark, combined with my youthful appearance, undoubtedly convinced him that I was irresponsible and that I had no idea of the value of money. The rest of the conversation, if such

---

[6] Frank Moore Collins, (b. 1872), was chief accountant of the ILO (1920–33). (Ed.)

[7] Sir Herbert Brown Ames (1863–1954) was a Canadian businessman and from 1904 to 1920 Member of Parliament for the Conservative Party of Canada. He served as Financial Director of the League of Nations after 1919. (Ed.)

it could be called, consisted mainly of a homily by Sir Herbert on the iniquity of the ILO's excessive expenditure and the dangers it involved. My attempt to explain the calls on the ILO and my assurance that the strictest economy would be observed were politely but firmly ignored. At last, apparently satisfied that, after this solemn admonition, the ILO would see the error of its ways, Ames wrote me a cheque for £5,000 and handed it over with a warning that he could make no promise about what amounts he might be able to provide in future.

With somewhat mixed feelings, satisfaction at the result and exasperation at the waste of valuable time, I hastened to my bank to open an ILO account. Here, I met with a disconcerting difficulty. No such account, I was informed, could be opened without evidence of a formal decision by the Governing Body. I explained that the Governing Body would not meet for another eight weeks and asked what I was to do meanwhile. "You can pay the cheque into your own account," replied the manager.

I had been under the impression that I knew something about banks – I had even succeeded in conveying that impression some years earlier to quite large audiences to whom I had lectured on the subject. But it was now painfully clear that I knew nothing about bankers, and very extraordinary people they seemed to be. Sir Herbert, after having devoted half an hour to asserting that he had no funds, had handed me £5,000. Now, the Midland Bank, which was supposed to take good care of money entrusted to it, was calmly proposing to place the ILO's cash in my personal account. I could think of no more unsafe place. The manager knew well that that account was not one of his best, and I was certain that Sir Herbert, with the strong opinion he held about overdrafts, would regard an account to which such calamities were not unknown as a wholly unsuitable place in which to deposit the ILO's resources. After some discussion I did at last obtain the concession of a second and distinct account which I could reserve for my ILO operations. This I thought solved the problem and I wondered why the manager had not himself suggested such an obvious course. "Don't you see", he said patiently, "that it is still *your* account and that any money in it is legally your personal property and that if you were to meet with a fatal accident it would belong to your heirs." I could think of no answer to this observation; so there the matter had to rest.

Every two weeks I made my call on Sir Herbert. Each time I listened to the same homily, and each time I came away with a cheque. All went well until I had to leave for Genoa. Ames at the time was preparing a full statement of the League's financial position. I put his chief accountant, Watterson, in touch with Collins so that he could get out a statement concerning the ILO in the form and with all the detail he might require. When the statement had been completed Ames sent

Watterson to ask me for an assurance that all unpaid liabilities had been included. I told Watterson about the cables that had been sent by the Colonial Office and the Foreign Office for the Organizing Committee some twelve months previously for which we had no figures because no bill had ever been sent in but for which a claim might possibly be presented. As I was just about to leave to catch the train, my explanation may have been rather rapid but it was certainly clear. For some reason Watterson merely reported to Ames that the only liability not included in the statement concerned a few telegrams. When Sir Herbert subsequently received a claim for something like £2,000, his consternation can be imagined and all his worse apprehensions about the ILO were confirmed. This unfortunate incident, for which the ILO was in no way responsible, undoubtedly played some part in the strained relations between the League and the ILO on budgetary questions which persisted for many years.

The Genoa Conference of 1920 has a special place in the ILO's history for several reasons: it was the first of a series of conferences dealing solely with maritime questions; although it figures in the *Record* as the Second Session of the International Labour Conference, it was the first to be prepared and held under the operation of the ILO's permanent machinery; and in many respects it was the most difficult with which any Director had to deal. Since I have described in considerable detail elsewhere some of the dramatic incidents that enlivened its proceedings,[8] I need only to mention here the circumstances that made it particularly difficult to handle. The first, and perhaps the most important, was a lack of cohesion among the delegates. The strong sense of being engaged in a new collective enterprise and the determination to make it a success that had prevailed in Washington was wholly lacking. Barnes, Fontaine, Mahaim and Delevingne were absent; the delegations included no personalities to whom was accorded, irrespective of their nationality, a special authority derived from the part they had played in bringing the Organization into being and to whom other delegates found it natural to turn for advice and guidance. On all sides an individualistic attitude predominated and the Conference approached its task in a spirit of conflict rather than of compromise. Other factors did nothing to soften the mood of delegates and put them in a better temper. Hotels were congested and most delegates were lodged in conditions of discomfort; many wartime food restrictions were still in force; the heat in June was stifling; owing to a strike no trams or buses were running, and perspiring delegates had to tramp back and forth from their hotels through streets that were like ovens. The hall in which the Conference met had

---

[8] Phelan: *Yes and Albert Thomas*, pp. 71–103. (Ed.)

historic associations but its acoustics were deplorable; the Conference's procedure was unfamiliar, the questions at issue were important and controversial, delegates were suspicious, irritated and excited; and to make matters worse the President's observations, admirable though they were in every other respect, were inaudible save to those in his immediate vicinity. Time and time again the proceedings would have degenerated into tumultuous anarchy had not Albert Thomas' dominating personality and powerful voice imposed discipline and kept the discussion within bounds.

His interventions were numerous and he was criticized for stepping outside what some regarded as the Secretary-General's proper role. But it is certain that without him the Conference would have collapsed. Its end was dramatic. The Convention on hours of work on board ship failed to secure the necessary two-thirds majority by a fraction of a vote. Albert Thomas was disappointed but he was not discouraged. On all the other questions on the agenda, satisfactory results were achieved, and in all the circumstances few would have dared to predict that the Conference could have secured so large a measure of real agreement.

The affairs of the Conference were not Albert Thomas' sole preoccupation at Genoa. He had also to deal with a meeting of the Governing Body and from it he obtained a decision of great importance which affected not only the ILO but also the League. He had become convinced in London that the ILO must settle into permanent headquarters as soon as possible and he had obtained an option on the Thudichum building in Geneva.[9] The Governing Body had approved this step; it corresponded to the obligation to establish the ILO at the seat of the League which the Covenant provided should be Geneva. At the peace conference opinion had been divided and a choice had to be made between Brussels and Geneva. President Wilson had thrown all his weight in favour of the latter and his view had prevailed. But when it had become apparent that there was no prospect of the United States becoming a member of the League, the question of its seat was reopened in a series of negotiations conducted with the greatest secrecy. Public opinion and confidence in the League would have been profoundly shocked if a provision of the Covenant had been openly and cynically disregarded. It was therefore planned to secure the desired result by creating a situation in which it would appear as the natural inevitable outcome of a state of fact; the first meeting of the Assembly would be held in Brussels in November where the secretariat would naturally be concentrated; and there the secretariat would remain

---

[9] This was the first location of the International Labour Office in Geneva, where it was housed from 1920 until 1926. The Thudichum building is currently the seat of the International Committee of the Red Cross. (Ed.).

occupied in carrying out the tasks entrusted to it until its continued presence in Brussels was accepted as a matter of course and could be given *de jure* recognition without exciting attention.

Albert Thomas was prepared to fight this plan for two reasons. In the first place the ILO would not be able to settle down in its permanent headquarters perhaps for a year or more; meanwhile, it would have to make shift with provisional arrangements, its work constantly interrupted and disorganized by having to move from one centre to another. In the second place he was profoundly disturbed by the idea that the League should appear as being the League of the victors, a political instrument at the disposal of the Supreme Council instead of an institution with a life of its own and a universal mission. He put these considerations to the Governing Body in vigorous language. The members of the Governing Body not unnaturally hesitated to involve themselves in a matter which was being discussed at the highest political level. They had never expected to be faced with responsibilities of this kind and they would gladly have found some way to evade them. But Albert Thomas, convinced that the whole future of the ILO was at stake, insisted vehemently that neither compromise nor delay was possible. In the end they followed his courageous lead and authorized him to take immediate steps "to establish the seat of the Office at Geneva". When the Genoa session of the Conference concluded its labours the staff accordingly moved to Geneva where, a few months later, the Brussels scheme having necessarily been abandoned, the secretariat of the League likewise set up its headquarters.

The establishment of the Office at Geneva in July 1920 came none too soon. With two sessions of the Conference to be followed up and another in prospect, and with regular quarterly meetings of the Governing Body each leaving a host of decisions to be implemented, it would no longer have been possible for the Office to work effectively if it had been compelled to continue a peripatetic existence.

Now that both staff and material arrangements were on a permanent basis I was relieved of the strain of successive organizational improvisations and I could leave in the hands of a staff which was quickly gaining experience more and more of the work which previously I had had to perform myself.

My satisfaction with this state of affairs was increased by the discovery that the diplomacy of the Division was not to be exercised solely on paper. The Council of the League was to meet at San Sebastian in August and among the questions on its agenda figured the League's budget in which had to be included provision for the ILO's expenditure. The references to finance in the ILO's Constitution were vague and the extent of the control which the League could exercise was open to various interpretations. I was deputed to go to San Sebastian to see that the

Council's decisions should not constitute any undue interference with the ILO's right to manage its own affairs.

The prospect of escaping from my desk, of getting a glimpse of Spain and of seeing the League machinery at work was highly attractive but I felt that my chances of successfully accomplishing such a mission were small. Sir Herbert Ames, by whose advice, as a Treasurer, the Council would be guided, would hardly be open to any suggestions I might make in favour of allowing the ILO the maximum possible freedom. The incident of the unexpected bill for cables I was sure still rankled, and my appearance on the scene would recall it, together with my unforgivable levity on the subject of overdrafts. Any attempt on my part to protect the ILO's freedom would only suggest that now was the chance to put an end to its spendthrift habits once and for all. Very reluctantly I decided I must inform Albert Thomas of these misgivings. He waved them aside.

"No one is better qualified than you to justify our figures and to defend our autonomy," he said. "Don't worry about Sir Ames. It is the Council that matters. I have written to Quiñones de León asking him to see you.[10] Make certain that he thoroughly understands our position."

Encouraged but not wholly reassured, I set out for San Sebastian. After having paid my respects to Sir Eric Drummond I went along to see Sir Herbert Ames. He was too preoccupied with a press conference, which he was just about to hold, to do more than greet me perfunctorily and invite me to be present. I readily agreed in the hope of getting some hint of what might be afoot. Along with a score of journalists I listened to a long and extremely solemn exposition of the system by which the contribution of each member State would be calculated. "How much will France have to pay?" was the first question when he had finished.

"That's what I have tried to explain," he replied and proceeded to repeat his exposé. "You must ask me that after the Council has decided on the amount of the budget," said Ames.

Much disappointed, the journalists departed. Concluding that I might expect the same unhelpful reply if I sought any enlightenment about the ILO's affairs, I congratulated Sir Herbert Ames on the clarity of his exposé and, having assured him that I was at his disposal if at any time he should wish to consult me, I went in search of Quiñones.

Quiñones de León was the Spanish Ambassador in Paris and the representative of Spain on the Council of the League of Nations. He was responsible for the

---

[10] José Maria Quiñones de León (1873–1957) was the representative for Spain at the League of Nations Assembly (1920–32) and Councils (1920–31). (Ed.)

invitation to the Council to meet in San Sebastian, and the arrangements for the Spanish Government's hospitality were in his charge. It seemed exceedingly doubtful that he would be able to spare the time to acquire the full understanding of the ILO's position which it was my mission to impart. My lucky star, however, was in the ascendant. The very reasons that led me to suppose that I might be a nuisance made my visit peculiarly welcome. It was the Council's method to allocate each item on its agenda to one of its members whose duty it then was to prepare a report for the Council's consideration. Quiñones had been asked to draft the report on financial questions and he had no idea what to say about the ILO. He had been given the ILO's budget and an extract of the legal provisions that applied; other than the Treasurer's view that the ILO's estimates were disproportionately high he had been given no guidance. He listened carefully to my explanation of the ILO's view and, although he did not commit himself, his questions gave me the impression that he wished to master all the arguments in its favour. This was as much as I could expect and I thought it would be unwise to attempt to secure anything more definite.

While waiting for developments I spent the next few days exploring San Sebastian and bathing in the warm waters of the bay. The meetings of the Council were private, the members of the secretariat were fully occupied, and there was nothing else to do. When at last I secured a copy of the report which the Council had adopted, I had every reason to be satisfied.

After citing the relevant article of the Treaty of Versailles it ran as follows: "The terms of this article show clearly that the Secretariat of the Council of the League can have no control over the decisions of the Budget Committee of the International Labour Office or over the total estimate for the budget itself. It is the duty of each Government to give its delegates on the Governing Body any instructions it deems necessary."

After this experience I resumed my work in Geneva with increased confidence, not because of the success of my mission, for which good luck had been mainly responsible, but because I was confirmed in my opinion that the Diplomatic Division was doing its job far more proficiently than the Secretariat of the League. The text of the Council's decision was, in substance, all that could be desired, but I was shocked by the terminological inexactitudes by which it was disfigured – "Budget Committee of the ILO" was a meaningless term in the context in which it was employed, and, since "each Government" had only one delegate on the Governing Body, the reference to "its delegates" was grammatically wrong or inexcusably ignorant. However modestly the Secretariat might conceive its role, it might at least have been expected to ensure that the Council's decisions were worded in less slipshod fashion. In the Diplomatic Division inaccuracies of this kind would have been severely dealt with and much more than accuracy was demanded. Years after I retired from the ILO one of the original members of the Division, recalling his early days in the Office, quoted the observations I made on a document he had drafted: "This is an excellent draft. It contains everything that is required, but it won't do. I understand it, and you understand it; but that's not enough. Take it away and bring me something that Mr 'X' will understand" (Mr "X" was a particularly stupid member of the Governing Body).

A still more difficult standard had to be achieved in the letters prepared for Albert Thomas' signature. Commendation was rare and almost never unqualified lest it give the impression that nothing better need be attempted. I was, therefore, much pleased when one day, after signing a batch of letters I had presented to him, he remarked, "The Diplomatic Division is to be congratulated. I never have to send its letters back to be revised." This observation implied much more than an admission that he had detected no errors in style or substance; it meant that the letters contributed, so far as the occasion allowed, to bring home to their recipients the importance and the value of the Organization. A great part of our official correspondence did not, of course, lend itself to any elaborate development for this purpose, but, within the range of the Division's activities, there was plenty of scope for bold and constructive initiative.

Once I had grasped the idea that the ILO should claim to be heard whenever social issues arose or might be ignored, I found many League activities in which the desirability of ILO intervention ought to be considered. In drawing attention to them I knew I was asking for trouble. Albert Thomas' invariable reply was to ask me to prepare a letter to the Secretary-General putting forward the arguments which supported our case. This was not always an easy task. When the League set up a commission to study the sanctions to be applied to a member which resorted to war in disregard of its obligations under the Covenant, I could see that its conclusions might affect matters in which the ILO was interested, for example commitments guaranteeing reciprocity of treatment of foreign workers. It consequently seemed desirable that in considering its recommendations the commission should be in a position to appreciate all that their application might involve. I raised these points in a brief note. The file came back to me with a long note by Butler pointing out that the whole question of sanctions was a burning political issue and concluding that the ILO abstain from any intervention. There followed a minute from Albert Thomas: "Prepare a letter to the Secretary-General taking into account Mr Butler's observations." I imagine his eyes must have twinkled behind his spectacles as he dictated this instruction. The challenge amused me and the letter that eventually went, with Butler's grudging approval, was I thought one of my best efforts. In the event nothing more was heard of the matter; the commission abandoned its task, the question of ILO representation had not to be considered.

Other initiatives concerning the affairs of the League, however, gave important results. The Director was accorded the right to participate in the discussion of the Council whenever any item on the agenda that might affect the ILO was under consideration. This was a major achievement only possible after the ground had been carefully prepared. It explained, incidentally, why Albert Thomas had sent me to San Sebastian on a mission that, in view of its importance, it would have been characteristic of him to undertake himself. I now realized that it would have been damaging to the prestige of the Organization if its Director had been obliged to appear in the guise of a lobbyist, and that he had been wise to keep out of the picture until appropriate arrangements had been made to give him direct access to the Council.

An almost equally important negotiation resulted in the appointment of a representative of the ILO to the Mandates Commission in an advisory capacity. The Constitution of the ILO contained an article providing for consideration of the application of ILO Conventions to colonies, protectorates and possessions. No corresponding obligation existed concerning mandated territories since the system of mandates had not been agreed on when the Constitution was adopted. The link now established with the Mandates Commission thus completed and extended the ILO's possibilities of influencing social progress in dependent territories; at the same time it added an element of realism to the Commission's work and contributed in no small degree to making it effective.

In the beginning the ILO's requests for representation on one or other League body created surprise and a certain irritation in the Secretariat. In its eyes the ILO was a minor institution to which had been confided a limited and purely technical task – the Secretariat, indeed, could hardly be blamed for holding a view which coincided with that held by many members of the Governing Body. If the Secretariat gave way, as it usually did in the face of the ILO's persistence, it was more out of impatience with a time-wasting discussion than out of any conviction that the ILO had a real case.

It came as a shock to the Secretariat to discover that a lack of effective contact between the two institutions could result in a situation of great embarrassment to the League itself. What happened has considerable historical importance, for it brought to general attention a realization of new forces stirring in the world that would henceforth increasingly influence political, economic and social thinking.

The conclusions arrived at by the Conference convened by the League in September 1920 to study the financial crisis and to make recommendations to remedy its effects make strange reading today. The Conference urged the governments to "abolish at the earliest possible moment all measures contrary to economic laws and having a purely artificial effect tending to hide from the people the real economic situation of a country. Amongst them should be included … the continuance of unemployment donations which tend to the demoralization of the worker instead of encouraging readiness to work."

The weight of authority behind this pronouncement was immense. It represented the considered opinion of the world's most eminent experts in the fields of finance and commerce and it reflected the views of all the outstanding political economists of the day. Nevertheless, Albert Thomas did not hesitate to challenge in the name of the ILO conclusions which he was convinced were out of date. In a letter to the Secretary-General, he pointed out that this pronouncement ran directly counter to the recommendation of the Washington Conference urging governments to establish systems of unemployment insurance and that such systems were now in existence in almost all the most important European countries. Having stated bluntly that the resolution adopted at Brussels would be regarded as reactionary and as hostile to the whole trend of modern social progress he concluded: "I do not know whether you will think it necessary or possible to take any steps towards mitigating the unfortunate effects which this resolution has produced. Personally, I feel that these effects may be so widespread, and so serious from the point of view of the reputation of the League, that some steps should be taken to counteract them."

Albert Thomas did not press the Secretary-General to take any direct action; he well understood that it would not be possible for the Secretary-General to disavow the conclusions of a League Conference. But, by printing his own letter in the *Bulletin* of the ILO, an official publication regularly distributed to the governments,[11] he was able to direct their attention to the ILO's reaction and to remind them of the principles to which their delegates at Washington had committed them.

After this incident the ILO's demands for representation on League bodies were received in a different spirit. It was clear that the ILO was a more important element in international life than had been supposed and that a full understanding of its views and activities would enable the League to avoid serious mistakes.

Although I was fascinated by Albert Thomas' personality and moved to enthusiasm by the boldness with which he seized every opportunity to enhance the prestige of the ILO, there were occasions when we differed. Such disagreements

---

[11] See ILO: *Official Bulletin*, 1921, Vol. 3, No. 23, pp. 649–54. (Ed.)

were, as a general rule, easily composed. One of the qualities that made him pleasant to work with was that he was reluctant to impose his view by an act of authority; he was always ready to expend time and effort on justifying the action he proposed to take; his desire was to secure intelligent collaboration and not mere acquiescence. But one had to be very sure of one's ground before challenging conclusions that were never the result of superficial consideration. Most of the arguments I had with him concerned internal administration. They were lively enough at times but they led to the establishment of administrative practices which were neither French nor English but combined elements of both and proved very successful in their application to an international staff.

On the larger questions of policy I recognized that his political experience was far greater than mine and I was inclined to follow his lead without question. On one such matter, however, our views proved irreconcilable and the argument between us was resumed at intervals over a long period. Some account of it must be included for it shows how insecure were the foundations of the ILO at that time.

Albert Thomas' conception of the ILO as the international organization into which should be channelled all the forces striving for social justice depended for its realization on securing the support of organized labour – without that support the ILO could not justify its name let alone accomplish anything worthwhile. Organized labour, however, had yet to be convinced that this vision of the ILO could be made a reality. In the dislocation caused by the war it was not surprising that events in Russia and threats of revolution even in countries as stable as Holland and Switzerland should have tempted the workers to believe that a revolutionary era had begun and that they would be able, by resolute action, to take into their own hands the control of industry and institute ideal working conditions. As against this mirage the ILO seemed to have little to offer and unless it could succeed in making effective the modest programme of reforms on which it had embarked it was in danger of being utterly discredited. In that programme there was one item to which the trade unions attached considerable importance, the institution of the eight-hour day. Albert Thomas, therefore, concentrated his efforts on securing the ratification of the Washington Hours Convention. France had an eight-hour law; if France could be persuaded to ratify, her example might well stimulate other countries; and the ILO would have gone a long way towards obtaining the confidence of organized labour.

The French Government, headed by Poincaré, was by no means sympathetic to labour. Albert Thomas could account it no small triumph when, after long and persistent efforts, he at last succeeded in persuading that intractable Prime Minister to agree that France should ratify. It then became the business of the French Ministry of Foreign Affairs to implement Poincaré's decision and it was over the procedure to be followed that the argument between myself and Albert Thomas arose.

To the Quai d'Orsay it was inconceivable that it should be required to depart from the sacred rules of traditional diplomatic procedure of which it considered itself the supreme arbiter. The Secretary-General of the French Foreign Office accordingly wrote to the Secretary-General of the League asking him to fix a date and place for a solemn ceremony of signature and the drawing up of a protocol recording that this diplomatic operation had been duly performed.

This letter Sir Eric Drummond communicated to the ILO for observations and it came to me during Albert Thomas' absence. In my view, it raised questions of the utmost gravity and I prepared a reply pointing out:

 (i)   that ILO Members had to submit all ILO Conventions to their parliaments;

 (ii) that, if its parliament approved, a Member had then to communicate its ratification to the Secretary-General of the League;

 (iii) that the obligation to follow this procedure was specified in the Treaty of Versailles and was binding on the Parties to that Treaty;

 (iv) that the procedure of signature had been deliberately excluded because it was incompatible with an obligation which applied to all Members including those who might have voted against the adoption of the Convention by the Conference and who obviously could not be obliged to sign a Convention to which they were opposed;

 (v)   that the Secretary-General of the League must therefore refuse to organize a ceremony of signature or countenance any procedure other than that specified in the ILO's Constitution.

I posted my draft to Albert Thomas. It did not meet with his approval and he dictated and signed a letter of his own which he dispatched to me to be sent on to Sir Eric. I was alarmed by its contents. It seemed to me that he had not appreciated what was at stake and that he was making concessions of a dangerous character. I therefore telegraphed to him saying that I was holding up his letter until his return so that he might have an opportunity of considering all its possible implications.

I was not surprised by his reply. His decisions were never lightly arrived at; he was prepared to listen to comments and suggestions before they were formulated but, once a matter had been disposed of, he regarded it as closed. His telegram expressed in curt terms his astonishment at my action and his intention to demand an explanation when he returned.

Although this was somewhat intimidating, I was confident of being able to justify what I had done. It did not prove as easy as I had expected. I saw the

Constitution as a victory that had emerged from a long and exhausting battle in Paris; I had a vivid recollection of every phase of that battle and how its fate had turned on certain points of fundamental importance: the equal status of government and non-government delegates, the adoption of Conventions by a majority vote, and the obligation on all Members of the Organization to submit to their parliaments the Conventions so adopted. All these made a revolutionary break with established diplomatic procedure and opened the way to far more effective international action than had been possible in the past. They were all interlocking parts of a single system and to abandon any one of them must inevitably destroy the whole achievement.

Albert Thomas could not be expected to share this rather emotional attitude to the Constitution. He was not acquainted with its history, and he was naturally less concerned with its long-term possibilities than with his immediate problem of winning over the workers to the support of the Organization. Just as my view was coloured by my recollection of the difficulties encountered at the peace conference, his attitude was influenced by the struggle in which he was engaged in Paris. The French ratification was within his grasp. It seemed to him wholly unrealistic to insist on an academic interpretation of the Constitution that must result in the loss of ground so painfully gained; what was the good of clinging to a rigid doctrine which could have no practical application if the Organization failed to achieve an effective existence?

Strong as this argument was, I could not feel that it was decisive. At last, I hit on the idea of restating my own case in political terms. I urged that, if a system of signature was accepted, the political consequences would be disastrous. As things stood, a Convention voted by the Conference had to be submitted to the national parliaments. If the system desired by France was instituted, the Conference would sink to the level of a mere drafting committee; its texts would be referred to a diplomatic conference composed of plenipotentiaries without whose approval they could not go forward to the parliaments. All delegates in the Conference possessed, as things stood, equal powers; but, if this new system were accepted, government delegates would be in a superior category. They would meet as plenipotentiaries at the end of the Conference and they alone would have the power to decide which, if any, of the Conference's decisions were to receive national consideration. The workers attached great importance to their equality of status. I ventured to doubt whether, if they understood what was at stake, they would be prepared to throw away that status and sacrifice their powers in respect of all Conventions in order to facilitate the ratification of only one.

This was an aspect of the matter which had not struck Albert Thomas and it made a considerable impression. He rewrote his letter embodying the main point in my original draft but he toned down its conclusions by saying that, if a government found itself obliged to follow certain formalities in submitting a Convention to its legislative authorities, such formalities must be considered as having a purely domestic character of which the Secretary-General of the League could take no official cognizance.

There the matter rested for the moment, but not for long. Poincaré was annoyed by the reception accorded to the French proposal. At their next meeting, he harshly upbraided Albert Thomas, accusing him of obstructing France's ratification and telling him that his interpretation of the ILO's Constitution was regarded by French legal authorities as totally unsound. Albert Thomas came back to Geneva furious at the way he had been treated and told me that, unless I could convince the French jurists that my view of the Constitution was correct, he would have to give way. I thought his irritation and impatience excusable and I admired his fairness in giving me a chance to make my view prevail.

I arrived in Paris in a confident mood. The ILO procedure was something quite new and it was understandable that the officials of the Quai d'Orsay, called upon to ratify an ILO Convention for the first time, should have automatically envisaged the application of traditional methods. Now they found themselves in a sorry pickle between the clear obligations of the ILO's Constitution and their much-feared chief, Poincaré, who was not the man to forgive an oversight which had placed him in a false position. Retreat, however, was the only course open to them and I was curious to see with what face-saving manœuvres they would conduct it.

The discussion which in fact took place was the very reverse of these anticipations. I was at first puzzled by a serene attitude in which polite condescension failed to mask entirely a sense of superiority. Then I gathered that, in the view of the two jurists to whom I had been handed over, I had no case at all. I read them the text of the Constitution. Did they agree that it had to be complied with? "Certainly," they replied. Then could I take it that they were prepared to do so? "But that is precisely what we are doing," was their gentle reply.

I was at a loss to understand by what process of reasoning this astonishing conclusion could be reached, and I pressed for an explanation. It was supplied with a certain pained patience. Was it possible that anything so elementary could be required? Could not the ILO have sent someone with whom intelligent discussion could be undertaken? I must be deplorably ignorant – not perhaps a complete imbecile, but diplomatically illiterate. The word "ratification" meant, and could only mean, the ratification of a document signed by plenipotentiaries; hence, since the Constitution contemplated ratification, it must necessarily contemplate signature by plenipotentiaries. True, it made no specific provision for this procedure but that was because it was unnecessary to do so.

The difference between us was now clear. My view was that the Constitution altered, and was intended to alter, existing practice. Their view was that existing practice decided the meaning of the text. I remembered Humpty Dumpty's imperious dictum: "A word means what I choose it to mean" and I was tempted to ask if they were relying on him as an authority. The discussion was being conducted in French and I doubted my ability to make the point without appearing offensive. Humpty Dumpty, however, contributed something of value, for it occurred to me that I might well adopt his tactics. I said that, although I would not presume for a moment to question their reading of the French text, I must remind them that both the English and the French texts were authentic. The English text, I could assure them, supported my view. If the two texts could not be reconciled, regard must be had to the intentions of the peace conference. Having participated in its proceedings, I was convinced an examination of its records would furnish ample evidence in confirmation of the interpretation I had put forward.

The discussion proceeded no further. The French gave no sign of modifying their attitude but I could sense that they were less confident. I guessed that in their traditional approach to the problem they had overlooked the new status accorded to the English language and that they were now feeling much less sure of their position. The first sign that this was so was that nothing more was heard of their original request to the Secretary-General. After an interval, France and Belgium made their own arrangements to sign a Convention incorporating the text adopted at Washington and drew up a protocol leaving this Convention open to adhesion by other Members of the International Labour Organization. This protocol the Quai d'Orsay communicated to the Secretary-General with the request that he be good enough to send copies to the member States.

This was a victory for the ILO but, although the Quai d'Orsay had abandoned practically all its ground, it had not left the field. It was evidently beginning a more subtle offensive which might prove as dangerous as the frontal attack which had failed. All that the Secretary-General was now asked to do was to let governments know, merely as a matter of information, what the French and Belgian Governments had done so that they might, if they so wished, follow their example. On the face of it this seemed a harmless request which it would be discourteous to refuse. But, if the Secretary-General made the communication, the Quai d'Orsay, pursuing its campaign through diplomatic channels as it must be expected it would, could urge that he had no objection to the procedure which the French Government thought appropriate. A system of signature might spread and the ILO's position be undermined.

Sir Eric, as on the previous occasion, prudently referred the Quai d'Orsay letter to the ILO for observations. I was greatly afraid that Albert Thomas would take the view that the Quai d'Orsay had accepted the compromise suggested in his earlier letter and that he would not be prepared to press the matter further. His reaction, however, was the same as my own and the terms in which he expressed it were as vigorous as I could desire. "The Secretary-General", he wrote, "could not comply with the request of the French and Belgian Governments without gravely infringing the provisions of Part XIII of the Treaty of Versailles."

It is unnecessary to tell the rest of the story in detail. The Secretary-General took the line indicated by Albert Thomas, eventually the attempt to apply the procedure of signature to ILO Conventions was abandoned and the simple and logical process required by the ILO's Constitution became accepted practice.

A more astonishing instance of how little reliance can be placed on treaty obligations was the dispute that arose over the right of the ILO to deal with problems of agricultural labour. It would be difficult to find any matter on which the decision of the peace conference had been more definitely formulated. In reply to a direct question from the Hungarian delegation, Clemenceau, the President of the Conference, replying on behalf of the Allied and Associated Powers, had stated the position in terms that admitted of no possible misunderstanding: "The International Labour Organization is concerned with all workers and may propose draft Conventions applying to industry, commerce or agriculture."

When in 1921 the Governing Body decided to place a number of agricultural items on the agenda of the Third Session of the Conference, some of its Members were opposed to this decision but no one dreamt of questioning its constitutional validity.

Opinion in farming circles was hostile and obtained a good deal of publicity in the press. There was a stormy debate in the French Chamber of Deputies and the Government, whose hold on office was none too secure, announced that it would ask the International Court of Justice to pronounce on the legality of the ILO's action.

Much more hung on the Court's decision than the specific point referred to it. If the Court should decide that the ILO had no power to deal with labour conditions in agriculture, the trade union movement would be more than ever convinced that it was right in thinking that the ILO could offer it nothing of value.

What was referred to the Court was not a "dispute" in the technical sense, but a request from the Council of the League for an advisory opinion. The French Government would naturally appear before the Court to argue the case against the ILO's competence but there was no certainty that the Court would have an opportunity of listening to any counter-argument. Other governments were entitled to intervene but governments favourable to the ILO's thesis were under no obligation to come to its assistance; political considerations might well make them disinclined to take an initiative which the French Government might regard as uncalled for. Moreover, even if a friendly government should intervene it could only express an individual opinion and would have no authority to speak for the Organization as a whole.

Albert Thomas was fully conscious of the danger this situation involved. He therefore asked the Court to hear the ILO and, his request having been granted, he decided to plead the case himself. In view of his nationality, this decision called for political courage of the highest order; but he undertook without hesitating what he considered to be his duty as Director and, by so doing, he set a memorable example of the loyalty which an international official owes to the institution to which he belongs.

I wondered, however, whether Albert Thomas was wise in this particular instance in assuming the task himself instead of entrusting it to some renowned international lawyer. De Lapradelle, the distinguished jurisconsult (jurist) of the French Foreign Office, [12] with the assistance of his legal staff, would certainly prepare his case with the greatest thoroughness. Albert Thomas had a thousand affairs on his hands, none of which he could neglect, and it seemed impossible that he would be able to find time to prepare himself adequately for a struggle with so experienced an advocate.

The Court began its hearings on 3 July 1922. Its proceedings were conducted with simplicity but with a solemnity and dignity befitting the world's highest tribunal. De Lapradelle made the opening statement and statements by the representatives of other governments followed. Albert Thomas' address occupied the morning and afternoon of the third day, and lasted altogether over five hours. I had listened to de Lapradelle with close attention and, although I remained satisfied that he had not really seriously damaged the ILO's case, I was troubled by the close reasoning with which he elaborated a series of subtle arguments which might make a special appeal to the legal mind. I was prepared for Albert Thomas to be eloquent but I was more than a little afraid that eloquence would be less effective before this particular audience than a relentlessly logical legal approach. Eloquent, Albert Thomas certainly was. He never faltered for a word; there was no pause while he reached for a document, no break while he passed from one group of arguments to the next; as an oratorical feat, it was a masterpiece to which the Court listened with evident pleasure. But eloquence was his servant and not his master. His arguments were none the less closely knit, none the less

---

[12] Albert de Geouffre de Lapradelle (1871–1955) was Professor of Law at the University of Paris, specializing in international law and the law of war. (Ed.)

pitilessly logical, because of an unexpected flash that suddenly illuminated and enforced their impact. Only in a few sentences at the end did he allow himself anything in the nature of an eloquent appeal. In closing his argument, he had explained how the uncertainty which had been created in the ILO's affairs when the present issue had been raised had made governments hesitant and had slowed down certain of the ILO's activities. Happily, the Court existed and henceforth hesitation and uncertainty would be removed.

"We are not a Super-State," he went on.

> Far from it! We are the humble servants of the fifty States, our masters, on whose pleasure we must attend. We are like the heroes of the ancient epics. We wait impatiently while our well-constructed ships lie becalmed, drifting helplessly in danger of going aground. High above us the gods debate, unable to decide our destiny. You will hand down your opinion. The gods will listen to your sovereign voice. They will loose again the winds that will fill our sails and carry us towards the open sea, towards that future of social justice of which a glimpse was given to mankind by the negotiators of the Treaty of Peace. [13]

Four weeks later, I returned to The Hague to hear the Court deliver its verdict. It was wholly in the ILO's favour. Technically, it was not a judgment but only an "advisory opinion" to which governments were not obliged to conform. France, however, at once announced that she accepted the Court's decision and our satisfaction was complete.

It is interesting to note that the first three affairs to come before the Court concerned the ILO. Thus, the diverse activities of the ILO in the early days of its existence, so often criticized as feverish and futile, not only established its own position but also served to bring into effective operation the machinery of the Court.

During this period, my relations with Albert Thomas grew more intimate and he invited me to accompany him on some of his journeys. My first such experience was a visit to London of which I have a vivid recollection, not only because to watch him at work was a political education but because it was my good fortune to be able to observe at close quarters two remarkable men whose personalities left on me a permanent impression. [14]

---

[13] The text quoted is a free translation of the last lines of Albert Thomas' speech. See ILO: *Official Bulletin*, 1922, Vol. 6, No. 4, pp. 164–97. (Ed.)

[14] The mission took place from 6 to 10 March 1921. See Cabinet Albert Thomas, CAT 1/21/3, ILO Historical Archives. (Ed.)

The programme that Albert Thomas set out to fulfil in the course of a single day was extraordinary; what was even more astonishing than the number of his engagements was the bewildering variety of the subjects discussed, the personalities encountered and the surroundings in which his conversations took place. In those days, the headquarters of quite important trade unions often consisted of no more than two or three rooms situated in one of the poorer districts. London taxi drivers are, I suppose, rarely startled by their clients. Ours had driven us from a shabby street off Gray's Inn Road to an equally mean street in Southwark and he was certainly doubtful whether he had heard aright when he was next told to take us to 10 Downing Street. He hesitated for a moment and then, with the air of a slow-thinking man who had found the answer to his unuttered question, he let in his gear. He had concluded, having heard us converse in a foreign tongue, that we were strangers in London who wished to see one of the sights. He watched dumbfounded when, having paid him off, we walked up the steps and rang the bell and he could scarcely believe his eyes when the famous door was opened and we passed within.

We were received by Megan, Lloyd George's youthful daughter, who welcomed Albert Thomas as an old friend. With her was Lord French,[15] who we found was to be the only other guest at lunch. A few minutes later, the Prime Minister appeared and we took our places round a small circular table just large enough to accommodate us with comfort.

In external appearance, Lloyd George and Albert Thomas were very different. Albert Thomas was stout; he was not untidy, but his beard and his hair, which he wore rather long, and his clothes, cut by a French tailor, all gave the impression that he was careless about how he looked. Lloyd George was light and graceful; he was neat to the point of being almost dapper; not a hair was out of place and *The Tailor and Cutter* could have found nothing to criticize in the perfect fit of his coat. But, in other ways, the two men were much alike.

Lloyd George had come straight to lunch from a long meeting of the Cabinet at which matters of exceptional gravity had been under discussion – it was no secret that Anglo-French relations had become strained almost to breaking point; at home, a critical situation had also to be faced and the Prime Minister was to meet a trade union delegation that afternoon. Although Albert Thomas' worries were of a less spectacular character, they were no less burdensome and his activities that morning would have exhausted any ordinary man. Nevertheless,

---

[15] John Denton Pinkstone French, first Earl of Ypres (1852–1925), served as the first Commander-in-Chief of the British Expeditionary Force in the Second World War. He then held the post of Lord Lieutenant of Ireland from 1918 to 1921. (Ed.)

both appeared as though they had not a care in the world, as gay and sparkling as men refreshed by a long holiday. Only the Field Marshal, on whom an earldom had just been conferred, and who might have been expected to be in high spirits, seemed unaffected by the general atmosphere. He seemed plunged in gloom and, when Lloyd George attempted to draw him into the conversation, he complained querulously that the College of Heralds was raising difficulties over his desire to include a reference to Ypres in his new title.

"Ah," said Lloyd George, "I'm afraid I can't help you on that. Those fellows wouldn't listen to me, even though I give them most of their business. They are a law unto themselves and you'll have to look out if you get into a fight with them – they give quarters but no quarter."

This jest, which I struggled vainly to translate for Albert Thomas, was received by the Field Marshal with something which I can only describe as a snort. Whether this expressed his opinion of the Heralds or of the impropriety of the Prime Minister's levity on so serious a subject, I could not determine. At all events, it concluded the Field Marshal's brief contribution to the conversation; and for the rest of the meal, he concentrated his attention solely on the contents of his plate. When lunch was over, he took himself off with a few grumpy words; Megan bade us goodbye; and Lloyd George led us into the Cabinet room for a private talk. The room itself was of graceful proportions but there was nothing to suggest that it might be other than the board room of some modest commercial enterprise. As I recalled to mind some of the famous historical figures who in these unpretentious surroundings had taken world-shaking decisions, I almost forgot the presence of their successor whom I was privileged to see in the flesh at a moment when, having no more laurels to gain at home, he was embarking on what Tom Jones has called "the most ambitious, the most heroic enterprise of his life".

His experience at the peace conference had led him to believe that world affairs offered him a sphere of action in which his special talents could find their full scope. He was convinced that the world was heading for another catastrophe and that he alone was capable of arresting its fatal progress. His argument ran roughly as follows. If Germany and Russia remained isolated, they would inevitably combine, and the menace of a second world war would arise. The political foundations for world peace which the Treaty of Versailles had sought to establish in the League of Nations had collapsed with the abstention of the United States. The problem should therefore be tackled afresh from the economic angle. All countries were becoming more and more concerned with economic difficulties and with rising unemployment. They all had a direct and urgent interest in general concerted action to put the world on the road to prosperity. His idea was to assemble a world conference in which Germany and Russia would participate and in which economic realities would prevail over political animosities.

This plan was already well on the way to execution and the main purpose of Albert Thomas' visit to Downing Street was to secure that the ILO should be represented at the proposed conference. Lloyd George admitted the strength of the ILO's claim to a place in any international discussion of the problem of unemployment but he maintained that, in this particular case, there were political considerations which it was impossible to ignore. The American Government would have nothing to do with a conference with which the League of Nations was associated. The ILO, despite its autonomous character, was part of the League; it could not be invited to attend without giving the impression that the conference was a League affair; suspicions would be aroused in Washington that the United States was being cunningly drawn into relations with the League, and all hope of American participation would disappear.

In spite of Albert Thomas' great gifts of persuasion, Lloyd George could not be induced to modify his attitude. "Don't be impatient," he pleaded. "You will have plenty of opportunities to get all you want for the ILO. I have only one to bring about this conference; don't increase my difficulties."

Albert Thomas refused to tie his hands by making any such promise. Nevertheless, the two parted on the friendliest terms. It may be added that Albert Thomas won in the end. He succeeded in getting the support of the French and Italian Governments and Lloyd George later agreed that an ILO delegation should be invited to attend.

We then crossed over to the Colonial Office to keep an appointment with Winston Churchill who at that time was Secretary of State for the Colonies. There was nothing to suggest in those days that Churchill would later emerge as a national leader whose renown would overshadow even that of Lloyd George. Everything, indeed, pointed the other way. He was regarded as impetuous, irresponsible, politically unreliable and childishly theatrical. His personal intervention at the head of armed police in the Sidney Street battle against anarchists and his dash to beleaguered Antwerp attired in the cocked hat and gold lace of an Elder Brother of Trinity House obscured in public memory less spectacular achievements. But, however dim his political future, he was easily the most picturesque figure in public life and the prospect of making his acquaintance was more than a little exciting.

He was quite unlike what his reputation had led me to expect. His room was utterly quiet; there was no sign of tempestuous energy and imperious action – no sign, indeed, of any activity at all. There was not a single paper on his desk, nothing but a blotting pad, which showed no mark of ever having been used, and an inkstand, a cigar box, and an ashtray, all of brightly polished silver. He greeted us without any of the effusion which politicians so readily display. And he seemed far more like a serious student than anything else as he at once began to question Albert Thomas about the political situation in the European capitals which he had recently visited. The details for which he asked showed a wide knowledge and an extraordinary memory. He rarely interposed any comment of his own and then merely to indicate agreement with some comment made by his visitor.

It was only when this political view had been completed that the subject of the ILO could be introduced. Churchill at once showed that he had a clear grasp of all the elements involved in the application of the ILO's Conventions to colonial territories. He readily promised that the attention of colonial governors should be drawn to the importance of considering in what measure the ILO's decisions could be applied to the areas for which they were responsible. These were matters left to the discretion of the colonies themselves but Churchill's action undoubtedly had a powerful and stimulating effect.

We had been with him for more than an hour when his private secretary entered to remind him that he was due to receive a deputation and offered him a file which presumably contained his brief. "Let them come in," said Churchill, waving the papers aside. As he accompanied us to the door expressing his regret at having to terminate the conversation, the deputation filed into the room through a door at the other end. Its members looked grim and determined. The private secretary, still clutching his wad of papers, looked extremely worried. Churchill was unhurried and unconcerned. The door closed behind us leaving me with the conviction that he would show himself fully master of whatever might be the subject the deputation had come to raise.

There were half a dozen more visits to be paid before the day's programme was completed. Some lasted only a few minutes, but each had a definite purpose; some concerned a relatively simple matter, others involved the discussion of some technical problem demanding both knowledge and concentration – for example, the conversation with the Chairman of the London and Northwestern Railway dealt with the difficulties of regulating hours of work in rail transport, [16] difficulties which it was alleged made it impossible for Great Britain to ratify the Washington Hours Convention.

Altogether, it was a dizzy experience and, when at last our taxi deposited us at our hotel, I was well content to call it a day. Albert Thomas seemed in nowise fatigued. A few minutes later, we were off to one of London's most famous

---

[16] Sir Josiah (later Lord) Stamp, the eminent economist. (E.J.P.)

restaurants where, having made his choice of food and wines with a gourmet's care, he enlivened the meal with conversation as amusing and light-hearted as he had contributed at the Prime Minister's lunch. Dinner, however, was only an interlude. When it was over, he returned to the hotel to dictate his notes and deal with his mail, a task which kept him busy till well after midnight.

A day as exhausting as that just described was by no means exceptional on Albert Thomas' journeys. I accompanied him on many other missions. The day's programme was always crowded, for he regarded time as precious, but there were occasions when the effort demanded from him made that day in London seem like a rest cure. There he was on familiar ground; he was known to the people he had to deal with; he knew the measure of agreement or disagreement he might expect to meet and the arguments he could most effectively employ. When he went further afield (and he took the world for his province), he was among strangers, obliged to struggle as best he might against barriers of indifference and incomprehension which it required all his resource and energy to overcome.

The lighter side of the League of Nations, Geneva

8

During my first years in Geneva, although my responsibilities grew more varied, I was never overwhelmed as I had been when the ILO was constantly moving its base of operations and when extemporized arrangements, perpetually on the point of collapse, monopolized all my time and energy. New problems were a welcome challenge instead of an additional harassment and, if I was usually to be found at my desk long after other members of the staff had left, it was only because I could then work undisturbed and, having cleared off all matters requiring my attention, be under no obligation to make an early appearance next morning. I never took papers home, and thus I was free, both in the evenings and at weekends, to seek such relaxation as Geneva had to offer.

During the war of 1914–18, large numbers of refugees had found a haven in Switzerland. Included among them were members of that cosmopolitan society whose sole object was the pursuit of pleasure and who had been forced to abandon their habitual resorts. Ironically enough, these wealthy voluptuaries converged on the City of Calvin where all kinds of luxury establishments sprang up to cater to their needs. Famous dress designers displayed their latest creations, jewellers' windows dazzled the eye with costly gems, restaurants served the choicest food and the rarest wines at prices reputed the highest in Europe, dancings were thronged till the early hours of the morning, and a small but richly furnished casino offered every facility to those who craved the excitement of playing for high stakes.

At the time of our arrival in Geneva, the playgrounds of Europe were opening again and their old clients were beginning to move back to their favourite haunts. An exotic interlude in the city's life was nearing its end but Geneva was still an expensive place for the foreigner, and particularly for members of the staffs of the ILO and the League. They were not only strangers in the city to which they had come but they might be in the lonely position of finding no one of their own nationality in the Organization they had joined. Some institution through which they could make social contacts with one another and with citizens of the town was an obvious need. I got together a small group consisting of two of my colleagues from the ILO, two members of the League secretariat and two Genevese of my acquaintance, with the object of exploring the possibility of founding an international club open to both international officials and citizens of Geneva. The first problem was to find premises at a rental that could be met out of the financial resources that we might hope to have available, and these could not be great since membership fees would have to be low enough to allow junior staff to join. After a long and discouraging search, only one possibility emerged. The departure of its clientele had caused the gaming establishment to close, the building had become the property of the city, and the municipal authorities, having no use for a structure which had been specially designed as a casino de luxe, were prepared to rent it to us on very moderate terms.

This accommodation, attractive though it was, presented as many problems as it promised to solve. The premises were extensive and to adapt them for our purpose would involve considerable expenditure. Moreover, neither members nor funds yet existed; our little committee had no authority to make commitments which the club would be bound to honour; and we might easily start the enterprise on a scale that would be impossible to maintain. Nevertheless, since the choice lay between taking these risks and doing nothing at all, it was decided to go ahead. An English billiard table, the only one in Geneva, was installed in one of the ground floor rooms, the adjoining room became a reading room with an impressive display of periodicals in different languages, the kitchen was handed over to a caterer who undertook to provide meals in a large hall on the first floor which was furnished as a dining room, the bar was stocked, a hall porter was recruited and provided with a uniform. A notice was then issued saying that the club would open at 6 p.m. on a specified date and informing all those who might be interested that they might exercise all the privileges of members during the evening without any obligation to join. The response exceeded our most optimistic expectations. The rooms were thronged until midnight; the bar and the restaurant did a roaring trade; and in the course of the next few days we enrolled a substantial membership. Other developments followed. A form of visitor's membership was instituted for representatives attending international conferences or committees; during meetings of the League Assembly lunches with a guest speaker on the American pattern, then unfamiliar in Europe, were organized; and the club became a notable feature in the international life of Geneva.

For some twelve years, I presided over its destinies as its president. The job was by no means a sinecure. Finance, and in particular the finance of the restaurant, was a perpetual problem; and there were occasionally crises of a political character as, for example, when the Genevese members of the committee threatened to resign in a body because Litvinov had been invited to be the speaker at one of the club lunches.[1] But if these problems were sometimes worrying, there were compensations.

Since the club was a general meeting place for people of varied tastes, its frequenters tended to form distinct coteries. There were for example those who came to browse over the periodicals, those who gathered in the bar, those who congregated round the billiard table, and those whose relaxation was talk. Into this last group I naturally gravitated, for talk was my favourite amusements and I had had few opportunities of indulging in it since leaving the Hampden Club in London. There it had been a light-hearted distraction, but now I found myself in the company of some of the best talkers of the time. Arthur Salter, Rajchman, Salvador de Madariaga, William Rappard, Pierre Comert and Paul Mantoux were stars of the first magnitude,[2] and equally brilliant were some of the visitors who came to get a personal impression of what was going forward in Geneva and who were introduced into the same group by one or another of its members. When these were present, the problems and prospects of the League naturally figured largely in the conversation. The ILO excited no comparable interest and indeed some of the visitors seemed scarcely aware of its existence. I had thus something to contribute and I neglected no opportunity to draw attention to its activities and to the importance of the innovations it had introduced into international practice. On other occasions when discussions developed on subjects of which I knew little, I was generally content to listen and learn, but sometimes I could not

---

[1] See Ch. 5, n. 4 above.

[2] For Arthur Salter, see Ch. 3, n. 9 above.

Ludwik Rajchman (1881–1965) was a Polish bacteriologist who joined the League of Nations Epidemic Commission to assist in the fight against the typhus epidemic in Poland in 1920–21. In 1921 he became Director of the League of Nations Health Organization (1921–39). When in 1945 the United Nations Relief and Rehabilitation Administration (UNRRA) was about to be disbanded, he succeeded in placing its residual resources in a special fund to help children. Thus the United Nations International Children's Emergency Fund (UNICEF) came into being on 11 December 1946 with Rajchman as its first Chairman.

Salvador de Madariaga y Rojo (1886–1978) was a Spanish diplomat. In 1921 he became a Member of the Press Section of the Secretariat of the League of Nations and later the Chief of the Disarmament Section (1922–28).

For William Rappard, see Ch. 6, n. 54 above.

Pierre Emilien Comert (1880–1964) was Director of the Information Section of the League of Nations from 1919 to 1932.

For Paul Mantoux, see Ch. 6, n. 48 above. (Ed.)

resist the temptation to plunge into the argument on one side or the other just for the fun of joining in the fray.

These verbal battles, which to me personally were the greatest attraction of the club, were fortuitous affairs arising spontaneously when a small number of people who enjoyed such contests happened to come together. Only those who actually took part in them were aware that the existence of the club made them possible. What impressed the ordinary visitor as giving the club a unique character was that it was used by so many celebrities attending the League meetings, and this was a feature sometimes described with picturesque inaccuracy. One day, a journalist brought me the manuscript of an article which he was about to despatch to an American periodical.

"I think you'll like this," he said. "I've given your Club a real boost."

"I'm afraid there are a few things you'll have to change," I said after reading his pages.

"What's the matter with it?" he asked, surprised and crestfallen.

"Well, you can't put this in," I replied, and read out the following: "There in a corner of the lounge, resplendent in his green turban, sits Sir Louis Kershaw,[3] one of the half-dozen men who govern India. And a little further on you will recognize the hunched figure of that famous English statesman, Lord Robert Cecil, son of the great Gladstone."

"What's wrong with that?" he enquired, obviously taken aback at this objection to a passage of which he was especially proud.

"Everything's wrong with it," I replied impatiently. "Indian civil servants never wear turbans, and Cecil is no relation of Gladstone – his father was Lord Salisbury."

"Who was Salisbury?" he asked.

"He was Prime Minister during the reign of Queen Victoria."[4]

"Nobody in America ever heard of him. But they've heard of Gladstone. He was Prime Minister too, wasn't he?"

"Yes," I said.

"Well," he said, triumphantly, "that makes it OK. They'll get the idea."

The function of the club in providing a social centre for the international

---

[3] Sir Louis James Kershaw (1869–1947) was Deputy Under-Secretary of State at the India Office. He attended the Paris Peace Conference in 1919 and was the British Government delegate to the First Session of the ILC in 1919. He represented India as government delegate at the ILC from 1921 to 1927 and the British Government in the ILO Governing Body between 1923 and 1926. (Ed.)

[4] Robert Arthur Talbot Gascoyne-Cecil, Marquess of Salisbury (1830–1903), was Prime Minister of the United Kingdom from 1885 to January 1886, from July 1886 to 1892, and from June 1895 to July 1902. (Ed.)

colony led incidentally to other initiatives of greater and, as it proved, more permanent importance. Various private international organizations were moving their headquarters to the world's new international capital. Out of the contacts which their representatives were able to establish in the club eventually emerged the Federation of Private International Institutions, the object of which was to secure for its constituent members a recognized status and certain facilities for their work. I incautiously took some part in the discussions that led to this result and then, much to my dismay, I found myself invited to assume the presidency of the new body, a request difficult to refuse since it was unanimous. As president of both the Federation and the International Club, and thus doubly qualified to voice the needs of the international colony, I was accorded a seat on the committee of the Intérêts de Genève. This liaison with local interests was instrumental in giving an impulse to the development of certain amenities much desired by the international community of which the most noteworthy was the provision of a golf course.

These new responsibilities were, however, not unduly burdensome. I still had time for disputation and a surplus of youthful energy which on one occasion enabled me to confound my opponents. The affair had its origin in a conversation with J.E. Herbert and Ernest Greenwood,[5] the ILO representatives in London and Washington, who were in Geneva during a session of the Conference in order to keep in touch with the press correspondents from their respective countries. My expression of disappointment with the meagre publicity that the Conference was receiving aroused their resentment. They pointed out that little or nothing connected with the Conference was "news" – the fate of some technical amendment, however important it might be in my view, was of no interest to the press – if, for example, a delegate were to shoot one of his colleagues, there would be plenty of publicity. I retorted that just to sit around waiting for a shooting affray between delegates hardly justified their presence in Geneva – if anything so unlikely happened the journalists would be well able to deal with it without their help. There were, I asserted, many novel features about an ILO Conference which it ought to be possible to present in a way that would arouse the interest of an intelligent journalist. They were nettled by my attack on their complacency and my insistence that, surely with a little effort, something could be done to improve

---

[5] Joseph Edward Herbert (1885–1955) was a British journalist (*Manchester Guardian, The Times*). He was appointed Director of the ILO London Office in 1920 and was transferred to Geneva as Assistant Chief of the Editorial Division in 1924. He resigned from the ILO staff in 1939. (Ed.)

Ernest Greenwood was Deputy Secretary-General of the First Session of the ILC in Washington, DC (1919) and ILO Correspondent in Washington (1920–24). (Ed.)

matters. The discussion grew warm. They waved aside with utter contempt one or two suggestions that I tried to get them to examine. These only showed how completely ignorant I was of the nature of the journalist's task. Finally, they said that it was easy enough to talk and that, if I was convinced that my ideas were practical, I ought myself to put them to the test. They were prepared to bet a hundred francs that I would fail to secure any result.

My immediate acceptance of this challenge was not as rash as it seemed. In those more tranquil times, the summer season was characterized by a general preoccupation with holidays and by the slowing down, or even cessation, of political and other feverish political activities. Newspapers were obliged to search for less serious topics and, sooner or later, rumours of the reappearance of the sea serpent might be expected to be given prominence in their pages if nothing so welcome as a horrible murder came to the relief of a hard-pressed editor. I saw no reason why Anthrax should not compete with the sea serpent for a share of the editor's attention and, with this as a starting point, I evolved a plan which I proceeded to put into operation.

I went along to the Café de la Régence on the Quai du Mont Blanc where I was well known to the proprietor and asked him to bring me a "white lead and anthrax". He looked at me blankly.

"What," I said, "don't you serve the new cocktail? Everybody is drinking it."

"Can you tell me how it is made?" he asked eagerly.

"Yes," I replied, "but only on condition that you keep its composition secret and that you display in the window a notice in French and English like this" – I handed him a piece of paper on which I had pencilled:

"The new ILO Conference Cocktail:
WHITE LEAD and ANTHRAX"

«Le nouveau cocktail de la Conférence du Travail:
CERUSE et CHARBON»

He readily accepted my conditions and I then visited a number of other establishments with which I easily succeeded in making the same bargain. Cocktails at that time were confined to a few standard varieties and barmen had not yet begun to compound their own "specials". The announcement of a new concoction with a gruesome name attracted attention and an immediate demand from amused and curious delegates started a demand that rapidly spread. The correspondent of the London *Times* sent in a dispatch recounting that a new cocktail with the startling name of "white lead and anthrax" had acquired an extraordinary vogue in Geneva. He explained that this name was derived from two items on the agenda of the International Labour Conference which was considering measures for the prevention of anthrax, a disease to which workers handling imported wool were exposed, and for the prohibition of the use of white lead pigments because of the prevalence of lead poisoning among painters. The cocktail, which was advertised by placards in all the bars and cafés, was repulsive in appearance, having a blackish-green colour appropriate to its nominally poisonous contents, and there was much speculation about its composition. It had, however, a pleasant taste and it possessed an unusual "kick" which no doubt partly accounted for its popularity. His story was given double headlines and nearly two-thirds of a column on the foreign page of *The Times*.

Another conversation concerning publicity led to far more important results. J. Sigfrid Edström, the Swedish employer on the Governing Body,[6] was, unlike most of the members of the group, himself the active head of a large industrial enterprise. A man with a progressive outlook, he was keenly interested in the ILO's activities and one evening he happened to say that it was a pity that so little was known in Sweden about the ILO and its work.

"Why don't you do something?" I replied. "Why don't you get the Swedish Government to invite the Governing Body to meet in Stockholm? All Sweden would then learn a good deal about it."

The idea made an immediate appeal to Edström's practical mind.

"That's an excellent suggestion," he said. "I'll take it up with the Prime Minister as soon as I get back."

I had not anticipated any such positive reaction to what I had intended as no more than a conversational challenge and, realizing that questions of policy might be involved, I took the first opportunity of telling Albert Thomas what had transpired. He was not inclined to think that any great importance should be attached to Edström's remark and he told me to warn him that expenditure would be involved for which no funds were available. I reported this to Edström but he was not the man to be deterred by difficulties. Some weeks later, Sweden invited the Governing Body to meet in Stockholm and accompanied the invitation with an offer to pay whatever additional expense would be incurred. Simultaneously, Denmark invited the committees, which normally met before the Governing Body went into session, to hold their sittings in Copenhagen.[7]

---

[6] Johannes Sigfrid Edström (1870–1964), a Swedish businessman, was an employers' group adviser at the First Session of the ILC in Washington, DC in 1919. A member of the International Olympic Committee from 1920 to 1952, he was also President of the Swedish Association of Machine Builders and attended several sessions of the ILO Governing Body (1920–22) and the ILC (1921–23) as an employers' delegate. (Ed.)

[7] The Eighth Session of the ILO Governing Body took place in Stockholm from 5 to 7 July 1921. The committees met in Copenhagen on 2 July 1921. (Ed.)

The example set by Sweden and Denmark was followed by other countries. It became almost a regular practice for the Governing Body to hold one of its meetings each year away from the ILO headquarters and sessions took place in Paris, Berlin, Warsaw, Madrid, Brussels, Rome and Prague.[8] The effect was twofold: the ILO ceased to be a remote and shadowy abstraction and became for the countries it visited a visible reality; at the same time, members of the Governing Body acquired a new sense of the importance and high status of their functions. Edström himself did not have the satisfaction of participating in these sequels to his initiative. His electrical company encountered financial difficulties which compelled him to leave the Governing Body in order to devote all his attention to his private affairs. Years later, after he had succeeded in re-establishing his fortunes, he again made a notable contribution to international life when, as President of the Olympic Games Organization, he played a major part in restoring its activities after the end of the Second World War.

[*Editor's note: The author continues this chapter with anecdotes about Geneva acquaintances and members of the Governing Body.*]

Postscript

At this point Edward Phelan's manuscript stops. His memories of the following quarter of a century, which would have been invaluable, were never written. But we have a partial record, in other forms, of what he would have said. Of his other writings by far the most important is *Yes and Albert Thomas*,[9] his moving tribute to the first Director of the ILO, which in effect continues the story until 1932; it has become and will remain a classic of the literature of international organizations. Any full story of the later years must now be by another hand; but a foretaste of what he would have said is available in a memorable series of seven articles concerning the ILO during the 1920s and the Second World War, which he published in the Irish review *Studies*.[10] These were originally intended as a

---

[8] The Governing Body also met in London but this was during the period between the Washington and Genoa Conferences when London was the headquarters of the ILO. London is therefore not included in this list. (E.J.P.)

The Governing Body was held in: Rome (12th Session 1922), Berlin (37th Session 1927), Warsaw (42nd Session 1928), Paris (48th Session 1930), Brussels (50th Session 1930), Madrid (60th Session 1932), Prague (81st Session 1937). For the interwar period, Phelan does not mention Paris (Second Session 1920), Interlaken (13th Session 1922) or London (85th Session 1938). (Ed.)

[9] See the Selected Bibliography of Phelan's writings in this volume. (Ed.)

[10] Three of these are reprinted in this volume: "Some reminiscences of the International Labour Organization" (1954), "The ILO sets up its wartime centre in Canada" (1955) and "The ILO turns the corner" (1956). (Ed.)

first draft of his memories of the later years but were never revised or completed, partly because of failing health and vigour, partly perhaps because, during the middle years of his retirement, the uncertain bent of world affairs made him increasingly reluctant to express in a more permanent form his judgements of events in which he had been so intimately involved. His story therefore remains incomplete, but incomplete though it may be it remains of permanent importance for the history of international organizations and social policy in the twentieth century. His place in the history of the International Labour Organization is, and in the nature of the case will always remain, unique; his place in the first rank of international public servants is equally assured.

C. Wilfred Jenks

Part III
Other writings of Edward Phelan

Some reminiscences of the International Labour Organization[1]

W hen I wrote a brief account of the ILO for *Studies* in 1925 the ILO was little more than five years old. It had made a remarkably successful start and it had a surprising number of substantial achievements to its credit. But many believed that fortuitous circumstances had favoured its precocious development and that once its initial momentum had exhausted itself, its pace would be moderated to the sober gait of a government department pursuing unobtrusively its appointed technical task. They attributed the intensity and variety of its activities, and the success that attended them even in the most unexpected fields, to the extraordinary driving force of the first Director, Albert Thomas. Delegates who felt the impact of his personality, who were carried along by his energy and eloquence, who were dazzled, or dismayed, by his endless initiative, not unnaturally came to the conclusion that without his brilliant leadership the ILO would have been, and would inevitably become, a much more modest institution. Instead of leading the ILO along sheltered paths appropriate to its youth and inexperience, Albert Thomas seemed to take delight in conducting it to the assault of dizzy precipices and in seeking out the most dangerous adversaries for it to confront. In the name of the ILO he even challenged the Supreme Council – in the days when that august body was all that its name implied; and with equal boldness he defied the Council of the League and established the headquarters of the ILO in Geneva, compelling the League to follow suit though he well knew that plans were far advanced for abandoning Geneva in favour of Brussels.[2]

---

[1] First published in 1954 in *Studies: An Irish Quarterly Review*, Vol. 43, No. 171, pp. 241–70. (Ed.)

[2] For an account of these and other incidents, see E.J. Phelan: *Yes and Albert Thomas* (London, Cresset Press, 1936), pp. 71–103. (Ed.)

His spectacular successes on these and similar occasions naturally attracted the spotlight of publicity and left in the shadow the purposes that in fact they were designed to subserve. Though the objects pursued were in themselves justifiable and important, these dramatic interventions were merely incidental to his wider objectives of teaching the ILO that it had constitutional responsibilities that it must not evade and of demonstrating to governments that a new international organization existed whose rights and competence could not with impunity be bypassed or ignored.

The ILO's heritage

Those who expected that the ILO would decline in vigour when death removed Albert Thomas from his post found that they had been blind to his real achievement. He left to the Organization an inspiration and a vision so compelling that it might almost be said to have inherited the personality of its late Director. Certainly he bequeathed to it a cohesion and an identity, a spirit and a character such as no other public international institution had possessed before or has since managed to acquire. It is not easy to convey in any brief fashion the real nature of Albert Thomas' contribution to the ILO's development without leaving the impression that it consisted wholly in imbuing the institution with a strong sense of the unique importance of its mission. That belief was indeed the mainspring of his activity and he was untiring in his effort to arouse and to spread the conviction that in the pursuit of social justice lay the only road to an enduring peace; but he believed with equal intensity that in the ILO the world possessed for the first time an effective instrument through which the cause of social justice might be steadily advanced. The real importance of his achievement, and what gave it a lasting character, was that he perfected the instrument given into his charge and with the instinct of genius revealed its unsuspected potentialities. What he accomplished will be better understood if we remember that a political, unlike a physical, machine cannot be subjected to tests and alterations before it is put into operation, and only on rare occasions is it ever possible to make such subsequent modifications in its structure as experience may suggest. Its success, therefore, depends not on constant improvement in design but on the discovery and development of skills in its use. If its first design is good so much the better, but, good or bad, what determines its fate is the vision and intelligence with which it is made to perform its task. It is from this point of view that Albert Thomas' contribution to the ILO overshadows even that of its creators. Great as their achievement was, it was limited to the plan for a new kind of international organization. The ILO was like a windmill, novel in its structure and embodying many innovations in its mechanism, but like all windmills it was wholly dependent for its successful operation on two things external to it – a breeze to turn the sails and customers to bring it business. Despite all the ingenuity of its designers, it might have experienced only short spells of activity alternating with long periods of stagnation had it not been that Albert Thomas, who was chosen as the Master Miller, combined an extraordinary talent of salesmanship with an inventive aerodynamical genius, the one producing a steadily increasing flow of grist, and the other so skilfully taking advantage of aerial currents that the wheels ground on without interruption and were ever equal to the task demanded of them. What he left to his successor was no longer an experiment but an established and renowned concern solidly based on a firm foundation of goodwill and equipped with newly discovered techniques for its successful operation.

In normal circumstances so strong a position would have been a sufficient guarantee of the ILO's future. But when Harold Butler became Director in 1932 the world economic crisis had swept through country after country with devastating effects and conditions had become steadily less favourable for international activity. He would have done well had he succeeded in maintaining the Organization at the level to which Albert Thomas had raised it and few would have thought it possible that he should do more.

The two men were very different. Albert Thomas was by instinct a politician and his career had lain in the political field; he enjoyed political battles as much as he welcomed political responsibility. It was on the political stage that he found the greatest scope for his gifts of magnetism and eloquence; and they were so dazzlingly displayed, as we have seen, his deeper purposes and his other abilities went largely unperceived. Harold Butler had inherited the tastes and instincts of a scholar and was by profession a civil servant; and he had many of the characteristics with which these two careers are commonly associated. In the human contacts that Albert Thomas could so easily translate into intimacy, Butler found it difficult to conquer a certain shyness and reserve that sometimes gave an impression of diffidence. Feeling strongly the responsibilities he had shouldered, he was cautious to the point of being often so non-committal as to lead people to think that he was being deliberately evasive. But in his case also these externals were deceptive; they masked a high intelligence, great powers of concentration and assimilation and the ability to reach by a process of study and synthesis conclusions on general policy. He lacked the politician's gift of being able to choose instinctively in the changing fortunes of debate the tactical position best adapted to secure progress to his objective; but his vision of the general political scene was acute and no one was quicker at seeing the dangers or the opportunities it might present. In addition to these qualities he possessed an unsurpassed knowledge of the ILO's history, a complete familiarity with its activities and techniques, and that special personal interest in its fortunes that naturally belonged to one who has had an important part in its creation and who had launched it on its career at Washington in 1919. He was now as Director to render further great services to the Organization and in particular to bring to fulfilment a hope which had once seemed reasonable but which for a long time had steadily receded as any prospect of its realization grew more and more remote.

Economic and political events in the United States

The world economic crisis which had progressively disrupted that world's economic and financial system struck the United States with the force of a tornado. The whole financial system of the country collapsed in chaos; the banks closed their doors; factories unable to sell their products were unable to pay their workers and were forced to suspend operations; bankruptcy and unemployment spread like a plague. In the distress and destitution that resulted, a violent political reaction was inevitable. The Republican Party, which had held almost unchallenged power since President Wilson had been defeated on the issue of the League of Nations, was disavowed by an immense swing of public opinion and Franklin Roosevelt entered the White House as President in March 1933. Butler was quick to see the possibilities of this new situation. Roosevelt had been Assistant Secretary of the Navy when the ILO held its first Conference in Washington in 1919 and had personally arranged for the provision of office space for the Conference staff in the temporary Navy Building. He had thus been associated with the ILO's earliest activities and was acquainted with its structure and purposes. Moreover, he had appointed as Secretary of Labor Miss Frances Perkins,[3] who was personally known to Butler and who had long shown a keen interest in the ILO's work.

It will be remembered that the Commission of the peace conference which had drawn up the Constitution of the International Labour Organization had been presided over by Samuel Gompers, the President of the American Federation of Labor, and it had been a blow to the Organization when United States membership became impossible because of the storm over the League of Nations.

---

[3] Frances Coralie Perkins (1882–1965), the first woman ever appointed to a US Cabinet position, served as Secretary of Labor from 1933 to 1945. She was a US Government delegate to the ILC in 1937, 1938, 1944 and 1945. In 1941 she was President of the ILC held in New York and Washington, DC. (Ed.)

Efforts had nevertheless been undertaken to secure some form of collaboration between the United States and the ILO, and Albert Thomas had even succeeded in 1923 in securing agreement for the regular attendance of workers' and employers' delegates. This agreement had been accepted by the American Federation of Labor and the United States Chamber of Commerce and had been welcomed by Mr Herbert Hoover,[4] who was then President Harding's Secretary of Commerce, but the rising tide of isolationist sentiment prevented its implementation. The ILO had, however, maintained a Branch Office in Washington and statistical and other information from the United States was made available. There had never been the same hostility to the ILO as to the League and now that a Democratic administration had come into power it seemed that the problem of United States collaboration with the ILO should be explored afresh.

A geographical solution to a political problem

Although there were now new and much more favourable factors in the situation, Butler was well aware that isolationist feeling was still strong and that therefore he must proceed with great caution. He wrote to Miss Perkins in an endeavour to discover what the possibilities might be of establishing some form of closer collaboration with the United States. Her reply was warmly sympathetic but not definite enough to give him any clear guidance. This was indeed understandable. As Secretary of Labor, she was in process of shouldering immense new responsibilities and was a central figure in the formulation of many of the new and daring measures for dealing with the national crisis. It was not to be expected therefore that she could do more than indicate her general interest and desire to be helpful. In these circumstances, Butler felt he must somehow get a clearer picture of what was happening in the United States before he could make any definite suggestions about the ILO. It was not easy from Europe to follow in any detail all the daring initiatives that were being taken in the social and economic fields and still less to attempt to form any judgment of their impact on American opinion. A personal visit would of course have enabled him to secure the answer to his problem but to this there were obvious and serious objections. A visit by the Director of the ILO to Washington at that time would inevitably attract attention; it would be given publicity and there was clearly a danger that it would give rise to speculation in

---

[4] Herbert Clark Hoover (1874–1964) was appointed Secretary of Commerce by President Harding in 1921. He later became President of the United States (1929–33). (Ed.)

the press that might do incalculable harm. Even if some less important official were to go over, it would be desirable that his presence should be susceptible of a wholly sound and harmless explanation. Butler hit upon an ingenious way in which this could be accomplished.

There was a genuine, and indeed an urgent, need for someone to visit Canada. Conditions in Canada, though they attracted less notice, were in many ways not less severe than those in the United States. The normal economic life of the country was disorganized and unemployment and its accompanying distress was rife. As one Canadian author put it, nearly a million Canadians waited in dismal queues to obtain a minimum of relief "just sufficient to keep together a hungry body and a despairing soul". The remedy of the Bennett Government was a policy of tariffs designed to prevent the importation into Canada of any goods that she could manufacture herself and the plan, pursued at the Ottawa Conference, to make the British Commonwealth a self-sufficing economic unit.

The social elements in the crisis were ignored.[5] The Department of Labour became an insignificant piece of administrative machinery pursuing in obscurity routine matters with, to all intents and purposes, no ministerial head. Since this Department was the channel of communication between the ILO and the Canadian Government, this meant that the Cabinet was not kept regularly informed of ILO activities and in consequence had little knowledge of their nature and, no doubt, even less sense of their importance. In these circumstances, it was not surprising that suggestions were mooted to make economies by moving for a reduction in the ILO's budget and by sending only an incomplete delegation, or possibly no delegation at all, to the next ILO Conference. These ideas did not derive from any hostility to the ILO and there was therefore reason to hope that personal discussion with the authorities in Ottawa would at all events succeed in placing the question of collaboration with the ILO in a different perspective. At the time when all countries were struggling with economic and financial difficulties, the dangers exemplified by the Canadian situation might well arise elsewhere and this pointed to the desirability of multiplying the ILO's direct contacts with its member States. It happened that Mexico was a country to which no ILO mission had ever gone and to which a visit by an ILO representative was long overdue. Butler decided to combine these two missions and asked me to undertake them, pointing out

---

[5] At a later stage the Bennett Government modified this attitude and introduced a wide "new deal" programme. (E.J.P.)

as he did so that, as I should be under the geographical necessity of passing through the United States in order to get from Canada to Mexico, I might naturally take advantage of the opportunity to make contact with some of our American friends.[6]

The attitude of the Roosevelt Administration to international institutions

After leaving Canada, I accordingly broke my journey in New York in order to get some first impressions of the American scene. It proved a fortunate starting point. Roosevelt had gone to the presidency from the governorship of the State of New York, and New York City was the centre from which he had drawn some of his friends to become his closest advisers. In those early days of his administration, New York was indeed almost a political suburb of Washington to and from which many of the brilliant individuals who came to be known as the "Brains Trust" regularly commuted. I had friends in New York, whose acquaintance I had made during my contacts with the American delegation at the peace conference, and I had expected to be able to talk with them in a leisurely and tentative fashion. I was astonished at the rapidity and energy of their behaviour, but I found that this was character- istic of the initiative and activity that Roosevelt's assumption of office seemed to have released in progressive intellectual circles. As soon as I had told them of my preoccupations, I was rushed round the city to meet a number of people whose names meant as little to me as mine to them; their offices were entered without ceremony or excuse; telegrams were sent, letters dictated and signed, and in a few hours I was on my way to Washington, more than a little breathless but equipped with introductions to and appointments with half a dozen of the personalities who were helping to formulate the new policies. In Washington, I was also fortunate in finding another old friend, Michael MacWhite, the Irish Minister.[7] No one else in the diplomatic corps had a better knowledge of the intricacies of the capital's political life, and, as he was one of Washington's most popular hosts, his hospital- ity made it possible for me to meet in the intimacy of social gatherings a number of Washington's more important figures. With all these contacts, I was soon able

---

[6] The mission took place between 10 and 31 May 1933. Phelan spent two days in Canada (10–11 May) and a week in Washington, DC before going on to Mexico City (22–25 May). On his way back to New York he stopped again in Washington and boarded ship on 31 May. For further information, see Mr Phelan's mission to Canada, the United States and Mexico (May 1933), XT 11/1/1, ILO Historical Archives (Ed.)

[7] Michael MacWhite (1883–1958), Representative of the Irish Free State accredited to the League of Nations (1923–29) was Vice-President (Government) of the ILC at its 11th Session (Geneva, 1928). (Ed.)

to feel that I had a pretty good understanding of the political background against which any discussion of the ILO's affairs must take place. As in New York, there was a readiness to explore all sorts of new ideas but a much more realistic view of what was politically possible. Much as many might deplore it, they regarded any gesture towards the League as out of the question: I was told with equal frankness that the ILO, admirable though it might be, could not expect to be given any consideration; that the only international interest of the United States was in the Economic Conference and that, if it should prove a failure, isolationism would become more pronounced than ever. This was not particularly encouraging but it suggested a line of argument that attracted attention. It had not been realized that the ILO was actively interested in international economic policy; that it had adopted at its last Conference a resolution proposed by Professor Alfred O'Rahilly on economic matters;[8] that it would be represented by a delegation at the forthcoming Economic Conference in London; and that therefore it was perhaps a mistake to dismiss it so summarily from consideration.

My most important conversation was of course with Miss Perkins. She had kept the greater part of a morning free for a discussion which she was willing to continue until every aspect of the question had been thoroughly explored, but although she was anxious to secure the closest possible collaboration with the ILO, she had no definite plan in mind as to what form it might take. She agreed with what I told her of the general impressions I had formed and was particularly interested in the link between the International Labour Conference and the forthcoming International Economic Conference which she asked me to explain to the Secretary of State. The idea of sending a delegation of observers to the ILO Conference appealed to her and she promised to seek the President's approval for the appointment of such a delegation by the Department of Labor – a procedure which had the advantage that congressional approval would not be required. Secretary Hull,[9] whom I saw later, proved equally generous with his time; he expressed great interest in the ILO and a readiness to examine with Miss Perkins what could be done to further collaboration with it.

The United States decides to explore the ILO

The following day Miss Perkins told me that she had seen the President and that he had given his approval to her proposal. Somewhat to my dismay she added

---

[8] Professor Alfred O'Rahilly (1884–1969), a mathematical physicist, led Irish delegations to the ILC in 1924, 1925 and 1932. (Ed.)

[9] Cordell Hull (1871–1955) was US Secretary of State from 1933 to 1944. He received the Nobel Peace Prize in 1945 for his role in establishing the United Nations. (Ed.)

that this approval must not be taken as final, but only as meaning that she could go ahead and get the proposal into detailed shape for a final decision at a Cabinet meeting. This indeed was as much as, or even more than, I could have hoped for and I felt I could inform Butler that things were going well and that prospects were favourable. There was of course still a danger that amid the feverish activity in Washington the proposal might get swamped in the flood of other and more pressing issues or that it would not secure final approval in the brief time remaining before the Conference was due to open. But on the whole, I continued to feel optimistic even though I became somewhat concerned when no news reached me in Mexico. However, when rather more than a couple of weeks after I had left Washington, I boarded the *Europa* at New York I found among my fellow passengers a delegation of United States observers bound for the ILO Conference. [10]

This was a great step forward and one that seemed to justify hopes that, if all went well, further developments might be possible in the future. That these would present difficulties was brought home to us by the discretion with which the observers felt it necessary to go about their task. While they were wholly sympathetic to the ILO and grew steadily more impressed with the atmosphere and efficiency of the Conference, they made it clear that they had no other interest in Geneva. They took up their quarters some distance outside the city and drove in each day to the Conference hall, thus keeping themselves as remote as possible from any contact with the seat of the League of Nations. Exaggerated as these precautions may seem, they were no doubt taken on instructions and were deemed to be necessary given the climate of public opinion that then prevailed in the United States.

The question of the relationship between the League and the ILO was bound of course to figure in any discussion of some more effective collaboration between the ILO and the United States. But it was a delicate political question that lay outside the competence of the observers whose mission, as they had made abundantly clear, was limited to reporting on the working of the Conference and on the ILO's social objectives. The task of reporting on the ILO's constitutional independence had therefore been confided by the State Department to the American Consul at Geneva, Prentiss Gilbert, [11] a career man in the diplomatic service whose intelligence, experience and objectivity well qualified him to examine in a completely unbiased fashion the somewhat intricate legal and constitutional issues involved. The fact that this careful study was being undertaken

---

[10] 17th Session of the ILC, Geneva, 8–30 June 1933. The US delegation of observers consisted of Mary Anderson, Edwin S. Smith, William H. Stead and Hugh Frayne. (Ed.)

[11] Prentiss B. Gilbert (1883–1939) represented the United States at the League of Nations. (Ed.)

was evidence that the United States did not consider that the attendance at the Conference of observers from the Department of Labor was the only form of collaboration with the ILO that might be envisaged. Butler, of course, was more than willing to give Prentiss Gilbert every possible facility for his enquiry. He was confident that it must show that, though the ILO was associated with the League and made use of the League machinery for certain purposes, the ILO was a completely independent body that formulated its own policies and administered its affairs without League interference or control. He was also satisfied that the report of the observers would be wholly favourable both on the working of the Conference and the results that it had achieved.

Roosevelt authorizes an approach to Congress

So far, Butler had only ventured to suggest to Miss Perkins in very general terms that the question of closer collaboration between the United States and the ILO should be explored. Now that that exploration had taken place and that the American Government was in possession of reports from its own representatives covering both the ILO's constitutional position and its methods of work, Butler felt that the ground had been cleared and that the possibility of United States membership might well be considered. He accordingly wrote to Miss Perkins suggesting that she should take up this question with the President. Miss Perkins has recorded how she reacted to Butler's request; [12] how she discussed the matter with the President; and how he told her to approach the leaders of Congress individually and attempt to secure their approval. He impressed on her that the first and most important step would be to see that they understood the whole question of the relations between the ILO and the League, and that they must be satisfied that joining the ILO would not involve the United States in any League obligations. This task Miss Perkins carried out with great skill and patience. Senators and congressmen were immersed in the discussion of innumerable domestic questions of the greatest urgency and it was by no means easy, even for a member of the Cabinet, to secure their attention for the consideration of a complicated legal argument concerning an international institution with which they were little (if at all) familiar and which was remote from all their pressing preoccupations. The process was necessarily slow – the President with his political wisdom

---

[12] See *The Roosevelt I knew*, Chapter XXVI entitled "Approaches to World Order", by Frances Perkins. (E.J.P.)

had specifically insisted that those approached should not be hurried and should be given plenty of time to come to their conclusions. Moreover, it had to be kept highly confidential; there must be no leakage that might precipitate a discussion before the leaders of Congress had become fully conversant with the matter and capable of defending the favourable opinion at which it was hoped they would arrive. For this reason, no communication could be made to Geneva, and as months went by with no news from Washington, it began to look as though Butler's hopes were doomed to disappointment. He was, nevertheless, not inclined to give up without a further effort, but he was confronted with the same difficulty as at the earlier stage of being unable to judge whether any intervention on his part might not do more harm than good. His perplexity was the greater because he felt that the most favourable moment must be passing, that the promising atmosphere at the end of the Conference must be fading and that it would be impossible to renew it if the opportunities it provided were now to go by default. It happened that I had been in correspondence for some time with Professor Shotwell of Columbia University in connection with the volumes on The origins of the International Labour Organization which he was editing for the Carnegie Foundation, and that a number of points had arisen which could not easily be settled without a meeting between us. This afforded a good reason for my going to New York, and Butler authorized me to visit Washington, but only on the express condition that I should first make absolutely sure that if I did so I should cause no embarrassment. A few telephone calls made as soon as I disembarked made it clear that I need have no such apprehension but that on the contrary my presence would be welcome; and exactly a week later I was again crossing the Atlantic in the opposite direction bearing the comforting news that all was ready for the submission of the question to Congress and that favourable action by that body might be considered as imminent. [13]

The International Labour Conference faces up to its responsibility

When the Conference opened on 4 June, there was an undercurrent of excitement. [14] Butler had of course to begin to prepare the ground and he had confidentially informed members of the Governing Body and heads of delegations that some approach by the United States might be expected. The journalists were alert,

---

[13] This mission took place in March 1934. For further information, see Mr Phelan's mission to the United States (March 1934), XT 61/3/1, ILO Historical Archives

[14] 18th Session of the ILC, Geneva, 4–23 June 1934. (Ed.)

having somehow discovered that something was brewing. Butler evaded them successfully. He felt that the first announcement must come from the United States and that any statement he himself might make, however general in its terms, might upset things in Washington while Congress was still considering its decision. The journalists pursued with more success, but with no greater satisfaction, the American delegation of observers who were unwilling or unable – probably the latter – to give them any information. [15] During these days, for reasons that will be given in a moment, Butler was under considerable strain, and that strain was intensified in almost comic fashion by two small incidents. On 6 June the American Consulate telephoned to say that they were sending up a cable from Washington. When Butler opened it, it proved to be a message from Miss Perkins regretting that she was unable to attend the Conference as she had hoped to do and asking that all possible facilities might be given to the American observers. Later the same day, the Consulate again telephoned that another cable was on the way. This, a much more bulky envelope, seemed likely to contain the expected communication, particularly as, when the envelope was ripped open, it was seen to be signed by Cordell Hull. It turned out to be the official, and somewhat belated, communication of the full names and titles of the American observers. Several more days were to pass before Butler learned that congressional action had been completed and was favourable, but he still did not know the exact terms of the decision and felt compelled to maintain his silence. It was only on 21 June that the text reached him accompanied by an authorization to communicate it officially to the Conference and he was then able to inform the journalists that an important announcement would be made the following morning. Though the decision of Congress, both in form and substance, was wholly satisfactory he had still, as will be seen later, many serious anxieties, and a brief delay was necessary to arrange the procedure that the Conference should follow, and to prepare the text of a reply that the Conference might be asked to approve.

Towards the end of the sitting the next morning, Butler communicated to the Conference a joint resolution of Congress that authorized the President of the United States to accept membership in the International Labour Organization, and he added that he had been given to understand that the American Government would consider favourably an invitation to this effect. After half a dozen

---

[15] The observers were: Elmer F. Andrews, Industrial Commissioner for the State of New York; Hugh S. Hanna, Chief of the Editorial Research Division, Bureau of Labor Statistics, American Department of Labor; Ethel Bagg Bullard; E. Arthur Baldwin, President of the American Chamber of Commerce in France and Vice-President of the International General Electric Company, New York; John L. Lewis, President of the United Mine Workers of America. (Ed.)

delegates had briefly expressed their satisfaction, the President of the Conference adjourned the sitting indicating that the Selection (or General) Committee would meet at 3.30 p.m. and that the Conference would reconvene in plenary sitting at 4.30. When the Conference reassembled punctually at the hour fixed, the Chairman of the Selection Committee laid before it a resolution for adoption. The text was short and clear. Its most important paragraph ran as follows:

> The International Labour Conference ... hereby decides to invite the Government of the United States to accept membership in the International Labour Organisation it being understood that such acceptance involves only the rights and obligations provided in the Constitution of the Organisation and shall not involve any obligation under the Covenant of the League of Nations.[16]

The Chairman of the Selection Committee made no speech beyond his opening sentence in which he informed the Conference that the Selection Committee had been unanimous in submitting its proposal. Other delegates imposed on themselves a similar restraint. Like the members of the Selection Committee, they realized the importance of allowing the terms of the resolution to express the decision of the Conference unaccompanied by any comment or paraphrase that might at some later time be quoted as shading its meaning. Only three or four delegates (including Frank Cremins,[17] representing Ireland) intervened to say in a few short sentences how warmly their governments welcomed the proposal. The President then put the resolution to the Conference and it was adopted unanimously.

The conflict between League and ILO policy

It may seem an exaggeration to accord to this decision of the Conference an importance equal to that of the action of the United States save in the sense that one was the complement of the other in order to secure the result desired by both. In retrospect, it would seem inconceivable that the Conference should

---

[16] For the complete text of the resolution, see ILO: *Conference of the International Labour Organisation: 18th Session, Geneva, Record of proceedings* (Geneva, 1934), p. 463. This resolution was adopted on 22 June 1934, at the 23rd sitting of the 18th Session of the ILC. (Ed.)

[17] Francis T. Cremins was the permanent delegate for Ireland to the League of Nations from 1934 to 1940, and government delegate for Ireland to the ILC from 1934 to 1937. (Ed.)

have followed any other course. But the matter was far from being as simple at that time as it must now appear. Just as Roosevelt had had a problem requiring careful and skilful handling extending over nearly 12 months, Butler also had a problem demanding caution on his side and one that laid on him a heavy burden of anxiety and responsibility.

There had long been a conflict between the ILO and the League over the question of the ILO's right to include in its membership States not members of the League of Nations. The view of the ILO was that while it was specifically provided that Members of the League were Members of the International Labour Organization this provision did not limit the right of the latter to admit other Members; and in support of this thesis it pointed to the fact that Germany and Austria had been admitted to ILO membership by the first Conference in 1919. It was argued on the other side that there was no text giving the ILO the right in question and that such a right could not be assumed merely on the ground that it had not been specifically excluded; and that the admission of Germany and Austria did not constitute a precedent since they had been admitted in special circumstances "in anticipation of their becoming Members of the League". The issue remained academic until Brazil, having withdrawn from the League, announced her desire of remaining in the ILO.[18] The Secretary-General of the League made a vigorous protest in the Fourth Committee of the Assembly, asserting that this was constitutionally impossible, but took no further steps. Brazil, her League membership having terminated, sent a delegation to the International Labour Conference: the credentials of the delegates were accepted, and their votes counted, without comment.

This, however, could not be held to settle the matter even by way of precedent. Brazil had become a Member of the ILO as a Member of the League and it could be argued that her ILO membership, thus constitutionally acquired, was unaffected by her subsequent withdrawal from the League.[19]

In the case of the United States, however, which had never been a Member of the League, and in which no special circumstances could be invoked as in the case of Germany and Austria, the issue was clear cut. That legal experts should hold different views on the constitutional points involved was not in itself particularly dangerous. What mattered was that any action by the ILO to admit

---

[18] Brazil withdrew from the League of Nations on 14 June 1926.

[19] On 6 June 1939 the Brazilian Government representative, Helio Lobo, informed the Governing Body that the Brazilian Government had, like the Government of the United States, agreed to assume the obligation of giving two years' notice in the event of its withdrawal from the ILO. See ILO: *Minutes of the 88th Session of the Governing Body* (Geneva, 6–13 June 1939), pp. 7–8. (Ed.)

to membership a State not a Member of the League ran directly counter to what had become a major element in League policy: the assertion that there could be no such thing as fractional membership allowing a State full rights of participation only in such League activities as especially appealed to it, and that a State could acquire such rights only by acquiring full membership in the League and in no other way. This policy did not exclude forms of association with the League's technical activities but such association amounted to something less than full membership. The advocates of this policy believed that it was the best way to enlarge the League's membership. It was their conviction that no Great Power (and in particular the United States, for it was United States membership at which the policy was aimed) could, or could for long, accept a position of inferior status in which it could express only technical views and in which it would have no voice in the financial decisions on which the practical carrying out of the technical activities in which it was interested must depend.

The prospect of the entry of the United States into full membership of the ILO appeared as a formidable threat to the maintenance of this policy as an effective weapon. How far would the League dare to oppose it? And if it did not openly oppose, how far might its influence, operating through various channels, not succeed in securing that government delegates at the ILO Conference would manoeuvre for the adoption of some formula that would at all events preserve in some degree the policy to which such fundamental importance was attached? These were real anxieties in Butler's mind and they had increased rather than diminished when the terms of the Joint Resolution of Congress was communicated to him. It was clear that the United States desired "membership" without qualification; that the President was not authorized to accept anything less; and that if the Conference proposed any alternative and less comprehensive formula it must not only be rejected but would be regarded as a rebuff that the United States would not easily forgive or forget. As we have seen, the response of the Conference was rapid, unambiguous and unanimous. The Organization showed the cohesion, the sense of responsibility for its own destiny and the jealousy of its independence with which Albert Thomas had striven to endow it; and as a consequence the United States became a Member of the ILO on 20 August 1934, the date on which President Roosevelt, exercising the powers conferred on him by Congress, accepted the invitation addressed to him. That date has its importance in the history of the ILO but it marks another event to which historians will no doubt attach a much wider significance, the beginning of the progress of the United States from extreme isolation to leadership in the creation of the United Nations and in the struggle to make that institution an effective guarantee of a peaceful world.

New financial regulations

The admission of the United States to membership in the ILO ran counter, as we have seen, to League policy, and though no overt protest was made relations between the two bodies became less cordial. Had this situation continued, it might have raised some awkward problems but, fortunately, it was of short duration. Indeed not long afterwards the League entirely reversed its previous policy and set out to group its own economic and social activities into a single organization of an autonomous character in which it hoped to include States not among its Members. Meanwhile, certain adjustments had to be made in League–ILO relations and as these have some importance in the ILO's history they must be briefly referred to.

The financial system under which the ILO's budget was incorporated in the General Budget of the League is far too complicated to be described here. It had evolved as a kind of modus vivendi between the two organizations and its successful operation depended entirely on the existence of a large measure of goodwill and understanding between them. In practice the system respected the ILO's independence but in form the legal basis for the collection of the ILO's contributions derived from the Assembly's adoption of the League's General Budget. In theory, therefore, the Assembly controlled the ILO's finances, though it had never exercised this power so as to interfere with the ILO's policies and activities. This situation, which derived from the original assumption that League and ILO membership would coincide, gave rise to no difficulty so long as the exceptions to such coincidence of membership were few and did not include any Great Power. With the advent of the United States, some new system had clearly to be devised. The problem was one of considerable delicacy but with good sense and much ingenuity it was solved and the necessary amendments to the League's Financial Regulations were adopted by the Assembly. [20] It was necessarily complicated because it had to provide for the operation of two parallel systems, the one a complete ILO system in which all ILO Members participated, the other a League system in which ILO Members who were also League Members played their part. It may seem that it would have been infinitely simpler for the ILO to have cut completely loose from the League and to have taken its financial machinery entirely into its own hands. But the ILO did not desire any such separation.

---

[20] The financial system thus worked out between the ILO and the League was a very interesting piece of international machinery. It is described in the chapter entitled "Finance" in the report on "Future policy, programme and status of the International Labour Organization", which I presented to the ILO Conference in 1944. (E.J.P.)

Under the circumstances prevailing at that time, there were great advantages in having the League responsible for securing the contributions of League–ILO Members and if those Members preferred to make their contributions through League channels, and were accustomed to do so, it would have been folly to impose on them a different method of payment. There were, of course, dangers of conflict in a dual system and it could easily have broken down. As a matter of fact, it operated astonishingly well and was one more proof that the secret of political institutions lies in the will to make them work and not in the perfection of their theoretical planning. The time was to come when the ILO would have to take complete responsibility for its own finances and, when it did, the experience gained in operating the dual system proved invaluable.

Harold Butler is succeeded by John Winant

The entry of the United States into the Organization was the outstanding event of Harold Butler's directorship, but it was far from being his sole achievement and in many other ways he showed that he was well fitted to be Albert Thomas' successor. Though he had to face new problems and though he brought to his task another set of qualities, the fact that the two men had been so long associated in the direction of the ILO's affairs had the consequence that, apart from the external impression given by their very different personalities, the ILO continued almost as if there had been no change. This continuity, extending over a period of some 17 years, was an important feature in the ILO's development since it permitted the ILO's methods of thought and action to acquire something approaching the character of a well-established tradition. The existence of such a tradition is of special importance to an international institution; it alone can imbue newcomers to the staff with an effective sense of the nature of international service and thereby inspire and perpetuate that loyalty without which an international institution cannot hope to function successfully or in the long run even to survive.

When Harold Butler resigned in 1938 to become Warden of Nuffield College, the Governing Body appointed John Winant to the post of Director. Winant was a well-known public figure in the United States, having been three times Governor of the State of New Hampshire and having had the further distinction, although a Republican, of having served as Chairman of the Social Security Board in Roosevelt's administration.[21] He was also well known in the

---

[21] The Social Security Act provided that the Social Security Board, which consisted of three members, should be bipartisan. Roosevelt chose Winant for the post of Chairman. (E.J.P.)

ILO, having been a United States delegate to the Conference, having presided over the ILO's Textile Conference in Washington in 1937, and having served for two brief periods as one of Butler's Assistant Directors. [22] The two years during which he was Director were unfortunately to see Europe engulfed in the chaos and destruction of the Second World War and there was therefore no opportunity to discover how his unusual gifts and a background of experience so different from those of his predecessors would have influenced the ILO's development. Brief though his tenure of office was, he rendered one great service to the Organization that made his directorship memorable.

The ILO in wartime

As soon as it appeared that there was grave danger of a European war, the ILO had taken steps to meet such emergencies as it could be foreseen might arise. The Governing Body laid down the principle that the Organization should continue to function; an Emergency Committee was appointed with full powers to act in place of the Governing Body if the latter should be unable to meet; governments were approached and their approval obtained for a procedure to avoid the dislocation of the ILO's staff by measures of national mobilization; and in consultation with the League an emergency procedure for the adoption of the budget was devised that could be employed if no meeting of the Assembly could be held. It was realized at an early stage in these preparations that it might become difficult, or even impossible, for the ILO to function effectively from Geneva, and an offer from the French Government to give the ILO hospitality in Vichy, if that eventuality should arise, was accepted. In the first months of 1940, as the situation grew more serious, various practical precautions were taken; a lease of the Pavillon de Sévigné at Vichy was negotiated and the ILO's most valuable archives, packed in some scores of boxes, were moved there, the Office retaining only current working files. This detail is worth recording because the sequel provides an example of the confused conditions in which other measures had later to be taken. When the French defences collapsed, German mechanized units penetrated to Vichy and even further south, and the Pavillon de Sévigné was for some weeks a German military headquarters. German staff officers took their meals in the Pavillon dining room along one wall of which were ranged the

---

[22] John Gilbert Winant (1889–1947) served as Assistant Director of the International Labour Office from 15 May to 1 October 1935 and from 11 August 1937 to 31 December 1938, and as Director from 1 January 1939 to 15 February 1941. (Ed.)

boxes containing the ILO's documents. Somehow these escaped their curiosity and after the armistice was signed the German forces withdrew northwards and the ILO was able to rescue its archives and bring them unnoticed safely back to Geneva, leaving the Pavillon de Sévigné to become the official residence of Marshal Pétain.

The Governing Body's decision that the ILO should continue to function was based on the knowledge that during the First World War social problems, far from losing their importance, had become more varied and more acute and it therefore concluded that there would be numerous fields for useful ILO activities. This proved to be correct, but various practical difficulties and problems arose that could not have been foreseen because there had been no experience of carrying on the activities of a general international organization in wartime conditions. As regards the staff, for instance, it had been supposed that the danger of its dislocation would come from the operation of measures of military mobilization. The precautions taken to secure that such mobilization should not unduly interfere with the ILO, however, worked satisfactorily. What was not foreseen was that, whereas a national civil service finds a greater cohesion and a stronger sense of the value of its activities in wartime, an international civil service was on the contrary likely to undergo a certain disintegration and that many of its members would feel that a higher duty called them to share the dangers and activities of their compatriots at home. This would have created a serious problem had it not been that the catastrophe in Europe rapidly attained such dimensions that the staff had to be drastically reduced for financial reasons. The question of finance indeed became a fundamental preoccupation. If, and the possibility could not be excluded, the League and the ILO should have to be wound up, they must be able to meet all their financial obligations. This meant that such modest reserves as existed must, so far as possible, be kept intact; it meant therefore that actual expenditure (as opposed to expenditure authorized by the budget) must be kept in line with income actually received; and as country after country was overrun and the prospect of receiving any contribution from them disappeared, reductions in expenditure on a massive scale became necessary. Since the greater part of the ILO's expenditure was in salaries, these reductions involved the dismissal of officials and the payment to them of the indemnities due under their contracts in such an eventuality. The reduction in staff had therefore to be more than proportionate to the loss of income; in the final upshot, while income declined by rather more than 50 per cent, only about 10 per cent of the staff could be retained. It will be readily seen that the problem of making so great a cut in staff and yet keeping a nucleus internationally composed and technically competent so that the ILO might still render a measure of useful service and be ready to expand when resources became available was one of considerable difficulty. But all this was overshadowed by a more fundamental question. The modest establishment that financial conditions thus imposed could only be maintained and its future extension hoped for if the ILO could in fact demonstrate that it had real functions to perform, as the Governing Body had believed, and that it could render real services to its Members. In order to be able to do so the ILO must have freedom: freedom of communications; freedom of movement for its staff to travel for purposes of consultation and technical assistance; and freedom to convene the representative meetings which were the very essence of its life and which alone could decide on the activities that it could most usefully pursue in the interests of its Members. Until the first days of April 1940, this problem did not become acute and it was still envisaged that the Conference would meet in Geneva in June. On 9 April the situation suddenly altered and catastrophe followed catastrophe with scarcely a pause. Denmark and Norway were invaded; the Netherlands, Belgium and Luxembourg suffered the same fate; the French defences collapsed and the British army was hemmed in at Dunkirk; Italy declared war on France and Great Britain; and by 14 June the victorious Germans had entered Paris and swept on to the south.

The decision to move the ILO to Canada

As this situation developed the position of Switzerland became more and more precarious. At one stage invasion was believed to be imminent; had the German thrust through the Argonne not succeeded, the alternative of turning the Maginot line by an advance through the valley of the Rhone might well have been undertaken. These were anxious weeks when the roads leading to Geneva were mined; when anti-tank defences were erected; and when, with Winant's permission, Swiss troops and light artillery occupied the ILO grounds to guard against the possibility of enemy forces landing from hydroplanes on the lake. As things turned out, Switzerland happily remained uninvaded; but she was surrounded and the ILO found itself practically isolated in the middle of a hostile Europe.

Well before this final stage was reached, Winant had decided that he must move the ILO if it was to escape paralysis or even possibly extinction. It was by no means an easy decision for him to take. The Emergency Committee could not meet and his constitutional power to take such a decision on his own responsibility was open to question. Such members of the Governing Body as he was able to consult individually were strongly opposed to the idea. The staff was unhappy and divided, partly because, as has been noted, national sentiments had come to the fore and most of the Europeans were against leaving Europe, partly because in the conditions prevailing many thought any attempt to operate the Office elsewhere would be a failure and that the best chance of saving the ILO was to "sit it out" as the secretariat of the League had decided to do. Views that he felt were influenced by personal ties or reflected a defeatist disinclination to take risks Winant was prepared to ignore. But other arguments were put forward that caused him deep concern. It was urged that the ILO more than any other international organization had intimate bonds with the peoples of its member States; that many of these peoples were clinging in their distress to any fragment of the world as they had previously known it that remained unsubmerged; that to many in Europe the ILO was such a fragment, powerless indeed to do anything to give any assistance, but still a symbol of hope; and that in these circumstances its departure would be regarded as "running away" – a flight and a betrayal. This view was shared by some of Winant's American friends and it made a strong appeal to the warmheartedness and sympathy for all in distress which were dominant traits in his character.

Nevertheless, he remained unshaken in his decision and took steps to carry it out. He had come to the ILO with the special blessing of President Roosevelt and it was naturally to the United States that he turned for assistance. He cabled to Secretary Hull explaining the Office's predicament and asking whether the American Government would be prepared to receive the ILO in the United States. The answer, though couched in most sympathetic terms, was definitely negative as regards any immediate move though it held out hopes that the matter might be reconsidered in several months' time. This was a severe and unexpected blow. Winant was unable to believe that the gravity of the ILO's situation had been really understood and he was also convinced that if the ILO did not get out of Geneva quickly it would be marooned there for the duration of the war and condemned to complete inactivity. He therefore decided to go at once to the United States, confident that he would succeed in overcoming whatever difficulties or hesitations had arisen. Having reached Lisbon he found he could fly to London and back before the departure of his clipper and be immediately decided to do so in the hope, which was fulfilled, that he would find in Great Britain support and encouragement for his plans. We had many days of acute anxiety in the ILO during which, beyond having learnt that he intended to visit London, we were left without any further news. Air travel to and from Europe was of course attended by risk and as no word reached us either from London or Lisbon our apprehensions grew. We did not realize that precisely because of these risks all movements of aircraft were kept highly secret for fear of German interference and no message could be sent that might even indirectly reveal an arrival or departure. This silence was only broken, and then in dramatic fashion, by a telephone call from the other side of the Atlantic in which Winant informed me, using a number of code words on which we had agreed before his departure,[23] that I was to proceed at once with some 40 members of the staff to Montreal and disperse the remainder according to our prearranged plan. He impressed on me that he had information pointing to the need for the swiftest possible action, and a few hours later a cable arrived emphasizing this injunction with the words "get the job done by tomorrow if possible period work all night".

Transportation and other difficulties

To work all night presented no difficulty but to get the staff away in anything like the time he suggested was a complete impossibility and he evidently had no conception of the complexity or difficulty of the arrangements involved. To begin with, I had not even the exact list of those who were to go; their names Winant had told me would be communicated to me by the American Consul who would have authority to give them visas for entry to the United States, and the necessary instructions to the Consul did not of course arrive as rapidly as Winant's brief personal cable. Other visas, not easy to obtain, were also required; Portugal, congested with refugees, would only give visas on the production of clear evidence, such as a steamship ticket, that the persons applying would not remain in the country; a Spanish visa was also necessary; two special visas had to be obtained in order to travel through France and these had to be specially authorized by the Ministry in Vichy; and of course all these visas and permits could only be obtained by successive operations as the passports had to be presented to each consulate or legation. These and other difficulties, for instance no trains were running in France and the ILO had to organize its own transport to the Spanish frontier, inevitably delayed the departure of the group for some ten days.

On one point, I had felt compelled to quarrel with Winant's instructions and that concerned my own movements. One of my responsibilities was finance and I was therefore seriously preoccupied with the question of a constitutionally adopted budget for 1941, since in the absence of such a budget the ILO would have no authority to spend money after the end of the year and no contributions

---

[23] The ILO telegram code was fairly basic: for example, Pétain was referred to as "father", Vichy was "mineral water", "Jane" meant Emergency Committee, and Phelan himself was simply "Ned". (Ed.)

from governments would be legally due. Under the Emergency procedure a valid budget could be adopted with the approval of the League's Supervisory Commission, and, as there were hopes that a meeting of this small body could be arranged in Geneva, I explained to Winant that I thought it essential to postpone my own departure until this meeting had been held. Winant waved all my arguments aside; he asserted his willingness to accept the responsibility for having no budget and his confidence that the difficulty could somehow be surmounted; he urged me to leave at the earliest possible moment, even ahead of the rest of the group once the arrangements for its departure were made; and he insisted again and again that I might be shut in. I remained unconvinced. I had had a long experience of the difficulties involved in financing an international institution and I was certain that these difficulties would be still greater in wartime. I felt, too, that Winant did not appreciate the fundamental issue involved, namely that in the absence of a legal right to collect its contributions the ILO would have to live on alms from charitable governments and would lose both its independence and its status, the very things that the move to Canada was intended to preserve. It was impossible of course to have any effective discussion of such issues by cable and Winant no doubt thought I was being unreasonably obstinate. In the end, however, he agreed, though reluctantly, to a compromise. I would stay for a fortnight and if by then I had no certainty of securing a meeting I would proceed to Lisbon and try to get one there. At the end of the agreed period it was clear that no meeting could be hoped for and I accordingly left Geneva accompanied by R.J.P. Mortished. [24]

A journey through stricken France

We drove south from Geneva keeping east of the Rhone. Under a summer sky the scenic beauty of Dauphiné was at its best. But the sunlit peace of mountain and valley only heightened by its contrast the atmosphere of gloom and despondency in the towns and villages through which we passed. They were curiously lifeless and silent. People moved listlessly as though in a torpor; they seemed like sleepwalkers whose eyes saw nothing of the world around them and whose minds were remote. There was no physical destruction to be seen but its absence brought out more poignantly how terrible were the spiritual wounds that France had received. It was not difficult to understand how great had been the shock

---

[24] Ronald James Patrick Mortished (1891–1961) was adviser to the Irish delegation at the ILC from 1923 to 1926 and an ILO official from 1931 to 1956. (Ed.)

that had so affected the French people. France had been the greatest military power in Europe: her prestige had dominated the continent; even when the storm of war had broken with a new and frightening violence and had overwhelmed with unparalleled rapidity other countries, the French people had believed themselves safe from invasion behind the impregnable Maginot line, and though they had known that they must face a struggle long and costly in precious French lives, they had been confident that in the end French valour and military genius would triumphantly drive back the aggressor. Now all had crumbled in almost instantaneous chaos and disaster; everything that had been France's pride and glory had vanished in a nightmare of incredible and ignominious collapse.

In the face of so great a catastrophe, going far beyond any imaginable military defeat, it is not to be wondered at that they saw no glimmer of hope, that they felt that British resistance must be futile, and that even if Great Britain herself survived, her survival could at the best be only the result of a stalemate that would leave the continent unaffected. And indeed they were not alone in thinking that the dimensions of the disaster made it irremediable. What other conclusion could the few small countries that remained be expected to reach? They might be spared invasion and occupation but how feeble and insecure must be their independence in a Europe dominated by a single great and ruthless military power. The time was to come when hope would revive, and the spark of resistance still alive in a few bold spirits would slowly spread and then burst into flame. But meanwhile, the attitude of resigned despair just described was general on the continent and it is only in its light that some of the incidents that will be later recounted can be readily understood.

When we crossed to the right bank of the Rhone, the scene became still more melancholy. Hitherto, we had encountered no refugees because all the bridges north of Avignon were down, but now we found masses of them camped on the roadside surrounded by such personal possessions as they had been able to carry with them in their headlong flight. The flood was beginning to turn. Small groups were making their way north again passing others who still struggled on towards the Spanish frontier. But the majority, exhausted both morally and physically, seemed unable to go either forward or back. What we saw, of course, was only a small fraction of a situation prevailing over a vast area but it was a spectacle not easily forgotten. Although all normal organization seemed hopelessly disrupted, life somehow went on in haphazard fashion through the enterprise and resource of individuals. We found beds in Avignon in a famous hotel but only after a long search through crowded streets were we able to discover a small obscure restaurant where we could obtain a simple meal which, incidentally, was extremely well cooked. In Perpignan, conditions were much more difficult and after an uncomfortable night we were glad to make an early start for the Spanish frontier.

An anxious moment at the Spanish frontier

Now that we were practically over what we had anticipated would be the most uncertain part of our journey, I began for the first time to feel an unreasonable anxiety lest I should, as Winant had so persistently warned, find myself unable to get through. Our road ran along the coast to Port Bou where, confined between the Pyrenees and the sea, it constitutes the main channel into Spain. I studied my map, and although our petrol supply was running low, I turned away from the coast along a small secondary road that was shown as having a customs station some few miles inland. After climbing up through a series of small wooded valleys, we reached the frontier and our special exit permits carried us past the French officials without difficulty. The Spanish post, a hundred yards or so further on, was a modest affair, but the care with which its two uniformed occupants studied my passport, scrutinizing each page with attention and then turning back and beginning the operation all over again while they whispered together as though confronted with a grave decision, caused me increasing apprehension. I mustered as much dignity and authority as possible and pointing to my passport said impatiently, "Diplomatic."

"Yes," replied the guard, and then after a pause that seemed ominous he asked shamefacedly: "What country, sir?"

It was an immense relief to discover that the source of his difficulty was that he had never seen an Irish passport before. He understood my reply in halting Spanish and smiled with pleasure. "The Irish Minister in Madrid," he said, nodding with satisfaction. I decided to let this pass as an assertion rather than a question and so I contented myself with repeating that I had diplomatic status and was proceeding to the United States via Lisbon, as the various diplomatic visas indicated. He listened patiently but evidently seemed to think this was going into much unnecessary detail. "The Irish Minister," he said firmly to his colleague with the air of a man who had solved a difficult problem with success, and bowed us courteously on.

Some weeks later, I had reason to bless the hunch that had led me off the main road. I learned that Seán Lester,[25] the Acting Secretary-General of the League of Nations, accompanied by the President of the Permanent Court of

---

[25] Seán Lester (1888–1959) was Ireland's permanent delegate to the League of Nations (1930–35), replacing Michael MacWhite. He became Deputy Secretary-General to the League of Nations in 1937 and Secretary-General in 1940. (Ed.)

International Justice and the Treasurer of the League,[26] had been stopped at the main frontier station on their way to the meeting of the Supervisory Commission at Lisbon and, after spending two days in futile telephone calls to Madrid, had been compelled to retrace their steps to Geneva. Just two days before I had entered Spain, instructions had been sent from Madrid to all frontier posts not to allow any League or ILO officials through. Either these instructions, which doubtless had their origin in a request from Berlin, had not reached the officials at the minor post through which I passed or their difficulties with the Irish language had so completely absorbed their faculties that my connection with the ILO had failed to attract attention.

On our journey through Spain, our route from Barcelona to Madrid passed through a region that had seen some of the severest fighting during the Civil War. Little or no reconstruction had taken place; towns still showed the marks of heavy bombardment, their streets half-choked with rubble above which half-demolished buildings hung precariously; bridges were either still down, or had been repaired only in the most makeshift fashion with a few beams and planks. Though the spectacle was not as tragic as in France, here was another corner of Europe that left a saddening impression. The whole note was one of poverty and exhaustion.

Portugal: An oasis

Portugal presented an astonishing and delightful contrast; everything was neat and orderly; houses gave the impression of having been freshly painted; the little towns were bright and clean and food was varied and abundant. What struck us forcibly in the circumstances of our journey was the petrol situation. In France there had been none at all; in Spain it was as scarce as gold and only to be procured in exchange for American dollars – and even then much patience and persistence was required before a source of supply could be located. In Portugal, it could be procured without difficulty in the normal way at any wayside garage. What struck us more forcibly still on arrival in Lisbon was the atmosphere of freedom and independence. Newspapers carried both the British and German communiqués – in Spain only the latter appeared – and we felt we were again in contact with the outside world. Lisbon indeed seemed a gay and happy city. A great

---

[26] José Gustavo Guerrero (1876–1958) was President of the Permanent Court of International Justice (1936–45) and subsequently the first President of the International Court of Justice (1946–49). The Treasurer of the League was Seymour Jacklin. (Ed.)

exhibition lined the banks of the Tagus in celebration of the 800th anniversary of Portugal's foundation and the third anniversary of her independence.

The exhibits in some scores of pavilions showed all aspects of her life and recounted the exploits of her great navigators and explorers who had carried her flag and her faith to vast undiscovered regions in all parts of the globe. I could remember no other exhibition that had so admirably and so colourfully fulfilled its purpose. But it may be that it made a special appeal at that moment giving as it did so dramatic a panorama not only of Portugal's great achievements but also of centuries of that civilization of Europe of which Portugal seemed now one of the last remaining fragments. Would she escape the fate that had overwhelmed almost the whole of the continent? As I made a round of visits to members of the diplomatic corps, I found that underneath the cheerful and carefree aspect of the city there was serious apprehension. The aerial attack on London was in full swing and as its intensity increased day by day few could believe or hope that Britain would be able to survive. Moreover, Portugal's stocks of food and petrol and the strategic value of her ports were tempting prizes that Hitler could take by lifting a finger; and her courageous charity in affording asylum to so many thousands of refugees from the territories under his control was in itself a defiance that might easily excite his anger and provoke his vengeance. As one Ambassador remarked, pointing to the map, "German mechanized forces could be in here in a matter of hours." In the event, Portugal, like Switzerland, escaped invasion but there is now plenty of evidence that the dangers that threatened them at that time were far from imaginary.

Vichy and the French staff

So far as the ILO was concerned, the immediate problem was that of securing passages across the Atlantic. This was no simple task as all shipping space was booked up for weeks ahead. Slowly, however, places were found whenever, at the last moment, because their papers were not in order or for some other reason, passengers cancelled their bookings. In the end, the whole ILO group got away, some on cargo steamers, others on Greek and Spanish and American liners.

Meanwhile another problem arose. The governments of member States had of course been informed of the transfer to Canada and of the reasons why it had been decided. I received a reply from the French Government in which it protested against the movement of staff to a belligerent country and demanded that the officials of French nationality should be sent back to Geneva.

This communication placed the French members of the staff in a most difficult situation and created a conflict between their national and their international loyalties. But it raised equally difficult problems for the ILO. If the ILO gave way, it would be a humiliating surrender of its independence and authority. On the other hand, if it refused, it could give its French staff no protection if they continued in its service, and the possibility of their being deprived of their passports and exposed to other sanctions could not be lightly dismissed. These were grave issues and there were also general political considerations to be taken into account that would have to be carefully weighed. Clearly, only the Director himself could take a decision and Winant accordingly flew to Lisbon to examine all the conflicting elements involved. The reply sent to the French Government maintained, so far as possible in the circumstances, the ILO's right to make use of members of its staff wherever in the Director's judgement they could render most effective service. Vichy was informed that the French members of the staff would be attached to the group remaining in Geneva and would not be asked to go to a belligerent country. This was a diplomatic formula that on the surface gave Vichy a measure of satisfaction without, in reality, conceding much in substance, since both groups were equally under the Director's control. The commitment that French staff would not be asked to go to a belligerent country left it open to use them elsewhere as occasion might require, and was no more than the admission that in war conditions the freedom of movement of particular members of the ILO's staff might suffer restrictions depending on their nationality. The French Government did not pursue the matter further, satisfied perhaps that they had covered themselves sufficiently against any complaint from Berlin. The French members of the staff were sent to Washington, where they could work in close contact with their colleagues in Montreal, and there they remained till the entry of the United States into the war obliterated the distinction it had been possible to draw between Washington and Montreal. By the time that happened, the position of Vichy as the sole centre that could claim French allegiance had been greatly weakened by the increasing importance in the number and quality of de Gaulle's adherents. In these circumstances, the totality of the ILO's small group was at last concentrated in Montreal without protest and without the members of the French contingent being exposed to any exceptional risk.

The jigsaw puzzle of the Supervisory Commission

After Winant's departure from Lisbon, I continued my efforts to secure a meeting of the Supervisory Commission. The Commission was a small body consisting of only seven members. [27] Two, however, were to all intents and purposes prisoners in occupied countries; another, who held a high official position in France, was clearly unavailable in view of Vichy's attitude to the League. The Chairman, Mr Carl Hambro of Norway, [28] was in the United States on an important mission for his country and the difficulties and delays involved in crossing the Atlantic made his attendance impossible. Of the remaining members, Sir Cecil Kisch, [29] the Vice-Chairman, was willing to fly from London; the Latin American member was expected to reach Lisbon on his way home in the near future, and there was hope of persuading the seventh member, who was a member of the diplomatic corps in Vichy, to attend. The terms of the Emergency Resolution had been deliberately made extremely wide so as to cover all contingencies and they did not exclude the securing of members' approval by correspondence, but for the purpose of adopting the budget, a meeting, however restricted in numbers, had many advantages. The readiness of countries to pay their contributions would certainly be increased if they had the assurance that proposals for expenditure had been carefully examined by independent members of the Commission meeting with the executive heads of the organizations concerned, whom they could question fully on the justification for the figures put forward. While this exploration of the possibilities of the situation was proceeding, Mr Hambro made the interesting suggestion that the President of the Council of the League, Mr Costa du Rels of Bolivia, [30] who was about to pass through Lisbon, could be co-opted as a member if the members attending the meeting agreed. Since their agreement might be counted on there seemed every prospect of reaching the figure of four, which had the merit of being a majority of the Commission's original membership of seven. An obstacle, that could not possibly have been foreseen but that was typical of the conditions that have previously been described, arose at the last moment. When the member of the diplomatic corps at Vichy arrived, he explained to his colleagues that he had only made the journey out of courtesy

---

[27] The Commission comprised: C.J. Hambro, Chairman; Harri G. Holma, Rapporteur; Sir Cecil Kisch, Carlos A. Pardo, Yves Bréart de Boisanger, Sir Adrian Carton de Wiart, H. Colijn. (Ed.)

[28] Carl Joachim Hambro (1885–1964), Norwegian politician, was President of the Assembly of the League of Nations Delegates from 1939 to 1940 and in 1946. He was also the Norwegian Government's delegate to the 90–94th Sessions of the Governing Body (1941–45) and to the ILC at its extraordinary meeting in New York in 1941 and in Philadelphia in 1944. He served as Chairman of the League of Nations Supervisory Commission in 1946. (Ed.)

[29] Sir Cecil Hermann Kisch (1884–1961) was an India Office official (1908–46) who served as Vice-Chairman of the League of Nations Supervisory Commission in 1946. (Ed.)

[30] Adolfo Costa du Rels (1891–1980) was a Bolivian delegate to the League of Nations (1930–46) and Bolivia's Ambassador to Switzerland and the Holy See (1937–43). He served as Chairman of the 107th Session of the Council of the League of Nations in 1939. (Ed.)

to them and in order to explain personally what he could not do by letter, that in the existing delicate situation of his country he could not take any part in the Commission's work. After much persuasion he consented to sit at the table while the Commission opened its session, it being understood that he would leave immediately after the preliminary formalities and so have no responsibility for any financial decisions the Commission might subsequently take. In opening the meeting the Vice-Chairman expressed the Commission's regret that they were not able to have his assistance and at the same time announced the acceptance of the Chairman's proposal for the co-option of Mr Costa du Rels.

The meeting presented one other unusual feature that is worth recording. As already recounted, the Acting Secretary-General and the League Treasurer had been unable to reach Lisbon and Seán Lester cabled asking me to represent him in the discussion. In the past (and as was to happen again in the future) the views of the ILO and of the secretariat on financial questions had often been at variance and it would have been difficult to imagine how the defence of their conflicting interests could have been undertaken by one and the same person. On this occasion, since both administrations had endeavoured to cut expenditure to the minimum, their common defence was easily possible.

At the end of three days, devoted to a careful scrutiny of every item, the Commission was satisfied that, after some minor adjustments, the proposals laid before them could be accepted and Mr Hambro, who had been kept in touch with their conclusions, likewise expressed his approval. Since the two members who were in occupied countries were clearly prevented by force majeure from expressing any opinion and must therefore be regarded as having ceased to be capable of performing their functions, the number of members of the Commission effectively in office was six. As four of these had now formally signified their approval, the League and ILO budgets for 1941 had in consequence been duly adopted under the emergency procedure.

So far as the League was concerned, the matter was finished. In the case of the ILO the other half of its dual system had yet to be operated so as to cover the position of its members who were not members of the League. This was done by submitting by cable the main figures of the budget to the members of the Governing Body. The great majority promptly cabled their acceptance of them and this telegraphic decision was subsequently confirmed when some months later the Governing Body was able to meet in the United States.

Across the Atlantic and out of the war zone

When the Supervisory Commission had drawn up its report my task in Lisbon was completed, and a few days later I embarked on the *Excambion* for New York. My anticipation that the ship would be crowded proved more than correct. All cabin space was of course filled to capacity but much other accommodation had been improvised. Only the dining room and a small bar remained in use for their original purposes; all the other public rooms had been stripped of their furniture and turned into dormitories by the simple expedient of spreading as many mattresses on the floor as could be fitted in. But there was no complaint from those to whom such places had been allotted and no protest at the discomfort and congestion they were compelled to endure; other emotions and preoccupations predominated in their minds: relief at having escaped from the horrors that had pursued them in their flight across half of Europe, and hope that they might at last be able to piece together in the new world such fragments as remained to them of the existence the old world had so cruelly and so brutally shattered. As the voyage proceeded in warm sunshine (for we were obviously following a southern route) and over a sea that was fortunately calm, faces became less strained and an almost happy concern with the problems of the future seemed to replace, or at all events to dull, the memory of past tragedies. It was, therefore, something of a shock when some days after leaving Lisbon the sudden appearance of a British destroyer speeding down from the horizon brought a reminder that although Europe lay far behind we were still in the zone of hostilities. Signals were exchanged as the destroyer slowed down and ran parallel to our course. Were we being inspected to make sure we were not a German raider in disguise or being warned of submarines lying in wait ahead? No explanation was forthcoming and speculation reawakened anxieties that these peaceful days in a deceitfully empty ocean had led us almost to forget. A call at Bermuda, where the ship's mail was unloaded and left for the purposes of censorship was, however, the only other incident of the voyage until the *Excambion* berthed in New York and one more group of refugees filed down the gangway to set foot in the land of freedom which had been the object of their hopes and struggles since their agony in Europe began.

The ILO sets up its wartime centre in Canada [1]

My first view of the ILO's quarters in Montreal gave me something of a shock. I found the staff occupying rows of plain wooden tables in a small hall, which, with its high windows and timbered roof, had a faintly ecclesiastical air – I learned later that it was in fact a disused chapel. At the end opposite the door two staff members with their tables were accommodated on a raised platform some six feet high. Had it not been for the clatter of typewriters and the sight of familiar faces I might have supposed that I had entered by mistake one of McGill's halls where an examination was in progress under the vigilance of the supervisors on the dais. As I made my way along a lane between the tables, greeting on one side and the other the colleagues who had preceded me from Lisbon, I was appalled to discover that the muster was complete and that therefore there was no other accommodation than this one big room. True, what we had transferred to Montreal was only a skeleton organization in which the various services had of necessity been reduced to their simplest expression, but even so, I had never imagined that whatever modest accommodation we might find would not allow for some measure of separation by function and responsibility. Here roneotists, typists, accountants, statisticians, translators, editors, experts and all the rest were camping out sheltered by four bare walls and a roof. How could intellectual work demanding a high degree of concentration be carried out in such conditions? How could experts confer or visitors be received? How could confidential discussions on Office policy be held?

---

[1] First published in 1955 in *Studies: An Irish Quarterly*, Vol. 44, No. 174, pp. 152–70. (Ed.)

The one cheerful note was the spectacle of the staff. Enthusiastically engrossed in their tasks, bobbing up and down between their tables and the tin boxes on the floor in which their precious documentation had been carried across the Atlantic, they seemed to have no regrets for the palatial accommodation they had left in Geneva and no misgivings about the lack of the facilities provided. I continued my way up to the platform and there I discovered that a door led into a steep and narrow stairway at the bottom of which I found Winant in a tiny dark room just large enough to contain a desk and one chair for a possible visitor. I suppose something of my discouragement must have been apparent in my expression for he hastened to assure me that the present arrangements were provisional. Two houses on the other side of McGill campus were being prepared for our use by the University authorities and to these it was hoped to move in a couple of weeks' time.

This was highly comforting news and in due course the move was accomplished. By that time I was able to realize how fortunate we had been. When Winant had discussed with Prime Minister Mackenzie King where the ILO should establish its working centre in Canada,[2] he had indicated his desire that it should be in some university city in which a good economics library would be available. Montreal, Toronto and Kingston were mentioned as fulfilling this condition but the Prime Minister left the decision entirely to Winant. Winant's choice was Montreal. It had the advantages that with its mixed population of French- and English-speaking Canadians it had something of an international character, and that it was in consequence well equipped for printing documents in French. Moreover, he had already tentatively explored its possibilities through his old friend and classmate at Princeton, Wilder Penfield, the Director of its famous Neurological Institute.[3] Penfield had put him in touch with Cyril James, Principal and Vice-Chancellor of McGill,[4] who had offered to place facilities at his disposal. But what weighed with him most, and ruled out any leisurely comparison of what might be available elsewhere, was his conviction that if the ILO did not leave Geneva at once it would never get away. Once the Prime Minister had given him a free hand he immediately accepted McGill's offer and made his telephone call to me in Geneva. His rapid decision was made just in time for, as I have already recounted, the Spanish frontier

---

[2] William Lyon Mackenzie King (1874–1950) was Canadian Prime Minister December 1921–June 1926; September 1926–August 1930; and October 1935–November 1948. (Ed.)

[3] Wilder Graves Penfield (1891–1976) was a Canadian neurosurgeon. In 1934 he founded McGill University's Montreal Neurological Institute, of which he remained Director until 1960. (Ed.)

[4] Frank Cyril James (1903–73) was Principal of McGill University from 1939 to 1962. (Ed.)

was closed to ILO officials only a few days after those bound for Canada had passed through.

The result, however, was to land the ILO into a city that was bursting at the seams. McGill itself was overcrowded; special training courses, set up to meet the needs of Canada's wartime industrial expansion, had increased the number of students and strained its resources to the limit; additional accommodation was impossible to find in the city which, as Canada's greatest industrial centre, was equally congested. The action of Principal James in placing two houses in University Street at the ILO's disposal was therefore much more than a friendly gesture. Not only did it mean the sacrifice of space badly needed by the University itself but the alterations necessary to adapt the premises to our needs involved the University in the expenditure of some $25,000.

The ILO was perforce operating under conditions of severe financial stringency. The costs of the transfer to Montreal had been greater than anticipated and even the smallest items of expenditure had, therefore, to be carefully watched. Since the management of the ILO's finances was my special responsibility, the problem of having to find an additional $25,000 would have been most unwelcome, and my gratitude for McGill's generosity was in consequence personal as well as official. Though no suggestion was made that the University expected this sum to be repaid, I nevertheless felt that the ILO's dignity and self-respect required that it be considered as an obligation to be honoured as soon as circumstances permitted. Some three years were to elapse before anything could be done. What happened then had its amusing side.

Our financial situation at that time had much improved but not to an extent that made possible the immediate payment of the whole sum. What I thought might be done was to deal with the matter by annual payments exceeding the rental value of our premises, and in order to treat the matter in this way it was necessary to discover what in McGill's view that rental value was since, if it was higher than what I could make available, I must wait till a larger sum was at my disposal. I accordingly went to call on Principal James with the idea of finding out whether I could make an appropriate proposal. The Administrative Building, which I believe is the oldest building on the campus and which I now entered for the first time, seemed to belong to another age. Its old-fashioned, gloomy entrance, with its grey walls and uneven stone floor, was not what I had expected as a setting for Cyril James' modern outlook and energetic personality. It reminded me of Gwydyr House in Whitehall in which I had made my first acquaintance with the British civil service some 30 years before. His own office on the first floor proved, however, to be a bright and attractive room in which utility and comfort had been most happily combined. After a brief preliminary conversation of a very cordial character, I approached the subject of my visit, saying that I thought it was unfair that McGill should be out of pocket on the ILO's account and asking what he thought would be a reasonable rent for our premises. At this his manner changed. He became at once the cautious administrator, coldly and efficiently very much on his guard, and told me he would prefer me to fix the figure for myself. This was exactly what I did not want to do. We fenced for a little but he steadfastly refused to be drawn. He had of course no idea of what I was at and no doubt concluded that my object was to negotiate for the lowest figure I could obtain. When the deadlock seemed complete I decided to reverse my tactics.

"What would you think of $5,000 a year?" I enquired.

He straightened up in his chair and looked as if he was asking himself if he had heard correctly. Then he burst out laughing and said, "I thought you were going to say something like $400 a year. That's what one of our schools would have offered."

"I was afraid you might have thought it too little," I replied.

"Good Lord, no," he said. "The University is very short of money at the moment and $5,000 will be more than welcome. The Board of Governors will be delighted when I tell them of the ILO's action. I can assure you that they will be impressed and highly appreciative."

Cyril James seemed to take an even livelier satisfaction in his anticipation of the Governors' reaction than in the payment itself. I suspected that some of them had not been over enthusiastic at his initiative in offering accommodation to the ILO when the University's needs were so pressing and that it gave him special pleasure to be able to inform them that it had been a sound move even from a narrow business point of view. Be that as it may, McGill's association with the ILO during the war years has now become part of the history of the development of international institutions. Among its many claims to fame, its friends and admirers can rank high that which is commemorated by a bronze plaque unveiled on its campus in 1950. The inscription reads as follows:

> To this campus the International Labour Organisation transferred its wartime headquarters in 1940 on the generous invitation of the Government of Canada and McGill University. From here the ILO directed its work of furthering world peace through social justice. This tablet records the lasting gratitude of the ILO to McGill University.

McGill, however, was not alone in lending the ILO a helping hand. There is another great university in Montreal and it in its turn was to afford the ILO facilities more extensive than those which McGill had been able to supply though for a much more limited period. When the time came to hold a Conference in Canada, Monseigneur Maurault,[5] the Rector Magnificus of the University of Montreal (who certainly lived up to his title), put at our disposal in the great building perched on the side of Montreal's "Mountain" not only a splendid hall, but committee rooms and office space for the Conference staff on a scale that rivalled our own accommodation in Geneva and far exceeded both in extent and convenience anything that we found elsewhere in America. Thus, both of Montreal's universities in different ways vied in generosity to the ILO in its time of need and both have a high place in the ILO's memories of Canadian generosity and hospitality.

Hospitality given so open-handedly certainly meant much but the ILO had wider and even more important needs and I must now turn back to my first days in Montreal when they called for my urgent attention. The ILO had left Switzerland because of the danger of being deprived of the freedom required for the performance of its international functions. Nothing would have been gained by the move unless arrangements could be made to ensure effectively its independence and freedom of action in Canada. This was by no means a simple matter. The arrangements under which the League of Nations and the ILO had operated in Switzerland had been negotiated in a world at peace and with a small country whose perpetual neutrality had seemed to make it peculiarly suitable for international headquarters. Canada was at war. There was therefore no precedent for the guarantees the ILO must now require, and the problem they presented was much more difficult than that involved in the arrangements with Switzerland. The fact that Canada was a belligerent meant that the guarantees to the ILO must necessarily cover a wider range and it equally meant that they must involve questions touching directly on measures of national security that the host Government would naturally and properly regard as of grave concern. Moreover, the decisions involved, dealing for example with such questions as passport control, censorship of letters and telegrams, foreign exchange, etc., were administratively intricate and many different governmental departments were responsible for one or other aspect of the questions they raised. It is impossible to praise too highly the way in which the Canadian Government and the able heads of her civil service dealt with these delicate and highly technical issues in spite of the tremendous pressure under which they were working at that time. The ILO's requests were met with a

---

[5] Olivier Maurault (1886–1968) was the Rector Magnificus of the University of Montreal from 1935 to 1955. (Ed.)

surprisingly full understanding of its international character and independence, and the necessary Orders in Council and administrative instructions were agreed on and issued with amazing rapidity. Few questions ever arose out of the working of the agreements made and these were easily and speedily settled. Certainly, the ILO was satisfied and I venture to think that the Canadian Government had never any reason to regret the arrangements into which it entered. It can take a legitimate pride in the knowledge that it thus created precedents concerning the relations between an international institution and its host country that made a contribution of immense value to the future development of international organization. How delicate were the problems Canada had to face and how much credit she deserved for having tackled them with such boldness and vision was brought home to me when I learned some time later that one of the principal reasons that had led the United States to refuse Winant's request for hospitality to the ILO was the reluctance of the State Department to approach Congress on arrangements of this kind.

While these negotiations with the Canadian Government were in progress, the ILO had steadily succeeded in resuming such activities as its modest resources and staff permitted. The new headquarters had made contact with member governments, information was flowing in, certain publications had begun to reappear and technical studies were in progress. In spite of the rigours of its first Montreal winter, there was a spirit of happy optimism in the staff born of the feeling that the ILO was once more a going concern whose survival, whatever difficulties might yet lie ahead, seemed secure. This cheerful optimism was abruptly shattered when it was learned at the beginning of the New Year that Winant was about to leave the ILO in order to go to London as American Ambassador. The dismay that this news created among the staff can easily be understood. They had been impressed by the courage and determination with which he had rescued the ILO from the perils that threatened it in Europe. They realized, however, that the establishment of wartime headquarters in Montreal was not in itself decisive, that the ILO would have an uphill fight to survive, and that, with Europe overrun and with Great Britain engaged in a life and death struggle, the ILO's future would largely depend on the degree of support it received from the United States. They regarded the presence of Winant at the head of the Office as the proof that that support could be counted on to the full. They knew that he enjoyed the esteem and confidence of President Roosevelt. Though his original plan of finding a haven for the ILO in the United States had not been accepted, their belief in the security his presence as Director afforded had not been shaken. Indeed, they felt that his influence in Washington had probably been enhanced and that, having been unable to meet his wishes on that occasion, the United States would be all the more ready to help him in other ways. Their dismay was the greater because the blow was so totally unexpected. They had been prepared to encounter all sorts of difficulties and uncertainties in the adventure on which they had embarked, but this was a catastrophe they had never anticipated, one that seemed indeed to have been ruled out from the start. They remembered that among the precautions taken by the Governing Body to ensure that the ILO's work should not be disrupted by extensive hostilities was the arrangement made with member governments that they would not call up their nationals in the ILO's service save after consultation with the Director, and that as regards the Director himself the Governing Body had stated that it assumed that no government would think of withdrawing him in such circumstances. Since this view had been unanimously expressed by the Governing Body when Winant himself was Director and when the Chairman of the Governing Body was also an American,[6] the news of Winant's departure was felt by many of the staff to augur ill for the future. If, they argued, the United States could so lightly neglect or forget a commitment concerning the ILO which it had so recently and so deliberately approved, what hope could there be of sustained and understanding support for the ILO once Winant had gone?

They did not, of course, raise these questions with Winant, and if they had it is unlikely that they would have been much enlightened. He rarely explained his decisions and never in terms of a closely reasoned argument. Logical exposition was not his mode of expression, and though he had no difficulty in understanding a case put to him in that way, his reply would often seem to be so vague and general that it gave the opposite impression. It was therefore never easy to understand how his mind worked. What one learned by experience was that he knew quite well what he wanted and even more definitely what he did not. This, however, did not always make things easier, since it by no means followed that he would reveal what his attitude was. He would choose his own time for making his decision known and even then one might learn of it only indirectly and still be left in doubt of its precise nature. It was said of him that his methods were oblique. Certainly, they were often baffling in the extreme.

Since he never gave in any but the most laconic form his reasons for accepting the London appointment, I can only record what I believe were the elements that converged in his decision. I think he saw the war as the climax of the struggle between good and evil. The ILO therefore did not figure in his thought as an

---

[6] Carter Lyman Goodrich (1897–1971), an American economic historian, was US Government representative to the Governing Body (1936–45) and Chairman of the Governing Body (1939–45). He opened the first post-war session of the ILC (Paris, 1945). (Ed.)

issue requiring special and independent consideration. It was part of something much wider, part of an attitude to life that the powers of evil were out to destroy. If the Axis won the war, the ILO would be involved in the destruction of all that gave it any meaning. He had placed it in Canada where, in the safest haven he could find, it must await the outcome of the conflict. There was no more that he could do for it within its own sphere. In the larger field he was now to enter he could hope to make a contribution to an Allied victory and that was the best service he could render to the ILO.

But his decision was not, I imagine, so much a conclusion logically reached as a passionate and almost mystic conviction that the fundamentals of all free existence were at stake and that in this apocalyptic struggle the opportunity would be given to him to help in some signal way the cause of freedom. And I also surmise that while this conviction was gaining strength there was running parallel to it on another plane in his mind a longing that, perhaps not consciously identified, had its part in his decision. He wanted to be in the danger zone. He wanted to be where the bombs were falling, to give the encouragement of his presence, if he could give no more, to those on whose sacrifice and courage all at the moment depended.

Though there may have been other elements in his decision, for he was a highly complex personality, I think that these, or something resembling them, were predominant. They correspond to different traits in his character and they explain his remarkable success as Ambassador in London. The impact that he made on people of all kinds in Great Britain by his warm sympathy, by the sincerity of his fervent belief in their cause, affords evidence of the spirit in which he came among them and it is not unreasonable to suppose that that same spirit moved him in accepting his appointment.

But whatever may have been the reasons for his decision and however much they might be held to justify it, the fact remained that it was a severe blow to the ILO and I therefore shared the misgivings of the staff. Indeed, I perhaps felt them even more acutely for I could foresee that his departure would confront me personally with difficulties and problems that it might well prove impossible to resolve. There was no possibility of a meeting of the Governing Body or of its Emergency Committee. Until such a meeting could be held, I, as Deputy Director, would take charge as Harold Butler had done when Albert Thomas died. The circumstances, however, were very different. On that occasion the interregnum had been a matter of only a few weeks and had any grave question arisen the Governing Body could have met at short notice. Now, the ILO's situation was critical in the extreme: new problems faced it at every turn; unprecedented decisions had to be taken day by day; and momentous decisions of policy would in all probability be required from time to time. Unless these responsibilities could be shouldered effectively, the ILO's chances of survival would be slim. I could, of course, appeal to the governments for support, but as a mere de facto Chargé d'Affaires lacking any properly conferred constitutional authority to be the mouthpiece of the Organization, how far would my voice carry and what attention would be paid to it? These considerations pointed clearly to the necessity of investing me with the fullest authority possible in the circumstances. They also suggested that all feasible measures should be taken to strengthen my position with member governments and particularly with the Government of the United States since with Winant's departure there would be no high-ranking official of American nationality on the staff through whom effective liaison could be maintained with Washington.

I tried to get Winant to give consideration to these problems whenever I could get hold of him, which was not often as he spent much of his time in Washington being "briefed" for his new post. On the first occasion, he listened patiently and sympathetically but his reply was too general to be satisfactory. "I'll see that you're all right," he said and then with a warm handclasp and a disarming affectionate smile off he went. The next time I pressed him more persistently. "I haven't forgotten," was his response, "but I can't do anything till the nomination has gone through the Senate. Then everything will be cut and dry and I'll get to work on it," and once more he was gone. Incidentally, whenever I asked to see Winant he always came into my office instead of summoning me to his. I once asked him why. "That's an old trick of mine," he replied grinning mischievously. "I always go to see the other fellow. Then I can go when I want to. If he comes to me I can't get rid of him so easily," and then he added with his attractive smile, "That doesn't apply to you. You come and see me whenever you want," an invitation which, though sincerely meant, was not as valuable as it appeared for it would rarely happen that I would know where he was to be found.

Events now began to move rapidly. It was clear that there would be no delay in the Senate and that very little time remained. I took it for granted that Winant would inform the Governing Body of his decision and I accordingly sent him the draft of a communication that he could adapt as he thought appropriate. After having stated as best I could the reasons why he felt it his duty to accept the London appointment, I added a phrase to the effect that he felt he could safely leave the Office in my charge. It seemed a necessary element in justification of his decision that he should say he had considered how the Office would carry on after his departure and that he was satisfied that it could do so.

I heard no more of my draft for he chose a different procedure, preferring to send his resignation by a letter addressed to Carter Goodrich, the Chairman of the Governing Body, in New York, rather than by a communication to all its members. I imagine his reason was that he wanted a single and rapid reply, and in the circumstances this was understandable. I did not see his letter till after it had been despatched on 13 February 1941. It was very different from the draft I had sent him and it can be summarized as follows. After its opening sentence, "This is to tender my resignation effective as from 13 February 1941," he confined himself to saying that the Office had been effectively established in Montreal, that the future of the Organization was involved in the maintenance of the free nations, that he had been asked by the President of the United States to accept the ambassadorship to Great Britain, that believing this to be his duty he must leave the Office, and that he wished to thank the Chairman and the other members of the Governing Body as well as his co-workers of the staff of the Office for their extraordinary efforts in these years of crisis.

On first reading, I found his letter puzzling. Apart from the first sentence, it amounted to little more than a recital of facts none of which was new. Governments and members of the Governing Body had been informed by a number of communications during the last four months that the Office had been established in Montreal, that work had been resumed and that the budget for 1941 had been approved. They were also well aware that Winant had always believed that the fate of the ILO was dependent on the issue of the war. There seemed to be no purpose in recalling these facts now unless they were to lead up to a reasoned statement justifying the decision with which the letter opened. Winant certainly had a case but it seemed to me inadequately expressed by the single word "duty". Duty to what? To the United States or to the ILO? There was no hint even that there were two duties and that he had had to decide between them, no explanation — and it could have been given with many powerful arguments — that, in the present abnormal circumstances, they coincided. Some of the material for such a case could be extracted from his letter by a selection of certain of his phrases and it could be argued that that was what he meant. But why had he deliberately, for I had no doubt that it was the result of a deliberate decision, left his justification unstated and in fact gone to some pains to hide it away?

On re-reading his letter I began to see some light. I had been looking at the matter from only one angle, the angle of the ILO. Winant had looked at it against a wider background. He was a figure in American politics. His appointment as Ambassador to London had created quite a stir and the American press was carrying stories every day about his career in New Hampshire and in Washington. Anything about him was news and the text of his letter of resignation was sure to be given wide publicity. His political career had been marked by dramatic incidents and in particular by his resignation from the chairmanship of the Social Security Board in order to campaign for Roosevelt's re-election although this meant taking the field against the candidate of his own party. This was something the Republicans could not easily forgive, and it may also be supposed that there were Democrats who were not a little jealous that he, a Republican, should have been chosen by a Democratic President for the coveted post of Ambassador to the Court of St James. It was the American readers of his letter that Winant had evidently had in mind and I could see that the terms in which I had narrowly conceived it as a communication from the Director of the ILO to the ILO's Governing Body were such as he could not possibly use. The idea that there might be obligations of loyalty to an international organization, as well as to one's own Government, that in certain circumstances the two loyalties might have to be weighed one against the other, was not an idea with which Americans were familiar, and one that his political enemies might well have exploited against him. Although there can be no question that these two loyalties, properly understood, are perfectly compatible, there still exists even today in certain quarters in the United States an opinion that loyalty to an international institution must mean a dilution, and possibly a dangerous dilution, of sincere patriotic sentiment. Winant, whose keen political instinct could sense this latent opinion before it found expression, had therefore good reason to choose his terms with the greatest caution. Those who set out to scale political peaks are aware, like other mountaineers, of the dangers of avalanches. When these are to be apprehended they know it is wise to proceed in silence. Only a fool or a madman would shout. Winant was neither but he had gone further than was perhaps prudent in speaking even in a sybilline whisper.

There was, however, another aspect of his letter to which these considerations did not apply that gave me grave concern. That was the omission of any reference to the fact that he was leaving the Office in my charge. I had urged him to take every possible step to strengthen my position and I had understood that he fully appreciated the need and was willing to do so. The first and most obvious measure was for him to inform the Governing Body that he was designating me to carry on. It was evident that I should have to exercise authority going far beyond my function of Deputy Director and the appropriate basis for this necessary extension of my powers was a commission from the outgoing Director. I could see no explanation for the omission save that in the midst of his political preoccupations this practical point had been overlooked. I put the matter to him and suggested that he should make a communication to the Governing Body saying that he was leaving the Office in my hands until such time as it could appoint his successor. His attitude both puzzled and perturbed me. He did not flatly refuse but he was so deliberately non-committal that I pressed him as strongly as I could, urging with all the emphasis at my command that it was something the Governing Body would expect; that the absence of any such statement would inevitably be interpreted as meaning that he had no confidence in me; that my authority would be gravely weakened and the difficulties of the Office increased. As he still remained mutely and bafflingly negative I asked him bluntly to tell me frankly whether I had his confidence or not.

He assured me emphatically that I had. "In all my experience," he said, "I have never had such splendid loyalty and such valuable help. No one could have given more." And then he added, and having just been pondering the nuances in his letter I was quick to see the value of the addition, "You could not have given more." Winant used few and usually very simple words, but they could on occasion convey very subtle and important distinctions. This tribute, emphatic though it was, however, carried matters no further. All I could get him to say was, "I thought my letter should deal only with my resignation. I don't want to add anything to it."

I still saw no reason why he should not send out a separate communication on the future administration of the Office and I continued my insistence. He broke into his charming smile. "I'll tell you what. I'll get Goodrich to do it," he said, moving towards the door with the air of having found a happy solution to all our troubles.

His attitude appeared to me so unreasonable and his explanation of it so unconvincing that I began to suspect that some plan was being hatched under which the Office would not be left in my charge. What could it be? I dismissed the idea of the immediate appointment of another Director. Only the Governing Body could make such an appointment and since this could not happen unknown to me there would be no point in not telling me that this was what was envisaged. Moreover, the operation would take some time, and meanwhile I, as Deputy Director, would automatically have to manage the ILO's affairs. This hypothesis, therefore, did not seem tenable. The only other possibility that occurred to me was that there might be a scheme for putting the Office under some form of joint control. This was an idea against which I reacted violently and not on personal grounds. The appointment of a new Director by the Governing Body would be the correct constitutional procedure. I had no ambition to succeed to the director-ship in wartime and I should have been fully content if the Governing Body were to appoint someone else to take Winant's place. The putting of the directorship into commission, however, would be utterly contrary to the Constitution. The whole internal history of the Organization had turned on the harmonious adjust-ment of the powers of the Conference, of the Governing Body and of the Direc-tor. To disrupt that equilibrium would destroy one of the most fundamental and valuable features of the Organization, one that it might well prove impossible subsequently to restore. Moreover, it would hopelessly cripple the Organization at a moment when its existence was at stake. I shuddered at the thought of the paralysis that would ensue and at the delays and disagreements that would inevitably confuse policy and hamper urgent action. If this was what was on foot, I was prepared to go to all lengths to oppose it. I made a last attempt to force Winant to an explanation. "That won't do," I said, rising and following him to the door. "If Goodrich makes a statement, it will only make things worse. Its only effect will be to draw attention to the fact that you abstained from making any such statement yourself."

Winant made no reply. He stood at the door with that almost tragic appearance of worried distress that so often evoked the desire to do anything possible to help him. But on this occasion, instead of reacting sympathetically, I resented a silence that I felt was a form of pressure. We looked at one another, he in mute appeal, I with growing irritation. Finally, I said, "Well, if you won't do it I will. I shall send out my own communication to the Members as soon as Goodrich replies accepting your resignation."

His answer was a complete surprise.

He nodded his head a couple of times in smiling agreement and said cordially, "That's all right," and then added emphatically, "Yes, you do it."

I remained, if anything, more puzzled than before. I had not gained my point but his unequivocal approval of the procedure I had stated I would follow was of substantial importance. It meant that there would be no hiatus and that my cable would go out while he was still Director. When Goodrich's letter arrived on the morning of 15 February, accepting Winant's resignation, I accordingly telegraphed to all the governments of the Members of the Organization the following:

> Chairman of the Governing Body has accepted Winant's resignation from his position of Director of the International Labour Office with effect from 15 February 1941. In his letter of resignation Winant who has been appointed American Ambassador to London reaffirms his faith in the continued ability of the Organisation to serve mankind. In assuming the responsibilities of the directorship of the ILO until the Governing Body appoints a new director in accordance with Article 8 of the Constitution I am confident I will receive the full support of yourself and your Government in maintaining the activities and prestige of the Organisation in accordance with the Constitution and in fulfilment of the policy laid down by the Governing Body and applied by Winant and his predecessors. This telegram has been sent to all Governments. [7]

---

[7] For the official text of the telegram, see ILO: *Minutes of the 90th Session of the Governing Body, New York, 25 October–5 November 1941* (Montreal, 1941), p. 38. (Ed.)

I also sent telegrams with essentially the same text to all members and deputy members of the Governing Body.

Four days later Goodrich sent out by mail copies of his correspondence with Winant accompanied by a brief covering letter which contained the following passage:

> As from February 16, Mr E.J. Phelan has taken over the responsibility of directing the continued functioning of the Office as Acting Director until such time as the Governing Body appoints a Director under Article 8 of the Constitution of the International Labour Organisation. For him and for the Organisation, I ask your fullest co-operation and support. [8]

This was followed several weeks later by Winant's farewell message addressed to "governments, employers and workers of member States", a lengthy printed document in which he surveyed the events of his directorship. In referring to his departure from the Office he wrote: "I leave it in the competent hands of the Deputy Director, Mr Edward J. Phelan, pending action by the Governing Body."

I never learned whether the passage in Goodrich's letter was inserted at Winant's suggestion, nor why Winant included in his message the statement he had so obstinately refused to make when I urged it upon him. To anyone who knew him the assumption that he changed his mind would appear unlikely. Actions of his that seemed contradictory were never susceptible of so simple an explanation; they had their place in some intricate pattern known only to himself about which speculation was usually futile.

I was nevertheless occasionally mildly irritated by my inability to make head or tail of his behaviour on this occasion. Whenever I looked back on the events in Montreal, it recurred to my mind as a kind of mental challenge. In the end I thought I could make sense of it on certain assumptions. *If* Winant had made a commitment not to send such a message, that would explain his obstinate refusal and it would be characteristic of him to stand by his commitment even though he was exposed to great pressure. *If*, however, he had come to realize more and more fully the undesirable results to which his inaction would lead, my declaration that I would send out my own statement would have appeared as a welcome solution – his commitment was limited and negative; it debarred him from acting himself but it did not oblige him to prevent action on my part and he was therefore free to agree that I should follow that course.

---

[8] For the full text of the covering letter, see ibid. (Ed.)

All that, however, is the merest conjecture. It may be that his baffling attitude had some other quite different explanation. In any case the matter ceased to have any importance as replies to my telegrams arrived in a steady stream containing welcome assurances of support and confidence.

This encouraging result was, however, yet in the future and I must turn back to recount certain other conversations with Winant before his departure. It might have been expected that at a time when we were so strongly divided on an issue that I believed to be of the greatest importance our relations would have been strained and our contacts reduced to such cold formalities as might be officially unavoidable. One proof that Winant was an unusual being was that, on the contrary, we remained on terms that can only be described as genuinely cordial. There were several questions, relatively small in themselves but important nevertheless, that it was urgent to get cleared up in the few days that remained. Winant had paid little attention to the general running of the Office or the performance of its well-established activities. These he was content to leave under my supervision. But he had initiated a number of affairs personally and kept them in his own hands. Some of them were of great interest since they were in a small way the beginning of what has now become a major international activity under the title of technical assistance. It was important that I should have a much clearer picture of what had been done in matters of this kind so that there might be no danger of disputes or misunderstandings at a later stage about the Office's exact obligations. This was the more necessary as Winant rarely put pen to paper except to sign his name. He was not in the habit of dictating a note of his conversations, and incoming letters or telegrams addressed to him were liable to disappear into one or other of his pockets and never afterwards to emerge. Such files as existed on these questions were therefore inadequate for my purpose and Winant readily agreed to go through them with me and fill in the gaps. When his last evening in the Office arrived, nothing had been done. On my reminding him that the matter ought to be dealt with he replied, "I haven't forgotten. I'll do it before I go." I pointed out that he would be going in an hour's time and suggested we get on with the task at once. "I can't do that," he said, "but you come down to my house at Concord on Saturday and stay over till Sunday. Bring your wife. I want you both to see Concord and there are lots of things I want to talk to you about."

Anxious as I was to get the job done, I demurred at the idea of breaking in on his last weekend with his family, but he waved my hesitation aside. "You won't be in the way. It's a big house and we are always having guests," and as though happily planning a house party he continued, "Bring Reymond [my private secretary].[9] He can take charge of all the papers. Tell him to bring his wife, too. You've all been working too hard and a quiet weekend in the country will do you good." It would have been more than discourteous to make any further difficulties about accepting an invitation so warmly given, but I asked him to leave the matter open and telephone me from Concord on Friday in case anything should arrive that interfered with his plans. This I thought would leave him an easy way out if he had acted on an over-generous impulse and would also ensure that Mrs Winant, who might well not welcome such an invasion on the eve of her husband's departure, would be consulted.

The telephone call came with a renewal of his invitation and in due course we arrived at the Concord airport, from which a car conveyed us to a large and attractive white house standing some distance back from a country road. The chauffeur, having deposited our bags beside the door and having rung the bell, drove off round the side of the house presumably to the garage, and then began a series of happenings that progressively became more and more bewildering. Nobody answered the bell. We stood in the snow, chilled by a bitter winter wind, anxious to reach the warmth inside. We rang again, and were about to ring a third time when we heard the rattle of a chain and the door was cautiously opened no more than an inch or two. A pair of malevolent eyes stared at us forbiddingly through the aperture. The scrutiny lasted a perceptible time and we thought we were going to be refused admittance. Then there was another rattle of the chain, the door was flung wide open and an impressive butler bowed us in. We found ourselves in a large hall in which a number of people were standing. They had a glum and dispirited air but we had barely time to glance at them before the butler, having taken our coats, ushered us into a large drawing room. A sense of unreality began to creep over us as we found that, like the hall, it was occupied by quite a crowd and that no attention whatever was paid to our arrival. Every available seat had been taken. Some of their occupants were reading crumpled newspapers, others gazed at nothing in particular in gloomy abstraction, others seemed asleep, and the whole atmosphere was one of boredom and despondency. There was also something peculiar about the butler. His dignity was tremendous — so much so that he seemed like a stage butler overplaying his part — but from time to time he breathed heavily as though beneath his mask he was repressing some

---

[9] Henri Ernest Reymond (1899–1998) joined the ILO in 1931 as Assistant and then Executive Assistant to the Director. He served under Albert Thomas, Harold Butler, John G. Winant and E.J. Phelan. He was Chief of the Administrative Section (1946–59) and then Director of the Liaison Office in New York. After his retirement in 1964, he served as Secretary of the International Civil Service Advisory Board (ICSAB) for two years. (Ed.)

violent emotion. Leaving us standing before the fireplace, he disappeared for a few moments and reappeared with some folding chairs which he placed at our disposal. Then having learnt that we had had no lunch he opened a bridge table, covered it with a spotless tablecloth and with Jeevesian efficiency laid before us an excellent cold meal accompanied by hot coffee. We lingered over this welcome repast. There was nothing else to do and nowhere else to go. We speculated in half whispers about our silent companions who continued to take no notice of us or of one another, and since speculation proved futile we too fell silent and, half dozing in the warmth of the fire, relapsing into semi-somnolent abstraction. The butler had long since disappeared, and without him and his ministrations there was nothing to connect us any longer with the normal world.

Whether I actually fell asleep I do not know but my mind drifted lazily between fact and fancy until finally they became indistinguishable. I remember thinking that we were part of a group of stranded travellers, waiting in patient boredom for a long overdue train, for whom the railway company had provided a luxurious waiting room with rich carpets and tapestried armchairs. Vaguely conscious that my own seat was hard and had no arms, I concluded that I must be travelling third class. As a compensation, however, we third-class passengers had been given an excellent free meal served with as much distinction as if we were directors of the company. Possibly this was some new experiment in social justice which I should investigate. The guard, whose uniform resembled a butler's, might know. No doubt he would appear again before we reached our destination. But when that would be and where, seemed of no importance.

Then suddenly I was aware that Winant had appeared in the doorway, and I woke up. "Have you been up to your rooms? Are you fixed up all right?" was his greeting. "You haven't. Come on. I'll take you."

We followed him with relief only to be plunged back into bewilderment as he halted us in the corridor outside with the words, "Wait here a minute. I'll have to get the keys from Robert. We have to keep your rooms locked."

He disappeared abruptly through a doorway, leaving us once more alone, perplexed by his announcement and somewhat dismayed at the idea that perhaps he would not return. His absence was only momentary and characteristically he picked up the conversation where he had left it, as if there had been no interruption. It required an effort on our part to catch his thread and to discover that Robert was the butler, as he continued, "He's terribly upset at the way he received you. He thought you were journalists! They invaded us this morning. Robert hurried round to barricade all the doors and windows but he was too late. They are all over the house, even in the bedrooms. He's furious. He thought you were some more of them, till he saw your grips."

As Winant showed us to our rooms, he explained that he had to make a farewell speech to the New Hampshire Senate but that meanwhile Mrs Winant would take us for a drive and afterwards we could pay a visit to her famous kennels. "When I get back", he added, "these journalists will have gone and we'll get our job of work done. I've discovered you can get too much publicity," he added ruefully.

Mrs Winant proved a charming and interesting guide to some of the beauties of Concord's surroundings and then we made our inspection of the kennels, an extensive establishment of some half dozen one-storeyed buildings comprising a kitchen, an infirmary, numerous fascinating young families of Scotch and Cairn terriers and a whole nobility of canine aristocrats whose silken banners hung above their separate stalls blazoning in gold and red and purple the titles they had won. There was plenty that was interesting to see but I was anxious to catch Winant on his return and I explained to the kennel master that we must go. He nodded his head understandingly. "I'll take you to the Ambassador," he said, and there was a tone of reverence in his voice as he proudly pronounced the exalted title. As we followed him towards the door he stopped before another blazoned stall and, pointing at its occupant, said in a voice of deep emotion, "Here is the Ambassador! The greatest dog ever shown in America." He seemed deeply offended when after a moment's startled silence his announcement was greeted with unrestrained laughter and was not greatly mollified when we suggested that the name had been prophetic.

Hardly had we arrived back at the house than Winant took me aside. "I've got a Catholic Monseigneur up in one of the bedrooms. He's come from the Bishop. I wonder if you'd talk to him for a few minutes until I can get away from some other people. He's awfully nice."

"Certainly," I replied, feeling a vague apprehension that these were the opening words of Act II of *A quiet weekend,* an apprehension that took more definite shape as Winant proceeded to explain what had happened. His only daughter, who had been at school in Peru, had made a runaway match with a young Peruvian a couple of days before and had arrived by plane with her husband. They had gone through a civil marriage but the family considered it essential that there should be a religious ceremony. Since the husband was a Catholic and the Winants Protestants, an authorization from the Catholic Bishop was required and hence the Monseigneur's presence and the desirability of treating him with every possible courtesy in the disturbed conditions in which he had perforce to be received.

These domestic events naturally modified the programme for the rest of our stay and any hope of getting hold of Winant to deal with ILO affairs had clearly to be abandoned. After dinner, one or two close friends of the family arrived and we all gathered round the radio in the big comfortable library listening to snatches of opera or watching the young couple giving, with admirable skill, demonstrations of the latest South American dances. It was a most pleasant evening. Winant and Mrs Winant were such admirable hosts that we in nowise felt that we were intruders. Conversation ran easily in spite of the fact that the bridegroom spoke only Spanish and could therefore only talk with the bride, a restriction that caused him evidently no regrets. Though this set them somewhat apart the glow of their happy absorption in one another radiated through the room and made the occasion genuinely festive. To watch Winant rolling back the carpet, fiddling with the radio in search of dance music, pulling books from his shelves, telling amusing stories and generally enjoying himself with the zest of a schoolboy arriving home for his holidays on Christmas Eve, was to marvel at his powers of recuperation after the exhausting day of private and public worries through which he had passed.

Next morning, the family went off to the wedding which, in the circumstances, was a strictly private affair. We packed our bags and made reservations to leave on the plane at noon. But when Winant returned from the church he would not hear of our departure.

"Don't do that," he protested. "Stay and have lunch with us and I'll go to Montreal with you on the 3 o'clock plane. I've got to see some people there and I've promised to say goodbye to the staff and then I take a late plane for Washington. I'll have plenty of time for our talk."

Again, his insistence bore down my reluctance to take him away from Concord earlier than he had intended and we altered our reservations accordingly. It would be wearisome to recount what happened during the five or six hours he spent in Montreal and the various complications that once more upset his programme. All the conversation I had with him was at the door of his taxi as he was leaving the staff's reception at the Faculty Club while his secretary was telephoning to the airport saying that he was on his way and asking that the New York plane be held until he arrived.

"I'm sorry we didn't get to do those papers," he said apologetically, "but you won't have any trouble. If there's anything you don't understand, call me up in London."

As I walked home I thought what an unusual person Winant was and what an extraordinarily wearing life he led. He was always getting himself caught between contradictory commitments and having to expend immense energy and much time and ingenuity in getting himself out of them. It was not the result of muddle in any ordinary sense. He always knew quite clearly what he was about but, like Lord Kitchener, he kept too many things in his own hands. He worked mainly by telephone and personal conversations and as he kept no notes it was beyond the power of the ablest private secretary to keep his path smooth. The very fact that he had the gift of securing from his immediate personal assistants an exceptional degree of devotion paradoxically made things worse. Impressed by the definiteness with which he accepted or refused a formula and by the silent and often prolonged reflection that preceded instructions given in a few brief words, they came to regard the latter as something sacred which it would be sacrilege to question and to which it was not their function to add any explanatory comment. "Not for them to make reply, not for them to reason why," and the result, though not tragic, was sometimes troublesome in the extreme.

Here is an instance that occurred after Winant had been some months in London. He sent me a message – it is worth noting that I received only one letter from him in the course of our long acquaintance and that contained less than 20 words. His message informed me that he had written an article on the ILO for the *Saturday Evening Post*, that I would receive a copy of his manuscript and that if I thought there was anything in it that required alteration I was to send the corrections to his representative who would forward them to the editor by whom they would be inserted in the text. An article in the *Saturday Evening Post* by Ambassador Winant would give most valuable publicity to the ILO's work. It would be read by millions and it was clearly most desirable that it should contain neither errors of fact nor any loosely worded phrase that might prove unfortunate. I accordingly read it with great care and forwarded my amendments through the prescribed channel. The result was a storm of impressive dimensions. The celebrated Ben Hecht, the autocratic and choleric editor of the *Saturday Evening Post*, blew up with a cyclonic violence that was unusual even for him. Winant, he thundered, had supplied the article only on the express condition that no change whatsoever would be made in its text. Ben Hecht's reaction was reported to me on the telephone by Winant's very disturbed representative, who suggested that my amendments might be withdrawn. Since they were important, I could not agree and so the matter had to be referred back to Winant in London. I could easily guess what had happened. Two quite separate things were involved: one of them Winant definitely wanted and the other he did not. On the one hand, he wanted me to vet the article so that it might contain no mistakes. On the other hand, he did not want the editorial staff of the *Saturday Evening* Post to follow their usual practice of editing contributors' manuscripts. The trouble arose from the fact that these two desiderata which could so easily have been coordinated had now precipitated a conflict. I can imagine how worried Winant must have been. The angry Ben Hecht had to be soothed at almost any cost – he was too vocal and powerful a figure for any politician to ignore – but equally the ex-Director could not allow an article containing errors about the ILO to appear under his name. I do not know how he managed to straighten the tangle. But while the politician and the ex-Director struggled with its complications, the Ambassador must have felt much as I did at Concord.

I have told these anecdotes about Winant in some detail because his personality was so complex and because in no other way can I convey what an unusual person he was. His range of mood and behaviour was so wide that it would present the most skilful biographer with a formidable challenge. What I have recorded amounts to no more than a few fragments of personal experience that remain vivid in my memory, and they are far from giving anything like a complete picture. But since they are concerned mainly with incidents that aroused feelings of frustration and impatience I should add that when I saw him in London during my wartime visits my experience was quite different. I was always able to secure access to him without difficulty and we had many long talks, any one of which exceeded in length all my conversations with him as Director put together. Incidentally, I found evidence on all sides of a respect and confidence in him that I imagine few ambassadors have ever enjoyed. In the circumstances of that time the United States was fortunate in having him as its representative and his intuition that he could render important service in his London post proved to be wholly correct. He achieved a personal success that was unparalleled and I was deeply grateful to him that in the midst of it he was always willing to give me so much of his time and to assist me in every possible way.

All this, however, lay in the future as I walked home that night in Montreal and began to survey the nature of the immense responsibilities that I must now shoulder alone.

The ILO turns the corner [1]

The events accompanying Winant's departure to take up the post of American Ambassador in London had made it impossible for me to give any consecutive thought to the responsibilities I would have to assume as his successor. As soon as I turned to survey them, I realized that the establishment of the ILO's headquarters in Canada was the beginning of a new phase in its existence and that therefore my first task must be to get some clear idea of the policy round which its activities should henceforth be coordinated.

I reflected a little ruefully, and perhaps unjustly, that such a policy was now much more difficult to define in Montreal than it had been in Geneva six months before. At that time the fundamental issue was limited to the choice between two alternatives, whether to go or to stay. Winant had decided to go; and thanks to his courage and determination the ILO had been rescued from encirclement, and its freedom of action assured. The question now calling for an answer was what was it to do with that freedom; what was the next step that would keep the ILO travelling along the road to survival? It was not a question that could be simply answered.

Winant had said in his letter of resignation that if the war was lost that would be the end of the ILO. And, since the ILO could do little or nothing to influence the issue of the conflict, he was no doubt right in deciding that his particular qualities would best serve its interests by being employed in a field of activity far outside its scope. But, while his statement furnished an argument for his own action, it defined only one of the dangers to which the ILO was exposed.

---

[1] First published in 1956 in *Studies: An Irish Quarterly*, Vol. 45, No. 178, pp. 160–86. (Ed.)

If the road to an Allied victory proved long and rough, as there was every reason to expect, many of civilization's valuable possessions might well be destroyed or damaged beyond repair, and many of the achievements of human progress perish unnoticed in the strains and stresses encountered on the way. Was it not possible, and even probable, that the ILO would be numbered amongst them? And, in comparison with the other losses entailed, would that of the ILO be considered as really important?

Personally, I believed that the loss of the ILO would have an importance difficult to overestimate. If that conviction should come to be widely shared, there would be sound grounds for optimism about its survival. But looking at the matter coldly and objectively I was driven to the conclusion that such sympathy and support as it now enjoyed would diminish rather than increase as the war continued; and that it would be a delusion to cherish the hope that its past record and present activities would be sufficient to guarantee its future. The former would become forgotten history, and the latter, because of its limited resources, could make no widespread appeal. If, however, the more fundamental implications of the ILO's existence in the perspective of the development of human institutions could be driven home, it might well hope for preservation, not out of sympathy or sentiment, but as an essential part of the organization of the post-war world.

Here at least was a positive idea, one that might well influence the issue if it was accepted in quarters that mattered. And that was perhaps not impossible, for solid reasons could be advanced to support the thesis that the ILO's survival would have a general importance.

The argument for the ILO's survival and a policy to achieve it

The argument, as I formulated it, ran briefly as follows. The whole experience of democratic institutions proves that they require time to mature before they can function effectively. They become of real value only when their operation, over a sufficiently long period, has created certain habits of thought and action; and this consideration applies with special force to institutions international in character.

The League and the ILO were the beginning of the attempt to provide the world with institutions for new forms of world political activity which, it was hoped, would provide a basis on which a peaceful world could be built. The League failed to fulfil the hopes placed in it, not because it was ill-designed, but because the magnitude and pace of events overwhelmed it before there was time for the use of its machinery to become a solidly established practice. The

ILO was more fortunate. Within its sphere, international collaboration steadily grew more intense and extensive in spite of the fact that political and economic conditions were little favourable to such a development. Collaboration between its Members had indeed become something approaching second nature, an involuntary response capable of setting in motion international activity over a wide economic and social field.

The situation that would have to be faced at the end of the war was evident. The reconstruction of the world's economic life, disrupted to a degree never before experienced, would raise problems of a formidable character, and those problems would be predominantly international in character. When these came to be dealt with, the existence of an international institution with a live tradition of successful international collaboration and a long experience of developing efficient techniques of international action would be an asset of incalculable value.

The general argument seemed to me wholly convincing but its application to the ILO might appear as no more than special pleading unless proof could be given that the Organization still possessed the qualities that had made its past achievements possible. This could not be supplied by the production of summaries of information and the sending of reminders to governments urging the fulfilment of certain minor obligations under a Constitution the major features of which would be steadily receding into the realms of pious memory. What had so far been saved was only the Office. What must be kept in being was the International Labour Organization as a living institution manifesting in action its qualities and its strength. If its Members lost the habit of using it, atrophy, paralysis and death would be the inevitable stages of its decline and final disappearance.

I had reason to fear that this decline had already begun and to believe that it would proceed far more rapidly in wartime than would have been the case if, for some reason, the activities of the Organization had been interrupted in time of peace.

It is worthwhile indicating why I entertained this fear because it arose from an element of weakness peculiar to international institutions. Whereas war strengthens national organizations, giving them an increased sense of responsibility and a greater cohesion, it produces exactly the opposite effects on an international organization. To understand why this was happening to the ILO it is necessary to remember that the Conference, the Governing Body and the Office are no more than an easily visible superstructure built on the foundation of member governments and their organizations of workers and employers. Each one of the elements in this foundation is itself a highly articulated organism composed in the last analysis of human beings, differing in rank and authority, but each possessing some special knowledge or experience out of which he makes, at his particular level, his contribution to the work of the organism as a whole.

Thus, when the ILO deals with a government, many individuals have a part to play and on their efficiency and on the coordination of their roles will depend the real strength of the bonds between the ILO and the government concerned.

With this picture in mind, it is easy to see how these bonds will be weakened when war supervenes. The civil service becomes burdened with new duties; staff has to be redistributed within a department or between departments; the whole pattern of both structure and function becomes subject to rapid and continuous change. The official dealing with some aspect of ILO affairs may find that other matters demand a share of his attention, or he may have been replaced by someone unfamiliar with ILO questions; or worse still, he may not be replaced at all. The civil servant at the top of the pyramid who must take the responsibility for the reply to the ILO will thus be left without the assistance on which he could previously count at the very time when other responsibilities are crowding on him. Inevitably, ILO questions will receive less attention than in the past. They will tend to be disposed of with a minimum of trouble rather than in a positive and constructive spirit.

Something like this was undoubtedly happening, not only in countries directly involved in the war, but also in others for which the war had precipitated a host of new problems. In the process of disintegration in the peripheral machinery of the Organization, which was thus occurring, lay, I thought, the fundamental danger to the ILO.

The Office could do nothing to remedy the situation. Only the member States themselves could repair or reinforce administrative instruments which were under their sole control. It was vain to imagine that, by some happy inspiration, they would individually be moved to take such action. Only by a renewed experience of their own collective function as Members of the Organization could it be hoped that they would become once more vividly aware of its potentialities and thus be led to restore, and thereafter to maintain, each in its own domain, a fraction of the Organization's machinery which was a necessary part of the whole. The practical conclusion that clearly emerged was that every effort must be made to secure a meeting of the International Labour Conference at the earliest possible date.

The idea was not new. It had been implied in the Governing Body's original decision that the ILO should carry on if war supervened, and in fact the main argument for the move to the American continent had been that there was no prospect of being able to convene the Conference in Switzerland. I had raised the question with Winant and Carter Goodrich, the Chairman of the Governing

Body, on several occasions after I had arrived in Montreal. At one such discussion, at which others were present, another idea was put forward, namely that, in view of the presence of so many European governments in London, a conference of the European Members of the Organization should be held in that city.

Although this suggestion received considerable support, I had strongly opposed it on the ground that the holding of such a conference would be resented by neutral Members in Europe, who would not attend, and by the great majority of non-European Members; both would feel that a meeting whose composition was the result of temporary circumstances external to the Organization could not be considered to be an ILO meeting in any proper sense of the term. A division of opinion of this kind would not serve the cause of the Allies and would weaken the unity of the Organization itself. These arguments were accepted as convincing and the idea was dropped. Though all were agreed that the alternative of a General Conference was desirable, I was far from feeling that its urgency was appreciated. Attention at that time was naturally concentrated on getting the Montreal office into running order and there was legitimate satisfaction at the success achieved. It seemed, however, to be too easily assumed that a meeting of the Conference would flow from this activity in due course. This I felt was over-optimistic and I continued to press my view that positive action was required, in the hope that Winant with his political experience would in due time find the right strings to pull.

Now that I had to face the problem after his departure, I realized that there was a difference between urging that something very desirable should be done and actually taking the responsibility for doing it. How great that difference is has been expressed by General Spears in the following words: "To command troops in battle and to be a Chief of Staff is as different as is riding in the Grand National and taking photos of the jumps."[2] While I did not state it in anything like so vivid a way, I was acutely conscious that the difficulties of getting the Conference to meet while the war was in progress, now that I viewed them from the angle of my new responsibility, appeared formidable indeed and even insuperable. Nevertheless, I could see no other policy that offered any chance of securing the ILO's survival. The only alternative was to juggle with the limited resources at the Office's disposal, concentrating them from time to time on some new small activity that might attract momentary attention, and to hope that in the end everything would turn out all right. My choice therefore was easily made. There

---

[2] Edward Louis Spears: *Assignment to catastrophe*, Vol. 1: *Prelude to Dunkirk* (London, Heinemann, 1954). Major-General Sir Edward Louis Spears (1886–1974) was a British army officer who acted as liaison officer between France and Britain in the First and Second World Wars. (Ed.)

would be fences to be taken one way or the other, but, if I was to break my neck over one of them, I preferred to do so while riding in what I believed to be the right direction.

It was therefore not in a particularly cheerful mood that I entered the ILO premises the following morning. I was heartened, however, by the messages that steadily poured in in reply to my cable announcing that I had taken charge of the ILO. Many of them from governments and from members of the Governing Body contained expressions of support and confidence and I was particularly encouraged by a letter from Prime Minister Mackenzie King that concluded with the words: "In the present crisis the fortunes of the ILO could be in no better or more competent hands." But personally gratifying as these communications were, and valuable for their effect on the morale of the staff, I knew that I must not exaggerate their importance and draw from them the conclusion that the proposal I had in mind would be readily accepted.

The problem that now occupied my mind was how to prepare the ground for its consideration by the Governing Body so that it would have the best possible chances of success. Since the Governing Body could not meet, the only way I could secure decisions from it was through correspondence with its members individually. This was a workable system so long as the questions put to them related to matters with which they were familiar and which could therefore be answered by a simple yes or no; but it clearly presented difficulties when the decision involved a startling new departure for which they were unprepared. Faced with a question of that kind, and one of exceptional importance, they would feel it impossible to give a reply without embarking on consultations with one another, particularly with a view to discovering the views of the principal governments. In such consultations I should be unable to play any part; I could neither secure that the case for holding the Conference would be effectively stated, nor that the arguments against it would be adequately replied to, and a negative result would, I felt, be a foregone conclusion.

Seeking support in Washington

The world situation being what it was, the attitude of the British and American Governments would in all probability decide the issue. If they were opposed, there would be no practical possibility of the Conference being able to meet whatever other Members might desire; and if they were favourable, many other Members would certainly wish to attend a Conference convened with such decisive support; London and Washington should, therefore, be my first objectives and I decided to begin with a visit to the latter. I realized that I must proceed with some caution for reasons very similar to those which had decided me against an immediate approach to the Governing Body. What I must attempt to secure from these governments was a firm and considered view, and such a view, as I have indicated above, is only arrived at after a survey of all its implications by the competent services of the government concerned. These services consult and argue with one another before they frame their advice to higher authority and the result of their deliberations, if it is definite, is unlikely to be overridden. To build on any opinion given by any single person, however eminent, in advance of this process would be to build on a very unsure foundation. On the other hand, if my proposal should be prematurely referred to the administrative machine and left to take its chance among all the more pressing questions of the moment, the prospect that it would emerge with a favourable answer was probably very slight.

The best course to follow would be to keep any definite proposal in the background until I had been able to get my general argument understood and, if possible, accepted by as wide a circle as possible. As this would be my first visit to Washington in my new capacity, it would be normal for me to make an extended round of visits and these would provide an excellent opportunity for a preliminary exploration of the ground.

My first call was naturally on the Secretary of Labor, and the obvious sincerity and warmth of Miss Perkins' greeting immediately removed any apprehension that Winant's departure might have lessened interest and confidence in the ILO. I had always been impressed by her quality of frankness and after I had explained that, as Acting Director, I had thought I should make a personal visit to Washington, her reply was typical of her general grasp of the situation and of her directness of expression:

"We are very glad to have you in charge of the ILO," she said: "If anyone can save it you can."

"I can't hope to do that," I replied. "I don't think the salvation of the ILO can be achieved by any individual. The International Labour Organization will only be saved if it saves itself."

"That is profoundly true," was her comment. "But I believe that the ILO has that spirit, and it is for you to show the ways in which it can be manifested."

I was strongly tempted to respond to an attitude that showed such an unexpected and clear understanding of the problem, but I remembered my reasons for proceeding cautiously and I confined myself to saying that I had had some ideas along those lines which I would like to discuss with her later when I was ready to put them into more definite form. She replied that she would always be at my disposal for such a discussion and would be glad to see me at any time.

My next important call was on Secretary Hull. I did not know him anything like as well as I knew Miss Perkins but he had received me twice before when I had come on missions to Washington. He remembered those conversations with surprising accuracy, and a little later he gave further proof of his remarkable memory. When I began to talk about the present problems of the ILO, he interrupted me to tell me of the part he had personally played in the decision of the United States to acquire membership in the Organization and in doing so he listed the senators and others whom he had called on the telephone in order to make sure that congressional approval would be forthcoming. After this digression, he told me that he regarded the ILO as an institution of great importance and fully accepted my argument that it was now of greater importance than ever. Finally, he assured me that I could count on his support and cordially invited me to come to see him any time I was in Washington.

A long round of visits, some official and some personal, followed during the next two days. It was a heavy programme as I was anxious to cover the ground as completely as possible during the short time I could afford to be away from Montreal, and when I at last stepped into the ILO's Washington Office to pick up my plane reservations for my return journey, I was feeling more than a little exhausted. To my dismay I was handed the following telephone message: "President Green would like you to come to a little dinner tonight to meet a few of the AF of L officials."

I had spent an hour with William Green the afternoon before. There was nothing more that I could usefully say to him at this stage and I was reluctant to change the arrangements for my return to Canada. On the other hand, he was an old friend of mine and an evening with him and a few of his close assistants in the American Federation of Labor offered the prospect of some hours of pleasant relaxation which I felt I both deserved and needed. And so, after some hesitation, I decided to postpone my departure and to accept his invitation.

I ought no doubt to have been more wary. I ought to have remembered that in United States terminology the word "officials" has a wider application than is given to it in English usage and that years previously I had been startled to find it used to describe the President of the Board of Trade and one of his colleagues in the British Cabinet.

As it was when I arrived at the Washington Hotel, I found that the "little dinner" comprised more than a score of guests including practically all the members of the Federation's Executive Council. Three or four of them I had already met and, though I welcomed the opportunity of making the acquaintance of the others, my satisfaction was more than counterbalanced by what I knew must follow. This was the kind of occasion that, in America, would inevitably conclude with speeches and to these I, as the guest of the evening (for as such I became uncomfortably aware I was regarded), would be expected to make a major contribution. In any other circumstances I would not have been greatly concerned. I had done a good deal of public speaking in the course of my career and I had even gained something of a reputation as a creditable performer before an after-dinner audience. But whatever talent I possessed for the kind of light-hearted fluency which those who have dined well can so easily be beguiled into accepting as wit would not serve on this occasion. President Green's speech made it clear that the purpose of the gathering was to introduce to the Executive Council the new head of the ILO and, as he proceeded to do so, I became more and more conscious that I was being subjected to a critical scrutiny and that much would depend on the impression I created when I came to reply.

Green did his best to smooth my path. He recalled at some length his own meeting with me at the peace conference in Paris in 1919 and how I had worked in close association with President Gompers during the meeting of the commission at which the ILO was born. All that was to the good: it gave me the standing of one whose contacts with the AF of L had extended over a long period. But the interest of his audience was, I felt sure, far more concerned with the qualities I might now possess than with those I had displayed 20 years ago. A number of other speeches followed from some of the most famous figures in the history of the American labour movement. With few and rare exceptions, members of the Executive Council are the heads of the most powerful and vigorous unions in the Federation. They have no exact counterpart in the trade unions of Europe for the reason that the United States is unique in its immense economic development and in the vast area over which it is distributed; the men who lead unions with a membership stretching from the Atlantic to the Pacific, and from Canada to Mexico, must in consequence possess and exercise a degree of power that would not easily be left to their discretion in a smaller area. As I listened to them, I was fascinated by their personalities and equally impressed by the fact that they constituted as formidable an audience as I had ever had to encounter and one that would have no hesitation in arriving at a rapid and utterly ruthless judgement.

Albert Thomas once told me that his best speeches were those about which he felt most nervous as he rose to deliver them. If that applied to my case, I must have spoken extremely well. My impression at the moment was, however, the exact contrary. As I watched the faces of my audience I felt with increasing discouragement that I was evoking no response – I was not then aware that nearly all its members were poker players of renown – and though I received generous applause when I sat down, I was unable to judge whether this was no more than as much as American courtesy always generously extends to a guest speaker however poor his performance.

When we passed into another room where we could mix around, I tried to discover from one of my friends what impression my speech had made.

"You needn't worry," was his reply, "Padway thought it was fine." Padway was the Federation's Legal Adviser, [3] and I concluded sadly that this was a polite way of telling me that I had over-elaborated some constitutional point which had bored everyone else. I did not know at the time that Padway's opinion on other than legal questions carried considerable weight in the Federation's inner councils and I was quite unprepared for the words that followed: "They are going to invite you to speak at the Convention."

Most non-American readers will not appreciate the distinction that such an invitation confers. In a country the size of the United States with a population of some 150 million, organizations really national in extent can hardly be said to exist. Even the two great political parties only take on something resembling a national character when once in four years they hold their conventions for the limited purpose of nominating their candidates for the presidency. In the interval their constituent sections are bodies concerned only with the local politics of the separate states. The American Federation of Labor, with its subsidiary state federations and its highly organized chartered trade unions, comprising a total membership (at that time) of some 8 million distributed over nearly the whole country, was therefore an organization possessing an almost unique national character. Its annual convention provided a rostrum which the most prominent figures in American public life were eager to be invited to occupy and it will therefore be easily understood that all my doubts about the success of my speech were completely removed by the announcement that I was to receive an invitation so highly prized.

An evening with Mackenzie King

As I reviewed my experiences in Washington during my flight back to Montreal, it occurred to me that it would be a good idea to make an exploratory visit to Ottawa. As the ILO's host, Canada was in a sense the ILO's special protector and she had indeed, with an admirable understanding of some of the problems involved, already acted effectively as such. She was therefore entitled to expect to be kept informed so far as possible of future plans and her attitude, though

---

[3] Joseph Arthur Padway (1891–1947), an American socialist politician, was General Counsel for the American Federation of Labor from the early 1930s to 1947. (Ed.)

not decisive, might well, if it were favourable, influence thinking in Washington and London. Moreover, my acquaintance with the Prime Minister was of long standing and I knew I could talk with him very frankly. I realized that I must be prepared for a cautious, and possibly a negative, reaction, but in any case his great political experience would make his counsel invaluable.

When a week or so later I arrived in Ottawa to keep my appointment with him, the good fortune that had accompanied me in Washington showed signs of having deserted me. I was told that an important debate required his continued presence in the House of Commons, that he would do his best to slip out for a few minutes to see me, and that meanwhile I could either wait in his room or listen to the discussion from the Distinguished Strangers' gallery. I chose the latter alternative and was soon deeply interested in the parliamentary drama taking place in what is one of the most beautiful and dignified legislative chambers in the world. The whole afternoon went by and at 6 p.m. the debate was still in full swing. I stepped out into the corridor to stretch my legs and there I met Percy Philips of the *New York Times* who invited me down to the Press Room, explaining that he would telephone the PM's secretary so that I could be found immediately, if required. This assurance led me to accept his invitation and, having retrieved my hat and coat from the gallery, I gladly accompanied him. Some 20 minutes later as we sat chatting in the otherwise empty room, Philips abruptly rose to his feet, saying, "The House is up." He had been alerted by a luminous signal behind my back which to me was invisible and I was taken by surprise. As he hurried out he almost collided with a junior secretary who came running in and who made directly for me saying, "The Prime Minister will see you now in his room. You must come quickly as he has to go in a couple of minutes."

Swept along by the wave of urgency that had so suddenly disturbed the calm atmosphere in which I had comfortably relaxed, I hastened to follow him up two or three floors and along several corridors to Mackenzie King's office. The Prime Minister was signing documents and, while I waited for him to finish, I admired the unhurried deliberation with which he performed his task. The pince-nez and the black silk ribbon to which it was attached gave him something of the air of an old-fashioned solicitor. What made the scene impressive was not his own appearance but the attitude of the secretaries standing on either side who watched his every move and the slightest change in his expression with the most concentrated attention.

When they had retired with the last of his papers, he came over to me apologizing for having kept me waiting so long. "I've had a difficult day; a difficult Cabinet to begin with that sat right through lunch time and then this business in the House."

"What!" I said, "Do you mean you've had no lunch?"

"That's of no consequence," he replied. "You know what happens when things get in a tangle and when you have to let a discussion go on till they work themselves out." I did know, and I knew, too, the tension and fatigue that such an experience involves.

"You won't want to be bothered talking to me at the end of such an exhausting day," I said. "Montreal is next door to Ottawa and I'll come up to see you again when you are not so hard-pressed."

"There's no guarantee that I wouldn't be equally hard-pressed the next time," he replied smiling. "Come and have dinner with me if you are free."

I could not believe that this was more than a very courteous way of insisting that he felt under a real obligation for having failed to keep an appointment which had brought me especially to Ottawa, and so I said that I could not think of trespassing on his hospitality in the circumstances and that I was prepared to take my chance of finding him with more free time on another occasion.

"I gather from that that you have no dinner engagement," was his answer. "I really would like you to dine with me. We have many interesting things to talk about quite remote from the questions I have been struggling with today and that's the kind of rest from which I get most benefit. Now," he went on, taking my consent for granted, "would you prefer to come out to my country home, my car will bring you back, or would you rather come to Laurier House?"

"Since you've had no lunch," I replied, and almost added "my good man" in a tone of expostulation, "let's make it Laurier House. You must be dying of hunger."

He called up his major-domo, on what was evidently a private phone, and told him that he was bringing a guest to dinner and was leaving his office at once.

As he was telephoning, I remembered that I had left my hat and coat in the Press Room and I realized with dismay that I should never be able to retrace my steps through the labyrinth of government buildings unassisted. I explained my predicament and asked the Prime Minister to let me have a messenger as a guide, telling him that I should then have no difficulty in getting to Laurier House.

"I'll take you," was his almost jaunty reply, and off we went through the long dimly lit deserted corridors, the Prime Minister walking with a buoyant step that showed not the slightest sign of fatigue.

Journalists are, I imagine, not easily surprised. It would be an exaggeration to say that the half-dozen who were in the Press Room when we entered were dumbfounded; but there was certainly a moment of astonished silence when the Prime Minister appeared in the doorway, and then they clustered round him bombarding him with questions on the day's political events. I made haste to retrieve my hat and coat, feeling guiltily conscious that my thoughtlessness had exposed him to still another fatiguing ordeal. To my amazement he seemed to be thoroughly enjoying it. The skill and good humour with which he answered or parried their questions, and the ease with which he finally disengaged himself from their curiosity, not even Roosevelt could have surpassed.

Laurier House has its place in Canada's history as the home of her two greatest Prime Ministers. Mackenzie King, out of veneration for Sir Wilfrid Laurier, had kept some of its rooms unchanged when it became his property, and into one of these I was shown on our arrival. It was singularly unattractive. It was overcrowded with uncongenial Victorian furniture and a large white marble bust of Laurier on a high pedestal gave it a cold funereal atmosphere. I was glad to leave it after a few minutes for other rooms on which Mackenzie King had left his own mark. From them the museum chill was wholly absent and they were pervaded by an aura of warmth and comfort such as bachelors rarely achieve.

During dinner I made no reference to the ILO; conversation wandered easily over all sorts of harmless topics, and so interesting were my host's comments on a variety of subjects, ranging from town planning to *Pickwick Papers*, that I was in some danger of forgetting the object of my visit to Ottawa. When we had finished our meal, which it should be added was excellent in every particular, a small and rather shaky lift conveyed us up to the Prime Minister's study. It was as crowded as the Victorian parlour downstairs but in every other respect it was different. A well-built-up fire burned in the grate; an inviting chesterfield was drawn up in front of it; and cheerfully reflecting its glow a silver cigarette box and ashtray added a final touch to my comfort, the more appreciated because I knew that my host was a non-smoker.

As I sank into the cushions of the chesterfield thinking, with an embarrassed sense of ingratitude, that I must now introduce the subject of the ILO, my eyes roved enviously round the book-lined walls and over the several tables on which still more books were piled.

Never was anyone in my predicament so gracefully and so generously given his cue.

"I see you are looking at my books," said Mackenzie King. "Your own is amongst them. He was a very great man, Albert Thomas, and he deserved your tribute. Now the ILO is in your hands. Tell me what you are going to do with it."

The general substance of my reply can be gathered from the preceding pages. The Prime Minister listened attentively. When I concluded the somewhat lengthy exposition of my argument, I waited with some anxiety for his comments. They showed at once that he had already given much thought to the problems that would arise when the war was over. His personal history and his political background would have led me to expect that he would emphasize their social and economic aspect but his approach was more general and was concerned with the fundamental problem of providing the world with international institutions that, if properly designed and wisely used, would give the nations a real guarantee of peace. He appreciated the great importance of preserving the continuity of established international cooperation and gave his full approval to the idea of holding a meeting of the International Labour Conference at the earliest possible date so that the habits of international collaboration in the ILO should not be lost. I could take it, he said, that that would be the Canadian Government's attitude, and he added that if I should find it useful in the course of my negotiations, I could affirm that the idea had his entire support.

I asked him if we could hold the Conference in Canada. He replied that Canada would be glad to have us do so, but suggested that it would be better, if possible, to hold it in the United States, adding that he was sure that President Roosevelt would like the idea of having the meeting held in the United States. I told him of my endeavours to prepare the ground in Washington, and then I ventured the suggestion that if at any time he had a suitable opportunity he might mention my plan to the President. I put this to him very tentatively, fearing he might think I was going too far, but he replied readily that he would keep the possibility in mind.

It was now nearly 11 p.m. and I rose to go, apologizing for having kept him so late.

"Don't go yet," he said, "My secretaries will be coming in with my papers for the weekend in a few minutes and then I'll take you along with me and drop you at your hotel." In due course they appeared with two large attaché cases crammed with documents, and these he carefully verified to make sure nothing had been forgotten, while I marvelled once more at his thoroughness and physical resiliency.

I had many other meetings with Mackenzie King during my years in Canada. I always found him courteous, generous, sincere and ready to go out of his way to be helpful. I was therefore puzzled by the fact that my impression of him was far from being shared in many circles with which I came in contact. Scraps of gossip about political personalities, exaggerated or distorted accounts of incidents in which they are made to appear in an unfavourable light, are a common feature of political life everywhere. Many of those told about Mackenzie King seemed rather pointless; they appeared to be inspired by a vague resentment or to afford the opportunity for some disparaging comments for which they provided little serious basis. Even those who defended his policy seemed little inclined to defend the man himself. No doubt he lacked the gift of arousing popular enthusiasm but that did not seem sufficient to explain why the many attractive traits in his character did not secure a warmer response.

If some future historian should draw a portrait of Mackenzie King from evidence of this kind, of which he could find plenty, he would do him less than justice. I venture to think that the explanation of the curious lack of sympathy with which he was regarded by so many who were close to the centre of affairs is to be found in the fact that the latter part of his political career coincided with the period in which Canada rose from the position of a small and negligible community to that of a near-Great Power. When the process began, Ottawa was, in every sense of the word, a small town; it has now become one of the world's important political centres. The immense expansion of Canada's industrial power was visible in a thousand ways. The growth of her political status was largely invisible; only the Prime Minister could sense to what it might lead. For him, more particularly during the war, it entailed secrets that he could not reveal and responsibilities that he could not share; and in consequence he must often have appeared unmoved by, and even strangely indifferent to, problems that others considered predominant. Even among his close supporters, the impression that he was becoming aloof and inscrutable must have been disconcerting, and among others a feeling of discontent and vague resentment might be expected to spread. When Moses went up to the mountain many of his people must have grumbled to one another, "Our Patriarch is getting peculiar and neglecting our urgent affairs."

Negative attitude of London finally changes

While I was exploring the situation in Washington and Ottawa, the attitude Great Britain might adopt remained a major preoccupation. It had become increasingly clear that I could not, at this stage, contemplate a personal visit to London. The absence of several weeks which such a visit would entail would compel me to abandon the central control of the Office's activities when it was more than ever necessary that it should be constantly exercised; and what was even more important, it would cut me off from Washington when everything might depend on keeping in touch with developments there and being able to intervene if need be.

Fortunately, M.R.K. Burge, the Director of ILO's London Office,[4] was in every way qualified to do what was required. He was on friendly terms with

---

[4] Milward Rodon Kennedy Burge (1894–1968) joined the ILO in Geneva in October 1921 after serving in the British delegation to the Paris Peace Conference and in the British and Egyptian civil service. Initially Private Secretary to Butler (then Deputy Director), he was appointed Director of the London Correspondence Office in January 1924, and held that post until he resigned in June 1945. (Ed.)

all the principal personalities in government, employers' and workers' circles in Great Britain and enjoyed their confidence. Moreover, he was an old friend to whom my thinking about the ILO was familiar, and with whom, therefore, I could keep in the closest touch by cable with the certainty that no misunderstanding would arise.

There was indeed a real advantage in having him undertake the task rather than myself. It was to be expected that London would be far more conscious of the practical difficulties involved in the proposal than either Washington or Ottawa, and that the idea might well be turned down out of hand on these considerations alone. It would be far easier for Burge than for me to persist in pressing it in the face of such objections. He would not be personally responsible for it, and he might even excite a certain degree of sympathy at having to put forward on instructions so "unrealistic" a suggestion. He would be able to display a pardonable obstinacy without exciting resentment, and succeed, as in fact he did, in keeping the question open through the first negative stages of its reception until other considerations could be more easily brought forward.

The first reactions he reported were definitely unpromising. The suggestion that high-ranking officials could lay aside their wartime responsibilities for an uncertain duration and embark on a journey across the Atlantic was greeted as absurd; and the attitude of the employers and workers was equally antagonistic. This was more or less what I had anticipated and so I readily agreed to Burge's suggestion that, while admitting the force of those objections, he should concentrate his efforts on trying to get the case for holding the Conference accepted in principle. This approach modified the workers' attitude to the extent that they declared themselves in favour of a meeting, though they added emphatically "not now". For practical purposes their position remained unaltered but there was nevertheless a tiny breach in the solid negative line, which left room for further discussion. I also asked Burge to talk informally with the Exiled Governments. Their reaction proved to be favourable and the lively discussions in which they engaged helped to keep the question alive. They felt the need of formulating and proclaiming new constructive social policies and their attitude therefore introduced a positive element which diluted, though it could not dispel, the wholly negative atmosphere that had first prevailed.

Meanwhile, progress in Washington went forward more smoothly and more successfully than I had anticipated. It would be wearisome, and indeed useless, to recount my various interventions in detail, for there was no means of knowing in what degree they influenced the course of events. What I did eventually become aware of was that considerations of high policy were steadily converging in the general direction along which I wanted the United States to move. The President and Secretary Hull were both becoming increasingly preoccupied with the question of post-war organization. They foresaw that the United States would have to shoulder great international responsibilities and they were acutely conscious that American opinion, with its long tradition of isolation, would be ill-prepared for their acceptance. Any opportunity that would enable it to acquire a closer acquaintance with, and a direct experience of, the working of an international institution was, therefore, something to be welcomed. Miss Perkins may well have suggested to them that a meeting of the International Labour Conference held in the United States would admirably serve this purpose; and it is also possible that Mackenzie King put the idea into the President's mind. I do not know, and I do not know what high-level communications passed between Washington and London, but I was not surprised when I heard that the British Government had reversed its attitude and was now in favour of the Conference taking place.

Defining the nature of the Conference and its task

Since there was now a solid foundation of support on both sides of the Atlantic, the next step was to obtain a decision from the Governing Body by correspondence with its members individually. Some of them raised points which, though they could have been disposed of rapidly in the usual process of verbal discussion, proved troublesome to deal with by this method and led to some delay. I had assumed that the Governing Body itself would meet at the same time and place as the Conference; the obstacle in the way of holding its meeting had been the question of transport and this obstacle the arrangements for the meeting of the Conference would automatically remove. The proposal that I asked the members of the Governing Body to approve therefore provided for a meeting of both bodies. Some members, however, while prepared to approve of a meeting of the Conference, held that the Governing Body could not meet because its three-year mandate had expired. This seemed to make no sense since if the argument was valid the Governing Body could not decide to convene the Conference.

A second point raised an issue of considerable importance. It was that when the Conference met it would be its duty to renew the Governing Body and that conditions were so abnormal and so unpredictable that it would be impossible for the Conference to carry out this task in a satisfactory way. The geographical composition of the Conference would, it was argued, in all probability be unbalanced, with the result that the elective seats might all be allotted to States fortunate enough to be able to attend, while those absent through no fault of their own might find their claims ignored. Remembering the less pleasant features of some elections in the past, I could easily see that a repetition of them might all too easily defeat the whole purpose for which the Conference was being held. Feeling would run high, for the claims of the absentees would certainly find defenders; the contending factions would inevitably be given political or regional labels; the press would carry headlines such as the "Struggle of America versus Europe" or "Belligerents versus Neutrals"; and the result would be to present a spectacle of conflict and division when the real object of holding the Conference was to manifest to the world the strength and unity of the ILO.

A third point that was raised drew attention to the fact that the Conference would have the power to adopt international Conventions and could thus impose on absent Members certain obligations. It seemed to be highly improbable that the Conference would act in this way, but the argument suggested a device by which this and the preceding point could be satisfactorily disposed of. I therefore proposed to the Governing Body that the conference to be convened should be a Special Conference not endowed with the normal constitutional powers and one which in consequence could neither proceed to elections for the Governing Body nor embark on international labour legislation. Nineteen members of the Governing Body gave this proposal their formal approval; none voted against it; and the remainder abstained. [5]

On 3 August 1941, I cabled to all the Members of the Organization informing them that the Conference would meet on 27 October in New York to survey the present and future possibilities of the Organization.

While all these negotiations had been going on, the Office had not been idle. It was clearly desirable that it should make every effort to demonstrate to the Conference the kind of services that it was equipped to render to Members. The staff worked with an enthusiasm and devotion that produced results little short of miraculous if account be taken of the limited resources which were available. Periodical summaries of information on labour conditions throughout the world were published, and as arrangements had been made to secure information on these subjects even from occupied Europe these summaries obtained wide press publicity; Office experts went on advisory missions to countries of North and South America; special studies were produced on a variety of technical subjects; and a series of tripartite meetings was organized to bring together United States

---

[5] Twelve government members (Belgium, Canada, Chile, China, India, Mexico, Netherlands, Norway, Poland, United Kingdom, United States, Yugoslavia), three employers' members (Forbes Watson, Gemmill and Harriman) and four workers' members (Andersson, Hallsworth, Joshi and Watt) gave their approval. Two members did not oppose (Oersted and Schürch) and the others did not or could not reply. See *Consultation of Members of the Governing Body*, D 600/X/1, 1941, ILO Historical Archives (Ed.)

and Canadian representatives to discuss the problems of labour supply for the purposes of national defence.

All these activities, although mainly technical in character, made considerable demands on my time. In ordinary circumstances they would have required no more than a minimum of supervision and coordination but, in the unprecedented conditions in which they had to be carried out, questions continually arose in which decisions had to be given with careful regard for political considerations. I was therefore unable to give my undivided attention to the next task which fell to my lot and which I felt was more difficult than any I had yet undertaken.

The principal item for discussion at the Conference was the Report of the Acting Director; on its content would largely depend the conclusions the Conference would reach; and since it must reach governments in time to allow them to give instructions to their delegates, only a few weeks could be devoted to its preparation. Directors' reports to previous Conferences had set a standard which it would in any case not be easy to approach. But on this occasion the report had to be much wider in scope than any previously submitted. If it was to fulfil its purpose, it must reassess the whole position of the ILO against the background of a totally different world in which new ideas were fermenting, and it must attempt to indicate positive ways in which the ILO could effectively respond to them.

I can indicate here only in the briefest fashion its main conclusions. After producing abundant evidence from the pronouncements of statesmen from all parts of the world, and from religious leaders of all denominations, that a great surge of new social thinking was already manifest, I summarized its tendency as the demand that future policy must be directed to ensuring for the individual not only better conditions of labour but also economic security; and I listed the headings under which practical measures would have to be taken if this worldwide demand was to receive satisfaction. I emphasized that both national and international action would be required to make these measures effective, and that in the international sphere the ILO would be indispensable. In order, however, that it should be able to fulfil its task when the time came to carry this programme into effect, two things were immediately necessary: first, it must be used from now on as the centre for the collection and distribution of information on post-war social planning; and, second, its position in the post-war scheme of world organization must be assured. Though the ILO would inevitably have a wider field of action, other international organizations would no doubt be created, each being assigned its appropriate share of the general task. Wasteful overlapping and dangerous conflicts of competence jeopardizing the whole effort could all too easily arise unless their assignments were carefully defined at the outset. The best way to avoid future confusion and friction would be to provide that the ILO, whose field of action was so varied and extensive, should be assured of representatives in any peace or reconstruction conference that might be convened. The argument of the whole report was intended to lead to this last conclusion which I considered of fundamental importance because in no other way could there be any guarantee that the ILO's future position would not be, wittingly or unwittingly, undermined.

The report went out, by airmail, six weeks before the Conference was due to open. I sent copies not only to member governments but also to outstanding personalities in the different countries who had had some past association with the ILO or who might be expected to be interested in the subjects it treated. Its reception was encouraging, and press comments were favourable. I received a number of personal letters of congratulations. One from Viscount Cecil ran as follows:

> I feel I must write a line to you to say how very much I admire your Report to the ILO. I have read it with the deepest interest, particularly the last section as to future policy. I hope very much that our Government will do something to draw attention to it or circulate it. Even if the paper shortage makes it impossible to reproduce the whole Report, the last section certainly ought to be circulated to all Members of Parliament. [6]

Shortly afterwards, information began to arrive about the composition of the delegations which would attend. A great deal now depended on the number of countries who would participate and the importance of the persons who would be appointed to represent them. The first news was curious and a little amusing. I heard that in one country prominent officials had announced that they did not wish to be members of the delegation. Their reason was that they were afraid that the public, and more especially their colleagues, would conclude that their responsibilities must be small if they could be so easily spared at such a time. Their hesitation vanished abruptly when they learned that the delegation concerned was to be headed by someone far more important than themselves.

This incident afforded interesting evidence that the decision favourable to the holding of the Conference had been, as I had guessed, taken as a result of very high-level communications which had been kept secret. As further information flowed in, it became clear that the composition of the Conference would be impressive. When all particulars had been received the figures showed that 35 countries would be represented by a total of 102 delegates accompanied by

---

[6] The letter is not in the relevant file of the ILO Historical Archives. (Ed.)

93 advisers. The government delegates included nearly a score of Ministers: among them figured Clement Attlee, Deputy Prime Minister of Great Britain; Henri Spaak, Foreign Minister, and Paul van Zeeland, former Prime Minister, of Belgium; Jan Masaryk, Foreign Minister of Czechoslovakia; Carl Hambro, President of the Norwegian Storting; a number of Ministers of State; and the Ministers of Labour of Canada, Chile, Greece, New Zealand, The Netherlands and Poland. The government delegates from the United States were Miss Frances Perkins, Secretary of Labor, and Adolf Berle, Assistant Secretary of State.

How President Roosevelt squared the circle

The inclusion of so many distinguished political personalities from so many different countries made it evident that governments were attaching great importance to the Conference. When this became apparent, I drew Miss Perkins' attention to what was happening and asked her whether it would be possible for President Roosevelt to come to a sitting of the Conference and address the delegates. She welcomed the suggestion, which she thought would appeal to the President, and promised to put it to him at the first opportunity. A week or so later she told me that, much to her regret, it had been found that the suggestion was not feasible. The difficulty lay in a structural feature of the Macmillan Theatre in Columbia University in which the Conference was to meet.

"You know of his infirmity," she said." It just would not be possible to get him on the platform."

I was not wholly convinced that the difficulty about the hall was the real explanation. It was not that I doubted Miss Perkins' sincerity but I was aware of the struggles for the President's time and how unscrupulously they were often waged. I therefore asked Miss Perkins whether the question could not be reconsidered, urging that the Conference could move to some other hall for that particular occasion, that the President would have a world audience of a unique character, that the impression of his personality would be carried directly into the Cabinets of a dozen countries and that his statement would thus have an immensely greater effect than if it took the form of a message.

Miss Perkins, though she listened with her usual patience to all I had to say, was clearly not willing to be drawn into any argument and merely replied that she could hold out no hope of the decision being changed. She added that, nevertheless, I could be assured that the President was keenly interested in the Conference and that I could count on a message from him "fully adequate to the occasion". And with this promise I had to be content.

When the Conference opened on 27 October 1941, Miss Perkins was elected to preside over its deliberations and in her presidential address she restated the main theme of my report in the following words:

> This Organization has continued during the War, and it will carry over into the peace in some form or other, I hope in extended and more important form … To build a new and better world we must build it upon foundations that are already in existence, and there is a large field of work in those activities in which the ILO has demonstrated its outstanding competence in the last twenty years. [7]

I listened with great satisfaction as she gave this lead to the Conference, knowing the importance delegates would attach to the views of the United States. I was surprised, however, when she concluded her speech without delivering any message from President Roosevelt. When she resumed her seat beside me I asked what had happened to the President's message.

"I haven't got it yet," was her answer, "but I hope to have it this afternoon."

At the opening of the afternoon sitting Miss Perkins greeted me with the words: "I've got the President's message. I think you'll be pleased with it. But I'll put through one or two items of formal business before I deliver it."

As soon as these had been disposed of, Miss Perkins rose and said: "The President of the United States has asked me to deliver a message to this Conference on his behalf. He is glad you are meeting here."

I noticed with dismay that she had only a half sheet of notepaper in her hand. The message "fully adequate to the importance of the occasion" was apparently to be no more than her own account of some brief comment presumably received by telephone. The impression was confirmed as she continued without any quotation: "He is sorry that he has been unable to arrange his affairs so that he might address a sitting of the Conference in New York City."

She paused and glanced at me as though to draw my attention to the fact that my proposal had really received his consideration and then she went on. "But in lieu of that he invites you to hold the last sitting of the Conference in the White House in Washington DC on 6 November."

If Miss Perkins had planned a surprise she certainly succeeded. There was a moment of silence before the delegates, having realized the full implication of

---

[7] ILO: *Conference of the International Labour Organisation: 1941, New York and Washington, DC, Record of proceedings* (Montreal, International Labour Office, 1941), pp. 7–12. (Ed.)

her statement, burst into a storm of applause. I shook her hand warmly, unable to find words to express my delight.

"I told you the message would please you," she said, smiling.

"It has indeed," I replied, "but how did the decision come to be changed?"

"Oh, it was the President's own idea. He loves meeting people, you know."

That was all I was to learn. I never discovered whether she herself had found an opportunity to reopen the question with the President but her words implied that there had been some further discussion with him at which he had characteristically settled the conflict between those who were for his going to New York and those who were against, by a decision that accepted the arguments of both sides and allowed him to do what he wanted.

The ILO ends its Conference in the White House

During the following days, the Conference got down to its work and after prolonged discussions adopted a series of resolutions on various subjects. One embodied the points to which I attached special importance. It called the attention of member governments "to the desirability of associating the International Labour Organization with the planning and application of measures of reconstruction"; it asked "that the ILO should be represented in any Peace or Reconstruction Conference following the War"; and it urged that the ILO should "be in a position to give authoritative expression to the social objectives confided to it in the rebuilding of a peaceful world upon the basis of improved labour standards, economic advancements and social security". [8]

Thus, what nine months before had seemed an almost hopeless enterprise had been attended by success. The Organization had asserted its will to survive in no uncertain terms; and it had staked out its claim to a position in the post-war world commensurate with the responsibilities that had been given into its keeping.

More the Conference could not do. It lay with other authorities to decide whether this claim should be accepted. In an important and perhaps decisive degree the final sitting in the White House would supply the answer.

Everything was going smoothly when an unexpected difficulty arose in connection with the journey of the delegates to Washington. An embarrassed Miss Perkins came to me to explain that the US Government would be unable to provide transportation as there was no way in which they could pay for it.

---

[8] Resolution on post-war emergency and reconstruction measures, paras. (a) and (f). See ILO: *Conference of the International Labour Organisation: 1941, New York and Washington, DC, Record of proceedings* (Montreal, International Labour Office, 1941), p. 163. (Ed.)

"It's very awkward," she added. "It's out of the question that the delegates should be asked to pay for themselves. Most of them have no dollars. Can you do anything to help?"

I hesitated over my reply, since the ILO's Constitution specifically provided that the expenses of delegates should be borne by the member governments. I was faced with the same difficulty as the American Government. Nevertheless, I felt that even this obstacle should not be allowed to jeopardize the meeting with the President and so I told Miss Perkins that if there was no other solution I would foot the bill. I did not mention the constitutional difficulty but I warned her that there would subsequently be a discussion in the Finance Committee of the Governing Body which would call into question the propriety of the expenditure and which might well be disagreeable for the United States.

"Well," said Miss Perkins glumly, "we'll just have to risk that. Our system is terribly inelastic and this is one of the cases in which we just can't do a thing. Anyway, thanks to you, we'll get them to Washington and that will be worthwhile."

Though I was satisfied that the decision I had taken was right, I was bothered by its implications and more and more convinced that in spite of the exceptional circumstances I must on no account get into the position in which I could be accused of not respecting the Constitution. The only alternative was to meet the cost out of my own pocket and I was ruefully speculating on what this would mean when the next day Miss Perkins reappeared in a much more cheerful mood and announced that a solution had been found.

"I've talked to some American employers and we are going round with the hat." I suppose I must have looked shocked at the idea of such a humiliating expedient for she added: "We often do that. It's in our tradition. When we can't get a thing done by Government, citizens get together and do something about it for themselves."

Possibly on this occasion the hat was insufficiently filled, or the railway was given too short notice, but, whatever the reason, some 200 representatives from the Conference, many of them in formal attire with carefully creased striped trousers and morning coats, found themselves on their way to Washington in some of the most dilapidated coaches that I imagine had ever left Pennsylvania station. The cars were dirty, many of the windows were cracked and all of them rattled so noisily that conversation was almost impossible. Many of the delegates had never been in the United States before and I could read ill-concealed surprise and even dismay in their faces as they compared this accommodation with the luxurious comfort of New York's hotels. Whatever unfavourable impression they may have received was effectively dissipated as they drove from Union station and caught a glimpse of Washington's palatial government buildings before arriving at the

White House, which always seems so uncannily quiet and dignified in spite of the crowded streets through which one approaches it.

Small as the White House appears, no doubt because of its harmonious proportions, the Conference was easily accommodated in one of its larger rooms which had been especially arranged for its reception. Rows of gilt chairs faced a curtained archway before which was a tall reading stand. The front row on the right corresponded to the platform of the Conference with seats assigned to Miss Perkins, myself as Secretary-General and the three Vice-Presidents. The front row on the other side was reserved for members of President Roosevelt's Cabinet, whose arrival the delegates watched with interest, and whose attendance indicated that the occasion was to be one of special importance.

Punctually at 3 p.m. Miss Perkins, standing beside the lectern, declared the sitting open and added that after the President had made his address the three Vice-Presidents of the Conference would each say a few words to mark the tripartite character of the Organization, the session would be closed and the delegates would file past the President, and be presented to him.

Miss Perkins was an impressive figure as she made this announcement and she spoke, as always on public occasions, with great self-possession and authority. As she ended her remarks the curtains opened; and the President, leaning on the arm of his aide, General Watson, advanced to the reading desk.

Everyone rose and one could feel an emotional tension in the room. It was a solemn moment for all present and particularly for those delegates who were evidently deeply moved at being in the presence of the man from whose power and humanity they hoped and believed the deliverance of their tortured countries would ultimately come. What impressed me even more, however, was that an emotion no less deep was manifest among the Americans. Miss Perkins seemed to grow smaller and the almost faltering voice in which she announced "The President of the United States" was strangely different from the assured tones in which she had just spoken. I realized how great is the place occupied by the President in the minds of the American people, not because of the great powers which he can exercise but because he is in a peculiar sense their sole representative and the embodiment of the traditions they cherish. The history of the American people is the history of its Presidents; and the man in the White House, on whom has descended the mantle of Washington, Jefferson and Lincoln, is the living symbol of the unity and will, so perilously forged in the past, which has made them a nation with a priceless heritage of freedom.

We resumed our seats and the President began an historic speech in which during 45 minutes he wove together with inimitable skill his answers to the questions that preoccupied not only his immediate audience but millions of men and women throughout the world. Characteristically, he started with a personal reminiscence, recalling that he had been associated with the Organization's first Conference in Washington in 1919. Then he continued:

> In those days, the ILO was still a dream. To many it was a wild dream ... Wilder still was the idea that the people themselves who were directly affected – the workers and employers of the various countries – should have a hand with Governments in determining labour standards. Now 22 years have passed and the ILO has been tried and tested. ... Today, you, the representatives of the 35 nations, have met here in the White House for the final session of your Conference. It is appropriate that I recall to you, who are in a full sense a parliament for man's justice, some words written in this house by a President who gave his life for justice. Nearly 80 years ago Abraham Lincoln said: "The strongest bond of human sympathy, outside of the family relationship, should be uniting all working people, of all nations and tongues and kindreds." [9]

After this general introduction, he turned to the struggle in which the world was now engaged, building up in graphic detail a picture of the ordeal of Europe and referring to "the extremely limited sacrifice" the United States had "so far" been called upon to make. The significance of the words "so far" did not escape his audience. He had evidently chosen this occasion to make an important political pronouncement and this was confirmed as he proceeded.

> So far as we in the United States are concerned that struggle shall not be in vain ... The American worker knows that his own liberty and the very safety of the people of the United States cannot be assured in a world which is three fourths slave and one fourth free.

More he could not then say, but there was no doubt that in this dramatic way he was at one and the same time drawing together strands of American opinion and giving it a definite lead.

Then he looked still further ahead.

> In the process of our working and fighting for victory, however, we must never forget the goal which is beyond victory. ... We must plan now for the better world

---

[9] The excerpts from Roosevelt's speech do not entirely reflect the official text. See ILO: *Conference of the International Labour Organisation: 1941, New York and Washington, DC, Record of proceedings* (Montreal, International Labour Office, 1941), pp. 156–58. (Ed.)

we aim to build. In the planning of such international action, the International Labour Organization, with its representatives of labour and management, its technical knowledge and experience, will be an invaluable instrument for peace. Your Organization will have an essential part to play in building up a stable international system of social justice for all peoples everywhere.

Thus did the President put the seal of his approval on the ILO's claim.

Though I felt a warm glow of satisfaction, I was not inclined to exaggerate the part I had played in achieving this happy result. Many great forces had converged to bring it about. Perhaps I had only been carried along on their tide, or perhaps I had been the tiny catalytic agent that had provoked their combination at a particular moment. One thing was certain, and it was sufficient cause for rejoicing. Though the road that lay ahead might be long and arduous, its direction was clear. The ILO had turned the corner.

Selected bibliography
of Edward Phelan's writings

1914

Milan (London, George Lunn's Travel Books).

1923

The necessity for international labour organisation: An address delivered to the League of Nations Union Summer School, Geneva, August 1923 (London, League of Nations Union).

1925

"The International Labour Organisation: Its ideals and results", in *Studies: An Irish Quarterly*, Vol. 14, pp. 611–22.

1926

"Ireland and the International Labour Organization: Part I", in *Studies: An Irish Quarterly*, Vol. 15, pp. 1–18.

"Ireland and the International Labour Organisation: Part II", in *Studies: An Irish Quarterly*, Vol. 15, pp. 380–98.

1927

"The sovereignty of the Irish Free State", in *La Revue des nations*, No. 3, pp. 35–49.

"Current progress of international labour legislation", in *The problems of peace: Lectures delivered at the Geneva Institute of International Relations at the Palais des Nations, August 1926*, Vol. 1 (Oxford, Oxford University Press), pp. 63–89.

1928

"The progress and problems of the International Labour Organization", in *The problems of peace*, 2nd series, *Lectures delivered at the Geneva Institute of International Relations at the Palais des Nations, August 1927*, Vol. 2 (Oxford, Oxford University Press), pp. 46–70.

1929

"Tendencies in international legislation", in *The problems of peace*, 3rd series, *Lectures delivered at the Geneva Institute of International Relations at the Palais des Nations, August 1928*, Vol. 3 (Oxford, Oxford University Press), pp. 96–129.

1931

"International co-operation and unemployment", in Q. Wright (ed.): *Unemployment as a world problem: Lectures on the Harris Foundation* (Chicago, University of Chicago Press), pp. 151–248.

"The British Empire and the world community", in *The problems of peace: Lectures delivered at the Geneva Institute of International Relations at the Palais des Nations, August 1930*, Vol. 5 (London, George Allen & Unwin), pp. 253–83.

1932

"L'Empire Britannique et la communauté internationale", in *Revue des sciences politiques* (Paris, Librairie Felix Alcan), Vol. 47, July–Sep, pp. 393–417.

1933

"Industrial and social aspects of the economic crisis", in *The problems of peace: Lectures delivered at the Geneva Institute of International Relations at the Palais des Nations, August 1932*, Vol. 7 (London, George Allen & Unwin), pp. 107–29.

1934

Albert Thomas, homme international: Discours prononcé par E.J. Phelan à la cérémonie commémorative du 2ᵉ anniversaire de la mort d'Albert Thomas, organisée par la Confédération Générale du Travail au Palais du Trocadero, le 9 mai 1934 (Annemasse, Granchamp).

"British preparations", in J.T. Shotwell (ed.), *The origins of the International Labor Organization* (New York, Columbia University Press), Vol. 1, pp. 105–26.

"The Commission on International Labor Legislation", in J.T. Shotwell (ed.), *The origins of the International Labor Organization* (New York, Columbia University Press), Vol. 1, pp. 127–198.

"The labor proposals before the Peace Conference", in J.T. Shotwell (ed.), *The origins of the International Labor Organization* (New York, Columbia University Press), Vol. 1, pp. 199–220.

"The admission of the Central Powers to the International Labor Organization", in J.T. Shotwell (ed.), *The origins of the International Labor Organization* (New York, Columbia University Press), Vol. 1, pp. 259–82.

1935
"The United States and the International Labor Organisation", in E.J. Phelan, M.O. Hudson and J.T. Shotwell (eds), 'The International Labor Organisation: Membership of the United States and its possibilities', *International Conciliation*, No. 309, April (Carnegie Endowment for International Peace, New York), pp. 107–19.

1936
Yes and Albert Thomas (London, Cresset Press).
Albert Thomas et la création du BIT (Paris, Bernard Grasset).

1937
"The International Labour Organisation and the future of the collective system", in *The problems of peace: Lectures delivered at the Geneva Institute of International Relations at the Palais des Nations*, August 1936, Vol. 11, pp. 127–44.

1941
Social services and defense (New York, Columbia University Press).

1942
"The ILO stands ready", in *The Christian Science Monitor* ("The world we want" series), 12 Oct. 1942.
"Labor in the peace to come", in *The Christian Science Monitor* ("The world we want" series), 14 Oct. 1942.

1946
The ILO and the United Nations (Montreal, ILO).
L'Organisation internationale du Travail et les Nations Unies (Montreal, ILO).

1949
"The contribution of the ILO to peace", in *International Labour Review*, Vol. 59, No. 6, pp. 607–32.

1951
"The contribution of the ILO to the social sciences", in *International Social Sciences Bulletin*, Vol. 2, No. 1, pp. 123–32.

1953
Albert Thomas y la Oficina Internacional del Trabajo (Mexico City, J. Mendez Rivas).

1954

"Some reminiscences of the International Labour Organisation", *Studies: An Irish Quarterly Review*, Vol. 43, No. 171, pp. 241–70.

1955

"The ILO sets up its wartime centre in Canada", *Studies: An Irish Quarterly Review*, Vol. 44, No. 174, pp. 151–70.

1956

"The ILO turns the corner", *Studies: An Irish Quarterly Review*, Vol. 45, No. 178, pp. 160–86.

1957

"After Pearl Harbour: ILO problems", *Studies: An Irish Quarterly Review*, Vol. 46, No. 182, pp. 193–06.

Further reading on ILO history

Alcock, A. 1970. *History of the International Labour Organisation* (London and Basingstoke, Macmillan).

Barnes, G. 1926. *History of the International Labour Office* (London, Williams & Norgate).

Béguin, B. 1959. *ILO and the tripartite system* (New York, Carnegie Endowment for International Peace).

Bonvin, J.-M. 1998. *L'Organisation internationale du Travail. Etude sur une agence productrice de normes* (Paris, Presses Universitaires de France).

Follows, J.W. 1951. *Antecedents of the International Labour Organisation* (Oxford, Oxford University Press).

Ghebali, V. Y. 1988. *The International Labour Organisation: A case study on the evolution of UN specialised agencies*, International Organization and the Evolution of World Society, Vol. 3 (Dordrecht, Nijhoff).

ILO. 1931. *The International Labour Organisation: The first decade* (London, George Allen & Unwin).

Jenks, C.W. 1970. *Social justice in the law of nations: The ILO impact after fifty years* (London, Oxford and New York, Oxford University Press).

Morse, D. 1969. *The origin and evolution of the ILO and its role in the world community* (Ithaca, NY, Cornell University Press).

Rodgers, G. et al. 2009. *The International Labour Organization and the quest for social justice, 1919–2009* (Geneva, ILO).

Ruotsila, M. 2002. "'The great charter for the liberty of the workingman': Labour, liberals and the creation of the ILO", in *Labour History Review* (London and Cambridge, Maney), Vol. 67, No. 1, pp. 29–47.

Schaper, B.W. 1959. *Albert Thomas. Trente ans de réformisme social* (Paris and Assen, Presses Universitaires de France and Van Gorcum).

Shotwell, J.T. (ed.). 1934. *The origins of the International Labor Organization* (New York, Columbia University Press), 2 vols.

Thomas, A. 1921. "The International Labour Organization: Its origins, development and future", in *International Labour Review* (Geneva, ILO), Vol. 1, No. 1, pp. 5–22; repr. in *International Labour Review* (1996), Vol. 135, Nos 3–4, pp. 261–76.

Van Daele, J. 2005. "Engineering social peace: Networks, ideas, and the founding of the International Labour Organization", in *International Review of Social History* (Cambridge, Cambridge University Press), Vol. 50, No. 3, pp. 435–66.

More information on ILO history reading can be found at:
www.ilocentury.org
www.ilo.org/public/english/century/information_resources/ilo_library.htm

Index

Note: In subheadings Edward Phelan is abbreviated as E.J.P.